National Academy Press

The National Academy Press was created by the National Academy of Sciences to publish the reports issued by the Academy and by the National Academy of Engineering, the Institute of Medicine, and the National Research Council, all operating under the charter granted to the National Academy of Sciences by the Congress of the United States.

Biographical Memoirs

NATIONAL ACADEMY OF SCIENCES

NATIONAL ACADEMY OF SCIENCES
OF THE UNITED STATES OF AMERICA

Biographical Memoirs

VOLUME 52

NATIONAL ACADEMY PRESS
WASHINGTON, D.C. 1980

The National Academy of Sciences was established in 1863 by Act of Congress as a private, non-profit, self-governing membership corporation for the furtherance of science and technology, required to advise the federal government upon request within its fields of competence. Under its corporate charter the Academy established the National Research Council in 1916, the National Academy of Engineering in 1964, and the Institute of Medicine in 1970.

INTERNATIONAL STANDARD BOOK NUMBER 0-309-03099-4

LIBRARY OF CONGRESS CATALOG CARD NUMBER 5-26629

Available from

NATIONAL ACADEMY PRESS

2101 CONSTITUTION AVENUE, N.W.,

WASHINGTON, D.C. 20418

PRINTED IN THE UNITED STATES OF AMERICA

CONTENTS

PREFACE   vii

LEASON HEBERLING ADAMS   3
  BY R. E. GIBSON

NORMAN LEVI BOWEN   35
  BY HANS P. EUGSTER

MILTON NUNN BRAMLETTE   81
  BY JAMES GILLULY

ERNST CLOOS   95
  BY AARON C. WATERS AND
  STEVEN M. STANLEY

GEORGE OLIVER CURME, JR.   121
  BY AUGUSTUS B. KINZEL

DAVID MATHIAS DENNISON   139
  BY H. RICHARD CRANE

JESSE W. M. DuMOND   161
  BY W. K. H. PANOFSKY

LUIGI GORINI 203
  BY JONATHAN BECKWITH AND
  DAN FRAENKEL

PERCY LAVON JULIAN 223
  BY BERNHARD WITKOP

KARL FRIEDRICH MEYER 269
  BY ALBERT B. SABIN

GEORGE SCATCHARD 335
  BY JOHN T. EDSALL AND
  WALTER H. STOCKMAYER

THEODORE SHEDLOVSKY 379
  BY RAYMOND M. FUOSS

VESTO MELVIN SLIPHER 411
  BY WILLIAM GRAVES HOYT

WILSON STUART STONE 451
  BY JAMES F. CROW

LORANDE LOSS WOODRUFF 471
  BY G. EVELYN HUTCHINSON

PREFACE

The *Biographical Memoirs* is a series of volumes, beginning in 1877, containing the biographies of deceased members of the National Academy of Sciences and bibliographies of their published scientific contributions. The goal of the Academy is to have these memoirs serve as a contribution toward the history of American science. Each biographical essay is written by an individual familiar with the discipline and the scientific career of the deceased. These volumes, therefore, provide a record of the lives and works of some of the most distinguished leaders of American science as witnessed and interpreted by their colleagues and peers. Though the primary concern is the members' professional lives and contributions, these memoirs also include those aspects of their lives in their home, school, college, or later life that led them to their scientific career.

The National Academy of Sciences is a private, honorary organization of scientists and engineers elected on the basis of outstanding contributions to knowledge. Established by a Congressional Act of Incorporation on March 3, 1863, the Academy works to further science and its use for the general welfare by bringing together the most qualified individuals to deal with scientific and technological problems of broad significance.

BRYCE CRAWFORD, JR.
Home Secretary

CAROLINE K. McEUEN
Associate Editor

Biographical Memoirs

VOLUME 52

LEASON HEBERLING ADAMS

January 16, 1887 – August 20, 1969

BY R. E. GIBSON

L EASON HEBERLING ADAMS was born in Cherryvale, Kansas, the son of William Barton and Katherine, née Heberling, Adams. Early in his life the family moved to Taylorville in southern Illinois, where with his father, a schoolteacher, he roamed the fields and the woods, learning to observe nature and gaining self reliance. In later years he frequently spoke with great pleasure of his early experience in this part of the country.

At the age of fifteen he entered the University of Illinois, his family having moved to Champaign-Urbana, and graduated with the degree of Bachelor of Science in 1906 when he was nineteen years old. His next degree came thirty-five years later, when Tufts University conferred on him the honorary degree of Doctor of Science, in recognition of his outstanding contributions to several fields of science. In the meantime, his education had progressed at an amazing pace, for Adams was endowed not only with an insatiable curiosity, but also with the discipline, the will, and the energy to satisfy his curiosity with solid and exact knowledge. He drank deep from the Pierian Spring. For example, in his early years at the Geophysical Laboratory, he developed an interest in chemical thermodynamics. To satisfy his interest, he and several colleagues (E. D. Williamson and G. W. Morey)[1]* studied the original works of Willard Gibbs, extracting their surpassing insight and wisdom page by page, and line by line. He became an outstanding authority on chemical thermodynamics.

After graduation from Illinois, young Leason spent two years in industry, first as a chemist with Morris and Company of Chicago, and next with the Missouri Pacific Railroad Company in St. Louis. These years had a great influence on his subsequent career. They gave him a lasting immunity to the lures of industry and its rich monetary rewards, but they also cultivated in him an appreciation of the practical problems of the engineer and of the disciplined use of time and money. Throughout his career, Adams was never intimidated by the difficulties of the practical problems presented by nature—he just set about mobilizing his own intellectual resources and ingenuity to solve them.

The year 1908 was a very significant one for young Adams. On January 25 he married Jeannette Maude Blaisdell of St. Louis, beginning an affectionate and harmonious partnership, the foundation of a secure, pleasant home, long remembered by the many who tasted of its hospitality. They had four children: Leason Blaisdell, William Muirhead, Madeline Jeannette, and Ralston Heberling. Later in the year he began what proved to be a long and productive career as a research scientist in Washington, D.C., first as a member of the staff of the technological branch of the U.S. Geological Survey, and two years later as a physical chemist on the staff of the Geophysical Laboratory of the Carnegie Institution of Washington. The move was a very natural one. In 1906 the Carnegie Institution had authorized the construction, in a then rural part of the District of Columbia, of a laboratory to support and extend novel experimental investigations of the

*See Appendix for numbered footnotes.

physics and chemistry of rock formation, started by Dr. Arthur L. Day and his colleagues in the technological branch of the Survey. In July 1907 a laboratory well equipped for these investigations was open for business with A. L. Day as director, and E. T. Allen, E. S. Shepherd, Walter P. White, G. A. Rankin, F. E. Wright, and J. K. Clement as members of the scientific staff.[2]

As research associate of John Johnston,[3] Adams began research on the effects of pressure and temperature on the behavior of physicochemical systems, particularly those of geological and petrological significance, an interest which he maintained throughout all the phases of his fifty-year-long career. These were days when precise scales for the measurement of high temperature and high pressure were still undeveloped. Adams' published works of that period (1910–1920) reflect his skill and meticulousness as an experimenter. They dealt not only with effects of environmental factors on solids, but also with experimental methods for measuring pressure and temperature consistently and accurately. At the same time, his capacity for critical thought, catalyzed by Johnston's incisive mind, impelled him to take nothing for granted. The paper "On the Effect of High Pressures on the Physical and Chemical Behavior of Solids" (1913) by Johnston and Adams is a model of critical scholarship.

The entry of the United States into World War I in 1917 brought into sharp relief the astounding fact that not only did the United States depend on German and Bohemian sources for optical glass, but U.S. technology had little or no knowledge and understanding of the chemical and physical processes required to produce glass of a quality demanded by the optical instruments so important to the support of the combat army and navy. In common with all his colleagues at the Geophysical Laboratory, Adams interrupted his researches to study the "optical glass problem," focusing his attention on the physics of the annealing process. The fundamental approach taken by Adams and Williamson yielded excellent practical results that were adopted by the industry. For this work, Adams received the prestigious Edward Longstreth Medal of the Franklin Institute in 1924.

Birefringence due to strain in glass and its elimination by annealing continued to be one of Adams' interests for many years. The paper "A Method for the Precise Measurement of Optical Path Difference, Especially in Stressed Glass" by Goranson[4] and Adams (1933) illustrated this continuing interest, Adams' skill as an experimenter, and his ability to explore in depth a strange field (Friedel optics) and find gold.

In passing, it should be noted that perusal of a list of Adams' publications, approximately 100, will reveal that many, in fact the majority, were published jointly with other investigators. It was a well-known fact among his colleagues, however, that Leason Adams never allowed his name to appear on a paper unless it contained an original contribution of his own and he endorsed the contents without reservation.

After World War I, Adams resumed his studies of the properties of materials under high pressures and the development of apparatus for making precise measurements over large ranges of pressure and temperature with special interest: (1) in the elastic properties of minerals and rocks; and (2) in fundamental studies of the effects of pressure on simple binary systems, mostly aqueous solutions.

The first line of investigation led him deeply into seismology and other branches of geophysics, particularly those dealing with the nature and composition of the interior of the earth. In the early decades of this century, seismologists were learning how to measure and interpret the velocities of longitudinal and transverse waves traveling deep into the interior of the earth, the famous Oppau explosion furnishing valuable data for the European sector. Adams devised apparatus for measuring the isothermal compressibility at 25°C of selected rocks and minerals between 2000 and 10,000 bars (approximately atmospheres), and with certain plausible assumptions he computed their density as a function of depth within the earth and the velocity of sound waves through them. Comparison of the velocities computed from laboratory measurements and those computed from seismic data indicated that below 60 km there existed material more basic than gabbro and approaching dunite (olivine) in composition. A chapter in the *Smithsonian Report for 1939* gives Adams' ideas on "The Earth's Interior, Its Nature and Composition."

In the course of his investigations of minerals, Adams determined the compressibility of diamond. His paper in the *Journal of the Washington Academy of Sciences* (1921) gives the first measured value obtained for this most incompressible of all minerals and a scholarly discussion of the results in the light of the current theories of solids propounded by Einstein, Gruneisen, Lindemann, and Debye.

In order to extend the range of temperature over which high-pressure effects could be measured, Adams devised a "bomb" in which systems could be studied at pressures up to 3000 bars and from 25 to 800°C. Three papers of geophysical significance came from this development: (1) "The System, Calcium Oxide-Carbon Dioxide" by Smyth[5] and Adams (1923); (2) "The Influence of Hydrostatic Pressure on the Critical Temperature of Magnetization for Iron and Other Materials" by Adams and Green[6] (1931); and (3) "The Influence of Pressure on the High-Low Inversion of Quartz" by Gibson,[7] *Journal of Physical Chemistry* 32(1928):1197.

Adams' second interest at that time, equilibrium in binary systems under pressure, resulted in a number of papers on the behavior of concentrated aqueous solutions of certain salts and their hydrates over a pressure range from 2000 to 12,000 bars. In the course of these pioneering studies, themselves classical examples of meticulous experimental work, Adams critically examined the thermodynamic concepts and logic then coming into wide use by students of solutions, particularly solutions of electrolytes. He had nagging doubts about their consistency and rigor. His paper on "Activity and Related Thermodynamic Quantities; Their Definition and Variation with Temperature and Pressure" (1936), a masterly piece of reasoning, gave for the first time a satisfactory proof of the variations of "activity" with temperature.

His experimental work in this field led to a number of papers by him and R. E. Gibson, of which we may cite "Equilibrium in Binary Systems under Pressure. I. An Experimental and Thermodynamic Investigation of the System, $NaCl-H_2O$, at 25°" by Adams (1931). This was truly pioneering work; it developed experimental methods for measuring accurately the appropriate thermodynamic quantities and rigorous methods for interpreting the data to determine the effects of pressure up to 10,000 bars on equilibria in heterogeneous binary systems.

In 1936, upon the retirement of Dr. Day, who had been director of the Geophysical Laboratory for thirty years, Dr. Adams was appointed acting director and a year later, director. Despite the pressures of administrative work and his constant efforts to encourage and support the staff in the development of their lines of research, Adams continued to work and write on the subjects mentioned above, but then encountered another interruption. Within two years the dark clouds of another world war were rising in the clear sky of American complacency. Along with many of his scientific colleagues, both in and out of the Carnegie Institution, Leason Adams heeded their portent. Putting the interests of the country ahead of his own desires, he interrupted his researches and placed his and the Laboratory's talents at the service of the nation.

In June 1941 he was appointed chairman of Section A, Division A (and a year later chairman of Division I), of the National Defense Research Committee with the task of investigating, among other things, the erosion of gun barrels caused by the action of hot propellant gases under high pressure and the rapid travel of projectiles along the bores of guns. This problem, which had taxed the ingenuity of ordnance specialists for many decades, was becoming acute, since gun erosion placed more and more severe limitations on the accurate life of guns as the muzzle velocities of shells were increased to meet urgent military requirements. With characteristic thoroughness, Adams set out to master available information and experience on gun erosion and assembled a group of scientists and engineers, backed by industrial firms and military arsenals, to study the problem and develop practical solutions.* This team effort did produce very significant results leading to improvements in ordnance that were adopted by the armed services and brought high-level recognition to members of the group. Adams himself was awarded the Presidential Medal for Merit in 1948.

Shortly after the cessation of hostilities, officially August 1945, Adams instituted a comprehensive review of the scientific policy and practices of the Geophysical Laboratory in the light of irreversible changes brought about by World War II. Some prewar programs were dropped, the investigators having moved into other fields; some were strengthened in the light of advances in instrumentation arising from the war effort. An excellent account of Adams' philosophy, his views

---

*For further information see John E. Burchard, ed., *Rockets, Guns and Targets* (Boston: Atlantic Monthly Press, Little Brown, 1948).

of the Laboratory's objectives, and an account of its programs are given in his annual report for the year 1947–1948 (*Carnegie Institution of Washington Yearbook,* 47), of which the first paragraph is quoted here.

> Studies of the earth have as their objective the determination of the nature of the processes whereby the whole earth and the materials of which it is composed have come into being and have acquired the forms, the disposition, and the mutual relations in which we find them. If we may be permitted to borrow terms from our biological colleagues and to expand their meanings somewhat, it might be said that earth processes are studied *in vivo, in vitro,* and *post mortem.*

The Laboratory program was to follow these three approaches with greatest, but not exclusive, emphasis on *in vitro,* that is, controlled experimental techniques.

The general policy and *modus operandi* as stated originally by Dr. Day remained unchanged. The staff members of the Laboratory, chosen for their keen interest in the Laboratory's broad objectives, were given free rein to formulate their own problems and to solve them. Many scientists who have since gained international reputations joined the Laboratory during Adams' term as director.

Upon his retirement in 1952 at the age of sixty-five, Leason Adams left an organization whose morale, enthusiasm, and ever increasing record of excellent scientific productivity remained outstanding after nearly fifty years, an achievement not often equalled.

In the postwar years, Dr. Adams resumed his personal studies of the effects of high pressure and temperature on the properties of rocks and minerals and of seismological exploration of the earth's crust. He worked with Dr. H. S. Yoder, Jr.[8] (now director of the Laboratory), on the design and use of apparatus for measuring the thermodynamic properties of solids including polymorphic transitions at pressures up to 12,000 bars and temperatures above 600°C, a project that made available vast areas of geophysical knowledge. Adams' paper on the stability of jadeite (1953) gives an example of this work. Advances in electronics during the war had placed in the hands of the Department of Terrestrial Magnetism (DTM) of the Carnegie Institution powerful new resources for the sensitive and precise measurement of motion and time from which were constructed very sensitive seismographs. In a cooperative program involving the DTM, the Navy, and the Geophysical Laboratory, these seismographs were deployed in the field and used to measure the travel time of shock waves initiated by suitably placed charges of explosives. Adams himself participated in the collection and interpretation of these data.

After his retirement, Dr. Adams served as a technical consultant to the National Bureau of Standards in the field of measuring and interpreting the effects of high pressures on a variety of materials.

These years were not kind to him personally. Jeannette Adams, his wife, with whom he had shared the vicissitudes of forty-seven years, died in 1954. His oldest son, Leason Blaisdell, died in the same year, and within a few years of the death of Ralston Adams, his youngest son.

The year 1957 saw the start of a new career for Leason Adams. He accepted an invitation from the University of California, Los Angeles, to become visiting professor of geophysics in the Institute of Geophysics and Planetary Physics. Together with his second wife, the former Freda R. Ostrow, whom he had married in July 1956, he pulled up his roots in Washington, sold their home, and established a new home in Pacific Palisades, California. Both Dr. and Mrs. Adams became thoroughly enthusiastic about West Coast living, and their hospitality is still remembered with pleasure by faculty members and former students alike.

At the Institute for Geophysics and Planetary Physics there was at that time a group actively working on the stability of rocks and minerals under high pressure and high temperature. Adams immediately started to implement his own interest and experience in this field by designing, constructing, and using an apparatus whereby changes in the crystallographic parameters of solids could be measured by analysis of their X-ray spectra, obtained directly as their pressure and, later, temperature environments were varied over very wide ranges. He adapted the anvil device originally developed by P. W. Bridgman in which the sample was placed between two opposing Carboloy anvils mounted in a powerful hydraulic press. Because Carboloy is not adequately transparent to X-rays, Adams first explored diamond as an anvil material, but found experimental difficulties, which could be overcome, but which were really unnecessary. After a year or so, Adams and his graduate student assistant, Briant L. Davis (now research professor of geophysics at the South Dakota School of Mines and Technology) turned to beryllium as their anvil material. The choice proved to be a very happy one—the strength and low atomic number of beryllium were appropriate for the transmission of high pressure to, and X-rays through, the specimen under study. By using an X-ray goniometer rather than a photographic method, Adams and Davis were able to make *continuous* series of measurements, extending over several hours, of the cell constants of specimens and, therefore, study the reaction kinetics of polymorphic transformations as well as the properties and regions of stability of the different polymorphs. This apparatus was finally developed to achieve pressures in excess of 25,000 bars and 500°C. It was unique at that time, but was soon reproduced by other investigators in the Institute and elsewhere, and, as was to be expected, has undergone refinements that have led to even better quantitative observations of the properties of solids over wider ranges of pressure and temperature.

Among the many systems he studied with his colleagues, Adams returned to a problem that had been on his mind for forty years—the calcite-aragonite transformation. At last he was able to study the kinetics of this transformation over a wide range of pressure and temperature, and with Dr. Davis he drew from the results some conclusions of geological interest (*Journal of Geophysical Research,* 1965).

As a result of his work at UCLA, Adams published some eight papers, all of them, in the words used by mathematicians, nontrivial. The majority, written with B. L. Davis, concerned the thermodynamic and kinetic properties of solids at high pressures and temperatures, and improved apparatus for extending these studies. Another paper, "Enthalpy Changes as Determined from Fusion Curves in Binary Systems" by Adams and Cohen (1966), was inspired by a problem brought to him by Lewis H. Cohen, then a graduate student (now professor of geophysics at the University of California, Riverside). In it, Adams returns to one of his early loves, the use of the thermodynamic reasoning of J. Willard Gibbs in solving problems presented by systems of potential geological applications.

Dr. Adams relinquished his professorship at UCLA and returned to Washington in March 1965. Failing eyesight had made experimental work more and more a strain on him, but it is not at all out of the question that half a century of life and work in the Washington area acted as a magnet against whose effects the wiles of California were powerless.

Two remarks made by his former associates at UCLA have a familiar ring to those who knew Adams before his retirement. Dr. Cohen wrote, "Through this gentleman from a generation long before mine, I derived more of a continuity with the past than I have from anyone else. When he left

UCLA in March of 1965 to go back to Washington, he inscribed his copy of Bridgman's *Physics of High Pressure* to me. I still cherish that volume more than any other book I possess."* Dr. Davis wrote, "One of the great qualities of Professor Adams was his willingness to allow the graduate student to pursue independent lines of thinking without structuring his thoughts or curtailing these independent probes into new areas. He would also take time to review papers or articles prepared for publication, which though not in his direct areas of interest, were studied by him for their content and presentability to the scientific community.... Professor Leason Adams has unquestionably left a mark on the scientific community, not only through his basic contributions to the field of geophysics, but also through the betterment and scientific development of his colleagues and students."†

Leason Adams was a gregarious man. He loved to exchange ideas and match wits with his fellows. Those who once tasted his soft spoken humor, his ready wit, and his encyclopedic knowledge gave him every opportunity to do so. He found outlets for these propensities in many ways, of which a few may be recalled here.

Participation in the activities of scientific societies afforded him greatest intellectual pleasure and contributed a great deal to his education. In this connection we might recall a remarkable, perceptive statement of Joseph Henry:

> Man is a sympathetic being, and no incentive to mental exertion is more powerful than that which springs from a desire for the approbation of his fellow men; besides this, frequent interchange of ideas and appreciative encouragement are almost essential to the successful prosecution of labors requiring profound thought and continued mental exertion. Hence it is important that those engaged in similar pursuits should have opportunities for frequent meetings at stated periods.... Furthermore, a society of

---

* Personal communication.
† Personal communication.

this kind becomes a means of instruction to all its members, the knowledge of each becoming, as it were, the knowledge of the whole.*

In the first three decades of this century, the scientific life of Washington was young, vigorous, and uncomplicated. Organizations such as the Bureau of Standards, the Naval Observatory, the Coast and Geodetic Survey, the Bureau of Chemistry of the Department of Agriculture, the Surgeon General's Office, the Hygienic Laboratory, the Carnegie Institution, the Naval Research Laboratory, the Geological Survey, the Smithsonian Institution, the Bureau of Ethnology, and others had attracted men of outstanding scientific caliber, who, while engaged in research inspired by practical problems, retained a deep interest in the fundamentals of their specific disciplines, keeping themselves abreast of the progress of these disciplines not only for their intellectual satisfaction, but also as sources of material for their applied researches. Those men and women pooled their knowledge and experience in the meetings of the various scientific societies.

Because the career of L. H. Adams was to a great extent influenced by the scientific climate in Washington, and in turn exerted reciprocally a constructive influence on this environment, it may be appropriate here to delineate the characteristics of the societies that reflected this environment. The oldest, the Philosophical Society of Washington, held its first meeting on March 13, 1871, with Joseph Henry in the chair. The Society "embraced *all sciences,* except those, if they be sciences, of speculative thought."† In those days a

---

*Joseph Henry, Anniversary Address to the Philosophical Society of Washington (1871), *Bulletin of the Philosophical Society,* 1 (1874): v–xiv.

†See W. J. Humphreys, "The Philosophical Society of Washington through a Thousand Meetings," *Journal of the Washington Academy of Sciences,* 20(1930): 245–316. This paper includes photographs of the presidents of the Society from 1871 through 1930. F. N. Frenkiel in "Origins and Early Days of the Philosophical

well-educated, intellectual man could be expected to take an intelligent interest in the whole spectrum of the sciences from mathematics to descriptive biology. Recognizing this, Joseph Henry, in his first presidential address (November 1871) remarked, "With so many facilities as exist in the City of Washington for the pursuit of science, this Society would be derelict in duty did it fail to materially aid, through communication of thought and concert of action, the advancement of the great cause of human improvement." In 1980 people are still trying feverishly to implement, without much knowledge of the past, the wisdom of Joseph Henry. Although the Philosophical Society made provision for the establishment of sections to accommodate members with specialized interests, this arrangement proved to be inadequate to cope with the rapid advances in all branches of science. As a result specialists formed societies of their own—the chemists in 1874, the anthropologists in 1878, the biologists in 1880, the entomologists in 1884, the geographers in 1888, the geologists in 1893—so that for a long time the chief interest of members of the Philosophical Society lay in the fields of the more mathematically dependent sciences—physics, astronomy, geodesy, geophysics, meteorology, and the like.

Prior to the end of World War II, the meetings of the Philosophical Society of Washington were devoted chiefly to papers and informal communications by members, or local people introduced by members. It formed a valuable forum where an investigator could present a recently completed piece of work for the edification and criticism of his fellows, or where interesting pieces of information gained by reading or experience could be aired.

Furthermore, through the *Bulletin* of the Society, and

Society of Washington," *Bulletin of the Philosophical Society of Washington*, 16(1963):9–24, gives an even more detailed account of the antecedents, the founding, and the history of the Society.

later minutes published in the *Journal of the Washington Academy of Sciences*, the priority date of the presentation of a paper was established. (This was before the days when newspapers became a common vehicle for the early publication of scientific results and also before the lecturer from out of town with accompanying expenses became popular.)

Adams was elected a member of the Philosophical Society in 1910 and for many years participated enthusiastically in its activities. He read a number of papers before the Society, contributed regularly to the discussions, and took on some of the chores of planning and operating the Society through membership on committees or election to office. In 1929 he was elected the fifty-first president of the Society.

In 1909 Leason Adams joined the American Chemical Society, which automatically made him a member of the Chemical Society of Washington (CSW). He soon took part enthusiastically in the activities of this Society, both scientific and social. The intellectual fare served up at the meetings of the CSW was excellent—the membership consisted of chemists, mainly hand-picked men and women attracted to Washington by senior officials of international reputation and by the opportunity to work on vital and interesting problems.

Compared with the somewhat serious and staid physicists, the chemists were a rather convivial bunch. They smoked pipes, enjoyed a glass of beer, played poker, and had an inexhaustible supply of diverting anecdotes in addition to tastes for music and other arts. Adams found their company much to his liking. His capacity to down a tankard of beer in record time became legendary. In later years, after his retirement, his visits to Washington were a signal to certain chemists and their comrades in other disciplines to organize a poker party.

It was not surprising that his services as a leader in organizing the meetings of the CSW were in great demand and that he was elected president for the year 1925. Among other innovations he introduced into the CSW was the establishment of the Hillebrand Prize, the first of which he presented to R. F. Jackson in 1925. Adams' presidential address, "Chemistry as a Branch of Mathematics," was a good example of the breadth of his scientific interest.

Adams also took part in the affairs of the national society, the American Chemical Society. He served as councillor (1926–1929), associate editor of the *Journal* of the Society (1934–1948), and regional director (1940–1945).

Between 1910 and 1926 or so, there existed in Washington an unorganized body known as the Metachemical Club. It was composed of chemists who met at irregular intervals for dinner and discussion of metachemistry—any subject beyond chemistry. The name of the Club is probably ascribable to John Johnston. Adams may have been in at the founding of the Club; he was certainly one of the early members.

In the last three decades of the nineteenth century, the number and variety of scientific activities in Washington, noted by Joseph Henry, grew exponentially and, indeed, has done so ever since. The consequent proliferation of specialized societies suggested the desirability of an organization to act as a federating agency to which various societies might adhere, loosely perhaps, but providing a vehicle for interdisciplinary communication and concert of action. Local leaders, led by the Philosophical Society, moved to establish a Washington Academy of Sciences, which was incorporated on February 18, 1898. Leason Adams was elected a member (now called a fellow) of the Academy in 1912. Among other activities related to the Academy, he became very interested in the welfare of its *Journal.* Being concerned that the vitality of an academy journal depended on the variety as well as the quality of the papers published, he tried to persuade his friends in the physical sciences to publish at least some of their work in the *Journal* (there was no dearth of papers in the descriptive natural sciences). He himself contributed some fourteen papers in the *Journal* between 1912 and 1931, among these his classical paper on the compressibility of diamond. He was elected president of the Academy in 1932.

Adams' growing interest in geology, the chief source of material for *in vitro* investigation of the earth, inspired his membership in a number of societies specializing in discussions of, and publication about, this subject—the Geological Society of Washington (of which he was elected president in 1950), the Geological Society of America, and the Mineralogical Society of Great Britain and Ireland. In addition, he took an active part in two informal dynamic groups in Washington, the Petrologists' Club and the Pick and Hammer Club, who held meetings in various places, often in the Geophysical Laboratory.

The American Geophysical Union (AGU) was created in 1919 as an Executive Committee of the National Research Council of the National Academy of Sciences to function as the American National Committee of the newly formed International Union of Geodesy and Geophysics. Its diverse scientific agenda were carried out by six sections, specializing in the fields of geodesy, seismology, meteorology, terrestrial magnetism and electricity, oceanography, and volcanology, corresponding to the associations of the International Union (later two new sections were added—hydrology in 1930 and tectonophysics in 1940). Within a year after its foundation, Leason Adams was selected as a member of the AGU and was soon loaded with new responsibilities. He was president of the Section of Volcanology from 1922 to 1924, president of the Section of Seismology (1926–1929), vice president of the Union (1929–1930, 1941–1944), and the first president of the Section of Tectonophysics (1940–1943). He was elected president of the AGU for the term 1944–1947 and also had the honor of serving as vice president of the International Union of Geodesy and Geophysics for the years 1948 through 1951.

In presenting Dr. Adams for the Bowie Medal, the highest award of the AGU, M. A. Tuve remarked on May 1, 1950, "I am privileged to recommend to the Union for the honor of the Twelfth Annual Award [of the Bowie Medal] a geophysicist who not only meets in the fullest the requirements of attainment and contribution in the advancement of geophysics for over forty years, but is also an outstanding example of devotion to his chosen field."

For fifty-four years, from the date of his election in 1915 to his death in 1969, Leason Adams derived great pleasure and no little pride from his membership in the Cosmos Club.* Here he had the opportunity to mingle with men from all over the world distinguished in a wide variety of learned professions, to exchange views with them in the lounge or the dining room, to match wits with them over the bridge table. From 1932 through 1936 he served on the Committee on Admissions, a most exacting assignment, as its secretary in

---

*According to Dr. Humphreys ("Philosophical Society of Washington"), the original inspiration for the founding of the Cosmos Club arose in the Philosophical Society, which for many years held its meetings in the Surgeon General's office in the Old Ford's Theatre Building. At the close of the scientific meetings, members fell into discussions of general topics that more and more frequently had to be continued over beer and pretzels in the more relaxed environment of a nearby tavern. The pleasure and profit derived from these discussions led to the idea of creating a club where members of the scientific community might be joined in a dignified, convivial atmosphere by their fellows, interested and practicing in the fields of literature, the fine arts, public service, and the like. A period of gestation ensued. During this time the desirability of such a club in Washington seems to have occurred to a number of people, including those who had pleasant impressions of similar institutions in London and New York. The written histories of the Cosmos Club make no mention of the role of the Philosophical Society in its inception. However, the fact that the entire Board of Managers of the new club were members of the Philosophical Society and that by resolution of the Club on December 12, 1878, all members of the Society were invited to become original members of the Club indicates that the accounts of Humphreys and Frenkiel are substantive.

1932, and chairman in 1934 and 1935. Recognizing his stature as a scientist, his acknowledged good judgment, and his devotion to the Club's welfare, his fellow members elected him vice president in 1938 and president in 1939.

In recognition of his contributions to geophysics, the National Academy of Sciences elected Dr. Adams to membership (rather belatedly perhaps) in 1954. Among other honorary memberships he held were fellow of the Royal Astronomical Society (London), Sigma Xi, and Phi Lambda Upsilon.

Leason Adams enjoyed teaching, particularly the instruction of advanced students. Unfortunately, the demands of other duties prevented him from indulging his taste for teaching as much as he would have liked. However, he taught physical chemistry and thermodynamics at the George Washington University (1927–1928) and never refused an invitation to address students of other universities both in and out of Washington. His experiences as visiting professor at UCLA have already been outlined. Adams' formal lectures were more solid and systematic than entertaining, but in an informal question and answer seminar his performance was superb. An onlooker could see that he soon established a complete rapport with the students, and as the seminar progressed their faces lighted up with understanding as his sympathetic answers to questions or his lucid explanations of points of interest proceeded. Adams was an "opener of doors" to his students and younger colleagues, an educator in the best sense of the term.

No biography of Leason H. Adams would be complete without an account of his extra-professional activities, which were motivated by the same curiosity and carried out with the same informed thoroughness that characterized *all* his undertakings.

He was one of the early radio fans; starting with crystal

sets and headphones, he built a series of radio receivers that reflected the rapid advances in technology occurring during the second and third decades of this century. Visitors to his home on 39th Street, N.W., were entertained by a progression of radio entertainments, first through headphones, then from horn loud speakers, and finally from a succession of cone speakers of ever-increasing quality. His early interest in what is now called electronics is reflected in papers he published in 1919 and 1924.

While a member of the staff of the Geophysical Laboratory, he designed and supervised in detail the building of two houses. The first, built in 1916, was situated about a block southwest of Chevy Chase Circle; the second, built in the 1930's, on a large tract of land at Bradley Boulevard and Burdette Road in Maryland, then far out in the country. By this time Adams had become a very knowledgeable gardener, and laid out his property somewhat in the style of an English landscape garden, a formal garden centered around a large lily pool and surrounded by indigenous trees and wildflowers.

His love of the outdoors, probably cultivated during his boyhood in southern Illinois, manifested itself in many ways, of which a few may be mentioned here. In the late 1920's he spent many weekends with his colleagues, J. Frank Schairer[9] and others, clearing out trees and underbrush to blaze part of the Appalachian Trail in the mountains of Virginia. He was one of the pioneers in making this now famous recreational asset.

He played golf and was a member of the Kirkside Golf Club, a small but attractive course situated west-southwest of Chevy Chase Circle, but long since fallen a victim to real estate developers. He was also a member of a group called the "Early Birds" or the "Oily Boids," which met frequently on the first tee of Rock Creek Golf Course promptly at 6:00 a.m., to complete a round before work of the day began. In the early 1930's he studied the art of sailing with customary diligence; to practice it he built in his garage, with the help of his oldest son, a Snipe, a sixteen foot sailing boat, and sailed out of West River, Maryland. He soon showed practical as well as theoretical mastery of the art.

His retirement years between his departure from UCLA in 1965 and his death on August 20, 1969 were peaceful ones. His home life was relaxed and happy. He retained an active interest in the scientific and social activities of his former colleagues, both young and old, and was often seen in the Cosmos Club. During these years his unquenchable curiosity led him to explore those areas that lie beyond the boundaries of systematic experiment and theory and into the realm of first sources—the realm of the thinkers, prophets, and poets who saw the hand of one God in all the phenomena of nature and of human experience. He took particular pleasure in conversations with rabbis and other students of the Old Testament.

The life and work of Leason H. Adams might be epitomized by the statement that he was truly a representative of the nineteenth century American school of pragmatic natural philosophers, a self-reliant school that took no man's word for it but looked to Nature herself for answers to its questions. Like those he admired and emulated—Joseph Henry, Willard Gibbs, Benjamin Silliman, Percy Bridgman, Theodore Richards, Richard Tolman, Arthur Day—his inquiring mind was disciplined by a passion to "get the facts" and link them together in terms of operationally-defined concepts and rigorous mathematics. Speculation and dogma were luxuries he felt he could not afford. His curiosity led him into many fields of science, and words paraphrased from Samuel

Johnson's epitaph of Oliver Goldsmith may aptly apply to Leason Adams:

> *Qui nullum fere scientiae genus non tetigit,*
> *Nullum quod tetigit non ornavit.*

THE AUTHOR ACKNOWLEDGES with deep gratitude information and assistance provided by Professors George Tunell, Briant L. Davis, and L. H. Cohen, and by Mrs. Freda Ostrow Adams. He is particularly indebted to Dr. Hatten S. Yoder, Jr., for many valuable suggestions that have improved this paper and, indeed, for the opportunity to write it at all.

APPENDIX

*Notes on Members of the Geophysical Laboratory
Mentioned in the Text*

1. Erskine D. Williamson (1886–1923): M.A., B.Sc., Edinburgh University; Mathematician and Physical Chemist, Geophysical Laboratory, 1914–1923.
   George W. Morey (1888–1965): B.S., University of Minnesota; Chemist, Geophysical Laboratory, 1912–1957; Acting Director, 1952–1953.
2. Arthur L. Day (1869–1960): B.A., Ph.D., Yale University; Director, Geophysical Laboratory, 1907–1936.
   E. T. Allen (1864–1964): A.B., Amherst College; Ph.D., The Johns Hopkins University; Chemist, Geophysical Laboratory, 1907–1932.
   E. S. Shepherd (1879–1949): A.B., Cornell University; Chemist, Geophysical Laboratory, 1907–1946.
   Walter P. White (1867–1946): A.B., Amherst College; Ph.D., Cornell University; Physicist, Geophysical Laboratory, 1907–1935.
   G. A. Rankin (1884–1963): A.B., Cornell University; Chemist, Geophysical Laboratory, 1907–1916.
   F. E. Wright (1877–1953): Ph.D., Heidelberg University; Physicist, Geophysical Laboratory, 1907–1944.
   J. K. Clement (1800–?): B.S., Trinity College; Ph.D., Göttingen University; Chemist, Geophysical Laboratory, 1907.
3. John Johnston (1881–1950): D.Sc., St. Andrews University; Chemist, Geophysical Laboratory, 1908–1916; Sterling Professor of Chemistry, Yale University, 1919–1927; Director of Research, U.S. Steel Corporation, 1927–1946.
4. Roy W. Goranson (1900–1956): B.A., British Columbia University; Ph.D., Harvard University; Petrologist, Geophysical Laboratory, 1926–1951; Physicist, Los Alamos Scientific Laboratory, 1951–1956.
5. F. Hastings Smyth (1888–1960): A.B., Hamilton College; Ph.D., Massachusetts Institute of Technology; Chemist, Geophysical Laboratory, 1919–1925; Priest, member Cowley Fathers, 1927–1960.
6. J. W. Green (1874–1971): Physicist, Department of Terrestrial Magnetism, 1920–1938; prior to 1920, Observer, U.S. Coast and Geodetic Survey. Assigned to the Geophysical Laboratory by DTM to conduct cooperative studies of the effect of pressure on the magnetic inversion of iron.
7. R. E. Gibson (1901–): B.Sc., Ph.D., Edinburgh University; Physical Chemist, Geophysical Laboratory, 1924–1946; Applied Physics Laboratory of The Johns Hopkins University, 1946–; Acting Director, 1947; Director, 1948–1969; Professor of Biomedical Engineering, The Johns Hopkins University School of Medicine, 1969–1978.
8. Hatten S. Yoder, Jr. (1921–): S.B., University of Chicago; Ph.D., Massachusetts Institute of Technology; Petrologist, Geophysical Laboratory, 1948–; Director, 1971–.
9. J. F. Schairer (1904–1970): B.S., Ph.D., Yale University; Petrologist, Geophysical Laboratory, 1927–1970.

BIBLIOGRAPHY

1911

With J. Johnston. The influence of pressure on the melting points of certain metals. Am. J. Sci., 31:501–17.

With J. Johnston. The phenomenon of occlusion in precipitates of barium sulfate, and its relation to the exact determination of sulfate. J. Am. Chem. Soc., 33:829–45.

With J. Johnston. Der Einfluss des Druckes auf die Schmelzpunkte einiger Metalle. Z. Anorg. Chem., 72:11–30.

1912

With J. Johnston. A note on the standard scale of temperatures between 200° and 1100°. Am. J. Sci., 33:534–45.

With J. Johnston. A note on the standard scale of temperatures between 200° and 1100°. J. Wash. Acad. Sci., 2:275–84.

With J. Johnston. On the density of solid substances with especial reference to permanent changes produced by high pressures. J. Am. Chem. Soc., 34:563–84.

With J. Johnston. Die Dichte fester Stoffe, mit besonderer Berücksichtigung der durch hohe Drucke hervorgerufenen dauernden Änderungen. Z. Anorg. Chem., 76:274–302.

1913

With J. Johnston. On the effect of high pressures on the physical and chemical behavior of solids. Am. J. Sci., 35:205–53.

With J. Johnston. Über den Einfluss hoher Drucke auf das physikalische und chemische Verhalten fester Stoffe. Z. Anorg. Chem., 80:281–334.

A useful type of formula for the interpolation and representation of experimental results. J. Wash. Acad. Sci., 3:469–74.

1914

With J. Johnston. Observations on the Daubrée experiment and capillarity in relation to certain geological speculations. J. Geol., 22:1–15.

With J. Johnston. Über Daubrées Experiment und die Kapillarität in Beziehung auf gewisse geologische Probleme. Centralbl. Mineral. Geol. Paläontol., 171–83.

Calibration tables for copper-constantan and platinum-platinrhodium thermoelements. J. Am. Chem. Soc., 36:65–72.

1915

Some notes on the theory of the Rayleigh-Zeiss interferometer. J. Wash. Acad. Sci., 5:265–76.

The measurement of the freezing-point depression of dilute solutions. J. Am. Chem. Soc., 37:481–96.

The use of the interferometer for the analysis of solutions. J. Am. Chem. Soc., 37:1181–94.

1916

With J. Johnston. On the measurement of temperature in boreholes. Econ. Geol., 11:741–62.

1919

With E. D. Williamson and J. Johnston. The determination of the compressibility of solids at high pressures. J. Am. Chem. Soc., 41:12–42.

With E. D. Williamson. Some physical constants of mustard "gas." J. Wash. Acad. Sci., 9:30–35.

With W. P. White. A furnace temperature regulator. Phys. Rev., 14:44–48.

With E. D. Williamson. Temperature distribution in solids during heating or cooling. Phys. Rev., 14:99–114.

With R. E. Hall. Application of the thermionic amplifier to conductivity measurements. J. Am. Chem. Soc., 41:1515–25.

Tables and curves for use in measuring temperatures with thermocouples. Bull. Am. Inst. Min. Metall. Eng., 153:2111–24.

With E. D. Williamson. The relation between birefringence and stress in various types of glass. J. Wash. Acad. Sci., 9:609–23.

1920

With E. D. Williamson. Note on the motion of the stirrers used in optical glass manufacture. J. Am. Ceram. Soc., 3:671–77.

With E. D. Williamson. A note on the annealing of optical glass. J. Opt. Soc. Am., 4:213–23.

With E. D. Williamson. The annealing of glass. J. Franklin Inst., 190:835–70.

1921

The compressibility of diamond. J. Wash. Acad. Sci., 11:45–50.
Note on the measurement of the density of minerals. Am. Mineral., 6:11–12.

1922

With H. S. Roberts. The use of minerals as radio-detectors. Am. Mineral., 7:131–36.
Temperature changes accompanying isentropic, isenergic, and isenkaumic expansion. J. Wash. Acad. Sci., 12:407–11.

1923

With E. D. Williamson. On the compressibility of minerals and rocks at high pressures. J. Franklin Inst., 195:475–529.
With F. H. Smyth. The system, calcium oxide-carbon dioxide. J. Am. Chem. Soc., 45:1167–84.
With E. D. Williamson. Density distribution in the Earth. J. Wash. Acad. Sci., 13:413–28.

1924

A physical source of heat in springs. J. Geol., 32:191–94.
With H. S. Washington. The distribution of iron in meteorites and in the Earth. J. Wash. Acad. Sci., 14:333–40.
Temperatures at moderate depths within the Earth. J. Wash. Acad. Sci., 14:459–72.
Thermostats for very high temperatures. J. Opt. Soc. Am. Rev. Sci. Instrum., 9:599–603.

1925

With E. D. Williamson. The composition of the Earth's interior. In: *Smithsonian Report for 1923*, Publ. 2767, pp. 241–60.

1926

With R. E. Gibson. The compressibilities of dunite and of basalt glass and their bearing on the composition of the Earth. Proc. Natl. Acad. Sci. USA, 12:275–83.
With R. E. Gibson. Die Kompressibilität des Dunits und des basaltischen Glases und ihre Beziehungen zur Zusammensetzung der Erde. Beitr. Geophys., 15:241–50.

Calibration tables for selected thermocouples. In: *International Critical Tables*, 1:57–59.

Chemistry as a branch of mathematics. J. Wash. Acad. Sci., 16:266–76.

1927

A note on the change of compressibility with pressure. J. Wash. Acad. Sci., 17:529–33.

1929

With R. E. Gibson. The elastic properties of certain basic rocks and of their constituent minerals. Proc. Natl. Acad. Sci. USA, 15:713–24.

1930

With R. E. Gibson. The compressibility of rubber. J. Wash. Acad. Sci., 20:213–23.

With R. E. Gibson. The melting curve of sodium chloride dihydrate. An experimental study of an incongruent melting at pressures up to twelve thousand atmospheres. J. Am. Chem. Soc., 52:4252–64.

1931

With R. E. Hall. The influence of pressure on the solubility of sodium chloride in water. A new method for the measurement of the solubilities of electrolytes under pressure. J. Wash. Acad. Sci., 21:183–94.

With J. W. Green. The influence of hydrostatic pressure on the critical temperature of magnetization for iron and other materials. Philos. Mag., 12:361–80.

With R. E. Hall. The effect of pressure on the electrical conductivity of solutions of sodium chloride and of other electrolytes. J. Phys. Chem., 35:2145–63.

Equilibrium in binary systems under pressure. I. An experimental and thermodynamic investigation of the system, $NaCl-H_2O$, at 25°. J. Am. Chem. Soc., 53:3769–3813.

The compressibility of fayalite, and the velocity of elastic waves in peridotite with different iron-magnesium ratios. Beitr. Geophys., 31:315–21.

With R. E. Gibson. The cubic compressibility of certain substances. J. Wash. Acad. Sci., 16:381–90.

1932

Equilibrium in binary systems under pressure. II. The system, K_2SO_4-H_2O, at 25°. J. Am. Chem. Soc., 54:2229–43.

With R. E. Gibson. Equilibrium in binary systems under pressure. III. The influence of pressure on the solubility of ammonium nitrate in water at 25°. J. Am. Chem. Soc., 54:4520–37.

1933

The annealing of glass as a physical problem. J. Franklin Inst., 216:39–71.

With R. E. Gibson. Changes of chemical potential in concentrated solutions of certain salts. J. Am. Chem. Soc., 55:2679–95.

With R. W. Goranson. A method for the precise measurement of optical path-difference, especially in stressed glass. J. Franklin Inst., 216:475–504.

1936

A simplified apparatus for high hydrostatic pressures. Rev. Sci. Instrum., 7:174–77.

Activity and related thermodynamic quantities; their definition, and variation with temperature and pressure. Chem. Rev., 19: 1–26.

1937

The Earth's interior, its nature and composition. Sci. Mon., 44: 199–209.

With R. W. Goranson and R. E. Gibson. Construction and properties of the manganin resistance pressure gauge. Rev. Sci. Instrum., 8:230–35.

Annual report of the Acting Director, 1936–1937. Carnegie Inst. Washington Yearb., 36:109–34.

1938

The freezing-point—solubility curves of hydrates and other compounds under pressure. Am. J. Sci., 35-A:1–18.

The Earth's interior, its nature and composition. In: *Smithsonian Report for 1937*, Publ. 3459, pp. 255–68.

Annual report of the Director, 1937–1938. Carnegie Inst. Washington Yearb., 37:105–36.

The significance of pressure and of volume in geophysical investigations. In: *Cooperation in Research,* pp. 37–47. Wash., D.C.: Carnegie Institute of Washington Publ. 501.

1939

Elastic properties of materials of the Earth's crust. In: *Internal Constitution of the Earth,* ed. B. Gutenberg, pp. 71–89. N. Y.: McGraw-Hill.

Annual report of the Director, 1938–1939. Carnegie Inst. Washington Yearb., 38:33–35.

1940

Annual report of the Director, 1939–1940. Carnegie Inst. Washington Yearb., 39:29–54.

1941

Annual report of the Director, 1940–1941. Carnegie Inst. Washington Yearb., 40:35–56.

Equilibrium in heterogeneous systems at high temperatures and pressures. Chem. Rev., 29:447–59.

1942

Annual report of the Director, 1941–1942. Carnegie Inst. Washington Yearb., 41:29–37.

1943

Annual report of the Director, 1942–1943. Carnegie Inst. Washington Yearb., 42:27–29.

1944

Annual report of the Director, 1943–1944. Carnegie Inst. Washington Yearb., 43:21–22.

1945

Annual report of the Director, 1944–1945. Carnegie Inst. Washington Yearb., 44:19–20.

1946

Annual report of the Director, 1945–1946. Carnegie Inst. Washington Yearb., 45:23–35.

1947

Annual report of the Director, 1946–1947. Carnegie Inst. Washington Yearb., 46:27–41.
Some unsolved problems of geophysics. Trans. Am. Geophys. Union, 28:673–79.

1948

Annual report of the Director, 1947–1948. Carnegie Inst. Washington Yearb., 47:27–51.

1949

Annual report of the Director, 1948–1949. Carnegie Inst. Washington Yearb., 48:29–55.

1950

Annual report of the Director, 1949–1950. Carnegie Inst. Washington Yearb., 49:27–59.

1951

Annual report of the Director, 1950–1951. Carnegie Inst. Washington Yearb., 50:33–63.
Elastic properties of materials of the Earth's crust. In: *Internal Constitution of the Earth*, 2d ed., ed. B. Gutenberg, pp. 49–80. N. Y.: Dover Publications.
With H. S. Washington. The chemical and petrological nature of the Earth's crust. In: *Internal Constitution of the Earth*, 2d ed., ed. B. Gutenberg, pp. 81–106. N. Y.: Dover Publications.

1952

List of systems investigated at Geophysical Laboratory. Am. J. Sci., Bowen Vol.: 1–26.
Annual report of the Director, 1951–1952. Carnegie Inst. Washington Yearb., 51:35–63.

1953

A note on the stability of jadeite. Am. J. Sci., 251:299–308.

With H. E. Tatel and M. A. Tuve. Studies of the Earth's crust using waves from explosions. Proc. Am. Philos. Soc., 97:658–69.

1954

With F. A. Rowe. The preparation of specimens for the focusing-type X-ray spectrometer. Am. Mineral., 39:215–21.

1962

With B. L. Davis. Reexamination of KNO_3IV and transition rate of $KNO_3II \rightleftarrows KNO_3IV$. Institute of Geophysics, University of California, Los Angeles, Publ. No. 246.

With B. L. Davis. Rapidly running transitions at high pressure. Proc. Natl. Acad. Sci. USA, 48:982–90.

1963

With B. L. Davis. Transition rates of KNO_3 high-pressure polymorphs. J. Phys. Chem. Solids, 24:787–94.

1964

With B. L. Davis. X-ray diffraction evidence for a critical end point for cerium I and cerium II. J. Phys. Chem. Solids, 25:379–88.

With B. L. Davis. High pressure polymorphs in the silver iodide phase diagram. Science, 146:519–21.

1965

With B. L. Davis. Continuous observation of polymorphic changes under high pressure. Am. J. Sci., 263:359–83.

With B. L. Davis. Kinetics of the calcite $\rightleftarrows$ aragonite transformation. J. Geophys. Res., 70:433–41.

1966

With L. H. Cohen. Enthalpy changes as determined from fusion curves in binary systems. Am. J. Sci., 264:543–61.

NORMAN LEVI BOWEN

June 21, 1887–September 11, 1956

BY HANS P. EUGSTER

In the history of experimental research in petrology, in particular the study of heterogeneous equilibria in silicate melts, he was the great pioneer, in fact his position is unique, for no one has broken so much new ground, nor contributed in such rich measure to the solution of fundamental problems of petrogenesis.

Tilley (1957, p. 18)

NORMAN LEVI BOWEN, the leading figure of the century in igneous petrology, died more than twenty years ago. This time lapse is both a disadvantage and a challenge. Personal details have faded, but we are perhaps better able to appreciate his enormous contributions and influence. I do not intend to assess Bowen's work in the light of today's knowledge. That would be unfair, because since 1956 we have lived through a revolution in the earth sciences. Many basic tenets had to be abandoned or severely modified, including some of Bowen's ideas on igneous rock evolution and parentage. Rather I propose to illuminate, by a careful reading of his principal published works, the sources and evolution of his ideas from *within* his time and his work. We will learn how he chose his problems and how his concepts developed; this will afford us an intimate glimpse of an unusual mind at work. At the conclusion we contemplate briefly what Bowen's work means to today's petrologist.

I did have the pleasure of being associated with Dr. Bowen at the Geophysical Laboratory, but only late in his career, after his retirement. Nevertheless, it was an unforgettable experience to watch him work with O. F. Tuttle on the granite system. I particularly remember a characteristic episode. One afternoon I gave Bowen an account of my unruly and seemingly contradictory data on the system muscovite-paragonite. The next morning I received a sheet of paper on which was drawn the only possible phase diagram, neatly solving my problems. Here was his legendary kindness and willingness to help.

BIOGRAPHICAL DATA

Norman Levi Bowen was born at Kingston, Ontario on June 21, 1887. His father, William Alfred Bowen, was a native of Chigwell, England, and his mother, Elizabeth McCormick, was from Kingston. Norman had one brother, Charles, born in 1879. Bowen was educated in local schools and attended Queen's University from 1903 to 1909. He completed a B.Sc. degree in mineralogy and geology, and subsequently studied at MIT from 1909 to 1912 where he obtained his Ph.D. In 1911 he married Mary Lamont of Charlottetown, Prince Edward Island, Canada, and they had a daughter, Catherine Lamont Bowen, born December 18, 1914 in Washington, D.C.

Bowen worked at the Geophysical Laboratory of the Carnegie Institution of Washington from 1910 to 1911, 1912 to 1918, 1920 to 1937, and 1947 to 1952, when he retired. During the period from 1919 to 1920 he taught at Queen's University and from 1937 to 1947 at the University of Chicago. Bowen became a naturalized U.S. citizen in 1933.

Honorary degrees were conferred upon him by Harvard, Queen's, and Yale Universities in 1936, 1941, and 1951. He was elected a member of the U.S. National Academy of Sciences in 1935, a foreign member of the Royal Society of London in 1949, and a member of Societies and Academies of London, India, Finland, Halle, Rome, and Belgium. He received the Bigsby Medal of the Geological Society of London (1931), the Penrose Medal of The Geological Society of America (1941), the Miller Medal of the Royal Society of Canada (1943), the Roebling Medal of the Mineralogical Society of America (1950), the Wollaston Medal of the Geological Society of London (1950), the Hayden Medal of the Academy of Natural Sciences of Philadelphia (1953), and the Bakhuis Roozeboom Medal of the Royal Netherlands Academy (1954).

During his last two years his health was failing and he died on September 11, 1956.

1907–1917: INITIAL SCIENTIFIC CONTRIBUTIONS

During his studies, Bowen put particular emphasis on chemistry, a fact of central significance in his later career. Equally important was his early and long association with geological field parties, to this day a typical and valuable aspect of Canadian geological education. The first summer, 1907, was spent at Larder Lake in Eastern Ontario, and the subsequent summers of 1908 and 1909 at Abitibi and Gowganda Lake, respectively, all parties being supported by the Ontario Bureau of Mines. During these studies, Bowen observed the intimate association of granophyre with diabase, and this observation may well have been the critical impetus for his lifelong involvement with igneous rock parentage and evolution. Originally, he accounted for the granophyre as a hydrothermal product between diabase and the surrounding slate, but he later changed his mind (1915c, p. 49).*

---

*Years in parentheses without authors refer to Bowen's publications.

During his studies at Queen's, and because of his double involvement with chemistry and geology, Bowen became aware of the pioneering work of J. H. L. Vogt in Norway on silicate liquids (Vogt, 1903) and decided to make this his field of inquiry. Vogt did not encourage study in Norway and hence Bowen decided to enroll at MIT in the fall of 1909. After one year he joined the Geophysical Laboratory in Washington to carry out his thesis project. Meanwhile, in the summer of 1910, he had his own field party in the Thunder Bay area of Lake Superior, where he encountered large masses of plagioclase enclosed in diabase. This observation awakened a permanent interest in monomineralic rocks, such as anorthosites and ultramafics.

The choice of thesis topic, the system $NaAlSiO_4$-$CaAl_2Si_2O_8$ (nepheline, carnegieite-anorthite), was probably strongly influenced by Dr. A. L. Day, director of the Geophysical Laboratory. Day and Allen (1905), in a pioneering study, had investigated the plagioclase feldspars, and what was more natural than to add a feldspathoid to anorthite? Again that choice had a profound effect on Bowen's future work, because it produced a lifelong interest in alkaline rocks. The question of technique was easily answered: In addition to the well-established heating curves, very useful except in viscous silicate melts, Shepperd and Rankin (1909) had recently introduced the quench method, which is more tedious and time-consuming, but also less equivocal. Bowen (1912d) lost no time in applying both methods and produced his first phase-equilibrium paper, which became a model for his later contributions. The essential raw data are given, and from this an equilibrium diagram is constructed. That diagram is then fully discussed in terms of crystallization paths. Next detailed optical data are given for both glasses and mineral phases. Comparisons with earlier results follow, and the paper concludes with a section on applications to natural rocks. Steeped in Bowen's approach, modern petrologists find the discussions of the ternary liquidus diagrams easily accessible, but we can imagine how forbidding this material must have been for the majority of the contemporary petrologists.

A brief application of thermodynamics, referenced to the classic text of Ostwald on physical chemistry, is included in the nepheline-anorthite paper (1912d). The experimental work apparently was completed in one year, 1910–1911, as Bowen returned to MIT in the fall of 1911 and received his Ph.D. in the spring of 1912. He then joined the Geophysical Laboratory as a staff member and there ensued three years of exceptional activity, culminating in his first major statement on igneous rock evolution (1915c). Looking at his productivity, one can conjure up the image of a happy young fellow who had been handed the key—the quenching method—to open those doors behind which he would find the answers.

While still at MIT, he wrote another seminal paper (1912c), entitled "The Order of Crystallization in Igneous Rocks." It would eventually lead to the famous reaction principle paper (1922c). Though I cannot trace the source of the original ideas, it touches upon questions any thin section course raises: how to read the sequence of crystallization from textural information. Furthermore, the quench method allowed a direct determination of the crystallization sequence, though the rock types he was considering were still well beyond his experimental grasp. Curiously enough, Bowen reached a rather negative conclusion. He decided that because of the random sections through the three-dimensional fabric, it was impossible from thin section studies to deduce the order in which minerals appeared. Rather, textural studies would only give information on when they *ceased* to crystallize. In a brief but illuminating paragraph, he considered the effect of crystal settling on differentiation, another topic which was to assume central significance in later years.

The summers of 1911 and 1912 were again spent in the field, this time in British Columbia, working for the Geological Survey of Canada. These were the last full field summers, but by now Bowen had become a professional field geologist, an important asset in terms of his eventual impact. From now on, his major energies would be devoted to laboratory studies, but contact with the field was maintained continuously through field trips and sample collecting.

When Bowen assumed his new job at the Geophysical Laboratory in the fall of 1912, he had important choices to make: what system should he tackle first? Between 1912 and 1915, the sequence goes: albite-anorthite, MgO-SiO_2, diopside-forsterite-silica, albite-anorthite-diopside, and it reveals his uncanny knack for finding the jugular. Except for Fe- and H_2O-bearing systems, these four systems form the cornerstones of his petrogenetic deductions and contributions. The first choice was obvious. Bowen had successfully dealt with feldspars and feldspathoids in his thesis and had come to fully appreciate the importance of solid solutions. Then what more obvious solid solution was there than albite-anorthite? Day may have given his permission somewhat reluctantly, because the classic plagioclase study of Day and Allen (1905) had led to the founding of the Geophysical Laboratory. But, though able to demonstrate isomorphism, Day and Allen (1905) could not define the melting interval. That had to await the development of the quenching method (Shepperd and Rankin, 1909). In 1912, everything was ready for Bowen to step in, and he produced what is still one of his most famous studies: "The Melting Phenomena of the Plagioclase Feldspars" (1913a). That study, not improved upon to this day, has one unusual aspect not common to most other papers of Bowen's, in that it contains a detailed calculation of the liquidus and solidus curves based on thermodynamic theory. Using ideal solution theory, Bowen closely followed arguments presented by Van Laar (1906), but he demonstrated that he was in full command of the subject. The agreement between calculated curves and experiments is spectacular and makes it doubly curious that in his subsequent writings, with two notable exceptions (1922e and 1935a), Bowen never again used a quantitative thermodynamic argument. We can only surmise that he must have considered his ternary systems too complex for this approach. In any case, his purely geometric deductions gave him all he needed.

For the next choice of topics we must read between the lines:

> In the course of work on two supposed binary systems of which $MgSiO_3$ was one component, the writers have found that $MgSiO_3$ is unstable at its melting point and can itself be treated only as part of a binary system and not as a separate component. The supposed binary systems mentioned must therefore be treated as ternary systems and before proceeding to the study of our separate ternary systems we have worked out jointly the binary system $MgO\text{-}SiO_2$ which is common to both. [Bowen and Andersen, 1914, p. 487]

The two ternary systems alluded to are diopside-forsterite-silica (Bowen, 1914) and anorthite-forsterite-silica (Andersen, 1915) and the originally chosen "binary" systems must have been enstatite-diopside (or wollastonite) for Bowen and enstatite-anorthite for Andersen. Bowen's choice was logical, but not inevitable. Though he was clearly aware of the importance of pyroxenes to basic igneous rocks, he was probably looking for another simple binary system. Also, $MgSiO_3$-minerals had previously been studied by his colleagues (Allen et al., 1906). But now fate intervened. As he and Andersen found out quickly, $MgSiO_3$ melts incongruently to forsterite and a siliceous liquid at atmospheric pressure. They joined forces and produced the brief but highly significant paper on the system $MgO\text{-}SiO_2$ (Bowen and Andersen, 1914). Actually Bowen did not realize the full significance of the incongruent melting of enstatite until later that year, when he was working out the ternary system forsterite-silica-diopside (1914). They clearly recognized the crystallization and then resorption of olivine: "This resorption takes place as a necessary result of equilibrium . . . during the normal course of crystallization as a simple result of cooling. . . " (1914, p. 499).

They also pointed to the possible discrepancies between chemical and mineralogical classifications: "We have then what might be termed an olivine-bearing lava in simplified form, though the actual total composition of the mixture shows no olivine but an excess of free silica" (1914, p. 500).

Having clarified the behavior of $MgSiO_3$, Bowen could proceed to $MgSiO_3\text{-}CaMgSi_2O_6$, but now in the context of the ternary system diopside-forsterite-silica (1914). That paper closely follows the earlier models, but it also contains an explicit discussion of binary and ternary solid solution in ternary systems that shows Bowen had absorbed Schreinemakers' many papers. These principles are applied in the detailed discussion of crystallization paths in the system diopside-forsterite-silica, which are quite complex, because the L (Fo, Px) boundary crosses the En-Di join. In other words, enstatite (En) melts incongruently, whereas diopside (Di) melts congruently. He points out that under certain conditions, forsterite (Fo) may first crystallize, then be resorbed and finally again crystallize. Two central ideas are clearly expressed now. The difference between equilibrium crystallization ("first type") and fractional crystallization ("second type") is stressed, and Bowen shows that zoned crystals indicate fractionation. Secondly, differentiation by gravitational settling of early crystals is discussed in detail, and Bowen feels "that the settling out from a basic magma of the more calcic plagioclases and the pyroxenes rich in magnesia and iron is the dominant control in the differentiation of the ordinary lime-alkali series of igneous rocks" (1914, p. 260). The die was cast, and Bowen was to elaborate, extend, and defend this idea for the next forty-two years.

The final system of this group Bowen turned to next (1915b) is the system diopside-albite-anorthite, a system he considered to represent simplified basaltic or dioritic magmas. It shows solid solution in a limiting binary system and a ternary cotectic curve which crosses the entire ternary system. A new argument enters, based on the abundance of mafic constituents: "as the plagioclase becomes more alkalic the percentage of diopside (colored constituent) decreases rapidly" (1915b, p. 183). We have the explicit statement, "the more acid types are not original magmas . . . the more acid magmas are regarded as derived from basic material, being, as it were, successive mother liquids from the crystallization of the basic magmas" (1915b, p. 184).

The basic experimental work is now completed and the main arguments have been assembled for an assault on the accepted ideas for the origin of igneous rocks. Missing only is the direct demonstration that crystal settling can actually occur. Using artificial melts, Bowen (1915a) next showed that forsterite and pyroxene settle, while tridymite floats, with the effects visible in a few hours. He calculates viscosities from Stoke's law and shows that the olivine layer of the Palisades sill probably formed by crystal settling in the gravitational field.

Next follows Bowen's first major statement, delivered in an eighty-nine-page paper entitled "The Later Stages of the Evolution of the Igneous Rocks" (1915c). This contribution, an important stepping stone towards Bowen's book on igneous rock evolution (1928a), cemented his rapidly growing international reputation. It contains few new ideas, but it marshals much evidence, experimental and field, to support the contention that basaltic magma is the parent material for all igneous rocks and that gravitational crystal differentiation is the principal evolutionary mechanism. Assimilation and liquid immiscibility are dismissed. The normal "line of descent" is basalt → diorite → granodiorite → biotite granite → syenite → nepheline syenite. In other words, the alkaline rocks are the final differentiation products. At this stage, volatile constituents also become important. On page seventy-five (1915c) Bowen gives a table of crystallization products which is tantalizingly close to the famous reaction series of 1922. Also touched upon is the problem of forming monomineralic rocks, such as peridotites, pyroxenites, and anorthosites. Many of the ideas expressed in this paper had been espoused by others, such as his teacher R. A. Daly, but never before had so much experimental and field evidence been assembled to support them. Also, Bowen went beyond most petrologists by making basaltic magma the parent for nearly all igneous rocks and differentiation the sole mechanism.

At the age of twenty-eight, Bowen had clearly carved his niche. His unusual effectiveness was due to his mastery of both classical petrology and physical chemistry. He had steeped himself in the phase theory of the Dutch school (Bakhuis-Rooseboom and Schreinemakers) so essential for interpreting his diagrams. He had adopted a new technique, the quench method, and had determined several of the most important diagrams. He wrote clearly and convincingly, and he had no hesitation to repeat his results and conclusions in print (the albite-anorthite and albite-anorthite-diopside diagrams each appear in at least nine of his publications). No wonder that his influence increased rapidly. By now, most of the ideas of his subsequent career had been touched upon.

In a paper entitled: "The Problem of the Anorthosites"

(1917b), Bowen points out that melting points of individual minerals are too high for such rocks to be emplaced as liquids, and he suggests a crystal mush instead, formed by crystal accumulation, which accounts for the cataclastic texture and the absence of dikes, as well as the intimate association with gabbros and syenites.

1917–1928: GLASSES, DIFFUSION, ASSIMILATION, LIQUID IMMISCIBILITY, ALKALINE AND ULTRABASIC ROCKS

The First World War brought an interruption. Day had accepted the challenge of producing optical glass (see also Abelson, 1975). Together with other staff members, Bowen moved for a time to Rochester to the Bausch and Lomb factory. This work had an obvious effect on his scientific interests, and he subsequently published a number of papers directly related to problems of glasses, the best-known being the paper entitled "The Significance of Glass-Making Processes to the Petrologist" (1918a). His interests in diffusion in silicate melts (1921) and liquid immiscibility (1926) were also fostered during this period.

From 1918 to 1920 Bowen was professor of mineralogy at Queen's University, Kingston, Ontario. Meanwhile, his differentiation theory of crystal settling was attacked as inadequate by some of the foremost petrologists, such as Daly, his former teacher, as well as Grout and Harker. The objections were manifold, but revolved principally around Bowen's rejection of assimilation, diffusion, liquid immiscibility, and convection currents as significant processes. Bowen (1919e) answered his critics in detail. He does not yield much ground but he does use the occasion to sharpen his ideas. About the only substantive change is a shift in emphasis: filter pressing of liquids now receives equal billing with crystal settling and zonation.

At Queen's, Bowen had no opportunity for experimental work and it is not surprising that he returned to the Geophysical Laboratory in the fall of 1920 to begin an extraordinarily fruitful period of association that lasted until 1937.

The first experimental problem to be tackled stems directly from his involvement with silicate glasses (1921a). Bowen was anxious to substantiate his contention that diffusion in magmas was a slow, small-scale process and he succeeded probably beyond his own expectations. Using diopside and plagioclase melts, he measured diffusivities of 3×10^{-6} to 2×10^{-7} cm²/sec at 1500°C and he concluded "that the movement of large quantities of material through long distances by diffusion in a magma cannot be credited when the relatively rapid rate at which the magma must cool is considered" (1921a, p. 316).

He also showed that the Soret effect, diffusion in a temperature gradient, is insignificant in geologic settings, and that diffusion is important only for the formation of reaction rims. The diffusion paper is characteristic of Bowen's approach. He begins with a petrologic problem, devises a method for obtaining the data needed, gets the data, and then immerses himself in the theory necessary to interpret the results. In this case he must have read most of the literature on diffusion and heat flow and acquainted himself with Gaussian distributions and error functions. Very few petrologists of his generation had that much courage, and this explains, in part, Bowen's effectiveness. But we should not overlook the advantage he had in being surrounded by physicists and physical chemists.

There now follows a seminal paper for petrologic theory and one which was immediately accepted by many of its practitioners: "The Reaction Principle in Petrogenesis" (1922c). The chief conclusion, in the form of a simple flow sheet of mineral reactions, found its way into every text on igneous petrology:

REACTION SERIES IN SUBALKALINE ROCKS

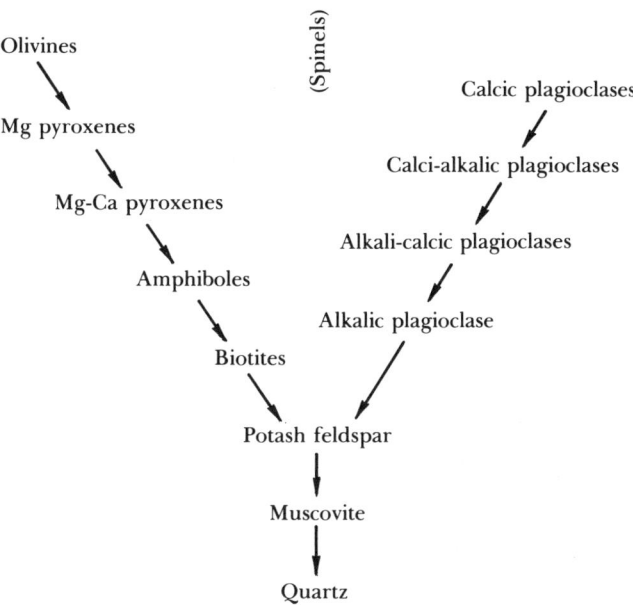

It is the contribution of Bowen's best known to geologists in general, and yet when we analyze the paper in detail, we find no radically new ideas. But there is a subtle shift, even in style. We have here the mature Bowen: elegant, persuasive, and in complete control of his material. The central problem remains unchanged: How to explain the bewildering variability of igneous rock compositions. For this purpose, J. H. L. Vogt had used eutectic systems and Bowen once more shows the inadequacies of such models. Using his favored systems, Ab-An, Ab-An-Di and Fo-Q, he defines two reaction series between minerals and liquids, a continuous reaction series represented by solid solutions and a reaction pair or discontinuous reaction series as exemplified by incongruent melting. Then, going back to his earlier ideas on the order of crystallization in igneous rocks (1912c and 1915c), but curiously enough, using a table from Harker (1909) as his take-off point, he devises the reaction series in sub-alkaline rocks. It is greatly simplified from the 1915c version and for that reason alone more easily acceptable. In the words of Schairer (1957): "One of the great ideas developed by Bowen is the significance of the reaction principle in petrogenesis. Pentti Eskola of Finland called it the most important contribution to petrology of the present century" (p. 118).

Order of crystallization and the theory of magmatic differentiation have now been linked successfully and inextricably, and Bowen had surpassed his mentors, Vogt in Norway, Harker in Britain, and Daly in the USA.

Building on earlier ideas (1915c), Bowen next turned to assimilation (1922e) in an extensive paper on the behavior of inclusions in igneous magmas. Extracting heats of mixing from liquidus curves, he points out that such heats between silicate liquids are small compared to heats of solution and that the common assumption that acid and basic materials mix with evolution of heat is not warranted. He then evaluates the effect of adding plagioclase to liquids in the system Ab-An-Di. Using the just developed concept of the reaction series (1922c), he concludes that "a liquid saturated with a certain member of a reaction series is effectively supersaturated with all preceding members of that series" (p. 568), and hence, "saturated granitic magma cannot dissolve inclusions of more basic rocks" (p. 539).

It does react with them, however. A discussion of the effect of adding limestone, with particular reference to the origin of alkaline rocks, of quartzites and of shales, with reference to ultrabasic rocks, concludes with the characteristic statement: "It is doubtful whether the presence of foreign matter is ever essential to the production of any particular type of differentiate."

Assimilation had been the "deus-ex-machina" of his teacher Daly for explaining igneous rock variability, and Bowen leaves no doubt that he holds this position untenable. This paper (1922e), like many others, makes it clear why critics found it so difficult to refute Bowen's conclusions. Taking advantage of every scrap of experimental data, Bowen argues his case quantitatively for a highly simplified situation, then extrapolates to the natural case, and bolsters his extrapolation by quoting observations from the field. The weak link is the extrapolation, but this is difficult to attack without further data, and hence many rebuttals become little more than battles of faith. In the end, as we shall see, Bowen often did extrapolate beyond safe ground.

Looking over the papers between 1922 and 1928, we detect a distinct shift in working habits. Before 1922 only one paper was coauthored (1914a) and that more by default than by choice. After 1922, Bowen frequently joins forces, first with G. W. Morey, J. W. Greig, his former Queen's student, and R. W. G. Wyckoff, and finally with J. F. Schairer and O. F. Tuttle. New topics are tackled but, at least between 1922 and 1928, the work is more diffuse and less obviously planned. Nevertheless, for Bowen everything contributes to his central concern: the evolution of the igneous rocks.

To the rich harvest of 1922 belongs one more paper (1922d), in which Bowen can hardly suppress his glee. Morey had, using water pressure, synthesized pure K-feldspar for the first time, and he invited Bowen to help out with optical and petrologic interpretations. To their surprise they found that K-feldspar melted incongruently to leucite + liquid at 1170°C. This gave Bowen a chance to forge a genetic link between the subalkaline rocks of the "reaction series" and the alkaline rocks of his thesis (1912d) and his 1915c and 1917a papers:

> It is with considerable satisfaction, therefore, that we announce a laboratory demonstration of the fact that a mass consisting in one part of feldspar and quartz and in another of feldspar and feldspathoid can form from a single homogeneous liquid. The method of formation of these contrasting parts, which may be referred to as subalkaline and alkaline, respectively, is the method of fractional crystallization. . . ." [p. 20]

Discovering unsuspected incongruent melting among minerals seems to have been Bowen's special province. In the assimilation paper (1922e), Bowen had noted that "as a consequence of . . . the instability of sillimanite in contact with liquid rich in anorthite or magnesian silicates, alumina is set free as corundum" (p. 570), and he interpreted noritic material as the reaction product between basaltic melts and aluminous sediments. Thomas (1922) described examples, from the Island of Mull, where the liberation of corundum at the contact took place in the presence of ample silica ("Sillimanite" buchites containing corundum and glass, p. 240–41).

Clearly something was wrong with the accepted congruent melting of sillimanite. When J. W. Greig joined him, they decided to reinvestigate the system Al_2O_3-SiO_2 (1924a), so important to the ceramic industry. They concluded: "Corundum is frequently formed from shales and clays when these are attacked by natural magmas . . . even when there is plenty of silica present to form sillimanite. This . . . suggested that sillimanite itself must melt incongruently, breaking up into liquid and corundum" (p. 254).

Indeed, the stable compound at 1 atm was found to be not sillimanite ($Al_2O_3 \cdot SiO_2$), but $3Al_2O_3 \cdot 2SiO_2$, later named mullite (1924b). Mullite melts incongruently to corundum + liquid at 1810°C and is an ideal material for high-temperature ceramics. The technological applications of

Bowen's work now spanned the glass and ceramic industries and were soon to encompass the steel industry.

In the summer of 1923 Bowen sailed for Europe, first to visit the igneous rocks of the Island of Skye under the guidance of A. Harker, and then to Norway to see J. H. L. Vogt and to study the alkaline rocks of the Fen area recently described by Broegger (1920). Two papers resulted from the Fen trip (1924c, 1926e), both proposing carbonate replacement of silicates rather than carbonate magmas. The latter Bowen rejected because of the high temperatures necessary.

A brief note on assimilation in the norite sheet of Sudbury (1925c) contains a clever use of two-component mixing diagrams of the type later used in his book (1928a). Bowen points out ". . . the remarkable similarity of the less siliceous portion of the diagram with an ordinary variation diagram of a normal calci-alkalic series of igneous rocks" (p. 827). Consequently, he dismisses assimilation as a reasonable hypothesis for the Sudbury sheet.

One more major contribution follows before the close of the 1917–1928 period, one which stems from his interests in monomineralic rocks (1927b) and must have been nurtured by his trips to Skye in 1923 and 1926 with A. Harker who had mapped the area and examined the ultrabasic dikes with him. He restates his conviction that: "anorthosites and probably other monomineralic (ultra-basic) rocks were formed as a result of the accumulation of crystals from a complex melt and that there were probably no liquids of the composition of these extreme rocks" (p. 89). He adds, with a note of triumph: "but the assumption is usually made that the accumulated crystals have been redissolved or remelted in depth. Since his recent conversion to crystallization-differentiation Vogt has been a champion of this assumption" (p. 89).

Next, using a statistical approach based on the chemical analyses in H.S. Washington's (1917) tables, an approach he later employed so successfully for granites (1954), he demolishes the idea of remelting. He points out the difference in the plagioclase compositions between porphyritic and non-porphyritic basalts and concludes: "The most calcic composition of the total plagioclase of a . . . fine grained or aphanitic, basaltic rock appears to be about $Ab_1\ An_2$. . . . There is thus no escape from the conclusion that the process of accumulation of crystals is not supplemented by significant remelting or re-solution of the accumulated crystals" (p. 100).

He proceeds to document a similar conclusion with respect to olivines and remarks that olivine phenocrysts must have been present before extrusion. He states that: "there are no liquids corresponding in composition with . . . ultra-basic rocks. They must originate through the local accumulation of crystals of either plagioclase or olivine which are not significantly re-melted or re-dissolved" (p. 108). Thus his ideas and conclusions first put forth in the anorthosite paper (1917b) are fully confirmed and extended to all monomineralic igneous rocks.

1928: THE EVOLUTION OF THE IGNEOUS ROCKS

In the spring of 1927, Bowen was invited to Princeton University to deliver a series of seminars at the suggestion of A. F. Buddington, who had been a former colleague at the Geophysical Laboratory. The lecture notes were later expanded and published in book form as Bowen's famous text (1928a). It was a revolutionary text both in its contents and its effect on the field. As Tilley (1957) reminds us: "In this vigorous presentation of the problems of the igneous rocks, Bowen provided a survey and synthesis which has exerted a profound influence on petrologic thought" (p. 13).

Based largely on Bowen's previous writings, the book is an excellent and convenient summary of his major contributions up to this period. I will briefly trace the sources of the material.

Opening with a concise statement in favor of a genetic link between igneous rocks of different compositions as exemplified by "natural series" and "petrographic provinces," Bowen emphasizes his belief in the "parental nature of basaltic magma" and the principle of fractional crystallization. He dismisses liquid immiscibility with arguments from his 1919e paper, shored up by recent experimental work by Greig (1927). The three mechanisms leading to fractional crystallization—crystal settling in the gravitational field, zonation, and filter pressing of the liquid, ideas enunciated in 1915a, 1915c, 1919e, and 1922—are elucidated. Next follows, as chapter IV, a brief course in phase theory with the aid of silicate melt diagrams principally determined by Bowen himself. Nothing reveals his enormous *experimental* contribution to this data quite as dramatically, and every diagram presented illuminates a different aspect of crystallization behavior. The reaction principle follows naturally and is essentially an abbreviated form of the (1922c) paper. In discussing the crystallization of basaltic magma, Bowen defends his position that "plagioclase and pyroxene crystallize out together at a very early period." He takes to task his own colleague, C. N. Fenner (1926), for holding a differing opinion and thereby precipitates a lifelong animosity.

Using a mixing diagram of the type presented in 1925c and material from the Mull Memoir (Bailey et al., 1924), he demonstrates that the non-porphyritic central magma cannot be formed from plateau magma by assimilation, but that settling of olivine and plagioclase does the trick. Quartz can also be freed by crystallization of biotite, he maintains in a section taken verbatim from the (1915c) report.

Chapter VII presents an approach Bowen has not employed previously: variation diagrams to delineate liquid lines of descent. He points out that when oxides are plotted against silica, smooth curves are formed for differentiating liquids. This holds for the Mull rocks as well as Fenner's own Katmai series. In a daring extrapolation beyond experiments, Bowen considers the effects of $KAlSi_3O_8$ and SiO_2 on crystallization paths involving pyroxene and plagioclase. Daly's averages from basalt to rhyolite define a generalized variation diagram into which ultrabasic rocks emphatically do not fit.

Having acquired an important new line of evidence, Bowen concludes: "In many igneous series all the rocks from basic to acid can be plotted on curves that require little smoothing and this fact, taken in conjunction with the evidence of the control of crystallization, points to the basic (basaltic) magma as the parental liquid" (p. 124). This approach, with less notable success, is extended to the glassy rocks.

In his paper, "The Later Stages of the Evolution of the Igneous Rocks" (1915c), Bowen has a brief section entitled "The Earlier Stages of Igneous Rock Evolution Not Revealed" (p. 73), in which he says that he assumes the existence of a parental basaltic magma, but does not know where it comes from. In his paper on ultrabasic rocks (1927b), and again in chapter VII, he states clearly why ultrabasic rocks cannot be the parents of basaltic magmas, but that such rocks are the result of crystal sorting. This conclusion is amplified in chapter IX, with material mostly from the 1927 (b) paper, except for a central section on peridotite dikes of Skye. A summary of his ideas on anorthosites stems from the 1917b contribution. The conclusion of part I (chapter X on assimilation) again is familiar to us from the 1922 (c) paper, which is reproduced in toto.

Part II opens with a section on K-feldspar liquids, and a chapter (XII) on the genesis of alkaline rocks. In 1915 (1915c, pp. 55–66), Bowen discussed the production of nepheline syenites from granites by fractional crystallization in the presence of high concentrations of volatiles. A desilication reaction was held responsible, such as the formation of biotite from K-feldspar. In 1919 (1919e, p. 426) he emphasized filter pressing of liquids rather than crystal settling, but in 1922 (1922d, pp. 16–20) a more convincing mechanism was presented in the form of the incongruent melting of K-feldspar to leucite and a siliceous liquid. This idea is exploited in chapter XII for trachytes and nepheline syenites, by constructing "skeleton diagrams" involving feldspars, feldspathoids and silica. These extrapolations are quite considerable, though by using natural assemblages Bowen presents a rather convincing case with respect to the location of field boundaries. Also of concern to him is the unknown effect of the presence of FeO.

A brief chapter on lamprophyres (XIII) is concerned directly with one special class of these rocks, the alnoites, which carry olivine, mica, and melilites. The material is taken largely from a paper entitled "Genetic Features of Alnoitic Rocks at Isle Cadieux, Quebec" (1922a). The presence of melilites is accounted for by the reaction of diopside with nepheline, and the olivine lamprophyres are the product of the interaction of an alkalic liquid with accumulated femic crystals (p. 269). The final chapters (XV–XVIII) are all brief and concerned with ancillary matters, such as fractional resorption, reverse zoning, volatiles, geophysics, and rock classification. Particularly revealing are Bowen's statements with respect to volatiles and geophysics.

In G. W. Morey and Paul Niggli, Bowen had two associates who advocated the importance of volatile constituents in the magma. On the other hand, as the leading experimentalist on the crystallization of dry silicate liquids, Bowen felt that "to many petrologists a volatile component is exactly like a Maxwell demon; it does just what one may wish it to do" (p. 282), and he concludes his discussion with a quote taken from Vogt (1922, p. 672): "I cannot endorse the statement that the volatile components have been the important factor in magmatic differentiation" (p. 302).

Bowen does, however, grant the effect of volatiles in lowering crystallization temperatures and viscosities, effects he was later to document himself forcefully in collaboration with O. F. Tuttle.

In the penultimate chapter, Bowen marshals those geophysical facts which bear on magma genesis and he concludes: "we can see little chance of escape from the necessity of deriving all magmas *ultimately* from matter much more basic than basalt and probably from peridotitic substance as represented in stony meteorites" (p. 311). Some of his conclusions with respect to partial melting of mantle material have a decidedly modern ring.

In writing his book (1928a), Bowen selected material of his fifty-five published papers that he felt was most significant, and he included entire sections word-for-word. Thus the book represents less of a beginning than of a summing up. Except for the chapter on liquid lines of descent (VII), new material and ideas are subordinate. Nevertheless, writing the book had a cathartic effect, and it presented Bowen with the opportunity for a new beginning, an opportunity which was reinforced by the appearance of a young collaborator, J. F. Schairer. It should not surprise us that Bowen clearly recognized his chance and took advantage of it brilliantly.

1928–1937: IRON-BEARING SYSTEMS AND "PETROGENY'S RESIDUA SYSTEM"

For Bowen, a new beginning does not mean a break with the past, and hence the new direction is linked to previous problems. Not surprisingly, therefore, Bowen and Schairer first tackled the system leucite-diopside and the melting of acmite (1929a and b). Both systems are concerned with alkaline rocks, one with leucitites and the other with the effect of iron. Acmite, $NaFeSi_2O_6$, a member of the pyroxene family, is common in alkaline rocks and its melting relations can be determined in air. Should we be surprised to learn that acmite melts incongruently? Bowen and Schairer (1929b) conclude that: "when there is an incongruent melting of a silicate compound it is always of such a nature as to throw excess silica into the liquid" (p. 373; see also 1928a, p. 298). This assertion was later to be qualified (1933e, p. 278). The acmite studies were extended to the ternary system Na_2SiO_3-Fe_2O_3-SiO_2 and the results were published in 1930c.

In 1929 Bowen attended the International Geological Congress in South Africa and on his return he visited alkaline volcanoes both in the western (Mufumbira volcanics N of Lake Kivu) and eastern (principally in the Lake Naivasha area) Rift Valley. An early account appeared in 1930 (1930a), with more interpretative results to follow (1937a, 1938b).

Next follows a series of contributions (1932, 1933a, 1933c) that lead up to the two monumental papers on the systems CaO-FeO-SiO_2 (1933e) and MgO-FeO-SiO_2 (1935a) with a combined 160 pages. These studies demanded innovations in experimental techniques as well as utmost mastery of the theory of ternary phase equilibria, but they yielded a rich harvest of petrologic insights and technological applications. They represent one culmination of the new direction begun in 1928, the other being the granite memoir with O. F. Tuttle (1958).

The first problem to be solved was the oxidation of iron during melting experiments. As pyroxenes and olivines contain iron in the ferrous form, the effects of oxidation had to be excluded. This was achieved by placing the charges in crucibles of metallic iron and passing a stream of nitrogen through the furnace. Any changes in bulk composition due to reaction with the crucible walls were evaluated by chemical analysis. Oxygen could not be excluded quantitatively, and hence some Fe_2O_3 was always present in the liquid. It was recalculated to FeO to be able to treat the equilibria in a ternary system.

In iron crucibles, fayalite was found to melt incongruently with separation of iron (1932). The join Ca_2SiO_4-Fe_2SiO_4 (1933c) also brought some unexpected results: "It is rather surprising that Ca-Fe olivines of the series we have prepared are not found in nature" (p. 292); and "The finding that $CaFeSiO_4$ forms a complete series of solid solutions with fayalite, which in turn almost certainly forms a complete series with forsterite, renders it rather surprising that the ordinary rock-forming Mg-Fe olivines do not contain more CaO" (p. 293).

The impetus for working on the system CaO-FeO-SiO_2 seems to have stemmed from an earlier, unsuccessful attempt to determine the relations on the join diopside-hedenbergite (1933e, p. 193), a fundamental join of the pyroxene quadrilateral. In working out the liquidus surface, Bowen and his co-workers confirmed the observation that iron lowers liquidus temperatures substantially. They found no ternary eutectic liquids, but they did encounter hedenbergite, $CaFeSi_2O_6$, but only below 965°C. It forms a series of solid solutions with $FeSiO_3$, ferrosilite, but the $FeSiO_3$ composition itself is represented by fayalite + tridymite.

Wollastonites presented another puzzle: "the remarkable feature of β-$CaSiO_3$ (wollastonite) is that it is capable of taking some 76 percent $FeSiO_3$ into solid solution yet this series of solid solutions is not known in nature . . ." (p. 269). They point out that ". . . metasilicate solid solutions . . . melt with separation of free silica and consequent throwing of excess of bases, especially iron, into the liquid, and the lowest melting liquid . . . is the iron-rich liquid . . ." (p. 278). "The possibility of alternative residual liquids, the one silica-rich, the other iron-rich, has been brought out in another system . . ." (p. 278).

The system $MgO-FeO-SiO_2$ (1935a) was to be considerably richer in petrologic implications. No less complex, it encompasses one of the most important substitution pairs in silicate minerals, $Mg^{++} \rightleftarrows Fe^{++}$, and three solid solution series: the wüstites, olivines, and pyroxenes, the latter two as fundamental to petrology as the plagioclases. No ternary eutectic appears, and the liquidus surfaces slope down towards the FeO corner. The olivines proved to be even more regular than the plagioclases, and the calculated liquidus and solidus curves agree well with the experiments as far as the latter could be taken. As we have made a point of Bowen's sparse use of thermodynamics, we should note his remark with respect to the use of ideal solution theory by Van Laar (1906): "The method of derivation of the equation is not altogether acceptable in these times" (p. 205).

The heat of fusion combined with a volume change estimated from the law of Gladstone and Dale gives an evaluation of the pressure effect on melting, which Bowen finds to be small for moderate pressures.

The pyroxenes present greater difficulties. Extensive solid solution was found, but again the composition $FeSiO_3$ (ferrosilite) is represented by fayalite + quartz. Perhaps the most important information contained in the join $MgSiO_3$-$FeSiO_3$ presented by Bowen and Schairer (p. 164) is the location of the orthopyroxene-clinopyroxene inversion. Synthetic orthopyroxenes could not be obtained in their pure form and the inversion was located with natural material, some of which had to be fluxed. For many years, this inversion curve has formed the backbone of pyroxene interpretation. Curiously enough, Bowen and Schairer themselves were not too clear about its meaning. At first they considered the orthopyroxenes primary and most pigeonites (or clinopyroxenes) as "formed metastably during rapid crystallization" (p. 203). But, in a footnote, they express less certainty: "Plainly it is necessary to investigate pyroxene compositions of more complex character before a satisfactory general explanation of pigeonites is forthcoming" (p. 203).

The high melting temperatures of olivines and pyroxenes confirmed Bowen's earlier contention that "rocks . . . made up entirely of pyroxene or of olivine . . . were not formed by simple crystallization of a melt of their own composition but rather by accumulation of crystals from a complex magma" (p. 204).

Emplacement is connected "with perhaps some special mode of intrusion of a crystalline mass. . . ." (p. 205).

Fractional crystallization based on the incongruent melting of clinoenstatite also presents a problem, because as little as 20 percent $FeSiO_3$ changes the pyroxene behavior to congruent melting (p. 211). On the other hand, the presence of anorthite stabilizes the incongruency.

Except for some brief subsequent papers (1935d, 1935e, 1936c) and the link-up of fayalite with feldspars (1937a, 1938a), Bowen's involvement with iron-bearing systems is terminated with the system $MgO-FeO-SiO_2$ (1935a).

The paper entitled "The Broader Story of Magmatic Differentiation, Briefly Told" (1933d) is an important foray into problems of ore deposits. Bowen had previously written a summary on geothermometry (1928b) for a volume on economic geology, but its scope was limited. He now specifically focuses on the "hyperfusible" or volatile components and concludes once again that they do not modify the fundamental course of fractional crystallization. If boiling occurs, however, acids accumulate in the gas phase and condensation may yield very corrosive solutions. He concludes:

Under less deep-seated conditions the residual liquid of crystallizing salic magmas frequently boils and a fractional-distillation column is set up. . . . This action results in the formation of an acid aqueous solution and it is such acid solutions that are probably the principal ore bringers. The solutions deposit their load as a result of reaction with the rocks. . . . They thus become neutral and finally alkaline. . . ." [p. 128]

We now turn to the other principal thrust of the Bowen-Schairer team: the system $NaAlSiO_4$-$KAlSiO_4$-SiO_2. The results are contained in the 1935c, 1937a, 1938a,c, 1947b, 1955, and 1956 papers. Bowen's address at the Tercentenary Conference of Arts and Sciences at Harvard University, September 1936, where he received an honorary degree (1937a), combines three interests: feldspar-feldspathoid equilibria, iron minerals (fayalite), and African Rift lavas. He shows that the additions of anorthite, diopside, and fayalite to the feldspathoid-silica systems all produce residual liquids enriched in alkali-alumina silicate. This conclusion is contrary to Fenner's (1926) assertion of iron enrichment in residual liquids and his own experience in the CaO-FeO-SiO_2 and MgO-FeO-SiO_2 systems (1933e, 1935a), which he rationalizes by stating that "absolute enrichment of iron silicate does not occur but rather only enrichment in iron silicate relative to magnesian silicate" (1938a, p. 408).

The residual liquids are closely approximated by the system $NaAlSiO_4$-$KAlSiO_4$-SiO_2, henceforth dubbed "Petrogeny's Residua System." Bowen points to the existence of a "belt of low-melting temperature, the lowest valley upon the fusion surface. . . ." (1937a, p. 12) that straddles the alkali feldspar join. He shows that his African lavas, as well as Daly's averages of alkaline rocks, granites and rhyolites, all fall in this trough and he concludes: "The process exerting the dominant control over the composition of liquids . . . has been fractional crystallization" (p. 18).

Mindful of assimilation, he modifies this to "The factor exerting the dominant control . . . has been crystal $\rightleftharpoons$ liquid equilibrium" (p. 19).

Bowen's involvement with the alkaline lavas from E. Africa surfaces once more (1938b), in an unsuccessful attempt to correlate magma chemistry with tectonics.

The final data relating to Petrogeny's Residua System were not published until 1955 and 1956, in papers by Schairer and Bowen on the systems K_2O-Al_2O_3-SiO_2 and Na_2O-Al_2O_3-SiO_2. Although Bowen must have been substantially involved in the data collection over the many years, the papers are principally Schairer's contribution and show little of Bowen's hand. Perhaps the most significant petrologic implication comes from the demonstration that the silica-feldspar-feldspathoid join in both systems is a binary section. In other words, this thermal divide cannot be crossed by liquids from the high-aluminous to the alkaline side and vice versa, in part, negating Bowen's own contention (1945): "There may develop also residual liquids very rich in alkali silicates, which . . . coupled with the inevitable concentration of water, will give rise to a waterglass-like residuum . . ." (p. 75).

1937–1956: LIMESTONES, FELDSPARS, AND GRANITES

In the fall of 1937 Bowen accepted an appointment as Charles L. Hutchinson Distinguished Service Professor of Petrology at the University of Chicago, a position he held until 1947. During this period a number of papers appeared which are concerned with matters already discussed (1938a,c, 1942, 1947b,c) and others which are summaries or addresses (1938d, 1939, 1940b, 1941b, 1943).

One particularly famous paper is entitled "Progressive Metamorphism of Siliceous Limestone and Dolomite" (1940a). It is Bowen's first paper on metamorphism and it was occasioned by teaching duties. Brilliantly argued, it gives us an inkling of what might have happened to metamorphic petrology had Bowen turned his mind to it earlier. Following the approach pioneered by V. M. Goldschmidt (1911), he identifies a series of decarbonation reactions to be expected during the progressive metamorphism of impure dolomitic limestones involving silicates such as tremolite, diopside, forsterite, wollastonite, and others. Assuming a dry system, the reactions are univariant and can be represented by curves in P-T space. These curves ". . . cut the general P-T diagram up into a grid which we may call a petrogenetic grid" (1940a, p. 274).

Calibration of the qualitative grid Bowen provided has kept and will continue to keep experimental petrologists busy.

At Chicago, Bowen continued his interests in alkaline rocks with the help of a number of students. Some of the work was published in the Daly volume (1945), where he stresses fractional crystallization as an alternative hypothesis to Daly's limestone assimilation: "Recent studies . . . in portions of the . . . system, Na_2O-CaO-Al_2O_3-SiO_2, show that . . . there can thus develop by fractional crystallization . . . a series of differentiates which may be referred to as simplified melilite nephelinites, tephrites and phonolites" (1945, p. 75).

A delightful presidential address before the Geologic Society of America (1947a) leads up to our next topic and also demonstrates the flexibility of Bowen's mind. It is entitled "Magmas" and it takes cognizance of the granite controversy which was heating up at the time. In it, replying to a jibe from H. H. Read, he coins the famous phrase: "We can, indeed, for rough purposes, separate petrologists into the pontiffs and the soaks" (p. 264). And he concludes:

Yet it is not to be supposed that I do not have an open mind on the possibility of some granitic magma being the product of refusion of granite (Bowen, 1928, p. 319) or of selective refusion of geosynclinal sediments. To one who believes that both the laboratory and the field point to a granitic liquid as a late-crystallizing residuum of fractional crystallization . . . , the hypothesis that granitic liquid would likewise be an early product of selective fusion . . . cannot fail of sympathetic reception. [p. 275]

The next installment (1948a), entitled "The Granite Problem and the Method of Multiple Prejudices," was delivered again from the Geophysical Laboratory which he rejoined in 1947. It is part of a symposium on the origin of granites and it is fascinating principally because of the tone. Bowen, at sixty, had spent forty years perfecting his beloved theory that granites resulted from basaltic magmas by fractional crystallization. In the minority, and attacked vociferously, he becomes defensive for the first time.

Referring to the magmatist's position on the origin of granitic magma: "There is the view that it formed by fusion of geosynclinal sediments, or . . . by the refusion of . . . the granitic layer . . . or, finally, that it is the product of differentiation of basaltic magma as such. These are again arranged in the order of decreasing respectability today" (1948a, p. 87). And even more dramatically: "Nevertheless the disgraceful representative of the lowest group who now speaks to you . . ." (p. 87).

While said in jest, some of the criticism must have hit its mark and he might have begun to wonder whether he had bet on the wrong horse. It did not prevent him from demolishing H. H. Read, one of his chief antagonists: "Pushed to its logical consequences for a large mass, that corollary of wet granitization, the 'basic front,' is thus a basic affront to the intelligence of the geologic fraternity" (p. 88).

One final confession is contained in "The Making of a Magmatist" (1950c). Referring to Larsen's work on the San Juan region and the Southern California batholith, Bowen reiterates his belief in basaltic magma as the parental material for granites. For these examples, at least, partial melting is rejected emphatically.

The publication of 1949 introduces a new collaborator: O. F. Tuttle. While this team existed for but a few short years, it had an astonishing effect on petrology, still felt today. The substance of the contribution is contained in four papers (1949, 1950a,b, 1958).

Like liquid immiscibility and assimilation, volatile constituents had often been used by others to support unsubstantiated claims, but again, it was up to Bowen to provide the quantitative evidence. The effects of volatiles had occupied his mind for some time, and when the opportunity presented itself, Bowen was quick to recognize it. Through the efforts of G. W. Morey and R. W. Goranson, considerable experience had been accumulated at the Geophysical Laboratory in handling high water pressure, but the equipment was cumbersome. When Tuttle (1948) designed a simple hydrothermal quenching apparatus the way was open to evaluate the role of the volatiles and to attack one of the most pressing problems, equilibria in the system granite-water. First, Bowen and Tuttle (1949) chose a relatively simple system, the system $MgO-SiO_2-H_2O$. An extension of an early system of Bowen's (1914a), it promised information on the emplacement of peridotites and and serpentines. The locations of five univariant curves involving talc, brucite, serpentine, forsterite, enstatite, and periclase were determined at pressures up to 3 kb. No liquids were encountered below 900°C and: "Our results seem to exclude the possibility of the intrusion at comparatively low temperatures of a magma of serpentine composition which crystallizes, wholly or in part, directly to serpentine" (p. 453).

Next, as a stepping stone to the granite system, the alkali feldspars were studied in the presence of the water (1950a,b). Results were startling. Referring to K-feldspar and albite, we learn that, "At high temperatures they appear to form a complete series of solid solutions showing continuous variations of lattice spacings. . . . When crystallized at still lower temperatures, the complete solid-solution relation no longer obtains, and two feldspars form side by side" (1950a, p. 489).

We can only surmise how pleased Bowen must have been by these findings, as they provided a link to his earliest work on the solid solutions of the other feldspars, the plagioclases. With respect to the role of water Bowen and Tuttle note "that the principal function of water is a fluxing one, . . . but it affects equilibrium positions . . . only moderately. . . ." (p. 510) and hence ". . . crystal-liquid equilibrium is the dominant control in the development of these rocks" (p. 509).

An address given by Bowen (1954) upon receipt of the Hayden Medal of the Academy of Natural Sciences of Philadelphia on November 14, 1953 represents a final summing up of his views (1954), but it also contains some exciting new results on the granite-water system.

In the long-standing argument with his colleague C. N. Fenner with respect to silica vs. iron enrichment in residual liquids, Bowen remains firm: ". . . the final residual liquid from fractional crystallization will be an alkali-alumina-silica-rich liquid. . . . The contention that there will be absolute enrichment in iron oxides in final residual liquids is not supported by the experimental results . . ." (p. 6).

Exciting progress has also been achieved with respect to the question of the origin of granite. Referring to the results on the system albite-K-feldspar-quartz–water obtained with Tuttle, Bowen notes: "The existence of a lowest-crystallizing composition near the center of the triangle . . . is now readily established. This, then, is the composition toward which the liquid should migrate in the fractional crystallization. . . ." Analyses of natural granites fall near this temperature trough and, "We can conclude only that such clustering of composition of granites is strong confirmation of the hypothesis of their origin by crystallization of the liquid which is a residuum of fractional crystallization" (p. 10). But just to be safe: "There is, however, one other possibility. This minimum crystallizing liquid would also be the first liquid formed in the selective fusion (melting) of random rock material" (p. 11). And in conclusion: "In their extreme clustering about the composition of the liquid of minimum crystallizing temperature, the vast majority of granites loudly proclaim their origin through crystallization of that liquid" (p. 12).

These are just about the last printed words we have which clearly come from Bowen's hand.

The full story of the work on the granite system was published much later (1958), but it was written by Tuttle after Bowen's death. Bowen contributed substantially to that monumental contribution, but understandably, the emphasis is on Tuttle's views: "It is proposed that this zone of melting, where temperatures are high enough to melt granite completely and more basic compositions at least partially, may offer a mechanism for producing large batholithic masses of granite" (p. 2).

Would Bowen have been willing to go this far, abandoning his beloved fractional crystallization? I doubt it. Nevertheless, the work on the granite system today remains unchallenged, a pinnacle of experimental petrology, the quantitative foundation compatible with either fractional crystallization or partial melting.

CONCLUSIONS

In the preceding pages I have attempted to bring some order into Bowen's scientific evolution, an evolution which was uniquely unified, with a minimum of "accidental" developments. Impressed by the bewildering range and variability of the igneous rocks and by the possibility of forging a genetic link among them, he adopted the theory of differentiation by fractional crystallization, a theory which he never relinquished. Beginning with early field observations on the granophyre-diabase associations and the crystallization experiments on the plagioclase feldspars, he accumulated field and laboratory evidence tirelessly to shore up this theory and to relegate liquid immiscibility, assimilation, diffusion, volatiles, and iron enrichment to minor roles. He elaborated, embellished and extended and extrapolated as far as deriving granites and alkaline rocks from a basaltic parent. Ultrabasic rocks seemingly did not fit into the fractionation scheme and this is perhaps why he lavished so much attention upon them. In his mind, his final triumphant contribution to the granite system fully justified his tenacity.

His desire and need to impose order upon nature at whatever cost was shared by other prominent contemporaries in the earth sciences: V. M. Goldschmidt, Paul Niggli, Pentti Eskola, Reginald Daly, Alfred Harker. It found expression in the elaborate classification schemes, such as those of Rosenbusch. In that sense, Bowen's style of research seems to be clearly rooted in the nineteenth century. Is it fortuitous that Darwin, the epitome of the nineteenth century naturalist, was the first to invoke fractional crystallization?

But Bowen was a true revolutionary. He forced his largely descriptive contemporaries to accept a more quantitative style of reasoning, based largely on laboratory experiments and physical chemistry. To retain his credibility, he sharpened and expanded his appreciation of critical field relations, traveling extensively in North America, Europe, and Africa. In that sense, he was the first modern petrologist, combining field work with experiments and theory. His approach is still valid today, but some of his more extreme extrapolations are not acceptable any more, largely because of new geophysical and isotopic evidence. While differentiation is still an important mechanism in certain well-defined circumstances, few petrologists would use it to derive granites from basalt, except on a small scale. According to modern views, basalts originate in the mantle, while large-scale granitic magmas are derived from crustal material by partial melting. Intermediate compositions, such as andesites, are accounted for by partial melting of subducted oceanic crust with subsequent fractionation. The energy source for partial melting, whose existence Bowen questioned so persistently, is associated with mantle convection.

Where should we fault Bowen, if he should be faulted at all? Perhaps in extrapolating too far, in imposing too much order. A crucial stumbling block to his unified scheme was known early in his career: By far the most abundant igneous rocks are basalts and granites, one extrusive and the other intrusive, with intermediate members subordinate. Bowen never satisfactorily accounted for this observation. His teacher Daly held a different, no less popular, opinion: "Amid so many uncertainties one truth stands fast: the more closely the process of differentiation is considered in terms of its possible or probable units, the more unsafe is the reference of the diversity among igneous rocks to only one mode of origin or any one mechanism of separation" (Daly, 1933, p. 332). Lest we forget, Bowen's contribution to igneous petrology remains unmatched. His many equilibrium diagrams, from the plagioclases to the granites, are a monument to his insight, zeal and plain hard work. They continue to be used to check new ideas and deductions. Even more important, perhaps, is Bowen's example of how to approach the earth sciences. His insistence on a quantitative, chemically sound method in place of vague assertions is so well embedded today that we forget how revolutionary it was at the beginning of the century. Among his contemporary practitioners such as Vogt, Van't Hoff, Goldschmidt, Boeke, and Niggli, N. L. Bowen surely stands as a giant.

REFERENCES

Abelson, P. H. Arthur Louis Day. In: *Biographical Memoirs*, 47:27–47. Wash., D.C.: National Academy of Sciences, 1975.

Allen, E. T., Wright, F. E. and Clement, J. K. Minerals of the composition $MgSiO_3$: A case of tetramorphism. Am. J. Sci., 22 (1906):385–438.

Andersen, O. The system anorthite-forsterite-silica. Am. J. Sci., 34(1915): 407–54.

Bailey, E. B., Clough, C. T., Wright, W. B., Richey, J. E. and Wilson, G. V. The Tertiary and post-Tertiary geology of Mull, Loch Aline and Oban. Mem. Geol. Surv. Scotland (1924), 445 pp.

Broegger, W. C. Die Eruptivgesteine des Kristianiagebietes. Vidensk. Skr. I, Mat. Nat. Kl., 9 (1920):1–408.

Daly, R. A. Igneous rocks and the depths of the earth. N.Y.: McGraw Hill, 1933, 598 pp.

Day, A. D. and Allen, E. T. The isomorphism and thermal properties of the feldspars. Carnegie Inst.. Wash. Publ. 31 (1905), 95 pp.

Fenner, C. N. The Katmai magmatic province. J. Geol., 34 (1926):673–772.

Goldschmidt, V. M. Die Kontaktmetamorphose im Kristianiagebiet. Vidensk. Skr. I, Mat. Nat. Kl., 1 (1911):1–483.

Greig, J. W. Immiscibility in silicate melts. Am. J. Sci., 13 (1927):1–44, 133–54.

Harker, A. The natural history of igneous rocks. N.Y.: MacMillan, 1909, 384 pp.

Schairer, J. F. Memorial to Norman Levi Bowen. Proc. Geol. Soc. Am., 1957, 117–21.

Shepperd, E. S. and Rankin, G. A. The binary systems of alumina with silica, lime and magnesia. Am. J. Sci., 28 (1909):293–333.

Thomas, H. H. On certain xenolithic Tertiary minor intrusions in the Island of Mull (Argyllshire). Q. J. Geol. Soc. London, 78 (1922):229–60.

Tilley, C. E. Norman Levi Bowen. Biogr. Mem. Fellows R. Soc., III (1957):7–22.

Tuttle, O. F. A new hydrothermal quenching apparatus. Am. J. Sci., 246 (1948):628–35.

Van Laar, J. J. Über den Verlauf der Schmelzkurven bei festen Lösungen (oder isomorphen Gemischen) in einem speziellen Fall. Z. Phys. Chem., 55 (1906):435–41.

Vogt, J. H. L. Die Silikatschmelzlösungen. Christiania Vidensk. Skr., Ma. Nat. Kl., 8 (1903):1–161.

Vogt, J. H. L. The physical chemistry of the crystallization and magmatic differentiation of igneous rocks. VI. The influence of the light volatile compounds. J. Geol., 30 (1922):659–72.

Washington, H. S. Chemical analyses of igneous rocks. U.S. Geol. Surv. Prof. Pap. 99, 1917, 1201 pp.

BIBLIOGRAPHY

1909

Diabase and aplite of the cobalt-silver area. Can. Min. Inst. J., n.s. 95–106.

1910

Diabase and granophyre of the Gowganda Lake District, Ontario. J. Geol., 18:658–74.

1911

a. Silver in Thunder Bay District. In: 20th Report, Bureau of Mines, Ontario, pp. 119–32. Ottawa: Ontario Bureau of Mines.
b. Notes on the salt industry of Ontario. In: 20th Report, Bureau of Mines, Ontario, pp. 247–58. Ottawa: Ontario Bureau of Mines.

1912

a. The binary system $Na_2Al_2Si_2O_8$ (nephelite, carnegieite)—$CaAl_2Si_2O_8$ (anorthite), Abstract of thesis submitted to the faculty of Massachusetts Institute of Technology in partial fulfillment of the requirements for the degree of Doctor of Philosophy, 15 pp.
b. The composition of nephelite. Am. J. Sci., fourth series, 33:49–54.
c. The order of crystallization in igneous rocks. J. Geol., 20: 457–68.
d. The binary system: $Na_2Al_2Si_2O_8$ (nephelite, carnegieite)—$CaAl_2Si_2O_8$ (anorthite). Am. J. Sci., fourth series, 33:551–73.

1913

a. The melting phenomena of the plagioclase feldspars. Am. J. Sci., fourth series, 35:577–99. Also in: Z. Anorg. Chem., 82:283–307.
b. A geological reconnaissance of the Fraser River Valley from Lytton to Vancouver, British Columbia. Geol. Surv. Can. Sum. Rep., n.s., pp. 108–114.
c. The order of crystallization in igneous rocks. J. Geol., 21:399–401.

1914

a. With Olaf Andersen. The binary system $MgO-SiO_2$. Am. J. Sci., fourth series, 37:487–500. Also in: Z. Anorg. Chem., 87:283–99.
b. The ternary system: diopside-forsterite-silica. Am. J. Sci., 38:207–65. Also in: Z. Anorg. Chem., 90:1–66.

1915

a. Crystallization-differentiation in silicate liquids. Am. J. Sci., fourth series, 39:175–91.
b. The crystallization of haplobasaltic, haplodioritic, and related magmas. Am. J. Sci., 40:161–85. Also in: Z. Anorg. Chem., 94:23–50.
c. The later stages of the evolution of the igneous rocks. J. Geol., 23 (Suppl.):1–89.

1917

a. The sodium-potassium nephelites. Am. J. Sci., 43:115–32.
b. The problem of the anorthosites. J. Geol., 25:209–43.
c. Adirondack intrusives. J. Geol., 25:509–12.

1918

a. The significance of glass-making processes to the petrologist. J. Wash. Acad. Sci., 8:88–93.
b. Crystals of barium disilicate in optical glass. J. Wash. Acad. Sci., 8:265–68.
c. The identification of "stones" in glass. J. Am. Ceram. Soc., 1:594–605.

1919

a. Devitrification of glass. J. Am. Ceram. Soc., 2:261–78.
b. Tridymite crystals in glass. Am. Mineral., 4:65–66.
c. Abnormal birefringence of torbernite. Am. J. Sci., fourth series, 48:195–98.
d. Cacoclasite from Wakefield, Quebec. Am. J. Sci., fourth series, 48:440–42.
e. Crystallization-differentiation in igneous magmas. J. Geol., 27:393–430.

1920

a. Optical properties of anthophyllite. J. Wash. Acad. Sci., 10:411–14.
b. Echellite, a new mineral. Am. Mineral., 5:1–2.
c. Differentiation by deformation. Proc. Natl. Acad. Sci. USA, 6:159–62.

1921

a. Diffusion in silicate melts. J. Geol., 29:295–317.
b. Preliminary note on monticellite alnoite from Isle Cadieux, Quebec. J. Wash. Acad. Sci., 11:278–81.

1922

a. Genetic features of alnoitic rocks from Isle Cadieux, Quebec. Am. J. Sci., 3:1–34.
b. Two corrections to mineral data. Am. Mineral., 7:64–66.
c. The reaction principle in petrogenesis. J. Geol., 30:177–98.
d. With G. W. Morey. The melting of potash feldspar. Am. J. Sci., fifth series, 4:1–21.
e. The behavior of inclusions in igneous magmas. J. Geol. 30:513–70.

1923

a. The genesis of melilite. J. Wash. Acad. Sci., 13:1–4.
b. With M. Aurousseau. Fusion of sedimentary rocks in drill-holes. Geol. Soc. Am. Bull., 34:431–48.

1924

a. With J. W. Greig. The system: Al_2O_3-SiO_2. J. Am. Ceram. Soc., 7:238–54.
b. With J. W. Greig and E. G. Zies. Mullite, a silicate of alumina. J. Wash. Acad. Sci., 14:183–91.
c. The Fen area in Telemark, Norway. Am. J. Sci., fifth series, 8:1–11; plates I-III.
d. With G. W. Morey. The binary system sodium metasilicate-silica. J. Phys. Chem., 28:1167–79.

1925

a. The mineralogical phase rule. J. Wash. Acad. Sci., 15:280–84.

b. With J. W. Greig. The crystalline modifications of NaAlSiO$_4$. Am. J. Sci., 10:204–12.
c. The amount of assimilation by the Sudbury norite sheet. J. Geol., 33:825–29.
d. With G. W. Morey. The ternary system sodium metasilicate-calcium metasilicate-silica. J. Soc. Glass Technol., 9:226–64.

1926

a. Concerning "Evidence of liquid immiscibility in a silicate magma, Agate Point, Ontario." J. Geol., 34:71–73.
b. Properties of ammonium nitrate: I. A metastable inversion in ammonium nitrate; II. The system: ammonium nitrate-ammonium chloride; III. A note on the system: ammonium nitrate-ammonium sulphate. J. Phys. Chem., 30:721–37.
c. With R. W. G. Wyckoff. A petrographic and X-ray study of the thermal dissociation of dumortierite. J. Wash. Acad. Sci., 16:178–89.
d. With R. W. G. Wyckoff and J. W. Greig. The X-ray diffraction patterns of mullite and of sillimanite. Am. J. Sci., 11:459–79.
e. The carbonate rocks of the Fen area in Norway. Am. J. Sci., 12:499–502. Also in: Centrabl. Min. Geol., Abt. A., n.s., 241–45.

1927

a. With G. W. Morey. The decomposition of glass by water at high temperatures and pressures. J. Soc. Glass Technol., 11 (Trans.): 97–106.
b. The origin of ultrabasic and related rocks. Am. J. Sci., fifth series, 14:89–108.

1928

a. *The Evolution of the Igneous Rocks.* Princeton, N.J.: Princeton Univ. Press. x + 334 pp. Reprinted with a new introduction by J. F. Schairer and a complete bibliography of the writings of N. L. Bowen, Dover Publications, Inc., New York (1956).
b. Geologic thermometry. In: *The Laboratory Investigation of Ores,* ed. E. E. Fairbanks, pp. 172–99. N.Y.: McGraw-Hill.

1929

a. With J. F. Schairer. The system: leucite-diopside. Am. J. Sci., fifth series, 18:301–12.

b. With J. F. Schairer. The fusion relations of acmite. Am. J. Sci., fifth series, 18:365–74.
c. With F. F. Kracek and G. W. Morey. The system potassium metasilicate-silica. J. Phys. Chem., 33:1857–79.

1930

a. Central African volcanoes in 1929. Trans. Am. Geophys. Union, 10th and 11th Annual Meetings, pp. 301–7.
b. With G. W. Morey and F. C. Kracek. The ternary system K_2O-CaO-SiO_2 (with correction). J. Soc. Glass Technol., 14:149–87.
c. With J. F. Schairer and H. W. V. Willems. The ternary system: Na_2SiO_3-Fe_2O_3-SiO_2. Am. J. Sci., fifth series, 20:405–55.

1931

a. With E. Posnjak. Magnesian amphibole from the dry melt: A correction. Am. J. Sci., fifth series, 22:193–202.
b. With E. Posnjak. The role of water in tremolite. Am. J. Sci., fifth series, 22:203–14.
c. With G. W. Morey. "Devitrite," (letter to editor). Glass Ind., June.

1932

With J. F. Schairer. The system FeO-SiO_2. Am. J. Sci., fifth series, 24:177–213.

1933

a. Crystals of iron-rich pyroxene from a slag. J. Wash. Acad. Sci., 23:83–87.
b. Vogtite, isomorphous with wollastonite. J. Wash. Acad. Sci., 23:87–94.
c. With J. F. Schairer and E. Posnjak. The system, Ca_2SiO_4-Fe_2SiO_4. Am. J. Sci., fifth series, 25:273–97.
d. The broader story of magmatic differentiation, briefly told. In: *Ore Deposits of the Western States*, pp. 106–28. N.Y.: American Institute of Mining and Metallurgical Engineers.
e. With J. F. Schairer and E. Posnjak. The system, CaO-FeO-SiO_2. Am. J. Sci., 26:193–284.
f. Note: Non-existence of echellite. Am. Mineral., 18:31.

1934

Viscosity data for silicate melts. Trans. Am. Geophys. Union, 15th Annual Meeting, pp. 249–55.

1935

a. With J. F. Schairer. The system, MgO-FeO-SiO$_2$. Am. J. Sci., fifth series, 29:151–217.
b. The igneous rocks in the light of high-temperature research. Sci. Mon., 40:487–503.
c. With J. F. Schairer. Preliminary report on equilibrium-relations between feldspathoids, alkali-feldspars, and silica. Trans. Am. Geophys. Union, 16th Annual Meeting, pp. 325–28.
d. With J. F. Schairer. Grünerite from Rockport, Massachusetts, and a series of synthetic fluor-amphiboles. Am. Mineral., 20:543–51.
e. "Ferrosilite" as a natural mineral. Am. J. Sci., 30:481–94.

1936

a. With J. F. Schairer. The problem of the intrusion of dunite in the light of the olivine diagram. *XVI International Geological Congress, 1933, Report*, pp. 391–96. Wash., D.C.: International Geological Congress.
b. With R. B. Ellestad. Nepheline contrasts. Am. Mineral., 21:363–68.
c. With J. F. Schairer. The system, albite-fayalite. Proc. Natl. Acad. Sci., 22:345–50.

1937

a. Recent high-temperature research on silicates and its significance in igneous geology. Am. J. Sci., fifth series, 33:1–21.
b. A note on aenigmatite. Am. Mineral., 22:139–40.
c. With R. B. Ellestad. Leucite and pseudoleucite. Am. Mineral., 22:409–15.
d. With F. C. Kracek and G. W. Morey. Equilibrium relations and factors influencing their determination in the system K$_2$SiO$_3$-SiO$_2$. J. Phys. Chem., 41:1183–93.

1938

a. With J. F. Schairer. Crystallization equilibrium in nepheline-albite-silica mixtures with fayalite. J. Geol., 46:397–411.

b. Lavas of the African Rift Valleys and their tectonic setting. Am. J. Sci., fifth series, 35-A: 19–33.
c. With J. F. Schairer. The system, leucite-diopside-silica. Am. J. Sci., fifth series, 35-A: 289–309.
d. *Mente et malleo atque catino* (Presidential address, 18th Annual Meeting, Mineralogical Society of America). Am. Mineral., 23:123–30.
e. With N. M. Fenneman, T. W. Vaughan, and A. L. Day. A possible program of research in geology. Geological Society of America, Proceedings, pp. 143–55.

1939

Geology and chemistry. Science, 89:135–39.

1940

a. Progressive metamorphism of siliceous limestone and dolomite. J. Geol., 48:225–74.
b. Geologic temperature recorders. Sci. Mon., 51:5–14.

1941

a. Certain singular points on crystallization curves of solid solutions. Proc. Natl. Acad. Sci., 27:301–9.
b. Physical controls in adjustments of the earth's crust. In: *Shiftings of the Sea Floor and Coast Lines* (University of Pennsylvania Bicentennial Conference), pp. 1–6. Philadelphia: Univ. of Pennsylvania Press.

1942

a. With J. F. Schairer. The binary system $CaSiO_3$-diopside and the relations between $CaSiO_3$ and akermanite. Am. J. Sci., 240:725–42.

1943

Petrology and silicate technology. J. Am. Ceram. Soc., 26:285–301.

1945

Phase equilibria bearing on the origin and differentiation of alkaline rocks. Am. J. Sci., 243-A:75–89.

1947

a. Magmas. Geol. Soc. Am. Bull., 58:263–80.
b. With J. F. Schairer. Melting relations in the systems Na_2O-Al_2O_3-SiO_2 and K_2O-Al_2O_3-SiO_2. Am. J. Sci., 245:193–204.
c. With J. F. Schairer. The system anorthite-leucite-silica. Soc. Geol. Finl. Bull., 20:67–87.

1948

a. The granite problem and the method of multiple prejudices. Geol. Soc. Am. Mem., 28:79–90.
b. Phase equilibria in silicate melts including those containing volatile constituents. Committee on Geophysical Sciences, Research and Development Board, Panel on Geology, 6 pp. Wash., D.C.: U.S. Govt. Print. Off.

1949

With O. F. Tuttle. The system MgO-SiO_2-H_2O. Geol. Soc. Am. Bull., 60:439–60.

1950

a. With O. F. Tuttle. The system $NaAlSi_3O_8$-$KAlSi_3O_8$-H_2O. J. Geol., 58:489–511.
b. With O. F. Tuttle. High-temperature albite and contiguous feldspars. J. Geol., 58:572–83.
c. The making of a magmatist. Am. Mineral., 35:651–58.

1954

Experiment as an aid to the understanding of the natural world. Proc. Acad. Nat. Sci., Philadelphia, 106:1–12.

1955

With J. F. Schairer. The system K_2O-Al_2O_3-SiO_2. Am. J. Sci., 253:681–746.

1956

With J. F. Schairer. The system Na_2O-Al_2O_3-SiO_2. Am. J. Sci., 254:129–95.

1958

With O. F. Tuttle. Origin of granite in the light of experimental studies in the system $NaAlSi_3O_8$-$KAlSi_3O_8$-SiO_2-H_2O. Geol. Soc. Am. Mem., 74:153 pp.

MILTON NUNN BRAMLETTE
February 8, 1896–March 31, 1977

BY JAMES GILLULY

MILTON NUNN BRAMLETTE—always known to his many friends as "Bram"—was born in Bonham, Texas on February 8, 1896, son of William Ambrose and Eula Lee Nunn Bramlette. His early youth was spent in Texas. He attended Principia School in St. Louis in preparation for college, whence he entered the University of Wisconsin in 1914.

At Madison he came under the distinguished instruction of C. K. Leith, Warren Mead, A. N. Winchell, and W. H. Twenhofel; his principal interest was in microscopic petrography and stratigraphy. His university work was interrupted by World War I. He enlisted in the aviation service, where he qualified as a pilot, but too late in the war to see combat. He was discharged as a Second Lieutenant early in 1919. He returned to Madison, where he graduated with high honors in 1921. During two of the summer vacations of the University he worked on the State Geological Survey, running magnetic traverses across the iron ranges of the north.

In June 1921, Bramlette joined the U.S. Geological Survey, skipping a normal grade because of his high academic standing and field experience, and thus qualifying as an Assistant Geologist. He was assigned to the party of Frank Reeves, on a mapping project in eastern Montana, in and south of the "Missouri Breaks." Here he showed himself to be a master of plane table surveying and an amazingly expert finder and collector of fossils. While the rest of the party would painstakingly hammer out a few badly mangled fossils, Bram would collect a hatful of beautifully prepared specimens, many worthy of museum preservation. Years later, he was widely known as the sharpest fossil finder in California—a reputation he fully deserved.

During the winter of 1921–1922 Bram commuted with other Survey novices from the Washington headquarters to Johns Hopkins for the famous course in stratigraphy taught by Professor Edward Berry.

As with most new employees of the Survey, Bram was given a series of various assignments to familiarize him with methods and varieties of geology before finding his particular research interests. Accordingly, he served on field assignments in Montana, Kansas, and the Black Hills rim in South Dakota before he began to draw assignments in one of the fields of his major interest—the study of clays. These he began in Louisiana, Mississippi, and Texas, where he discovered many hitherto unrecognized ash flow tuffs. He also found that many of the "heavy minerals," which had been considered as stable under normal sedimentary conditions, were subject to solution or etching and could not be relied upon in correlation studies. He was among the first to recognize the wide distribution of zeolites as cements in clastic sedimentary rocks.

In 1924 Bramlette took leave of the Survey and spent the academic year 1924–1925 in graduate studies at Yale. He then spent three years with the Gulf Oil Company in Latin America: Mexico, Venezuela, and Ecuador. His work was so outstanding that he had for many years a standing offer from Gulf for employment whenever he would prefer it.

Because his employment had been in foreign countries, Bramlette retained his status with the Geological Survey. He took two more graduate years at Yale and returned to the Survey in 1930. (He received his doctorate in 1936, utilizing one of his outstanding Survey studies as the thesis.)

His work shifted to California, where he began his long and close association with Wendell P. Woodring. These two outstanding stratigraphers supplemented each other perfectly. Woodring, a world authority on fossil molluscs, and Bramlette, the leading sedimentary petrographer—and soon to become an outstanding authority on foraminifera and other microfossils—produced a whole series of classic studies, as fine as have ever been published in North Amerca: the U.S. Geological Survey reports on the Palos Verdes Hills, the Kettleman Hills oil field, and the Santa Maria Valley.

Bram's petrologic studies dealt further with intrastratal alterations of minerals, with phosphatic deposits, and with zeolites. Here he began his classic work on the origin of the siliceous rocks of the Monterey Formation. This problem had fascinated geologists for two generations and theories concerning it were almost as numerous as the students. Bramlette, after thorough studies extending over nearly all the well-exposed sections of the formation, was able to demonstrate that these highly siliceous strata were derived from original diatomaceous strata. The siliceous tests of these tiny animals had been etched, dissolved and redeposited, with great shrinkage, into thinner strata virtually free of identifiable fossils. His arguments have proved so cogent that no further controversy has appeared in the twenty-five years since his publication.

At the same time that Bramlette was dealing with the petrography of the sedimentary rocks, he was also studying their foraminiferal content. He finally became so expert that he could identify many diagnostic species in the field with a hand lens only—a really remarkable feat.

Bramlette also utilized his skill with clay minerals in

diagnosing many deposits of bleaching clays in several of the southern states. He also studied the bauxite deposits of Arkansas and showed conclusively that all were formed in the relatively brief interval between the close of deposition of the Midway Formation and the beginning of deposition of the Wilcox. This sharp limitation on the time of formation of the ore deposit is a matter of prime economic importance. During World War II Bramlette was reassigned to the bauxite problem because our imports were critically interrupted by the submarine attacks. The strategic mineral program of the U.S. Geological Survey led to many significant increases in metal production; none were more successful than this project under the guidance of Bramlette.

Bramlette was a principal investigator, along with W. H. Bradley and Kenneth E. Lohman of the Survey, of the series of "Piggott cores" during the 1930's. The plethora of much longer cores accumulated since World War II has all but buried this pioneer study in oblivion. Nevertheless it was the first real study of seafloor stratigraphy and was highly significant in permitting the first correlation of American with European glaciations.

In 1940 Bram joined the faculty of UCLA, where he remained until 1951, except for two years during World War II. As noted above, he spent one of the war years with the U.S. Geological Survey on the bauxite deposits of Arkansas and Jamaica—both highly successful projects. A second year was spent with Gulf Oil Company in Venezuela.

In 1951 Bramlette transferred from UCLA to the Scripps Institution of Oceanography, also a branch of the University of California, at La Jolla. Here he began his pioneer studies of coccoliths, discoasters, and other nanofossils—studies which he continued for many years after his retirement in 1962. He found that these tiny drifting organisms sink so slowly in the sea after death that currents distribute them almost worldwide. Furthermore, they evolved so rapidly that the overlapping ranges of large assemblages of these fossils permit highly precise dating; they are virtually worldwide stratigraphic markers. Amazing as it may seem, fossils collected off New Zealand may include the same species as are found off Japan, Gibraltar, Norway, and Brazil. As guides to correlation the coccolithophores are unsurpassed. Bram's contributions to the development of such correlations was preeminent.

Bramlette was not only an extraordinarily skilled microscopist, he was also a superb field stratigrapher. Many experienced field students agree with the writer in considering him the best observer they had ever seen.

The record indicates something of Bram's energy, originality, and versatility. Further, he was a profound scholar, plunging deeply into whatever research he undertook. Conscientious beyond words, in preparing a single lecture on a subject with which he was thoroughly familiar, he would spend entire days in reading and organizing his material. He was a most effective teacher of both stratigraphy and micropaleontology. He insisted on clear distinctions between fossil stratigraphy, time stratigraphy, and lithostratigraphy. Critical of all work, he was most critical of his own. Many former students who have had successful careers in university, government, or industry credit Bram's teaching as most influential in their work.

Bram was married in 1931 to Valerie Jourdan of Bradford, Connecticut. They had one daughter, Emily (Mrs. M. M. Assami, of Damascus, Syria), who survives him, along with her five children. Valerie's death, in 1962, was a great blow from which Bram never really recovered.

He was a member of the American Association for the Advancement of Science, the Geological Society of America, the American Association of Petroleum Geologists, the Mineralogical Society of America, the Society of Economic Paleontologists and Mineralogists, and the Geological Society of France.

Bram was elected to the National Academy of Sciences in 1954 and received its Thompson Medal in 1964. He was awarded the Distinguished Service Medal of the Department of the Interior in 1963 and was awarded the degree of Doctor of Laws by the University of California in 1965.

He died of emphysema on March 31, 1977. Throughout life he was a modest gentleman.

BIBLIOGRAPHY

1924

Bentonite in the Upper Cretaceous of Louisiana. Am. Assoc. Pet. Geol. Bull., 8:342–44.

Volcanic rocks in the Cretaceous of Louisiana. Am. Assoc. Pet. Geol., 8:344–46.

1925

A subsurface correlation of the stratigraphic units from Russell County to Marion County, Kansas. Kans. State Geol. Surv. Bull., 10:86–93.

Paleozoic formations penetrated by wells in Tishomingo County, northeastern Mississippi. U.S. Geol. Surv. Bull., 781:1–10.

1928

Pseudo-stratification in core recoveries. Am. Assoc. Pet. Geol. Bull., 12:1167–69.

1929

Natural etchings of detrital garnet. Am. Mineral., 14:316–27.

1933

With E. Posnjak. Zeolitic alteration of pyroclastics. Am. Mineral., 18:167–71.

Heavy mineral studies on correlation of sands at Kettleman Hills, California. Am. Assoc. Pet. Geol. Bull., 18:1559–76.

1934

Rhythmic bedding in the Monterey rocks of California. J. Wash. Acad. Sci., 23:575.

1936

Geology of the Arkansas bauxite region. Ark. Geol. Surv. Inf. Circ. 8, 68 pp.

With W. P. Woodring and R. M. Kleinpell. Miocene stratigraphy and paleontology of Palos Verdes Hills, California. Am. Assoc. Pet. Geol. Bull., 28:125–59.

1940

Some bleaching and ceramic clays in western Tennessee and possible bleaching clays in Calloway County, Kentucky. U.S. Geol. Surv. Bull., 901:189–206.

With T. N. McKay. Some organic clays in Alabama. U.S. Geol. Surv. Bull., 901:207–27.

With A. K. Ray and A. C. Munyan. Bleaching clays in Alabama. U.S. Geol. Surv. Bull., 901:228–49.

With W. P. Woodring. Late Miocene and Pliocene stratigraphy and paleontology of the Santa Maria District, California. Oil Wkly., 99:60.

1941

The stability of minerals in sandstone. J. Sediment. Petrol., 11:32–36.

1943

With W. P. Woodring and K. E. Lohman. Stratigraphy and paleontology of the Santa Maria District, California. Am. Assoc. Pet. Geol. Bull., 27:1335–60.

1944

With C. E. Weaver and others. Correlation of the marine Cenozoic formations of western North America (Chart no. 11). Geol. Soc. Am. Bull., 55:569–98.

With S. N. Davies. Geology and oil possibilities of the Salinas Valley, California. U.S. Geol. Surv. Oil Gas Invest., Prelim. Map no. 24.

1945

With J. S. Loofborough and W. P. Woodring. Geology of Santa Rosa Hills, eastern Purisima Hills District, Santa Barbara County, California. U.S. Geol. Surv. Oil Gas Invest., Prelim. Map no. 26.

1946

With W. P. Woodring and W. S. W. Kew. Geology and paleontology of the Palos Verdes Hills, California. U.S. Geol. Surv. Prof. Pap., 207, 145 pp.

The Monterey Formation of California and the origin of its siliceous rocks. U.S. Geol. Surv. Prof. Pap., 212, 57 pp.

1947

Lateritic ore of aluminum in the Greater Antilles (Jamaica). Geol. Soc. Am. Bull., 58:1248–49.

Occurrence and origin of chert in the Monterey Formation. Am. Assoc. Pet. Geol. Bull., 31:239.

With A. A. Baker and others. Stratigraphy of the Wasatch Mountains in the vicinity of Provo, Utah. U.S. Geol. Surv. Oil Gas Invest., Chart no. 30.

1950

With W. P. Woodring. Geology and paleontology of the Santa Maria District, California. U.S. Geol. Surv. Prof. Pap., 222, 185 pp.

1951

With others. Correlation section across the Los Angeles Basin, California. Am. Assoc. Pet. Geol. Bull., 35:3633.

1954

With W. R. Riedel. Stratigraphic value of discoasters and some other microfossils related to the recent coccolithophores. J. Paleontol., 28:385–403.

1955

With R. R. D. Revelle and others. Pelagic sediments of the Pacific. In: *Crust of the Earth*, ed. A. Poldervaart. Geol. Soc. Am. Spec. Pap., 62:221–35.

Change in four groups of microfossils from the Eocene to the Oligocene of the Oceanic Formation of Barbados. Geol. Soc. Am. Bull., 66:1534.

1957

With G. O. S. Arrhenius and E. E. Picciotto. Localization of radioactive and stable heavy nuclides in ocean sediments. Nature, 180:85–86.

1958

Significance of coccolithophorids in calcium carbonate deposition. Geol. Soc. Am. Bull, 67:121–26.

1959

Pelagic sediments (invited lecture presented at the International Oceanographic Congress, New York). In: *Oceanography*, Am. Assoc. Adv. Sci. Pub., 67:345–66.

1960

Age relations in the early Tertiary of Europe and America as indicated by coccolithophorids and related microfossils. Geol. Soc. Am. Bull., 71:1832.

1961

With F. R. Sullivan. Coccolithophorids and related nannoplankton of the early Tertiary in California. Micropaleontology, 7:124–88.

With W. R. Riedel and others. Preliminary drilling phase of Moho Project, Part 2: Summary of coring operations (Guadalupe site). Am. Assoc. Pet. Geol. Bull., 45:1793–98.

1963

With E. Martini. Calcareous nannoplankton from the experimental Moho Project. J. Paleontol., 37:845–56.

1964

With E. Martini. The great changes in calcareous nannoplankton between the Maestrichtian and Danian. Micropaleontology, 10:291–322.

1965

Massive extinctions in biota at the end of Mesozoic time. Science, 148:1696–99.

1967

With J. A. Wilcoxon. Middle Tertiary calcareous nannoplankton of the Cipero section, Trinidad, W.I. Tulane Stud. Geol., 5:93–131.

With J. A. Wilcoxon. *Discoaster druggi* nom. nova pro *Discoaster extensus* Bramlette and Wilcoxon, 1967. Tulane Stud. Geol., 5:220.

Some remarks on calcareous nannoplankton. Committee on Mediterranean Neogene Stratigraphy, 4th Session, Bologna, Italy Proc. Pt. 2. G. Geol. (sec. 2). 35:127–28. Bologna: Bologna Univ. Press.

1968

With D. Bukry. Stratigraphic significance of Tertiary calcareous nannofossils. Tulane Stud. Geol., 6:149–55.

With D. Bukry. Summary of coccolith biostratigraphy. In: *Initial Reports of the Deep Sea Drilling Project*, vol. 1, *Leg 1 of Cruises of the Glomar Challenger, Orange, Tex. to Hoboken, N.J., Aug.–Sept. 1968*, pp. 621–23. Wash., D.C.: U.S. Govt. Printing Off.

With D. Bukry. Coccolith age determinations. In: *Initial Reports of the Deep Sea Drilling Project*, vol. 1, *Leg 1 of Cruises of the Glomar Challenger, Orange, Tex. to Hoboken, N. J., Aug.–Sept. 1968*, pp. 369–87. Wash., D.C.: U.S. Govt. Printing Off.

1969

With D. Bukry. Some new and stratigraphically useful calcareous nannofossils of the Cenozoic. Tulane Stud. Geol. Paleontol., 7:131–42.

1970

Calcareous nannoplankton. In: *Smaller Foraminifera of Late Eocene Age from Eua, Tonga*. U.S. Geol. Surv. Prof. Pap. 640, p. 18.

With D. Bukry. Coccolith age determinations, Leg 5, Deep Sea Drilling Project. In: *Initial Report, Cruise of the Glomar Challenger, San Diego, Calif. to Honolulu, Hawaii*, pp. 487–94. Wash., D.C.: U.S. Govt. Printing Off.

1971

With W. R. Riedel. Observations on the biostratigraphy of pelagic sediments. In: *The Micropaleontology of Oceans*, pp. 665–68. Cambridge, England: Cambridge Univ. Press.

With W. R. Riedel. Observations on the biostratigraphy of pelagic sediments. Scripps Inst. Oceanogr. Contrib., 41:489–92.

1972

With D. Bukry. Validation of *Pedinocyclus* and *Quinquerhabdus*, new calcareous nannoplankton genera. Scripps Inst. Oceanogr. Contrib., 42 (part 2):876.

Ernst Cloos

ERNST CLOOS

May 17, 1898 – May 24, 1974

BY AARON C. WATERS AND STEVEN M. STANLEY

ERNST CLOOS' activities spanned that extraordinary interval from the horse-and-buggy days to the space age, a period of time that to young minds hardly seems compressible into one lifetime. An internationally renowned geologist, he also will be remembered as a remarkable man whose warm friendliness, insight, and humanity affected the lives of hundreds of people. Although he spent long hours and nearly every weekend at his teaching and research, Cloos nevertheless found time to respond to requests for advice regarding personal problems of the lowliest student, typist, or laborer. He was equally adept at resolving differences of opinion at the highest level of University faculties, in meetings of committees of the National Research Council, and among board members of large corporations.

Cloos was born in Saarbrücken, Germany on May 17, 1898 and died in Baltimore, Maryland on May 28, 1974. His early childhood was spent in Cologne, but after the death of his father, when Ernst was six years old, Frau Cloos moved to Freiburg im Breisgau, where Ernst's brother Hans, who was older by thirteen years, was a student in geology at the University of Freiburg.

Young Ernst performed indifferently at the local public school and spent three years at a religious boarding school in the Black Forest. At age fourteen he was sent to the Hermann Lietz-Schule in Switzerland. Among the graduates of this unusual institution have been several luminaries, including Werner von Braun. It was here that the young Cloos found himself. Practical skills like woodsmanship were weighted equally with traditional academics. Agriculturally, the school was self-sufficient, and heavy outdoor work formed a major part of the program. The balanced curriculum appealed to Ernst, and he excelled. Whether the Hermann Lietz-Schule implanted traits in the boy or simply unlocked latent drives, his new enthusiasm for both academic and practical work was to last a lifetime.

Cloos' pre-university training, however, was interrupted by World War I. As a youth of seventeen, he volunteered for the Kaiser's army. Despite medical questions raised by the sound of his heart, he was granted admission to pilot school. He began the war pacifically enough by flying reconnaissance missions. Behind the cockpit of his biplane was stationed an observer-photographer. In the early days of the war, French and German pilots left the animosity of the conflict on the ground. Once aloft, they waved cordially in passing. As Cloos used to say, it was not until the damned American flyers joined in with their machine guns that his troubles began. One day over France, four of these villains appeared on his tail. Despite his best efforts at evasion, they gave pursuit for several miles and severely damaged his aircraft. This day, as every day, the young German flyer was mindful of the position of the Swiss border. With his engine failing, he glided to the safety of Swiss neutrality. Finding no area large enough for a normal landing, he brought his craft down in a field full of haystacks and set his course for one of them—the workers harvesting hay scattered as he approached. Years later, a son of one of these workers was by the sheerest coincidence a student in Cloos' classroom on the opposite side of the Atlantic. One day on a field trip, the son heard his professor tell of the crash landing. Returning home, the student repeated the tale to his mother, who responded with amazement: "I know that man! I was in the field in Switzerland where he landed."

What the student's mother and her comrades in the hayfield found when they rushed to the plane was a dead observer and a dazed pilot, slumped forward, with his head against the motor. They revived the pilot, gave him food and water, and summoned the police. Young Cloos' airplane, riddled with nearly forty bullet holes, was placed in a Swiss museum. He himself was no less a curiosity, as a uniformed hero in a peaceful land. He was interned with the family of a friend from school days and permitted to reenter the Hermann Lietz-Schule where he made good use of his time by completing the studies that prepared him to enter the University at Freiburg.

Released from Swiss internment with the coming of peace, young Cloos returned to the Germany of *All Quiet on the Western Front*, the Germany of a lost generation. He rejoined his family in Freiburg and enrolled at the University to prepare for a career in biology. Like nearly all veterans returning from war, Ernst Cloos had difficulties in concentrating on his studies. He nearly left Freiburg to fly airplanes in Mexico, but his biology professor persuaded him that continuing his studies offered a far better opportunity for building a career. Nevertheless, as his education in biology advanced, the student became more and more frustrated as he sat on a stool hunched over a laboratory bench peering at almost invisible animals. Did not his brother's profession offer a new opportunity, and far more freedom?

Ernst's brother, Hans Cloos, had studied geology at Freiburg, and later worked as a geologist in the Erongo Mountains of Southwest Africa and in the oil fields of Indonesia. In 1919, at age thirty-four, Hans Cloos was appointed to the

Chair of Geology at the University of Breslau (at present in Poland, and renamed Wroclaw). In his autobiographical book of geologic travels, *Gesprach mit der Erde* (R. Piper, Verlag, 1947), Hans Cloos speaks vividly of his astonishment at finding his younger brother on his doorstep in Breslau:

> "I have got to lay my hands on something solid," he said as for the last time he cleaned and laid aside the hair-fine glass needles which for a whole year he had been using to coax invisible abnormalities from his almost invisible animals, or to add them where none had been before. With this he put his hammer in his knapsack, and exchanged the dampest and greenest corner of Germany for that other corner where, through a thin forest cover, the bare rocks of the mountains look out, clear and enticing. . . .
>
> "I can't endure sitting down any longer," the big, broad-shouldered man said to his astonished brother. "I want an existence where I can move around freely, where I can tread as hard as I like without breaking something. I'm sick of tiny little lumps of slime. I want to lay my hands on big, hard mountains! I want to become a geologist!"*

At Breslau Ernst Cloos met and became firm friends with Robert Balk, born in Riga on the Baltic. Balk almost simultaneously had decided to give up his interest in hummingbirds and other "living organisms for the realm of the dead rocks."† Their friendship lasted a lifetime. Both were destined to come to the United States, where they had outstanding careers as university professors. Each student chose to work for his doctorate on the granites and gneisses of Bohemia, using the methods of "granittektonik" that the older Cloos had made famous in Europe. Food was scarce in Bohemia after World War I, and German money was almost worthless. At times the two students virtually had to "live off the land," but the rocks were exciting and well-exposed on mountain slopes and in numerous quarries. Moreover, a raw

---

* Hans Cloos, *Conversation with the Earth* (New York: Alfred Knopf, 1953), p. 351.
† *Ibid.*

potato or cabbage could sometimes be gleaned from the fields between. Each student completed the reports on his field work, and each was awarded the doctorate with highest honors in 1923.

To what extent the elder Cloos served as surrogate father to the younger can only be speculated upon, but the ability of the two to prosper as professor and student is a tribute to both men. Each brother held a great fondness and admiration for the other, and to this strong sibling bond Robert Balk was admitted as another close "brother." Yet the three were very different in temperament and in physical stature. Hans Cloos, a small wiry man of tough mind and principles, was a brilliant lecturer and writer. Robert Balk was quiet, introspective, and even-tempered. Ernst Cloos' difficulty with biology was not entirely a matter of intellectual boredom. The problem here was that the younger Cloos was also by far the larger brother. A giant for this generation, he stood well over six feet tall and weighed over two hundred pounds. Even as a septuagenerian, his friendly slap on the back could set one to coughing. The man simply was not built for glass needles and microscope slides.

Nevertheless, Ernst Cloos did reap a real reward for his years of studying biology at Freiburg: on receiving his doctorate at Breslau he returned to Freiburg and married Margret Spemann, the daughter of his biology professor! Many years later no one was prouder than Ernst Cloos when Professor Spemann won the Nobel Prize for his studies of the "little lumps of slime" that his awkward student had so cavalierly rejected!

Worthwhile positions in geology were almost nonexistent for new Ph.D.'s in the Germany of 1923. Robert Balk emigrated immediately to the United States. In the course of his graduate education, Ernst left Breslau for a brief interlude to study at Göttingen under the famous Hans Stille. Now, upon graduation from Breslau, he was offered a position as Stille's assistant, a miraculous opportunity in the perilous postwar economy. But on the night before the wedding, with the Spemann house filled with guests, a telegram arrived. Tragically, the state had cancelled the position with Stille. In this unforeseen crisis, the advice of Professor Spemann was for the couple to proceed with the wedding and to take up residence in Göttingen, hoping that a position might appear. The advice was heeded; Ernst did find work at a menial curatorial job in Stille's department, but the pay was a paltry ten pounds of flour a month!

Some thirty pounds of flour later, Cloos secured a position with one of the first companies ever to apply seismic exploration toward the discovery of oil. Lutger Mintrop, the founder of this company (Seismos), assigned Cloos to work first in the swamps along the Gulf Coast of Texas and Louisiana, and later in the scorched deserts of Iraq. Although the work was timely and interesting—it ultimately developed into the major method of discovering oil adjacent to salt domes, and in offshore parts of the continental shelves—the areas selected for study were not attractive places to bring a bride, or to start a family. Margret endured the humid Texas swamps, but was not permitted in the oil fields of Iraq. Moreover, after a few years Cloos became bored with the routine of "setting off huge blasts of dynamite and studying the squiggles that the artificial earthquake waves produce on a sheet of paper."

In 1930 Prussia's director of geologic studies made it possible, by a small grant from the Notgemeinschaft der Deutschen Wissenschaft, for Ernst Cloos to study the granitic rocks of the Sierra Nevada. He resigned his well-paying job with Seismos and headed for California.

During the next two field seasons Cloos roamed over the barren peaks of the high Sierra plotting on maps thousands of structural readings of the cracks, schleiren, lineations, mineral banding, dikes, and other subtle features that record the motion of granitic and granodioritic masses during the final stages of their emplacement and consolidation within the earth's crust. The science of "granite tectonics" was new in America, and his first report on the Sierra Nevada, although published in German, drew attention from American scholars, and also an awareness of the publications of his brother, Hans, who developed these techniques during investigations of European and African igneous massifs.

A fortunate turn of events for the Cloos family, and also for Appalachian geology, occurred in 1931 when Ernst Cloos was on his way to Europe after completing his Sierra Nevada field work. On a tip from Robert Balk, then professor of geology at Hunter College, Cloos drove his battered California field auto to Baltimore in order to visit the Geology Department at Johns Hopkins University and inquire about a possible opening for a lecturer. At the end of the visit E. B. Mathews, chairman of the Department, invited Cloos to "stay a little longer." Margret Cloos, on receiving this news, found temporary care for their two small daughters at a nursery home in the Black Forest and crossed the Atlantic to join her husband. The lectureship was renewed each year, but the young couple could not plan on the position becoming permanent.

In 1933 news of Hitler's ascendency reached the Clooses at a cocktail party in Baltimore. Other guests, knowing little about German politics, were surprised at the couple's great agitation. Ernst, forthright as usual, predicted the eventual onset of World War II, and announced to all that he would not return to Germany. Margret did, briefly, to gather up her children and the couple's personal belongings.

The decision to remain in America during the most bitter year of the depression required courage ("after all if I lose my job I can open a filling station in Death Valley," Ernst joked), but it also brought intangible benefits. The feeling of "marking time" while waiting for an academic position in Germany was ended. A more important benefit was that Ernst realized that he should now start on larger and more complex projects of the local geology, and bring them to completion.

Cloos' impact upon prevailing ideas of the geology of Maryland began almost from the moment he arrived in Baltimore. Much of his research time in his first two years at Johns Hopkins was spent writing reports (in English) on the Sierra Nevada work and in preparing a report on the Loon Lake batholith in eastern Canada, but whenever a free day appeared he used it to investigate the structure of the gneiss domes and granitic bodies near Baltimore. A year or two later he and his students were ranging farther afield among the greenstones, quartzites, slates, and limestones of the Appalachian Province at Harpers Ferry, Peach Bottom, South Mountain, and the Virginia Blue Ridge. Most American geologists had assumed that the geologic mapping of Maryland was completed, principally by state and federal surveys, but the remapping of certain areas in more detail with Hans Cloos' techniques brought major changes in geologic interpretation of some areas. Soon Cloos and his students were writing articles on Piedmont and Appalachian geology, giving examples of the application of the new structural methods to local rocks.

Cloos' methods of teaching proved as original and novel to his American colleagues as did his work on the local rocks. Unlike his brother Hans, Ernst Cloos deplored formal lecturing in the classroom, holding that discussions about rocks are more stimulating and most informative when held on the outcrop, where additional evidence can be garnered immediately if differences in interpretation arise. He scheduled his structural geology class for "All Day Saturday, in the Field," and this did mean "All of Daylight." Office discussions with a graduate student (or with a visiting colleague) were likely to end shortly with the invitation: "Let's go to South Mountain [or other appropriate locality] and see!" Gasoline ranged from 9¢ to 11¢ a gallon (including taxes!) in the nineteen-thirties, and a good second-hand field car could be had for thirty-five to fifty dollars. Moreover, Johns Hopkins was a mature university whose red tape was held to an absolute minimum. Cloos did not have to fight the battles with committees of "Educational Policy," "Scheduling," "Registration," "Safety," "Credits," and "Academic Policy" that would have cramped his style in a large American state university.

During the depression years few young faculty members in American universities dared raise questions of "tenure," but by 1937 the tenuous lectureship at Hopkins was straining Cloos' patience to the point where he began to look elsewhere. An offer of permanent status came from Wisconsin. When it was presented by Mathews to Isaiah Bowman, the University president, Bowman's response—long cherished by its subject—was, "Good for Cloos." Not an assistant professorship but an associate professorship was immediately offered and accepted. The attachment to Hopkins became permanent. At last Margret Cloos, her husband, and children had a home.

At first Cloos' reinterpretations of Maryland geology aroused strong objections from some local geologists who had relied solely on petrologic mapping, and had neglected structural methods in reading the record imprinted in the rocks. One cutting remark irritated, but also stimulated Cloos to widen the scope of his own inquiries: "The trouble with Cloos and his students is that they are so busy mapping the cracks and lineations in the rocks that they don't see the rocks between the cracks." Cloos decided he must learn how to use the petrographic microscope.

It is an interesting coincidence that George Huntington Williams, the first professor of geology at Johns Hopkins University, had elected to go to Germany to study for his doctorate. He brought home to America the new method of investigating rocks in thin sections by means of the petrographic microscope. Williams was the first great teacher of petrography in America. Among his early pupils who took their doctorates at The Hopkins were Andrew C. Lawson, Florence Bascom and William Herbert Hobbs. The petrographic microscope caused a major revolution in the geologic sciences near the end of the nineteenth century. Cloos, however, had never taken a course in petrography in college. By that time in Germany, mineralogy and petrography were well-established branches of the earth sciences, usually taught in a separate department. Williams, of course, had died long before Cloos arrived at Johns Hopkins, but the excellent collections of rocks and thin sections that he brought from many classical localities in Europe, and the extensive collections of local Maryland and New York State rocks that he added later, were in the Johns Hopkins laboratories along with several large bound ledgers filled with notes and descriptions written in Williams' exquisite classical penmanship.

Cloos' effort to become a "self-taught" petrographer with the aid of Williams' notes and collections was only partly successful. Always an innovator, he soon merged his new-found interest in the petrographic microscope with "gefugekunde"—generally translated into American English as "petrofabrics"—a new line of microtectonic investigations developed by Professor Bruno Sander of Innsbruck. After all, quartz and mica are readily identified under the petrographic microscope, and the plotting of their axes by means of a microscope equipped with a universal stage appealed to Cloos' almost military penchant for order, symmetry, and detail in everything he did. Cloos soon adapted Sander's method of presenting data in contoured petrofabric diagrams to his measurements of cracks, lineations, and other structural elements in the field. Now on Saturdays, if a snowstorm or muddy country roads prevented field work, Cloos and his students busily plotted their field and thin-section data into the "equal-area net," oriented with north at the top as in a map, and contoured the results into fabric diagrams.

Out of this happy symbiosis of old and new methods came many excellent publications. Moreover, Cloos' "education" in petrography and petrology received a great boost from a truly exceptional group of postdoctoral and predoctoral students who came to work with him. Many were well-grounded in petrography from studies at other universities. The joint monograph of Cloos with Anna Hietanen: "Geology of the 'Martic overthrust' and the Glenarm Series in Pennsylvania and Maryland," published in 1941 as Special Paper 35 (207 pages) by the Geological Society of America, affords an outstanding example. Trained under the world-famous petrologist Pentti Eskola in Finland, Anna Hietanen had also sharpened her expertise on petrofabrics through her investigations of Finnish quartzites. She worked with speed and precision in determining the petrography of the Maryland and southern Pennsylvania rocks. During her two-year postdoctoral fellowship at Bryn Mawr and Johns Hopkins, Cloos gained much help in overcoming his petrologic handicap. Their monograph put a stop to the old controversies, and as Francis Pettijohn wrote many years later, "This monograph went far toward building a solid foundation for understanding the fundamental problems of the Appalachian geosyncline. It was a 'quantum jump' ahead of earlier work and set a standard not yet surpassed."* Later, doctoral stu-

---

*Francis Pettijohn, "Memorial to Ernst Cloos 1898–1974, *Geological Society of America, Memoir* vol. 6 (1977).

dent James G. Moore helped Cloos revise a few of his interpretations of the Sierra Nevada rocks, and, contemporaneously, doctoral student Clifford A. Hopson showed that some "granite" massifs in the Maryland Piedmont were really metamorphosed sediments instead of igneous granites. Both cracks and rocks were now being looked at—and in great detail.

Cloos had already published papers about the South Mountain fold, but with these new tools he decided to detail the strain features shown in the oöids within the oolitic limestone deformed by this fold. Oöids are spherical, sand-sized grains, which commonly form on the seafloor in shallow tropical areas like the modern Bahama Banks. They frequently become incorporated into sedimentary rocks, like certain of the limestones that have been folded into the Appalachian Mountains. Under great pressure in the building of the Appalachians, spherical oöids became stretched into ellipsoids, tracking the course of deformation of the rocks that held them prisoner. With characteristic German thoroughness, Ernst Cloos measured myriads of these diagnostic grains. His view was that broad trends, extending over many miles, can be interpreted by extrapolation from highly detailed local analysis of the strain features in the oöids. His famous paper "Oolite Deformation in the South Mountain Fold, Maryland" (*Geological Society of America Bulletin,* 58 (1947): 843–917) reached a far greater audience than his papers on structural geology of granite. Demand for reprints was so great that Cloos had it republished at his own expense. This paper, and the joint monograph with Anna Hietanen undoubtedly gave the impetus for Cloos' election to the National Academy of Sciences (1950), and to the American Philosophical Society (1954). Meanwhile other new methods were casting light on the geologic evolution of the crystalline rocks of the Appalachians and Piedmont. After some false starts and early difficulties, radiometric dating suddenly "came of age." With the use of the concordia curve and of isotope studies, radiometric dates unraveled some snarls in reading the histories of the gneiss domes, the Glenarm Series, and equivalent rocks in other parts of the Piedmont. Although Cloos took no part in these geochronologic and geochemical investigations, he aided in getting the equipment and staff needed to modernize the laboratories at Johns Hopkins, and helped in arranging a joint program with the Geophysical Laboratory in Washington. Moreover he was a stabilizing critic in emphasizing that a batch of radiometric dates unrelated to structural and stratigraphic studies are no more informative of earth history than a barrel of miscellaneous rocks and fossils gathered at random.

The importance of these additional methods, and also of the contribution made by the program of paleocurrent studies which Professor Francis Pettijohn brought to Johns Hopkins in 1952 can be seen by leafing through the book *Studies in Appalachian Geology* (New York: Interscience Publishers, John Wiley, 1970, 460 pages). This book, planned to honor Cloos when he became Professor Emeritus in 1968, contains contributions by thirty-three of Cloos' former students and colleagues. The book is dedicated: "To Ernst Cloos who rekindled a spirit of inquiry into Appalachian geology."

A controversial problem discussed in this book is whether the basement rocks of the Piedmont were involved in the deformation that produced the Appalachian folds, or whether this deformation was "thin-skinned"—with the Paleozoic sedimentary rocks merely gliding over the basement rocks like a rug crumpled across a floor. With characteristic energy, Cloos turned his attention to this problem after "retirement." He knew that in the northern extension of the Blue Ridge (called South Mountain in Maryland) the crystalline rocks that lie beneath the oolitic limestones and Catoctin greenstone (a belt of slightly metamorphosed basalt lavas) are elevated to heights several kilometers above their level in the Ridge and Valley Province to the west, where they lie beneath folded sedimentary rocks. Could the strain produced by this period of folding, which he had so successfully measured by the changes in shape of oöids in limestone, be traced and correlated with other structures present in the greenstone and gneissic rocks, as well? Fortunately several patches of oolitic limestone are infolded with the much more voluminous greenstone and gneiss of the Blue Ridge to James River, 200 miles south of South Mountain. These patches became keys to a solution. During renewed visits to South Mountain during the late 1960's, Cloos noted that a relation exists between the direction of the longest axis of deformed oöids and the direction of certain lineations and streaks of new mineral deposition in the greenstones and gneisses. The refinement of these observations, and extension of the field work to cover an area 200 miles long and 30 miles wide enclosing the Blue Ridge is reported in a book *Microtectonics Along the Western Edge of the Blue Ridge, Maryland and Virginia* (Baltimore: Johns Hopkins Press, 1971, 234 pages).

The astonishing conclusion from this work is that during the folding of the sedimentary rocks, all formations, including those of the crystalline basement, received an imprint of easily recognized microtectonic structures over the entire area covered, and to a stratigraphic depth of at least six miles. On pages 78 and 79, Cloos lists the microtectonic structures that can be used for each formation, from the oldest Precambrian gneisses to the Devonian Romney Formation. The amazing uniformity of the pattern of deformation throughout this thick and widespread succession of rocks is best stated in Cloos' own words (page 79):

This simple pattern [of deformation] is universal in all diagrams and [for] all formations from the Precambrian gneisses to the Silurian. The deformation plan [for the whole area] is identical with that reported for South Mountain, Maryland. . . . The elements are common everywhere, can be identified in the field, in [sawed] specimens, and in thin sections. There can be little confusion if the coordinates can be so easily recognized.

Cloos' beautiful book, certainly a milestone in Appalachian geology, reveals much about its author as well as about the rocks. The text is short—it occupies less than one-third of the space in the book. Eighty-seven pages of half-tone plates, forty-seven carefully hand-drawn figures, thirteen tables, and twenty-three pages of an appendix labeled "Raw Data" make up the rest. Literally tens of thousands of field observations are recorded in diagrams. So great is the mass of data that it almost amounts to overkill. If only Professor Spemann had lived to see this memoir! Impatient long ago with "little blobs of slime," his student (and son-in-law) had now produced wonders from little blobs of rock through his patience and painstaking detail. Appropriately, Cloos dedicated the book "To the Memory of Robert Balk," who lost his life in an airplane crash.

Ernst Cloos' introduction of microtectonic techniques, of the sort pioneered by Bruno Sander and Hans Cloos in Europe, to problems of the Appalachians came at a logical time. By these techniques, small-scale rock deformations are analyzed both in the field and in thin sections, and the results extrapolated to the scale of mountains and valleys. The inception of the techniques in Europe presumably reflected the relatively early completion of regional geologic mapping, which was succeeded in the first half of this century by more detailed field work, and by micrometric analysis. Across the Atlantic, New World geologists were still assembling the broad geologic outlines of a vast continent. Not surprisingly, it was immigrants like Cloos and his friend Robert Balk who initiated microtectonic studies in America.

Thus far we have written about Ernst Cloos' accomplishments as investigator and teacher. He was equally gifted as a leader of people. Perhaps because of his commanding size and strong personality, his leadership was felt immediately in any group or committee. He was a forceful and decisive executive. As an arbiter who possessed an unusual sense of wisdom, he was elected to the Academic Council of the Johns Hopkins faculty almost every year from 1948 to his retirement. In this work he was noted for insistence on high standards, but also for the kindliness with which he terminated a "sticky problem."

In 1950 a Johns Hopkins evaluation committee recommended that the Geology Department be upgraded—after G. H. Williams' days it had declined in stature. President Detlev Bronk immediately appointed Cloos to the chairmanship. Within a year Cloos persuaded Francis Pettijohn and Aaron Waters to join the faculty, and later added younger men: Clifford A. Hopson and Hans Eugster. The small department regained the position it had once held among the nation's top graduate schools in geology. One indication was the outstanding graduate students (most of them bringing NSF predoctoral fellowships with them) who elected to work for their doctorate at Johns Hopkins. Those admitted came from widely different parts of the United States, Canada, and Europe, thus aiding in bringing diversity and new ideas to what had formerly been mostly a local student body. Many persons who become chairmen of academic departments at universities view their jobs as thankless undertakings appreciated only by a few local beneficiaries. Seldom does a chairman succeed so spectacularly as to be nationally acclaimed for his administrative efforts. Ernst Cloos was such a chairman.

Cloos chaired the Division of Geology and Geography of the National Research Council from 1951 to 1954. He accomplished this duty by spending every Friday in Washington, D.C.

Cloos served as acting director of the Maryland Geological Survey during 1963, and led the search for a permanent director. During this year he also completely rewrote the Survey's charter and changed its objectives, reducing regulatory activities and providing employees with greater freedom to engage in productive scientific research.

Throughout his career Cloos maintained an interest in those corporations that employed geologists. He was hired as a part-time consultant by numerous companies, but eventually narrowed these activities to the Thomasville Stone and Lime Company of Pennsylvania, and the Esso Production Research Corporation in Houston, Texas. As geologist for the Thomasville Company, he supervised exploration (by drilling) at their limestone quarry. When the surface outcrops had been largely removed, he persuaded the Company to follow the ledge underground in a mining operation. The huge caverns that resulted proved economically feasible, and the Company is still producing from them.

For Esso Production Research, one of the tasks that Cloos particularly enjoyed was running a seminar course in structural geology, or in his words as a "Maker of Mud Pies." Each year he went to Houston for a period of a week or ten days and set up scale-modeling experiments, using a soft white clay mixed with water until it was scaled down in strength to simulate approximately the behavior of rocks that are folded and fractured within the much larger dimensions of the crust of the earth. Before an appreciative audience of Esso trainees, geologists, executives, and other Texas geologists who were invited to participate, Cloos demonstrated his talents as master mud-pie maker by deforming the wet clay, and causing it to change before their eyes into miniature near-replicas of the folds, graben, salt domes, and basins of the kind that guided their search for oil. It is claimed that these sessions were conducted in a more relaxed atmosphere and with far greater levity than the same experiments done in the Johns Hopkins structural geology laboratories on snowy winter mornings. There, perhaps because the weather prevented the pie maker from teaching in the field, woe came to the unlucky student who drowsed off during the slow emergence of a structure, and thus did not immediately notice, measure, record, and sketch the appearance and changes in the cracks, striations, and minifolds as they evolved from the wet clay.

These scale-modeling sessions in Houston were the inspiration for another of Cloos' research papers. Through discussion with the Houston geologists he became interested in trying to model the structure of the entire Gulf Coast Province, an area where he had first worked in 1924 as a young recruit in geophysics for Seismos. Cloos' article, "Experimental Analysis of Gulf Coast Fracture Patterns," published in *American Association of Petroleum Geologists Bulletin* (vol. 52 (1968): 420–44), won for him the Association's Presidents Award.

He received many other honors. Already mentioned was his election to the American Philosophical Society and the National Academy of Sciences. He received a Guggenheim fellowship in 1956. He became a foreign member of the Finnish Academy. He received the Gustav Steinmann medal of Germany's Geologischen Vereinigung in 1968. He represented Johns Hopkins University at the celebration of the 500th Anniversary of the University of Basel in 1960, and also at the 100th anniversary of the National Academy of Sciences in 1963. His long and outstanding services to Johns

Hopkins University were recognized by the conferring of an L.L.D. in 1973.

In addition to the major American geological societies, he was a member or fellow of the Geological Society of Canada, Geological Society of London, Geologischen Vereinigung (the Geological Society of West Germany), and the Geological Society of Finland. Although his greatest contributions were to American geology, and especially to the structure of the Appalachians, his influence on the development of structural geology was worldwide.

For those colleagues and students who worked with Ernst Cloos, and who knew him well, the feelings evoked by news of his death are well summed up in two short sentences written by Professor O. M. Phillips, chairman of the Department of Earth and Planetary Sciences at Johns Hopkins University: "In my life I have known but few great men, a very few, and Cloos was certainly one of them. We will miss him more than we know."

Margret Spemann Cloos survived her husband, and now lives in Pennsylvania. The homes of their two daughters are also in the United States: Gisela (Mrs. W. R. Evitt) lives in California, and Veronica (Mrs. F. C. Evering) in Vermont.

MANY PASSAGES in this memoir are taken directly, or closely paraphrased, from a memoir that one of us (Waters) wrote for the American Philosophical Society. We have also had the advantage of access to data in Francis Pettijohn's Cloos memoir for the Geological Society of America. The bibliography up to 1968 is modified from the previously referenced book *Studies in Appalachian Geology*. Margret Cloos' kindness in checking dates, and providing information about Ernst Cloos' early life in Germany and America is greatly appreciated.

BIBLIOGRAPHY

1922

Tektonik des Granits von Gorkau (Kr. Nimptsch) im Schlesien. Abh. Preuss. Geol. Land., 89:93–102.

Tektonik und Parallelgefüge im Granit und Granitporphyr des nordlichen Schwarzwaldes. Abh. Preuss. Geol. Land., 89: 137–41.

1927

With Hans Cloos. Die Quellkuppe des Drachenfels am Rhein. Ihre Tektonik und Bildungsweise. Z. Vulkanol., 11:33–40.

With Hans Cloos. Das Stromungsbild der Wolkenburg im Siebengebirge. Z. Vulkanol., 11:93–95.

1931

Der Sierra Nevada-Pluton. Geol. Rundsch., 22:372–84.

Mechanism of the intrusion of the granite masses between Mono Lake and the Mother Lode. J. Wash. Acad. Sci., 22: 319–20.

1932

Structural survey of the granodiorite south of Mariposa, California. Am. J. Sci., 23(5th ser.):289–304.

"Feather joints" as indicators of the direction of movements on faults, thrusts, joints, and magmatic contacts. Proc. Natl. Acad. Sci. USA, 19:387–95.

1933

Structure of the Sierra Nevada batholith. In: *Middle California and Western Nevada,* Guidebook 16, XVI session, International Geologic Congress, Washington, D.C., pp. 40–45. Wash., D.C.: U.S. Govt. Print. Off.

Structure of the "Ellicott City granite," Maryland. Proc. Natl. Acad. Sci. USA, 19:130–38.

1934

Auto radio—An aid in geologic mapping. Am. J. Sci., 28 (5th ser.):255–68.

Auto radio als Hilfsmittel geologischer Kartierung. Z. Geophys., 10:252–58.

The Loon Lake pluton, Bancroft area, Ontario, Canada. J. Geol., 42:393–99.

With William D. Johnston, Jr. Structural history of the fracture systems at Grass Valley, California. Econ. Geol., 29:39–54.

1935

Mother Lode and Sierra Nevada batholiths. J. Geol., 43:225–49.

1936

Der Sierra Nevada-pluton im Californien. Neues Jahrb. Beilage-Band, 76:355–450.

With Howard Garland Hershey. Structural age determination of Piedmont intrusives in Maryland. Proc. Natl. Acad. Sci. USA, 22:71–80.

1937

The application of recent structural methods in the interpretation of the crystalline rocks of Maryland. Md. Geol. Surv. Report, 13:27–105.

1940

With Carl Huntington Broedel. Geologic map of Howard and adjacent parts of Montgomery and Baltimore Counties. Md. Geol. Surv., Geologic Map, Scale 1:62,500.

Crustal shortening and axial divergence in the Appalachians of southeastern Pennsylvania and Maryland. Geol. Soc. Am. Bull., 51:845–72.

1941

With Anna Marta Hietanen. Geology of the "Martic overthrust" and the Glenarm Series of Pennsylvania and Maryland. Geol. Soc. Am. Spec. Pap., no. 35, 207 pp.

Flowage and cleavage in Appalachian folding. Trans. N. Y. Acad. Sci., 3(ser. 2):185–90.

1942

Distortion of stratigraphic thicknesses due to folding. Proc. Natl. Acad. Sci. USA, 28:401–7.

1943

Method of measuring changes of stratigraphic thickness due to flowage and folding. Trans. Am. Geophys. Union (24th Annual Meeting), part 1:273–80.

With Carl Huntington Broedel. Reverse faulting north of Harrisburg, Pennsylvania. Geol. Soc. Am. Bull., 54:1375–97.

1945

History of geology in graphical representation. Geol. Soc. Am. Bull., 56:385–88.

Memorial to Edward Bennett Mathews (1869–1944). Am. Mineral., 30:135–41.

Correlation of lineation with rock-movement. Trans. Am. Geophys. Union (25th Annual Meeting), part 4:660–62.

1946

Lineation, a critical review and annotated bibliography. Geol. Soc. Am. Mem. 18. 122 pp.

1947

Boudinage. Trans. Am. Geophys. Union, 28:626–32.

Oolite deformation in the South Mountain fold, Maryland. Geol. Soc. Am. Bull., 58:843–917.

Tectonic transport and fabric in a Maryland granite. Comm. Géologique de Finlande, 140:1–14.

1949

With E. N. Goddard et al. Map symbols used in publications of the United States Geological Survey. Calif. J. Mines Geol., 45:109–16.

1950

The geology of the South Mountain Anticlinorium, Maryland. Baltimore: Johns Hopkins Univ. Studies Geol., Guidebook 1, no. 16. 28 pp.

With Judson Lowell Anderson. The geology of Bear Island, Potomac River, Maryland. Baltimore: John Hopkins Univ. Studies Geol., Guidebook 2, no. 16. 13 pp.

With John Calvin Reed. Memorial to Robert Ellsworth Fellows (1915–1949). Geol. Soc. Am. Proc. 1949:159–62.

1951

History and geography of Washington County, pp. 1–16; Stratigraphy of sedimentary rocks, pp. 17–94; Igneous rocks, pp. 95–97; Structural geology of Washington County, pp. 124–63; Mineral resources of Washington County, pp. 164–78; Ground water resources, pp. 179–93. In: *The Physical Features of Washington County (Maryland)*. Baltimore: Department of Geology, Mines and Water Resources, Washington County, Report 14.

With Charles Wythe Cooke. Geologic map of Prince Georges County, Maryland and the District of Columbia. Maryland Department of Geology, Mines and Water Resources, Geologic Map, Scale 1:62,500.

1953

Appalachenprofil im Maryland. Geol. Rundsch., 41:145–60.

With Charles Wythe Cooke. Geologic map of Montgomery County and the District of Columbia: Md. Geol. Surv., Geologic Map, Scale 1:62,500.

Lineation—Review of literature 1942–1952. Geol. Soc. Am., Mem. 18 (Suppl.), 14 pp.

1955

Experimental analysis of fracture patterns. Geol. Soc. Am. Bull., 66:241–56.

1956

Fabric at a granodiorite-schist contact, Bear Island, Maryland. Tschermaks Mineral. Petrogr. Mitt., 4(Folge 3):81–89.

Memorial to Robert Balk (1899–1955): Geol. Soc. Am. Proc. 1955: 93–100.

1957

Cost of educating one geologist. Am. Assoc. Petrol. Geol. Bull., 41:2364–68.

Blue Ridge tectonics between Harrisburg, Pennsylvania and Ashville, North Carolina. Proc. Natl. Acad. Sci. USA, 43:834–39.

1958

Lineation und Bewegung, eine Diskussionsbemerkung. Geologie, 7:307–11.

Structural geology of South Mountain and Appalachians in Maryland. Baltimore: John Hopkins Univ. Studies Geol., Guidebooks 4 and 5, no. 16. 85 pp.

1959

Memorial to Robert Milton Overbeck (1887–1958). Geol. Soc. Am. Proc. 1958:161–64.

1960

With Donald U. Wise. The Martic problem and the New Providence railroad cut. In: *Some Tectonic and Structural Problems of the Appalachian Piedmont Along the Susquehanna River: Pennsylvania Geologists, 25th Annual Field Conference, 1960 Guidebook,* pp. 39–48, 51–52.

1961

Bedding slips, wedges, and folding in layered sequences. Société Géologique de Finlande. Compte Rendu, 33:105–22.

1964

History and geography of Howard and Montgomery Counties, pp. 1–10; Review of the post Triassic rocks, pp. 18–26; Structural geology of Howard and Montgomery Counties, pp. 216–59. In: *The Geology of Howard and Montgomery Counties.* Baltimore: Maryland Geological Survey.

Wedging, bedding-plane slips, and gravity tectonics in the Appalachians. In: *Tectonics of the Southern Appalachians.* Memoir 1, pp. 64–70. Blacksburg, Va.: Virginia Polytechnic Institute, Department of Geologic Sciences.

Appalachenprofil 1964. Geol. Rundsch., 54:812–34.

Memorial to Joseph T. Singewald, Jr., State Geol. J., 16:314.

1968

Experimental analysis of Gulf Coast fracture patterns. Am. Assoc. Petrol. Geol. Bull., 52:420–44.

Thomasville Stone and Lime Company, Thomasville, Pennsylvania. In: *Guidebook for 33 Annual Field Conference of Pennsylvania Geologists, 1968, Harrisburg,* pp. 16–24. Harrisburg: Bureau of Topography and Geological Survey.

1969

Reply [to discussion of] "Experimental analysis of Gulf Coast fracture patterns" [1968]: Am. Assoc. Petrol. Geol. Bull., 53:435–36.

1971

Microtectonics Along the Western Edge of the Blue Ridge, Maryland and Virginia. Johns Hopkins Univ. Studies Geol., no. 20, Baltimore: Johns Hopkins Press. 234 pp.

1972

Experimental imitation of the upturned Precambrian surface along the Blue Ridge, Maryland and Virginia. In: *Appalachian Structures; Origin, Evolution, and Possible Potential for New Exploration Frontiers,* pp. 17–37. Morgantown: West Virginia University and West Virginia Geologic and Economic Survey.

1973

With F. J. Pettijohn. Southern border of the Triassic basin, west of York, Pennsylvania: Fault or overlap? Geol. Soc. Am. Bull., 84:523–36.

Memorial to Edward Hollister Wisser (1895–1970). Geol. Soc. Am. Memorials, II:143–46.

1974

Edward Wilber Berry. In: *Biographical Memoirs,* 45:57–95. Wash., D.C.: National Academy of Sciences.

GEORGE OLIVER CURME, JR.
December 24, 1888–July 28, 1976

BY AUGUSTUS B. KINZEL

GEORGE OLIVER CURME was born in Mt. Vernon, Iowa on Christmas Eve, 1888. He was the third child and first of two sons in a family of rugged individualists. His father, a professor of Germanic languages and literature at Mt. Vernon's Cornell College, was to gain such recognition in the field of philology that his namesake always referred to himself as G. O. Curme, Jr. His mother (Caroline Chenoweth Smith) was one of America's early women graduates with a diploma from DePauw University, and while his parents frequently held dissimilar views on many subjects, they were agreed on rigid and high intellectual and performance standards for their children. A cardinal rule in this Victorian household was, "whatever you do, do it well," followed closely by an insistence on precision in expression.

In 1896 George's father was appointed professor of German philology at Northwestern University, and the family moved to Evanston, Illinois. There George, Jr. attended the public schools and, in keeping with his peers, played tennis, baseball, and the mandolin and studied the "classics"—science not being included in the secondary curriculum at that time. Like his peers, he watched and played baseball, but unlike them he was an individualist. For example, he set some sort of a record by walking from Evanston, Illinois to St.

Louis, Missouri to see the "World's Fair" (the Louisiana Purchase Exposition) of 1904. It was at this time that he set as his personal goal the words of the baseball player, Wee Willie Keeler, "Hit them where they ain't."*

CHEMISTRY

At Northwestern University George O. Curme, Jr. was elected to Sigma Alpha Epsilon, served on the staff of the 1909 yearbook, appeared in his junior class play, managed and was elected captain of his class baseball team, and graduated with honors in 1909. What distinguished this period of his life to George Curme, however, was his introduction to chemistry and to a vision of what it might mean. This vision was far from universally held. As he recalled: "My own interest in chemistry began in 1905. . . . A few years later when I had decided to specialize in chemistry, I was urged by friends of our family to reconsider the matter on the grounds that there was no future in chemistry."† In addition, he noted the great cleavage that existed between the study of pure science and its beneficial, profitable applications: "I recall one of my much loved professors, who stated that if it was ever found that any of his research had commercial importance he would drop it immediately."‡ However, always an individualist, he disagreed. He said: "I just happened to be a character who thought that science was so wonderful that the public ought to be given a chance to benefit by it."§

To fit himself to help provide the public with this opportunity, he spent two summers in the stockroom of the University's chemical laboratory and following his graduation

---

* Personal communication, George O. Curme III.
† Remarks, Willard Gibbs medalist presentation, American Chemical Society, May 25, 1944.
‡ *Ibid.*
§ Remarks, Princeton University Conference, April 14, 1958.

enrolled at Harvard for graduate study. Following the death of his Harvard mentor, he transferred to the University of Chicago. Here, as he was later to discover and admit, even his Utopian view of chemistry was short of the mark:

> I recall as a graduate student at the University of Chicago attending the lectures of Professor McCoy who was at that time one of only two professors in the country offering courses in what is *now* called "atomic energy." It was a most interesting experience and for many years thereafter I thought of this field of science as the most fundamental of all, the least likely to have any practical value.*

In 1913 he was one of four candidates to receive the doctoral degree in chemistry from the University of Chicago. In his own words, the employment potentials outside the groves of academe looked bleak, even though, to his mind, the future was unbounded: "Growth as a part of management was not conceived in these days. The attitude of all industry was that the scientist was a saboteur trying to obsolete the Company's plants."†

GERMANY

Germany, however, was taking a far more opportunistic look at chemistry and had established world leadership in synthetic organic chemistry. In addition, young Curme had often heard his father speak with great enthusiasm about German education at the time of his studies at the University of Berlin in 1890. As a result, in 1913 G. O. Curme, Jr. enrolled at the Kaiser Wilhelm Institute to study for one semester under Fritz Haber, the discoverer of a synthetic ammonia process, and Professor Nernst. According to his heirs and friends, it was obvious that George Curme recognized that this course, together with the course that he took the

---

*Remarks, Pittsburgh Section, American Chemical Society, December 18, 1952.
†Interview with G. O. Curme, Jr., by Ms. Marion Merrill.

next semester at the University of Berlin under Professor Emil Fischer, were high points of intellectual stimulus and especial satisfaction to him, particularly since he was the coauthor of a paper with the renowned Emil Fischer. Of this he was quite proud.

Fate, in the form of shortage of funds, intervened to get the enthusiastic scholar out of Germany before World War I was declared. He had had time, however, to see what was being done in Germany and to foresee what could be done in the field of chemistry. He was convinced that America should put this fantastic tool to use industrially as well as academically. Despite his father's opinion that he should return to the academic world and the general lack of interest expressed by most industries in synthetic chemistry, George Curme was determined to find some way to bring reality to his vision.

DISCOVERIES

Dr. E. R. Weidlein, director of the Mellon Institute of Industrial Research, provided the key by hiring him as a fellow for the Prest-O-Lite Company, a firm engaged in manufacturing acetylene lamps for bicycles and autos. The purpose of this fellowship was to discover some cheaper source of acetylene than the calcium carbide that the Union Carbide Company was producing. At a salary of $3,000 a year, including apparatus, on November 15, 1914 George O. Curme, Jr. became the Prest-O-Lite Illumination Fellow at Mellon Institute.

The next year G. O. Curme, Jr. made two discoveries that were probably the most important ones of his life. The first, in point of time, was that by using organic liquids in exothermic processes, he could produce not only acetylene, but also a hydrocarbon gas rich in ethylene. The second discovery occurred at the dinner party at which he met Lillian Grace Hale, a very pretty and lively home economics teacher. They were married on June 29, 1916 and had two sons and three daughters. Recounting the fateful meeting, George Curme continually expressed surprise that such a lovely and well-spoken young lady as his beloved "Billy" should have paid any attention to him, especially since he had had a wisdom tooth pulled that very afternoon.

"WHERE THEY AIN'T"

Although he had discovered a new source for acetylene, George Curme realized that the economics of production demanded that some profitable use be found for the by-products. This obviously provided him with an opportunity to enter an area in which little academic or industrial interest was evidenced, even though ethyl alcohol had been produced in the laboratory of Michael Faraday by Hennell as early as 1828.

The need to find use for the synthetic acetylene by-products became increasingly important as the reason for his fellowship seemed to vanish in 1917 with the formation by merger of a technological combine known as Union Carbide and Carbon Corporation. Since the Union Carbide Company and Prest-O-Lite Company were joined in this new corporation, the need for an alternate source of acetylene was certainly less pressing. The combine also included the Linde Air Products Company, whose oxygen burned with acetylene to achieve high temperature in the new welding torches. The Linde people were skilled in low temperature phenomena and the separation of gases, while the other merging companies, the Electro Metallurgical Company and National Carbon Company, had long histories in high temperature and physical phenomena. Thanks primarily to the vision of John M. Price of the Electro Metallurgical Company, this combine, instead of discouraging Curme, continued to support him at Mellon. As the work progressed, Curme's belief in the potential for successful ethylene, propylene, and acetylene production increased and convinced him that a new unit of the Corporation should be formed to focus on this area.

Dr. Weidlein recalls that it was sometimes difficult to keep Curme from going straight to the Corporation's headquarters in New York to elucidate to its management the "short sightedness" of their ways in not "immediately" adopting his ideas. In a more tactful approach, Dr. Weidlein submitted to Union Carbide's management G. O. Curme, Jr.'s report on "The Possibilities of a Chemical Industry Based on the Simple Hydrocarbon Gases." The last paragraph of the introduction reads:

> In particular, ethylene, when complemented by acetylene and the by-products obtained in the production of these two substances from their various sources, provides the starting material for an organic chemical industry of almost unlimited proportions which might be extended as desired in any or all directions to cover a large part of the field of the existing chemical industry.

In the concluding paragraphs, the writer points out the obvious economics of using the plentiful supply of petroleum rather than the higher priced food and vegetable products as raw materials. In fact, George Curme visualized the petrochemical industry even before the word "petrochemical" entered our vocabulary!

Having aroused some interest on the part of management with the report, Curme went to New York with plans and estimates; with the encouragement of such men as Price of Electro Metallurgical Company, W. F. Barrett and J. R. Rafferty of Linde, and J. M. Moorhead of Union Carbide, the Carbide and Carbon Chemicals Corporation was formed on October 11, 1920. G. O. Curme, Jr., at the age of thirty-two, became manager and chief chemist of an operation he had literally inspired, even though as he later said: "We had not provided for raw materials, markets, financing, engineering, operations, shipping, publicity, accounting and a few such items . . . but we thought we were ready to go."*

ETHYLENE

The first plant of this new operation was a purchased one in Clendennin, West Virginia, and it was in this ancient, run-down gasoline compressor station that the future of the new venture was to be tried—and not found wanting. In reply to the question, "What was produced at Clendennin?" Curme's answer was, "Mostly mistakes," but he also added: "It was a revelation to realize that chemical processes functioned in a sheet-iron shack quite as well as under the best laboratory conditions."†

Selling the products that were produced was a more difficult task than had been anticipated. In a letter to his brother (December 7, 1920), he described how Rafferty and he, armed with samples, went out on selling trips: "I don't know whether I told you that we two now constitute the sales force. Well, we do . . . and I'm rather glad of it in a way, for that is the critical point of the development right now, and I'm glad to be on the firing line when the decision is made." The separation of gases provided them with a winning ticket—low-cost propane for home cooking and heating gas, and in 1922 the first tank car of PYROFAX gas was shipped from Clendennin. In 1923, J. G. Davidson was added to the staff and proved to be a remarkable salesman. He and G. O. Curme, Jr., became known as Carbide's "Gold Dust Twins."

Many products followed, particularly ethylene glycol, and by 1925 a "giant" (in terminology of the day) plant was constructed at South Charleston, West Virginia, chiefly for the manufacture of ethylene glycol, which was finding a major

---

*Aubrey D. McFayden, "American Contemporaries," *Chemical and Engineering News*, March, 1948.
†*Ibid.*

market under the PRESTONE trademark, the first "permanent" antifreeze for automobiles. In the language of one of Curme's many citations he was: "The father, grandfather, and great-grandfather of ethylene and her numerous progeny."*

EXPANSION

In 1929 George O. Curme, Jr. was elected vice president of research for the chemical operations. While this meant more administrative duties, his focus never shifted from the big picture of chemistry as the servant of mankind. In the thirties, while most of industry was cutting back on production, employment, and research and placing their main attention on weathering the depression, G. O. Curme, Jr. was worrying about a more distant future—one in which basic materials for production, such as rubber, would be in short supply. With this in mind, he directed the research into such areas as vinyl resins, coal hydrogenation, the production of butadiene, man-made fibers, agricultural chemicals, and toxicology studies. He took advantage of the newly completed, but not fully occupied, Linde laboratory at Tonawanda, New York to begin a research program in inorganic chemicals and persuaded the Corporation to allot monies for "blue-sky" or "seed-money" research.

In 1940, as war clouds darkened and as America's supply of essential rubber was threatened, his foresight was rewarded as he was able to make the first shipment of butadiene to Goodrich, and by 1944 Carbide had supplied over 62 percent of that needed for the war effort.† In addition, thanks to the research effort, the Tonawanda laboratory was able to provide synthetic gem bearings when war cut off the

---

* Willard Gibbs medalist presentation, American Chemical Society, May 25, 1944.
† Union Carbide Corporation records.

European supply, and Carbide produced quantities of vital polyethylene for the coating of radar cables within 100 days of the Navy's request. Again due to the unusual research and development experience, Carbide played a major role in the field of atomic energy. In Curme's words:

Two weeks after the Chicago pile, I received a call from Vannevar Bush to be on a committee to get a plant going. They were interested in UCC because of the large scale development work our company had done. No one was really qualified to do the job, but we had more experience than most in jumping from experiment to full-scale operation.* [Appointed to five-man planning board, Office of Scientific R&D to be "responsible for technical and engineering aspects of the work."]

HONORS

The work of George Curme was now being recognized from all sides. By 1944, when he was elected a member of the National Academy of Sciences, he had been presented with the Chandler, Perkin, and Eliott Cresson medals, the National Modern Pioneer Award, and the Willard Gibbs Medal. Other honors and appointments followed, but the one he cherished most was his degree of Doctor of Science from Northwestern University in 1933, when his father placed the hood over his head.

In 1951 he was elected Vice-President–Research, Union Carbide and Carbon Corporation, and the following year he was elected to the board of directors. From this eminence, he was ready and willing as ever to help generate further progress. As the Corporation had grown, he had seen the necessity for improved communication and had initiated a series of mutually beneficial briefings with researchers and members of the Corporation's service groups. He retired in 1955, but served on the board until 1961. In 1976 he died in Martha's

---

*Interview with G. O. Curme, Jr., by Ms. Marion Merrill.

Vineyard, where his wife "Billy" had been buried two years before.

THE MAN

George O. Curme, Jr. was a trim, compact man of average height with sharp eyes and a small, neat mustache. His quiet, almost humble stance belied a personality that was friendly and given to dry wit among his close friends. He often appeared brisk, ill at ease and sometimes even terrifying to many of his acquaintances and associates, for he was a stern believer in order and self-discipline. But while all might agree that he didn't have a humble bone in his body and did not tolerate fools gladly, they would also hasten to say that he was the first to give praise, to offer assistance, and to stand behind and support others if they truly believed in what they were doing. The trappings of power and prestige meant little to him. He was sure of himself because he always first made sure of the facts. He was a scientist in the truest sense of the word, and to those who had the opportunity of working with him or for him, he was a challenging leader with an exciting, but practical view of the present and the future. He often described himself as "The last of the Victorians."*

George O. Curme, Jr. was a wide reader, an early riser, a clean desk man, and a good listener. He enjoyed privacy, and when TV first came out, he wouldn't have it with "all those people" in his house, but in his later years, he could often be found before the TV set in his son's home watching a baseball game. He was adored by his grandchildren and respected by their pets, who knew exactly how close they could come to the dining room while he was in residence. He and his wife shared a mutual wedding anniversary with two other "Georges" from Union Carbide, and this was celebrated by

---

*Personal communication, G. O. Curme III.

dinners followed by plays or concerts for many years. Science was very close to G. O. Curme, Jr.'s heart, but his "Billy" came first.

RECOLLECTIONS

When I came to Carbide in 1926, George Curme headed all research in organic chemistry and, without title, was truly the sponsor, promoter, and godfather of all the Corporation's research. Since I was in the metallurgical side of the business, I only saw him occasionally if I happened to be present when he made his regular trips to the various company laboratories. He was always interested in the projects and experiments and would ask truly challenging and penetrating questions. If it was something you were enthused about and believed in, he would encourage and support you. But he let *you* do the job. His attitude was, "If you run into trouble, come see me. If not, bring me the answer." He had a great view of the future and knew that the future depended on what was coming out of research.

As the chemical business grew, and as pressures and temperatures were increased, equipment requirements became more and more demanding, and chemical problems became metallurgical ones. I was fortunately able to solve one such problem.

Subsequent to the successful operation of a pilot plant to produce vinyl acetate, a full-scale manufacturing plant was built. The pilot plant had produced white material. The full-scale plant initially produced pink material! The main reaction was being carried out in a stainless steel pressure vessel, and it was thought that the stainless steel, then a relatively new article of commerce, was defective because it must be corroding to provide the iron that produced the pink color. A vessel of essentially identical composition in the pilot plant did not produce the pink color. I checked specifications, analysis, and manufacturing procedure of the vessel and decided that it was not faulty. Somehow the feed to the larger vessel must have contained traces of chlorine which attacked the stainless steel. The local chemical engineers and I studied the possibilities. We found that the large plant differed from the pilot plant in that at an earlier point in the process, a small lead coil heat interchanger was used in the pilot plant, whereas a much larger copper heat exchanger was used in the full-scale plant. The lead had reacted with the traces of chlorine in the feed material, thus removing it. Of course copper would not do this. Solution: put some lead in the heat exchanger lines of the large plant; no need to replace the large stainless steel vessel. Simple! It worked. The product now had no trace of pink. George Curme was pleased. This brought me to his attention, and many years later helped in my succeeding to his post. He strongly believed that new tools make possible new findings.

He loved challenges. I recall visiting him at his home on Martha's Vineyard and seeing his great lawn. When he and Billy moved there in the thirties, there was no grass on the island. He changed that and was the first to grow an almost "putting green" lawn. To accomplish this, he had an irrigation system and powerhouse. I well recall that the whole system was truly a first-class chemical plant.

He was a complex character—somewhere between "Cal" Coolidge and Franklin Roosevelt. He combined reserve and a desire for facts with enthusiasm and political intuitiveness. I liked and respected him and so, I believe, did everyone who worked with or for him. Those who knew him and those who didn't know him are in his debt, for it was his vision and his courage, perseverence, and ability to make it come true that has done so much to provide all of us with a standard of living we now take for granted.

IT WOULD BE FUTILE to attempt to list all of my colleagues at Carbide, past and present, who provided information on which this memoir is based, but I would particularly thank Paul Cullen, who had been George Curme's secretary for many decades, and pay tribute to Ms. Marion Merrill, then of Union Carbide's technical publicity department, who interviewed families, Carbiders, and associates of George Curme, who searched the Carbide files, and did more than assist in the writing of the memoir proper.

BIBLIOGRAPHY

1913

Thermal decomposition of symmetrical diarylhydrazines. J. Am. Chem. Soc., 35:1143–73.

With Julius Stieglitz. Transformation of hydrazobenzene into azobensene and aniline—a first order reaction. Preliminary communication. Berichte, 46:911–20.

1914

With Emil Fischer. Lactal and hydrolactal. Berichte, 47:2047–57.

1921

Importance of the olefine gases and their derivatives. Chem. Metall. Eng., 25: I. Sources and uses of ethylene and propylene, 907–9; II. With H. R. Curme, Diethyl sulphate, 957–59; III. Ethylene dichloride, 999–1000; IV. With E. W. Reid, Isopropanol, 1049–50; V. With C. O. Young, Ethylene chlorhydrin and ethylene oxide, 1091–92.

1923

With C. O. Young. Ethylene glycol: its uses and properties. Chem. Metall. Eng., 28:169–70.

1925

With C. O. Young. Ethylene glycol. A contribution of chemistry to the automobile anti-freeze problem. Ind. Eng. Chem., 17:1117–20.

1933

Synthetic organic chemistry in industry (Chandler Medal address). Ind. Eng. Chem., 25:582–89.

1935

Industry's toolmaker (Perkin Medal address). Ind. Eng. Chem., 27:223–30.

1936

With S. D. Douglas. Resinous derivatives of vinyl alcohol. Ind. Eng. Chem., 28:1123–29.

1937

Recent progress in synthetic organic chemistry. Sci. Mon., 45: 100–105.

1938

Large molecules in synthetic organic chemistry. J. Franklin Inst., 226:187–202.

1942

Research in industry. Dedication of the new building of the Technological Institute, Northwestern University, June 16.

1944

Chemistry for the many (Willard Gibbs Medal address). Chem. Eng. News, 22:900–903, 928.

1950

Industrial research. In: *Seventy-fifth Anniversary Proceedings*. New Haven: The Connecticut Agricultural Experiment Station.

1952

With Franklin Johnston, eds. *Glycols*. N.Y.: Reinhold Publishing.

UNITED STATES PATENTS*

1919

1,315,540. Electrochemical Method and Apparatus for Producing Synthetic Acetylene from Organic Liquid.
1,315,541. Preparation of Pure Ethylene.
1,315,542. Preparation of Ethylene Dichloride.
1,315,543. Methods of Preparation of Acetaldehyde.
1,315,544. Preparing Acetone from Acetic Acid.
1,315,545. Preparing Ethyl Dichloride from Ethylene.
1,315,546. Preparation of Acetic Acid.
1,315,547. Process of Making Propylene Dichloride.

1922

1,422,182. Treating Gaseous Hydrocarbon Mixtures.
1,422,183. Process of Treating Gaseous Mixtures.
1,422,184. Process of Separating Ethylene and Other Components from Gaseous Mixture Containing Same.
1,422,838. Processes of Chlorinating Gaseous Hydrocarbons and Recovering Products Therefrom.

1923

1,442,386. With C. O. Young. Process of Making Glycols.
1,456,916. With C. O. Young. Process of Making Chlorhydrins.
1,460,545. With P. E. Haynes. Production of Ethylene.
1,463,255. With H. B. Heyn. Process of Preparation of Salts of Benzoic Acid and Benzoic Acid from Dibenzyl.
1,472,294. With H. E. Thompson. Process of Purifying Chlorine and Other Corrosive Gases.

1924

1,518,182. Process of Making Alkyl Chlorides.

1925

1,524,355. With P. E. Haynes. Process of Making Olefines.
1,545,742. Process of Making Isopropyl Chloride.

---

*The majority of George Curme's patents were registered in Canada, and many were duplicated in the industrial countries of Europe.

1927

1,638,434. With H. E. Thompson. Process and Apparatus for Generating Fuel Gases.
1,646,349. Re: 18,148. Thermal Decomposition of Hydrocarbons.

1928

1,695,249. With E. W. Reid. Process of Making Isopropyl Alcohol.
1,695,250. Manufacture of Glycols.

1931

1,817,893. Non-Inflammable Liquids.
1,832,534. With F. W. Lommen. Process for Making Ethylene Diamine.

1945

2,378,466. Improved Diesel Fuel and Method of Improving Diesel Fuel Ignition.
2,384,816. With H. C. Chitwood. Preparation of Amino Carboxylic Acids and Their Salts.
2,384,818. (Div. of #2,384,816) With H. C. Chitwood. Preparation of Amino Carboxylic Acids and Their Salts.

David M. Dennison

DAVID MATHIAS DENNISON
April 26, 1900–April 3, 1976

BY H. RICHARD CRANE

DAVID MATHIAS DENNISON, distinguished theoretical physicist and member of the National Academy of Sciences since 1953, died on April 3, 1976 at the age of seventy-five. His principal work concerned the application of quantum theory to the interpretation of the infrared spectra of molecules, a field in which he was a pioneer discoverer, and in which he remained a leader throughout his life. He made important contributions in other areas as well, including the first application of microwaves to spectroscopy, the exploration of the optical properties of thin films, and the theory of high energy accelerators.

David Dennison was born in Oberlin, Ohio on April 26, 1900. Since his father was a professor of classics, he grew up in an academic atmosphere. The family made several moves among academic settings: from Oberlin, Ohio to Ann Arbor, Michigan (the father's native state) when young David was two years of age; to Rome, Italy for a sabbatical year when young David was seven; and to Swarthmore, Pennsylvania when he was ten. David continued his schooling there, and graduated from Swarthmore College in 1921. His college years were difficult. His father died in 1917, the year in which David entered college. To make ends meet David obtained a scholarship, and his mother served as a housemother at a dormitory. As a further complication, upon the entry of the U.S. into World War I, David was enrolled in the Student Training Corps.

In 1921 David Dennison enrolled as a graduate student at the University of Michigan in Ann Arbor, the town in which he had lived as a boy. There he received the Ph.D. in physics in 1924. The summer of that year was an eventful one for him. He was married to Helen Lenette Johnson of Ludington, Michigan, he was granted a General Education Board (Rockefeller) fellowship for two years, and he and his bride departed for the Institute for Theoretical Physics in Copenhagen. The period of study in Europe was extended to include a third year, which was divided among three leading centers of physics: Zurich, Copenhagen, and Cambridge.

In 1927 the Dennisons returned to Ann Arbor where David had an instructorship in the Physics Department of the University of Michigan waiting for him. He remained a member of the faculty of the University for the rest of his career, and he served as chairman of the Physics Department from 1955 to 1965. He retired to become Professor Emeritus in 1970, but continued to be active in physics research until the end of his life.

It is always interesting to try to see how talented scientists first become interested in science. In this case we are fortunate to have the transcript of a lengthy interview with Dennison conducted by Professor Thomas S. Kuhn of Princeton University in 1964 for the Sources for the History of Quantum Physics Project (see acknowledgement). The interview is revealing in many ways, and it is rich in the history of physics, for David Dennison was a good teller of stories, including those about himself. Much of the information that follows has been drawn from that source.

It often turns out that one's choice of a career can be traced to the influence of a friend or a teacher encountered at an early age; Dennison's case was no exception. There were two such individuals: one was an Episcopal minister and the other was a technician for a mustard company. Both were ardent amateur scientists and tinkerers who lived in the neighborhood and welcomed interested high school students after school hours. David was a regular visitor, and he worked with, or learned about, electrostatic machines, telescopes, spectrographs, arc lights, replica gratings, double pendulums, lathes, surface tension phenomena, and many other things. Using what he learned, he later set up, on his own, a spectrograph, a double pendulum, and a water-motor that drove a dynamo. He was tremendously excited about all of this. The enthusiasm with which he recounted these early adventures to his interviewer would surely lead one to think that he would have followed the track of experimental science—but that was not to be the case. During his college years he gravitated toward the mathematical approach to physics, which was to be the theme of his life work. We shall try to trace how this attraction grew.

After entering Swarthmore College, further adventures in experimental science were opened to David. Immediately he was allowed to use the College's 6-inch telescope. A little later he became involved in a program of systematically recording the parallaxes of certain stars, and that gave him access to the College's 24-inch telescope. In an electrical engineering course he was given the project of building a Tesla coil that would give a 6-foot spark. To his great satisfaction, he succeeded. He did not lack for opportunities to experiment at any time. Nevertheless, before he progressed very far in his college career, his primary interest turned toward understanding physical problems by mathematical, rather than experimental, methods. The elegance of that approach appealed to him, and he found that he could understand the mathematics with ease. Real physical systems remained his primary interest, but his method of analyzing them had moved toward the theoretical. There is no better evidence of the strong tie Dennison retained between his interests in theory and real "hardware" than the fact that throughout his life both his home and his office were replete with instruments that exemplified simple principles of physics.

An interesting sidelight, indicating that Dennison did not "catch on" to the ease with which he could solve problems by theory until he was well into college work, is found in the taped interview. He remarked that the introductory physics course failed to capture his attention, and he did poorly, receiving a grade of C. He remarked further that during his first two years he had to work hard on all of his courses, but that at the end of two years he had somehow learned the trick of working the examinations, so that from then on, he got straight A's. He said he supposed that after he had acquired the trick of it he learned much less!

Dennison's first encounter with research physicists came in the summer of 1920, between his junior and senior years. The General Electric Research Laboratory at that time was offering summer appointments for students, and the engineering professor who had coached Dennison in building the Tesla coil encouraged him to apply for an appointment. The experience proved to be a great eye-opener. David was assigned to assist Irving Langmuir, who was trying to understand and use the new Bohr model of the atom. David had just studied the model in a course, so they started on an even footing and learned together. Later that summer, David was assigned to assist A. W. Hull, whose interests were the diffraction of X-rays from powdered materials. Dennison's work during the summer was mainly to attempt to interpret Hull's data by means of theory, but he did at times have a chance to operate the apparatus. With Hull's help, he published a paper—his first. What he got from the summer was primarily, of course, the introduction to real research scientists in a real and vigorous laboratory. He returned to the same laboratory for two later summers, 1922 and 1923. At those times he worked mainly with Saul Dushman, who studied thermionic emission problems. Dennison's association with the Laboratory resulted in an offer of employment at the conclusion of his Ph.D. program, but he declined because he was intent on continuing his studies of theoretical physics.

To go back a bit, when in 1921 Dennison presented himself at the Physics Department of the University of Michigan to begin his Ph.D. program, he announced that he wanted his thesis to be in theoretical physics. Professor H. M. Randall, then Department chairman, was, the story goes, quite astounded, in view of the outstanding experimental program in the Department, and the fact that no theoretical thesis had so far been sponsored. But Randall acceded.

The first part of David's graduate program was rather uneventful: he was a teaching fellow, and he took graduate courses, some (as he remarked) good and some bad. In the latter part of the program he became immersed in the theoretical interpretation of the infrared spectrum of methane, which Randall and others in the laboratory were measuring. He worked mainly with Walter F. Colby, H. M. Randall, and with a visitor from Copenhagen, Oskar Klein. During that period the laboratory had the honor of a visit by Niels Bohr, and it was through that brief but exciting association that Dennison made up his mind to find some way to go to Copenhagen as soon as he received his Ph.D.

Dennison's way of getting to Copenhagen is interesting. He applied for and was awarded a National Research Council fellowship. But because it contained a new proviso that it was to be used only in the U.S., he declined it. Through the efforts of one of his former Swarthmore professors, he was granted a General Education Board (Rockefeller Foundation) fellowship to go to Europe for two years. He was able to extend his stay for a third year with the help of funds from the University of Michigan. Professor Randall arranged for the extension as what now would be called a "holding pattern." He wanted to hire David, but he would not have the position to offer for another year.

Dennison's years in Europe coincided with a period of great excitement in physics. He was in the right places at the right times and got to know most of the important persons. Among these were Werner Heisenberg, Niels Bohr, and Erwin Schrödinger. He became especially interested in the new (and controversial) matrix mechanics that were being developed by Heisenberg, and he applied it to what seemed to him a very challenging problem, that of the rigid, symmetric rotator. His work may have been the first application of the new quantum theory to anything beyond the simple two-body system. It resulted in a publication. But what did most to establish Dennison in the world of physics was a piece of research he did quickly and just at the end of his stay in Europe. This occurred at Cambridge University, and through an interesting chance happening, as David recounted it in a talk he gave much later.*

Dennison related that during his time in Copenhagen he had become acquainted with R. H. Fowler of Cambridge, who invited him to visit Cambridge before returning to the U.S. When he arrived, Fowler was giving a seminar course on statistical mechanics, and he invited David to give three of the talks about matters of his own choice. Preparation for these out of material David already knew went smoothly as far as such material lasted, but it fell short of what would be needed to fill the three sessions. In the search for material to fill the gap, he decided to have another look at a perplexing problem

---

*"Recollections of Physics and of Physicists During the 1920's," *American Journal of Physics*, 42(1974):1051–56.

he had worked on with no success while in Copenhagen: the theoretical calculation of the specific heat of hydrogen gas. This had long been a real puzzle. Excellent measured values were available, and they were in striking disagreement with careful calculations that had been made by several theorists, including Dennison himself. The discovery of the spin of the electron in 1925 had aroused hopes that the problem would be solved if a spin were assigned to the proton, but that tack had come to naught. Dennison, in rethinking the problem for his seminars, retained the spin of the proton and, in a rare insight, added a new condition, namely, that the ortho and para states of the molecule were very long lived and that the ortho-para ratio did not change appreciably during the time in which the temperature was varied in the measurements. To quote from Dennison's 1927 note in the *Proceedings of the Royal Society* (see bibliography): "The coupling of the nuclear spins with the spin of the molecule which determines the transitions between symmetrical and antisymmetrical terms will indeed be very small, much smaller than the coupling forces between the electronic spins and the orbits which give rise to the very weak transitions between ortho- and para-helium. Let us make the assumption that the time of transition between a state symmetrical in the rotation, and a state antisymmetrical is very long compared with the time in which the observations are made. In this case we have in effect two distinct gases..." (all earlier calculations had, in effect, assumed rapid equilibration between the ortho and para modifications). By using this new postulate, and by using for the ratio of populations of the antisymmetric and symmetric forms of hydrogen the value three, which he could justify on quantum theory grounds, Dennison obtained a curve for the specific heat that agreed with the experiments exactly.

With the simple matter of the lifetime of the ortho-para

states cleared up, a much more fundamental aspect of the agreement became evident. Since the agreement depended on assigning a spin of exactly $\hbar$ to the proton, it constituted (turning the argument around) the first quantitative (although indirect) measure of the value of the spin of the proton. Naturally, Fowler, in whose seminar course this was described, urged David to write his work up for publication. In writing the manuscript, however, David did not remark explicitly about the implication of the result for the spin of the proton because, as he recalled in a seminar talk* in later years, "It was so obvious there seemed to be no need to belabor the point. Like the names of the streets in the center of town; there is no need for signs because everyone knows the names." It remained for Niels Bohr, to whom David sent the manuscript, to urge David to make the point explicitly, which he then did. He also added a remark about the possibility of physically separating the ortho- and para-hydrogen gases. The work on the specific heat of hydrogen formed a most successful conclusion to Dennison's three-year experience in Europe and established his reputation in molecular physics.

Upon returning to the University of Michigan and taking his place in the midst of a burgeoning program of experimental infrared spectroscopy, Dennison found an abundance of raw material to feed his interest in molecular theory. He became especially interested in explaining the spectra of the simple molecules of water vapor, methane, carbon dioxide, ammonia, and methyl alcohol. All of these molecules were being worked on at Michigan in the large experimental program headed by H. M. Randall. Throughout these years Dennison worked very closely with the experimentalists, and

---

*Remarks, University of Michigan, Department of Physics Colloquium, November 15, 1968.

to him should go a great deal of the credit for the leadership the laboratory enjoyed in the field of infrared spectroscopy.

If Dennison's molecular work had a special theme, it can be found in his concentration on simple molecules whose physical constants happened to be in just the right range to elucidate particular basic phenomena; examples are carbon dioxide with its Fermi resonances, water vapor with the full complexity of an asymmetric rotator, ammonia with its inversion frequency, and methyl alcohol with all the features of rotational tunneling. He was very discriminating, working not to turn out papers, but always to follow some subtle and basic point that intrigued him. He never lacked for such questions; his work on methyl alcohol, which began in the 1930's, continued, with publications, until the end of his life. About forty-five of his papers concern the interpretation of molecular spectra. He almost continuously supervised doctoral students in that subject—about twenty in all.

A short time after Dennison joined the Michigan faculty (1927), the Department greatly expanded its capacity in theoretical physics. This was due to the efforts of H. M. Randall, the chairman, and Walter Colby, the resident theorist. Three promising young theorists besides Dennison were hired: Otto Laporte, whose work was in optical spectroscopy, and George E. Uhlenbeck and Samuel A. Goudsmit, who togehter had discovered the spin of the electron two years earlier. The four young theorists, with the vigorous backing of Randall and Colby, expanded the Department's summer session into a symposium of international importance, which continued until it was stopped by World War II. Dennison was a key organizer throughout the series.

A most interesting episode took place in the early 1930's. In 1932, Dennison and Uhlenbeck had discovered a vibration mode in the ammonia molecule that should give rise to the absorption of radiation at a remarkably long wavelength—about 1.6 cm. The three hydrogen atoms in the ammonia molecule form a triangle, and the nitrogen atom lies in the center, but not quite in the plane of the triangle. The nitrogen can occupy symmetrical positions on either side of the plane (the situation has been referred to as the "reversing umbrella"). This configuration is unique to ammonia, and it is responsible for the long wavelength absorption. By coincidence, Professor Neil H. Williams and a graduate student, C. E. Cleeton, had been working in the Physics Department on the development of magnetrons of very small size that could generate radiation in the range of a centimeter or less. Dennison saw the opportunity there and persuaded them to collaborate with him in an attempt to measure the 1.6 cm wavelength absorption in ammonia gas with the magnetron radiation. The experiment, which required a large room full of venetian blind–size diffraction gratings, parabolic dishes, and a balloon of ammonia gas, was completely successful. The year was 1933, and the experiment constituted the birth of microwave spectroscopy, a technique that much later came into widespread use. But it was before its time—Williams, Cleeton, and Dennison carried it no further, and it was not reborn until after World War II.

During the war years, Dennison worked on problems associated with the VT (radio proximity) fuze. Much of his work was on the evaluation of the performance of the fuze, resulting in recommendations for changes in its characteristics to make it more effective. In the early years of the war he used data that he helped generate through scale-model experiments (a project at the University of Michigan), and later he used data that were transmitted to him from the battles in the Pacific Theater, where the ammunition was in daily use. For his contributions in this program, he received a citation for exceptional service from the U.S. Navy.

Dennison's work with the scale-model VT fuze experiments had an interesting delayed result. The experiment involved "flying" model airplanes past radio oscillators. Since the experiments were supposed to simulate the effects in free space, the reflections of the radiation from the ground had to be eliminated. This was done in the way that had been used by Winfield Salisbury, of the University of California at Berkeley, which was by stretching a sheet of poorly conducting cloth at a height of one-quarter wavelength above the conducting ground plane. (The cloth, which was made in quantity by the United States Rubber Company, came to be known as "Salisbury's shirt tail.") Dennison was intrigued at the time with this technique, and made many calculations about it. In retrospect, it should have been obvious that revolving in his mind was the possible application of the scheme (but on a microscopic scale) to infrared measurement problems. Immediately after the war he turned his efforts to that application. He and a thesis student, Lawrence N. Hadley, employed evaporated layers of transparent materials to create nonreflecting surfaces and band-pass filters for the infrared. Today, evaporated nonreflecting and filtering films have a multitude of uses, including, of course, the coating of all photographic lenses.

In the first few years after the close of World War II, Dennison explored yet another subject that was new to him. This was a study, with Theodore Berlin, on the stability of the orbits or particles in a new type of high-energy accelerator. It was occasioned by a proposal by H. R. Crane to modify a synchrotron into the form of two half-circles separated by straight sections, called, for obvious reasons, a "racetrack." While the straight sections would offer many practical advantages, the problem was that construction of such a machine could not be undertaken unless it could be proven that the particle orbits would be stable. Dennison and Berlin rose to the challenge and devoted about a year to the study.

The result was a paper that set forth the general conditions for the stability of the particle orbits in an accelerator having any even number of straight sections. It showed that such an accelerator could operate stably, and it therefore gave the go-ahead signal for the Michigan "racetrack." (The study showed that there would be an advantage in having four straight sections rather than two, and that change in the design was made.) The paper by Dennison and Berlin served as a text for other accelerator builders as well for some time to come. I understand why Dennison was immediately intrigued by the problem of an accelerator with straight sections. He saw it as a beautiful and complex example of a stability problem involving the Mathieu equation, which he had discussed for many years in his course in theoretical mechanics. He even had among his classroom props a simple mechanical model that demonstrated the principle.

Mention must be made of another interest Dennison had, which occupied him for a few years beginning in about 1939 and again in the early 1950's—the effort to apply his methods of treating molecules to the determination energy levels in nuclei. The oxygen-16 nucleus was particularly suitable, because he could think of it as a "molecule" of four alpha particles. He made the simplest assumption as to the configuration, namely, that the alpha particles were at the points of a tetrahedron, and then proceeded to apply the quantum conditions and selection rules to their vibrations and rotations. The results were encouraging, but the experimental data to which they could be compared were at the time rather meager. Later, in the 1950's, when the data were much better, Dennison returned to the problem and published another paper. The study represented an approach to energy level calculations that was different from that taken by the nuclear theorists of his time, and it proved to be a forerunner of later active studies of light nuclei according to the alpha-cluster model.

In the preceding few paragraphs, some wide-ranging problems that captured Dennison's interest and to which he was able to make contributions have been mentioned. For the most part, they were problems that came to his attention during his wartime experience. But it should be emphasized that his main interest, molecular rotations and vibrations, was remarkably durable. He returned solidly to it after every side-adventure.

Dennison accorded no less importance to teaching than to research. For decades he gave a major graduate course each semester, changing off among the subjects of theoretical mechanics, quantum mechanics, and electricity and magnetism. There is little doubt that the theoretical mechanics was his favorite. Past graduate students of all ages, when recalling their experience at Michigan, will mention Dennison's theoretical mechanics course as a high point (and a not inconsiderable hurdle).

Dennison's interest in teaching went beyond the preparation of the material to an interest in the process itself. He frequently had advice to give to young instructors or teaching assistants. A set of notes that he evidently made for himself in order to give a talk on teaching to a group of graduate students has survived—and is illuminating (also still good advice). The pity is that the illustrative stories he mentions were in his head and so are lost to us. The notes are repeated here in full, for they tell more about the man than would ten times as many words by this writer.

> What can I tell you about how to teach? Very little. Great distrust of all educational systems. Nevertheless:
> First: and most important point: want to be a good teacher—willingness to put in the time and energy in preparation.

<u>Second</u>: Analyze other teachers and colloquia speakers—what they do right—what they do wrong.

<u>Third</u>: Always watch your audience. Bored? Cannot follow? Watch for the sparkle and smile.

(The Fermi Story)

<u>The mechanics of teaching</u>:
1. Start on time—2 minutes of resume.
2. Stop on time. Resist the temptation to finish a subject.
3. Write clearly and speak slowly. Be sure you give the audience time to take notes.
4. Try to encourage questions, but <u>discourage</u> screwballs.
5. Always prepare—understand every point and more. 10 hrs. for a point that takes 5 minutes.
   (Story of suddenly discovering a flaw).
6. Allow some latitude in presentation, but not complete.
   (Story of Klein and of writing for Bohr.)
   (Story of Kramers)
7. Give enough problems, but not too many. Always work your own problems. Why?
8. Give enough blue books. Ask principles not tricks, not complicated algebra. Always work the questions yourself, in a blue book, and be able to complete them in 1/3 the allotted time.
9. Never get angry—unless on purpose.

<u>The wonderful experiences, and the tradition</u>:
The stories of:
Ehrenfest and Goudsmit
Ehrenfest and Uhlenbeck
Sommerfeld and Laporte
Bohr and me
Bohr and the idea that could not be expressed in words.

When it comes to hobbies, it should be said first of all that molecules and teaching were David's hobbies as well as his livelihood. Beyond that, his love of precise mechanisms led him to have in his house and office such things as a ship's chronometer, a precision lathe, fine cameras, a compound pendulum (by which he made beautiful Lissajous figures on photographic paper), a gyroscope from a World War II bombsight, and a surveyor's transit. Once he set up a Foucault pendulum in his basement, suspended from a floor joist, and found, after weeks of observations, that the deflection the pendulum produced in the house was the source of a systematic error! In all of these adventures he had pure scientific fun, without feeling that he had to break any new ground.

During his active career David Dennison was the recipient of many honors and prestigious appointments. Some have already been mentioned, namely, his election to the National Academy of Sciences and the citation by the U.S. Navy. In addition he received an honorary D.Sc. from Swarthmore College in 1950. He was appointed delegate to the Seventh General Assembly of the International Union for Pure and Applied Physics in 1951. He was selected as the University of Michigan's Henry Russel Lecturer in 1952 (the lectureship, the recipient of which is chosen by the Research Club, is the highest honor the University can bestow upon a faculty member for distinguished scholarship). He received a Distinguished Faculty Achievement Award from his University in 1963, and he was elected president of the Research Club of the University of Michigan in 1964. In 1966 he was appointed Harrison M. Randall University Professor. In 1975 he was invited as the principal speaker at the Fourth International Conference on Molecular Spectroscopy, at Tours, France. As a further high distinction, he was made an honorary citizen of the City of Tours (that was only the second time in the City's long history that the honor had been bestowed upon anyone). In 1976 the new physics and astronomy building at the University was named for Dennison, not only in recognition of his scientific achievements, but of the fact that earlier he had supplied the driving force that had brought the building into being.

Needless to say, Dennison performed many services

within the University, in addition to serving as chairman of the Physics Department for ten years. He was considered an elder statesman and was called upon in critical matters. An interesting sidelight on his way of operating, however, is the fact that he was quite determined (successfully) to sidestep what he termed time-wasting committee appointments.

David Dennison is greatly missed by all who were privileged to know him. He was a scholar and friend in the finest tradition. He is survived by his widow, Helen Dennison, and two sons: Edwin W. Dennison, who resides in California, and David S. Dennison, of New Hampshire.

THE AUTHOR WISHES to acknowledge the loan, by the Center for History of Physics of the American Institute of Physics, of the transcript of the taped interview with David M. Dennison conducted by Professor Thomas S. Kuhn of Princeton University (January 27–30, 1964) for the Center's Sources for the History of Quantum Physics Project. The author is also indebted to Professors Karl T. Hecht and William C. Parkinson of the Physics Department of the University of Michigan for much information and valuable advice.

BIBLIOGRAPHY

1921

The crystal structure of ice. Phys. Rev., 17:20–22.

1925

The infrared spectrum and molecular structure of methane. Astrophysics, 62:84–103.

Molecular structure of methane. Phys. Rev., 25:108–9.

1926

The rotation of molecules. Phys. Rev., 28:318–33.

The analysis of certain molecular spectra. Philos. Mag., 1:195–218.

Bemerkung zur Arbeit von C. Schaefer u. B. Philipps: Das Absorption-spektrum der Kohlensaure und die Gestalt der CO_2 Molekel. Z. Phys., 38:137–40.

1927

Wave mechanics and the rotation of homopolar molecules. Nature, 119:316–19.

A note on the specific heat of the hydrogen molecule. Proc. R. Soc. London, Ser. A, 115:483–86.

With S. Dushman and N. B. Reynolds. Electron emission and diffusion constants for tungsten filaments containing various oxides. Phys. Rev., 29:903.

1928

The shape and intensities of infrared absorption lines. Phys. Rev., 31:503–19.

A proposed experiment on the nature of light. Proc. Natl. Acad. Sci. USA, 14:580–81.

1930

With S. B. Ingram. A new band in the absorption spectrum of methane gas. Phys. Rev., 36:1451–59.

1931

Infrared spectra of polyatomic molecules, I. Rev. Mod. Phys., 3:280–345.

With N. Wright. A new long wave-length absorption band of CS_2. Phys. Rev., 38:2077–78.

1932

With J. D. Hardy. Parallel type absorption bands of ammonia. Phys. Rev., 39:938–47.
Vibrational levels of linear symmetrical triatomic molecules. Phys. Rev., 41:304–12.
With G. E. Uhlenbeck. The two-minima problem and the ammonia molecule. Phys. Rev., 41:313–21.
With J. D. Hardy and E. F. Barker. The infrared spectrum of H^2Cl. Phys. Rev., 42:279–89.

1933

With S. L. Gerhard. The envelopes of infrared absorption bands. Phys. Rev., 43:197–204.
With A. Adel. The infrared spectrum of carbon dioxide, I. Phys. Rev., 43:716–23.
With A. Adel. The infrared spectrum of carbon dioxide, II. Phys. Rev., 44:99–104.

1935

With G. B. B. M. Sutherland. The potential functions of polyatomic molecules. Proc. R. Soc. London, Ser. A, 148:250–71.
With M. Johnston. The interaction between vibration and rotation for symmetrical molecules. Phys. Rev., 47:93–94.
With M. Johnston. The vibration of symmetrical molecules. Phys. Rev., 48:868–83.

1937

With H. M. Randall, N. Ginsburg, and L. R. Weber. The far-infrared spectrum of water vapor. Phys. Rev., 52:160–74.

1939

With I. Z. Slawsky. The centrifugal distortion of axial molecules. J. Chem. Phys., 7:509–21.
With I. Z. Slawsky. The potential functions of the methyl halides. J. Chem. Phys., 7:522–29.
With N. Fuson and H. M. Randall. The far-infrared absorption spectrum and the rotational structure of the heavy water molecule. Phys. Rev., 56:982–1000.

1940

With B. T. Darling. The water vapor molecule. Phys. Rev., 57:128–39.

Excited states of the O^{16} nucleus. Phys. Rev., 57:454–56.

With J. S. Koehler. Hindered rotation in methyl alcohol. Phys. Rev., 57:1006–21.

The infrared spectra of polyatomic molecules, II. Rev. Mod. Phys., 12:175–214.

1941

With H. Sheng and E. F. Barker. Further resolution of two parallel bands of ammonia and the interaction between vibration and rotation. Phys. Rev., 60:786–94.

1946

With A. Adel. Notes on the infrared spectrum and molecular structure of ozone. J. Chem. Phys., 14:379–82.

With T. H. Berlin. The stability of orbits in the racetrack. Phys. Rev., 69:342–43.

With T. H. Berlin. The stability of synchrotron orbits. Phys. Rev., 70:58–67.

With T. H. Berlin. Racetrack stability. Phys. Rev., 70:764–65.

With L. N. Hadley. The microwave spectrum of ammonia. Phys. Rev., 70:780–81.

1947

With H. H. Nielsen. Anomalous values of certain of the fine structure lines in the ammonia microwave spectrum. Phys. Rev., 72:1101–8.

With L. N. Hadley. Reflection and transmission interference filters, I: Theory. J. Opt. Soc. Am., 37:451–65.

With F. B. Shull. The double focusing beta-ray spectrometer. Phys. Rev., 71:687.

1948

With L. N. Hadley. Reflection and transmission interference filters, II: Experimental, comparison with theory. J. Opt. Soc. Am., 38:483–96.

1951

With D. G. Burkhard. Molecular structure of methyl alcohol. Phys. Rev., 84:408–17.

1952

With G. E. Hansen. The potential constants of ethane. J. Chem. Phys., 20:313–26.

1953

With T. Chang. Centrifugal distortion effects of methyl chloride. J. Chem. Phys., 21:1293.

With Eugene C. Ivash. The methyl alcohol molecule and its microwave spectrum. J. Chem. Phys., 21:1804–16.

1954

Energy levels of the O^{16} nucleus. Phys. Rev., 96:378–80.

1957

With Karl T. Hecht. Hindered rotation in molecules with relatively high potential barriers. J. Chem. Phys., 26:31–47.

With Karl T. Hecht. Vibration-hindered rotation interactions in methyl alcohol. The $J = 0 \to 1$ transition. J. Chem. Phys., 26:48–69.

1959

With Donald G. Burkhard. Rotation spectrum of methyl alcohol. J. Mol. Spectrosc., 3:299–334.

1960

Note on the determination of the potential functions of polyatomic molecules. J. Opt. Soc. Am., 50:1267–70.

1962

Molecular spectra. In: *Quantum Theory*, vol. 2. N.Y.: Academic Press.

With W. T. Weeks and K. T. Hecht. Inversion-vibration and inversion-rotation interactions in the ammonia molecule. J. Mol. Spectrosc. 8:30–57.

1963

With H. A. Gebbie and G. Topping. The rotation spectrum of methyl alcohol from $20\,\text{cm}^{-1}$ to $80\,\text{cm}^{-1}$. J. Mol. Spectrosc., 11:229–40.

1967

Physics and the Department of Physics since 1900. In: *Research, Definitions and Reflections.* Ann Arbor: Univ. of Michigan Press.

1972

With Y. Y. Kwan. Analysis of the torsion-rotation spectra of the isotopic molecules. J. Mol. Spectrosc. 43: 291–319.

1974

Recollections of physics and of physicists during the 1920's. Am. J. Phys., 42:1051–56.

1975

With R. Gary Lee, Robert H. Hunt, and Farle K. Plyler. A high resolution study of the OH-stretch fundamental of methanol. J. Mol. Spectrosc., 57:138–54.

JESSE W. M. DuMOND
July 11, 1892–December 4, 1976

BY W. K. H. PANOFSKY

JESSE W. M. DuMOND died December 4, 1976, after a career characterized by extraordinary length and productivity. Jesse DuMond was a physicist, with that term encompassing all branches of the science. He was an experimental designer with extraordinary gifts, a skilled experimenter and an inspired interpreter of results, and a correlator of data gathered by others. He was, above everything else, driven by his notion of the inseparability of all phases of his work and by the wholeness of all physics. In order to have full confidence in the results obtained, he would delegate any component of his work to others only under extreme duress. For this reason, each item of apparatus, each calculation, and each interpretation was, wherever possible, a product of his own hand and brain.

Jesse DuMond was the most inspired mechanical designer I have ever known. He had an infallible sense of geometry, and he would prefer geometrical analysis and construction to any analytical or numerical method. His best-known work is his discovery of the broadening and fine structure of Compton scattering of X-ray photons. This work, born in some controversy, gave persuasive evidence of the dynamic nature of the Bohr atom by demonstrating the motion of orbital electrons.

Let me elaborate this glimpse of DuMond's contributions and work by outlining his career in more detail. Happily, in November 1972 DuMond had completed, under the farsighted sponsorship of the American Institute of Physics, a two-volume work entitled *The Autobiography of a Physicist*, to which the reader is referred for greater detail and for a poetic description of DuMond's career in his own words.

Jesse DuMond married Irene Gaebel in Paris in 1920. They had three children, two of whom married; they are (Mrs.) Desiree Andre Wilson, born in 1927 and (Mrs.) Adele Irene Panofsky, born in 1923. DuMond remarried in 1942 and is survived by his widow, Louise DuMond, as well as by eleven grandchildren.

EARLY EDUCATION AND MILITARY SERVICE

Jesse DuMond was born July 11, 1892 in France, of American parents. His mother died while he was an infant, and his father and his uncle were both artists of some renown. Interestingly, his early childhood reflects an attraction both to technical and artistic influences. He was brought up in the care of a maternal grandmother and great-aunt, but when his father remarried, his education and upbringing became the responsibility of his paternal grandfather, residing in Rochester, New York, and later in Monrovia, California. He went to high school in Monrovia and at the same time received a thorough exposure to the mechanical arts through his grandfather. DuMond's grandfather was a very unusual person. He was a self-educated man who had been a sailor and had engaged in various trades. He then decided to settle down and start a sheet-metal business. Despite, or possibly because of, his lack of a formal education, he had a deep respect for books, for poetry, and for learning in general, and at the same time had the highest standards of craftsmanship. Under his tutelage, DuMond acquired his deep understanding of geometrical and mechanical principles and the skills in mechanical design that were to serve him so well during his later scientific career.

DuMond's grandfather had a negative attitude about art as a career. Thus DuMond's dual interests, in art, and science and the mechanical arts, reflect his dual upbringing by his father and grandfather.

After completing schooling in Monrovia, DuMond held a number of jobs and then entered, in 1912, what was then known as Throop College, later to become the California Institute of Technology. At that time Cal Tech was not as yet a full-fledged graduate institution offering the Ph.D. degree, nor had it collected many prominent research people. Moreover, its president, the famous astronomer George Ellery Hale, felt that Throop College should produce not just engineers and scientists, but should offer a well-rounded education. It is characteristic that this task of balancing the technical education with some instruction in the humanities fell to a single professor, Clinton K. Judy, who apparently had a large influence on DuMond's increasing interest in poetry and the arts, in addition to his growth in physics and engineering.

DuMond completed his undergraduate education in 1916 with an excellent record, receiving several prizes. His thesis consisted of the construction of an harmonic analyzer, which at that time was considered to be a highly advanced calculating device. After receiving his undergraduate degree, DuMond took a job as a test man at General Electric in Schenectady, New York and continued part-time study at Union College. He had some contact with the famous C. P. Steinmetz, then considered to be the leading genius in electrical engineering. Steinmetz's extensive use of complex variable analysis of alternating current circuits inspired DuMond to design and construct a complex quantity slide rule, in essence a very ingenious, two-dimensional plotting table, which I had the privilege of using. Again, this development, which became his master's thesis, was indicative of DuMond's preference for using geometry rather than algebra whenever possible in the solution of difficult problems.

Apparently, after initial enthusiasm, DuMond considered his work at General Electric to be unpromising, too routine, and leading only to administrative or organizational positions. Accordingly, despite the successful efforts by the General Electric Company to defer DuMond from military service, he enlisted in the army and became a member of a sound-ranging battalion in France. In those days locating enemy batteries by sound ranging was far from a routine operation. In command of the army's sound-ranging effort was Professor Lyman of Harvard University, who attained the rank of colonel in this profession. Sound ranging by the enlisted men involved learning to distinguish the sound waves from the muzzle blasts of guns, which propagated at the ordinary velocity of sound, from the ballistic shock waves of the projectiles' flight, which did not. The whole technique of sound ranging was developed by Sir William Bragg of England. In short, sound ranging during World War I involved the leaders of U.S. and British physics. As a sound ranger DuMond served on the front under fire, but was never involved in personal combat.

POSTWAR EMPLOYMENT AND GRADUATE STUDY

The Armistice led to orders for DuMond to be honorably discharged back in the United States, but he attempted to stay in France to settle the estate of his recently deceased grandmother who had been responsible for his early upbringing. Combining his stay in France with discharge from the army proved to be impossible; thus after continuing various minor technical jobs for the Army, DuMond found it necessary to make a round trip to San Francisco to be discharged and then returned to Paris to settle the estate. To make this trip and stay in France feasible economically, DuMond decided to take a position with the Thomsen-Houston Company in France, which at the same time had reached an agreement with General Electric to standardize the design of large turbine generators to be marketed in Europe and the United States. DuMond's job consisted of translating the G.E. designs, down to the detailed blueprints, into a form suitable for production by French methods. Although this was a relatively routine task, it contributed substantially to his deep understanding of the detailed problems faced in engineering and production.

After this engineering interlude, caused primarily by the vicissitudes of U.S. military and French judicial bureaucracies, DuMond resumed his scientific career, first in a position with the National Bureau of Standards. He worked in a group headed by Harvey Curtis, who was at that time engaged in refining the determination of the absolute ampere by the classical current balance method. Although DuMond participated in this work in only a minor way, it kindled his lasting interest in work on precision determination of natural constants, and it impressed upon him the distinction between absolute units and those units established by standards of convenience.

DuMond's primary work at the Bureau was to assist Curtis in his work on the interior ballistics of guns. The work consisted of recording the recoil displacement of guns after firing as a function of time, and from this information computing the dynamics of firing. Again, this work, although relatively routine in nature, introduced DuMond to the intricacies of data analysis and curve fitting, using the relatively primitive techniques of those days.

In 1920 the National Bureau of Standards was a prime intellectual center in American physics. Visiting lecturers included the pioneers in atomic and quantum theory, and there was extensive discussion concerning the validity of the special theory of relativity. The atmosphere was congenial and led to much intellectual stimulation. Induced by this experience, together with the modest amount of money inherited by the settlement of his French estate, DuMond decided that more advanced education was a necessity for a career in physics. He therefore applied to Cal Tech to work towards a Ph.D. degree, and he was admitted in 1921.

DuMond's period of graduate study was a long one, leading to a Ph.D. degree in 1929 just short of his thirty-seventh birthday. His studies towards the Ph.D. were interrupted by two trips to France. Also, his field of investigation—X-rays—was one of his own choosing and not carried out under direct supervision of a more experienced member of the faculty. However, his thesis, dealing with the broadening of the Compton effect due to the internal motion of electrons in an atom, describes one of the truly classical experiments in atomic physics.

STUDIES OF THE MODIFIED COMPTON LINE
THE DYNAMICS OF THE ATOM

DuMond was acquainted with the discovery of the Compton effect. He recognized, however, that the usual derivation of the Compton shift assumed that the electron struck by the incident photon was at rest, and that therefore broadening of the Compton-scattered line should result if motion of the electron was taken into account. Accordingly, DuMond proposed detailed study of the modification of the Compton-scattered line as a valuable tool in studying the velocity distribution of electrons in atoms. Recently Richard Feynmann and Richard Wilson have given eloquent credit to DuMond's recognition of this fundamental fact. DuMond's measurements were accompanied by an extensive set of papers relating theoretically the shifted line shapes to the atomic electron motion.

DuMond's studies of the broadening effect of electron motion on the Compton line were beset both by technical and human difficulties. Intensities available from X-rays combined with X-ray spectrometry with single crystals gave insufficient intensity. DuMond's studies in classical optics made him aware of the properties of the Rowland circle, which had been in use for a long time in optical spectroscopy. He immediately realized that if a crystal operating in accordance with the Bragg reflection condition was to serve as the grating in the conventional Rowland configuration, then the radii determined by the focusing conditions and the Bragg reflection condition were incompatible by a factor of two. Starting from this conflict, he proposed that these two radii could indeed be independently created by either configuring a large set of independent small crystals along one of the radii while orienting each crystal along the other, or by bending a crystal so that the crystal planes would conform to the Bragg condition. While publishing both of these solutions, DuMond rejected the second one as impractical to the accuracy required and embarked on the construction of a multi-crystal spectrometer. At the same time other workers in Europe, notably H. H. Johann and Y. Cauchois, used DuMond's suggestions as a point of departure for the construction of curved crystal spectrometers. DuMond complained throughout his career that the priority of his proposal of the curved crystal spectrometer had never been adequately recognized by those who first reduced it to practice.

Using a spectrometer constructed with fifty separate crystals, DuMond, with Harry A. Kirkpatrick, then investigated what has since become a milestone in classical atomic physics: He measured the broadening of the Compton line and extended this work to a number of elements. Although credit for this work is being accorded to DuMond universally, publication of these results was not without controversy. In particular DuMond accuses, and I believe with considerable merit, A. H. Compton himself of particularly ungenerous conduct in connection with these discoveries. The chapter of the classical text on X-rays, "Compton and Allison," initially reproduced DuMond's data without discussing their significance. Moreover, in subsequent critical discussions of the shape and position of the Compton-scattered line, A. H. Compton gave a great deal of credence to the work of a student of his, Gingrich, which subsequently was almost certainly proven to be incorrect. The work of Gingrich used a much less "luminous" two-crystal spectrometer. DuMond and an associate (A. Hoyt) did a two-crystal spectrometer experiment also, obtaining results in disagreement with Gingrich.

In view of the above events, DuMond found himself embattled in a rather unproductive controversy about priorities and credibility of experiments. In retrospect, there is little question that DuMond's period of graduate study at Cal Tech encompassed two exceedingly fundamental contributions: the discovery of the focusing properties of curved crystal or multi-crystal assemblies for X-ray spectroscopy, and the discovery, initial exploration, and theoretical interpretation of the modified Compton-shifted X-ray spectroscopy.

X-RAY STUDIES ON NATURAL ATOMIC CONSTANTS

I mentioned previously that DuMond returned to graduate study at Cal Tech inspired by the revolutionary developments in atomic physics of the early 1920's as introduced to him at the National Bureau of Standards, and that he felt he could return to such studies because of his small independent income. It was characteristic of DuMond's general attitude in those days that he relinquished a paid teaching assistantship at Cal Tech in order to make these funds available to other, presumably younger, graduate students who had no other means of support. This history was to repeat itself after his Ph.D., in 1929, when Cal Tech was in a state of financial crisis. R. A. Millikan, as head of Cal Tech, was deeply impressed by DuMond's contributions as a student and offered him the position of research fellow at Cal Tech to continue his work—without salary. DuMond accepted. In 1931 DuMond was offered an associate professorship at Stanford University. He worked and taught there for three months to become acquainted, and he made many friendships that endured into later years, in particular with W. W. Hansen whom he greatly admired. However, despite the obvious professional attractiveness of the position at Stanford—and the fact that it involved a salary—he decided to return to Cal Tech to continue his research. DuMond felt that the intellectual opportunities at Cal Tech during that time were superior to those at Stanford, and he particularly admired Millikan's leadership in attracting inspiring leaders in physics. Not until 1938 did DuMond receive a salary as an associate professor!

In those days obtaining some financial support to carry out experimental research was no mean accomplishment. R. A. Millikan tried to be as helpful as he possibly could in furthering the work of the members of the Institute. Specifically, Millikan succeeded in interesting an ever-widening group of industrial and professional leaders in the work of Cal Tech, and he introduced DuMond to a Dr. Leon L. Watters, a wealthy businessman from New York. This contact led to a gift* by Watters in 1933 in support of DuMond's work, which greatly amplified DuMond's ability to carry out his fundamental work on X-rays and natural constants.

*$9,000 total—a princely sum for research at the time.

Although the Watters gift appears modest by current standards, it provided DuMond the means to engage in what in those days was surely considered by some to be "big physics." Quite apart from the then higher value of the dollar, the leverage of such funds was enormous. The work in which DuMond engaged was largely based on ingenious design and painstaking construction of extraordinary apparatus. He generally carried out the work by himself, assisted by a dedicated group of students, associates, and gifted mechanicians. Only outside purchases had to be covered by the Watters grant.

Within this pattern, DuMond proceeded to construct two major installations. One was a 300 kw X-ray tube operating at voltages up to 100 kv. The tube was entirely laboratory built using surplus transformer bushings as insulators; many other "scrounged" components constituted the power supply and ancillary apparatus. Some purchased components were incorporated in the power supply, which had to be carefully regulated for the research to be undertaken. The X-ray tube incorporated a gyrating anode, a major innovation in those days. DuMond devoted extraordinary mathematical efforts to the quantitative heat conduction design of this anode, and he also designed and built the entire vacuum system. An interesting note is that DuMond decided to avoid the use of the then conventional McLeod vacuum gauges and instead designed and built a set of Knudsen gauges, which utilize the momentum of thermal bombardment of residual gas molecules to deflect a suspended vane. It was DuMond's habit to personally draw each component and assembly to the highest standards of engineering draftsmanship, and also to prepare perspective drawings for publication, since he felt that they communicated technical content better than photographs. It is interesting to note as a sideline that when he published the meticulous description of the Knudsen gauges there was much demand from others who wished to use but not to build them. Accordingly DuMond, in cooperation with one of the superb mechanicians in the Cal Tech shops, marketed this gauge for a while and received sufficient returns to pay for a summer vacation!

In addition to the high-powered X-ray tube, which represented a large advance in equipment available at the time, DuMond, together with an engineering student (Douglas Marlowe), designed and built a precision two-crystal spectrometer, which made it possible to position large calcite and other crystals to a precision of a fraction of a second of arc. Again drawings were prepared to meticulous standards and many highly ingenious innovations were incorporated to reach the desired precision at low cost. One of the innovations in which DuMond took great pride was the driving mechanism that rotated the crystals. This consisted of precision-lapped driving screws which drove large worm wheels. These wheels were split into two halves, and a spring between the two halves prevented backlash. This concept was not new, but DuMond supplemented it with a mathematically elaborate systematic lapping scheme. The teeth of the worm wheels were lapped with the two halves of the wheel superimposed on one another in what he analyzed to be the optimum sequence to average out the initial machining errors. This instrument was a success; again requests were received from several laboratories to make precise copies, since the kind of design skill incorporated in the small physics group under DuMond just did not exist anywhere else in the world.

Armed with this advanced instrumentation and other less unusual pieces of equipment, DuMond and his students embarked on a series of X-ray experiments dedicated to advance the frontiers of knowledge on the fundamental atomic constants—Planck's constant and the charge and mass of the electron. The foremost discrepancy among the atomic constants at the time dealt with the value of the electronic charge. For over two decades the measurements published by Millikan in 1917 were accepted essentially uncritically. However, the indirect approach to measuring the electronic charge by measuring the absolute value of the lattice spacing of crystals using X-rays of wavelength determined by grating reflection resulted in an uncomfortable discrepancy of almost 1 percent. To derive the electronic charge from the lattice-spacing measurements one needs to know the density of that part of the crystal contributing to the reflection of X-rays, as well as auxiliary constants such as the Faraday. A possible alibi for the discrepancy was, therefore, that those few atomic planes that participate in Bragg reflection in crystals might have an anomalous density—and one of DuMond's colleagues (Zwicky) proposed an elaborate theory of possible crystal superstructures that might be responsible. To investigate this proposed explanation, DuMond undertook two programs. One was to substitute transmission rather than surface-reflection measurement of X-rays to determine crystal-lattice spacings, thereby sampling the crystal in depth. The other was to obtain X-ray crystal diffraction patterns from powdered crystals (the Debye-Scherrer method), thereby taking a random sample of surface reflections. The first approach in particular turned out to be more difficult than anticipated, but through painstaking effort in a series of experiments DuMond and his students succeeded in bringing both methods to fruition. The result agreed well with the original surface-reflection data, thus contradicting the explanation that crystal non-homogeneities were somehow responsible for the discrepancy between the Millikan oil-drop value of the electronic charge and the X-ray diffraction value. It was these results, together with the persuasive communications to Millikan by Professor R. T. Birge of the University of California at Berkeley, who was then the most highly respected reviewer of natural constants, that persuaded Millikan to reexamine all the assumptions of the auxiliary constants used in his old oil-drop determinations. As is now well known, this review led Millikan to question the correctness of the value of the viscosity of air that he had used in the old experiments, and he put a graduate student to work to remeasure this parameter. This remeasurement successfully removed the discrepancy, and the X-ray measurements proved to be correct.

The second major application of X-rays to natural constants initiated by DuMond dealt with the ratio of Planck's constant to the electronic charge. This number can be inferred through a precision determination of the voltage threshold at which X-rays of known wavelengths are produced by electron bombardment. Such a measurement requires precision measurement of the X-ray tube voltage, precision wavelength measurement of the X-rays, and enough intensity to permit measurement at very high resolution of all these quantities. A measurement was carried out by DuMond and one of his students (Bollmann) before the Watters apparatus was constructed. Some uncomfortable discrepancies remained in the consistency of these measurements with the charge of the electron, optical measurements of the Rydberg constant, and measurements of the charge to mass ratio of the electron by various methods. Accordingly DuMond and his associates and students (including myself) engaged in a series of measurements that brought the power of the new instruments to bear on this problem. The result set a new mark in accuracy of determination of the so-called shortwave limit of X-ray production. It turned out that at the precision in question (a few parts in 10,000 in those days), considerable attention had to be paid to solid-state phenomena governing the details of the final state which the electron can occupy after emission of the X-rays near threshold, to the surface cleanliness of the anode, and to precise analysis of the factors determining resolution.

This work led DuMond to engage independently from, but in good communication with, R. T. Birge in a critical analysis of the worldwide picture of the natural constants. In those days DuMond strongly emphasized his disdain for numerical and, to some extent, formal statistical methods, and superimposed his dominant interest in geometry. He devised the so-called "isometric consistency chart" in which the combinations of values of the electronic charge and mass and of Planck's constant as contained in each particular measurement were represented by straight lines accompanied by parallel lines representing the probable errors. The success or failure of these lines to intersect in a small region represented the consistency or lack thereof of the multitude of measurements. In subsequent years DuMond was to publish successive literature and experimental surveys of the atomic constants, plotting his findings in such a chart. As complexity and precision of experimental determination of the natural constants increased, DuMond found it progressively more difficult to deal with these questions alone and formed an association with E. Richard Cohen, with whom he collaborated on critical evaluations of the natural constants for the balance of his life. Cohen, as a member of the younger generation, brought a thorough knowledge of computational methods to supplement DuMond's geometrical intuition and detailed knowledge of experimental apparatus. The successive reviews of DuMond and Cohen of natural constants became standard references on the subject for a protracted period of time.

THE BEGINNING OF GAMMA-RAY SPECTROSCOPY

The Watters apparatus had made it possible for DuMond to extend the traditional methods of X-ray crystal spectroscopy to higher energies. Motivated by this success, and drawing on his earlier invention of the curved crystal spectrometer, DuMond embarked on the new direction of gamma-ray spectroscopy. Following a suggestion by Y. Cauchois, he found that the spacings of certain crystal planes in quartz were sufficiently narrow, and their structure functions for X-ray reflections sufficiently large, that there might be hope of success. Accordingly DuMond designed a large (two-meter radius) and elaborate curved crystal gamma-ray spectrometer. This instrument posed several formidable design problems stemming from the small magnitude of the Bragg angle at gamma-ray energies. DuMond realized that a principal problem was precision collimation to separate the very weak Bragg-reflected beam from the direct beam from the source, and that therefore the collimator and detector would be very massive devices, while the source, being simply a radioactive sample, could be relatively small. DuMond designed an instrument in which the traditional Rowland circle geometry was reversed; the detector is stationary, while the source moves along the circle. Based on this principle, DuMond devised an ingenious kinematic arrangement controlled by a precision feed screw, which moved a curved crystal holder and a radioactive source in the correct kinematic conditions designed to preserve both the Bragg angle and the relevant focusing conditions. An additional feature of his kinematic solution to this problem was that the scale of wavelengths bore a linear relationship to the feed screw setting controlling the device. DuMond, in his autobiography, considered this design to be the best among his instrumental achievements.

Design and fabrication of this instrument under DeMond's direction, again executed by the superb mechanicians in the Cal Tech shops, was well along when World War II started. Final assembly and commissioning of the instrument was delayed by almost a decade since higher priority items were placed in the machine shops, and DuMond himself went on a leave of absence to the East to engage in military work.

As it turned out, this delay was a very fortunate one indeed. It is doubtful that the intensity of the radioactive sources available before the war would have been adequate to carry out experiments that would have made significant contributions to gamma-ray nuclear spectroscopy. The advent of nuclear reactors made it possible to activate large varieties of substances to yield nuclear gamma-ray transitions of intensities unprecedented before the war. This fortuitous circumstance made DuMond's gamma-ray spectrometer an enormously productive instrument.

This new instrument led to a shift from DuMond's prewar research activities with X-rays below 100 KeV to his postwar activities dedicated primarily to nuclear spectroscopy. This latter field was not DuMond's primary area of expertise. Therefore the choice of research topics to which DuMond's high-precision X-ray spectroscopic methods were to be dedicated in the field of nuclear spectroscopy were largely left to others. It was the fortunate combination of highly experienced nuclear spectroscopists and DuMond's extraordinary gift of instrumental design that shaped the postwar research period. However, let me first turn back to DuMond's contribution to military work during the war.

CONTRIBUTION DURING WORLD WAR II

DuMond's war work did not follow the mainstream of participation of most American high energy physicists. DuMond's personal style was very individual. He insisted on very high standards and, when recognizing that he could do a certain job himself more ably than delegating it to associates, he generally preferred the former course. DuMond's style did not lend itself well to participation in the mass assault on the pressing technical military problems of World War II to which physicists have contributed so much—radar, the atomic bomb, and the development of rocketry.

DuMond's first wartime activity took him to the East. There he worked at the request of the Bell Telephone Labs on a problem relating to degaussing the magnetic field of ships so that they would not trigger enemy magnetic mines. He did a great deal of work on mathematical solutions of the degaussing problem by synthesizing the magnetic field of coils to cancel successively higher moments. Based on these calculations, he constructed a simulator for modeling the magnetic field of ships and compensating that field on a moment-by-moment basis.

As his next assignment, DuMond became associated with the rocket propellant activities at Indian Head near Silver Spring, Maryland. There he worked on processes to extrude what is known as rocket "grain," resulting in a product which would burn in a rocket motor at controlled rate and thrust. He designed what was possibly the first successful extrusion press for solid rocket fuel, and his work became incorporated into basic rocket technology.

DuMond then returned to Cal Tech in December 1941. In continuation of his work on rocket technology, he initially associated himself with the large-scale rocket work then conducted at Cal Tech under the direction of Professor Charles C. Lauritsen. At the same time DuMond set up a small project shop in another part of the Institute to pursue more specialized projects that utilized his unique design skills more specifically. Although he made some useful contributions, such as designing some new types of rocket launchers, his association with the big rocket project at Cal Tech was only partially successful. The reason was not that his technical and personal qualities were not appreciated by all—on the contrary, everyone spoke with admiration of DuMond's skill and ability—but that his working methods and insistence on personal control did not lend themselves to the world of compromises inherent in the execution of a large-scale project of this kind. He therefore concentrated his work more and more away from the central tasks of the rocket activities at Cal Tech and worked on smaller projects. One of these was the design and construction of a large aerial camera for intelligence collection. This device used Schmidt optics configured to result in very high photographic speed. This camera was mounted on a set of gimbals arranged to rock in such a manner as to compensate for the ground speed of the airplane, thus producing a stationary image. The device worked excellently at unprecedented optical speed and resolution, but to the best of my knowledge, it never reached production or regular military use because no follow-up to make this instrument producible was provided.

DuMond's contact with the rocket activities led him to what was to become his major wartime contribution. He participated in a field exercise in northern California where rockets were used as targets for ground-to-air antiaircraft gunnery exercises. He recognized that the principal problem in using target rockets, or as far as that goes, targets of any kind, as training tools for antiaircraft fire was error assessment. Since actual hits were only obtained in exceptional cases, no evaluation of training effectiveness or improvement in performance could be made. DuMond, together with his associate A. E. S. Green, proposed that a remote sensor be mounted on aerial targets, which by telemetry could broadcast the distance between the projectile and the target.

The first concept developed by DuMond and his associates to achieve this was the use of magnetic detection. Large configurations of magnetic coils were designed, contrived to cancel magnetic disturbance from external sources, but sensitive to the magnetic field from hardened steel armor piercing, and magnetized, ammunition. This attempt was basically unsuccessful, since the attainable sensitivity did not meet the objective of detecting bullets at relatively large miss distances from the target. However, DuMond proposed an alternate approach, derived from his observation of the "crack" of bullets traveling overhead associated with his early experiences as a sound ranger in military service in World War I. He proposed that the shock wave of supersonic projectiles be the handle for measuring the miss distance of such projectiles from aerial targets. This initiative led to a more substantial project dedicated to developing practical detectors that could be mounted on airborne tow-targets, on target drones, or target rockets. Development of this device, called the Firing Error Indicator (FEI), took well over a year, but field tests were very encouraging. For the first time, firing crews who were encamped in the desert areas of southern California to practice shooting at aerial targets had information whether their performance improved as a result of such training. The device was placed into commercial production, but the products did not see much service before the end of the war. One problem was that the increasing speed of aircraft led to what amounts to technological obsolescence of this device. Based on observation of the acoustic shock wave, the FEI would become very inaccurate as the target fired at approaches the speed of sound.

Concomitant with the actual development of this device, DuMond delved more deeply into the theory of shock-wave propagation. With his associates, he wrote a much-quoted paper that derived theoretically the acoustic wave shape of high-speed projectiles and the modification of this wave shape as it propagates. Also, some of the techniques in producing and testing the ultra-precision microphones required for acoustical detection of shock waves led to important technological advances in that field.

There was one interesting sideline connected with this work, apart from its own intrinsic significance. Luis W. Alvarez, then at Los Alamos, had been assigned the task of designing sensors to be used both during the initial test of nuclear explosives and during their actual operational use in order to measure their yield. He decided that observation of the acoustic shock wave of the explosions was what was needed. Upon reading the results of the work of DuMond and associates at Cal Tech, Alvarez decided that his problem was essentially solved, and that the Firing Error Indicator would easily be adaptable as a shock-wave detector for nuclear explosions. Accordingly, secret liaison arrangements were set up between DuMond's project at Cal Tech and Los Alamos. The relatively minor modifications of the firing indicator for this novel use were carried out, and a special receiver to display the frequency-modulated signals was designed and built. Such a receiving unit was intalled in a B-29 that overflew the first nuclear explosion in Alamagordo, but the FEI devices were never dropped due to bad weather conditions. However, the devices were actually used during the nuclear bombings of August sixth and ninth, 1945 of Hiroshima and Nagasaki, and provided the primary information on the yields of the nuclear explosions detonated. There was a further sideline, as the shock-wave detectors were dropped by parachute at considerable distance from the explosion and therefore escaped destruction. Alvarez and associates at Berkeley used this fact to tape a message to the battery case of the shock-wave detectors, addressed to Japanese physicists, some of whom had worked at Berkeley. The record shows that this message was actually delivered to the addressees and by them to the Japanese high command. Thus a strange chain of development, beginning with DuMond's idea of using shock waves from bullets to assess errors during aerial gunner training, led ultimately to a means of communication during wartime to an enemy who may have had difficulty understanding what tragedy overtook him as a result of the development and use of nuclear weapons by the United States.

RETURN TO NUCLEAR SPECTROSCOPY

During the latter part of the wartime activities, DuMond and his associates found enough time to make small progress on the assembly of the gamma-ray spectrometer equipment. As the war ended, this instrument was ready for use, and initial testing showed that, using radioactive isotopes produced in reactors, gamma-ray lines could be measured with precision unprecedented in the history of nuclear spectroscopy. One of the first measurements dealt with the two-photon annihilation radiation of electrons and positrons. This measurement yields directly a value of the ratio of Planck's constant to the electron mass. Thus, even as DuMond's X-ray work moved into the MeV region, a link to the natural atomic constants remained. Wavelengths of gamma-rays from more than thirty nuclides measured to an accuracy of a few parts in ten thousand were published by DuMond and his collaborators in a remarkable series of papers from 1949 to 1963.

The postwar era in DuMond's work was shaped by the availability of this first gamma-ray spectrometer, which DuMond had designed and almost completed before the war. This instrument added new power to investigations of nuclear spectroscopy. Joining DuMond were numerous distinguished associates whose specialty was nuclear spectroscopy and who benefitted from DuMond's great gifts of instrumental design and construction. Among these were David Lind, Felix Boehm—who is now in charge of the heritage of DuMond's work at Cal Tech—and for some time Rudolf Mossbauer.

The instruments supporting the program of nuclear

spectroscopy rapidly grew beyond the initial gamma-ray spectrometer. A further curved crystal spectrometer was constructed. In addition, it became clear that nuclear spectroscopy required beta-ray spectrometers also, and again DuMond's designs advanced the art considerably.

Triggered by the success of DuMond's first curved crystal spectrometers, which employed a 3" × 4.5" bent quartz crystal, demand increased from several institutions for DuMond to assist them in constructing similar instruments adapted to particular needs. An instrument using a quartz crystal of the unprecedented size of 11" × 11" was constructed for the Argonne National Laboratory in order to analyze gamma-ray transitions of extremely short-lived nuclides produced in a test reactor. Naturally, since this instrument had to be directly incorporated into the reactor configuration, the original concept of DuMond's first gamma-ray spectrometer could not be used because the kinematic solution he had adopted required motion of the source and not of the detector. The mechanical design of the Argonne instrument was done directly by the Argonne staff with DuMond acting as advisor.

David Lind, who had joined with DuMond to perform the first gamma-ray experiments after the war, starting in 1947, left Cal Tech in 1950 and worked for some time at the Nobel Institute in Stockholm. With the DuMond tradition being thus introduced into Sweden, an instrument was built at the Nobel Institute which permitted valuable cross-checks with the Cal Tech work.

To these variants of the initial design of a gamma-ray curved crystal spectrometer, DuMond and collaborators added another called the Mark III. It incorporated a large germanium crystal rather than a quartz crystal, since large germanium crystals are easier to obtain and bend. However, the degree of perfection so desired for such a crystal was more difficult to attain. The Mark III curved crystal spectrometer was more compact than the first design and had simpler kinematics. In particular the radiation source remained stationary. The design was so successful that it was copied by six institutions. A modified copy saw service at Livermore to analyze nuclear gamma-rays produced by the unprecedented intensity of the Livermore, so-called A-48, high-current deuteron accelerator, which was built as a model to demonstrate the feasibility of accelerator breeding of fissionable materials. This work was carried out as a result of a collaboration between DuMond and Hans Mark, then at Livermore.

Although as individual experiments the measurements of gamma-ray spectral lines as carried out by DuMond and collaborators may seem somewhat prosaic, their totality constituted a substantial fraction of the basis of the Nobel Prize award-winning proposal of Aage Bohr and Ben Mottelson on what is known as the collective model of the nucleus. Initial publications by Bohr, Mottelson, and associates relied heavily on the gamma-ray measurements made by the DuMond family of curved crystal spectrometers.

As mentioned above, the nuclear spectroscopists working with DuMond found it desirable to supplement the curved crystal gamma-ray spectrometer with beta-ray spectrometers also. There were two motives for this proposal: one was to provide a tool for beta-ray spectroscopy as such, and the other was to measure gamma-ray energies by observing the spectrum of Compton-scattered electrons in the forward direction.

To meet the first challenge, DuMond carried out a careful, systematic study of the optimization conditions that pertained to the design of beta-ray spectrographs of axial symmetry. Although many instruments of this general description had been built in the past, none of them was truly optimized to achieve the best compromise between luminosity, on the one hand, and energy resolution, on the other. DuMond showed that an optimum solution could be based on trajectories in a uniform magnetic field. If such a uniform field was used, DuMond showed that optimum luminosity for a given resolution would be obtained at a certain fixed cone of emission of electrons, and he showed that there existed a uniquely defined position for an annular slit to be mounted within the uniform magnetic field. Based on these fundamental considerations, DuMond designed an instrument in which the uniform magnetic field was produced by a set of coils placed on the surface of an ellipsoid, and where the entire apparatus was constructed of totally nonferrous materials. The required annular slit could be adjusted fully from the outside of the apparatus. The result was an incredibly complex design, and it speaks for DuMond's engineering genius that the apparatus was fully assembled from the parts as designed from his drawings without modification. Performance was exactly as predicted, and an important new tool was added to the arsenal of nuclear spectroscopists.

This instrument was not usable at the lowest energies of interest to beta-ray spectroscopists, and therefore one of DuMond's associates (Herbert Henrickson) designed a smaller matching instrument. In the time interval from 1951 to 1960 these instruments were the tools leading to analysis of the beta spectra of seventeen nuclides (incidentally, seven Ph.D. theses were produced). In addition to the instruments mentioned, a third spectrometer was built which was to serve the dual purpose of Compton electron spectroscopy and beta-ray spectroscopy. This instrument followed the classical solution of Siegbahn and Svartholm for a double-focusing spectrometer, which incorporates a magnetic field falling off radially with a field index designed such that horizontal and vertical focusing wavelengths become equal. Under those circumstances, focusing is obtained at a bend angle of $\sqrt{2}\,\pi$ radian from the source. Such an instrument was again constructed successfully with a bending radius of 35 cm and turned over to the nuclear spectroscopy activities of Felix Boehm and associates.

DuMond's retirement from teaching duties at Cal Tech was a gradual one starting at age sixty-five with decreasing duties, down to full retirement at age seventy. He continued research well beyond retirement—his last published papers date beyond his seventy-fifth birthday. It is noteworthy that his last research work reverted to his prime interest—the natural atomic constants. His last papers were review articles, written jointly with E. R. Cohen, of the status of the constants, and he joined his old and now retired friend and associate of his graduate student days, Harry A. Kirkpatrick, in a final, but not successful, attempt to solve the residual discrepancy in the absolute standardization of X-ray wavelengths. After that effort he stayed in contact with the researchers of his group and gave occasional lectures until ill health prevented him from continuing.

The above account gives only an outline of the highlights of DuMond's scientific work and only the briefest glimpse of his human qualities. He will be remembered for both of these for a long time. It is doubtful that the increasing specialization of physics will make it possible again for a single physicist to make as comprehensive contributions to design of apparatus, to precision measurements, and to theoretical interpretation as was done by Jesse W. M. DuMond during his lifetime.

BIBLIOGRAPHY

1915

Design and construction of an harmonic analyzer. Thesis, California Institute of Technology.

1925

Complex quantity slide rule. J. Am. Ins. Electr. Eng., 44:188.

1928

The structure of the Compton shifted line. Proc. Natl. Acad. Sci. USA, 14 (11):875–78.

Experimental confirmation for Fermi-Dirac degenerate gas theory of conduction electrons. Nature, 67(1767):452.

1929

Compton modified line structure and its relation to the electron theory of solid bodies. Phys. Rev., 33(5):643–58.

1930

With Archer Hoyt. The Seemann spectrograph tells the story. Radiology, 14:62.

A new parallel plate comparator. Rev. Sci. Instrum., 1:84–87.

With Harry A. Kirkpatrick. The multiple crystal X-ray spectrograph. Rev. Sci. Instrum., 1:88–105.

With Archer Hoyt. Energy of $K\alpha_3$ of copper as a function of applied voltage with the double-spectrometer. Phys. Rev., 36:799–809.

Breadth of Compton modified line. Phys. Rev., 36:146–47.

Evidence for the Richtmyer double jump hypothesis of X-ray satellites. Phys. Rev., 36:1015–17.

With H. A. Kirkpatrick. A study of scattered X-radiation and electron momenta with the multicrystal spectrograph. Science, 72(1868):404.

Multiple scattering in the Compton effect. Phys. Rev., 36:1685–701.

With Archer Hoyt. Design and technique of operation of a double crystal spectrometer. Phys. Rev., 36:1702–20.

1931

With H. A. Kirkpatrick. Experimental evidence for electron velocities as the cause of Compton line breadth with the multicrystal spectrometer. Phys. Rev., 36:136–59.

Breadth of the Compton modified line with the double crystal spectrometer. Phys. Rev., 37:1443–51.

With Archer Hoyt. A new k-series X-ray line due to Fermi-Sommerfeld electrons. Phys. Rev., 38:839–41.

With H. A. Kirkpatrick. Dependence of Compton line breadth on primary wavelength with the multicrystal spectrograph. Phys. Rev., 38:1094–108.

1932

Possible narrowing of Compton line breadth by preferentially directed electron momenta in Ceylon graphite. Phys. Rev., 39:166–68.

With H. A. Kirkpatrick and Lucas Alden. Search for preferentially directed electron velocities in crystalline graphite with the multicrystal spectrograph. Phys. Rev., 40:165–77.

With Archer Hoyt. Present status of the problem of measurement of X-ray intensity and quality. Radiology, 18:787.

The technic of stereofluoroscopy. Radiology, 19:366.

1933

The linear momenta of electrons in atoms and in solid bodies as revealed by X-ray scattering. Rev. Mod. Phys., 5:1–33.

1934

With B. B. Watson. Curved quartz crystal X-ray spectrograph. Phys. Rev., 46:316–17.

1935

With B. B. Watson and Bruce Hicks. Temperatures of continuously operated mobile X-ray focal spots. Rev. Sci. Instrum., 6:183–93.

Two applications of the sylphon bellows in high vacuum plumbing. Rev. Sci. Instrum., 6:285–86.

With P. Youtz. Selective X-ray diffraction from artificially stratified metal films deposited by evaporation. Phys. Rev., 48:703.

With W. M. Pickels, Jr. Superiority of a Knudsen type vacuum gauge for large metal systems with organic vapor pumps; its design and operation. Rev. Sci. Instrum., 6:363–70.

1936

With V. L. Bollman. New and unexplained effects in Laue X-ray reflection in calcite. Phys. Rev., 50:97.

With V. L. Bollman. Tests of the validity of X-ray crystal methods of determining e (Letter-to-editor). Phys. Rev., 50:383.

1937

With V. Bollman. Tests of the validity of X-ray crystal methods of determining e. Phys. Rev., 50:524–37.

With V. Bollman. A determination of h/e from the short wavelength limit of the continuous X-ray spectrum. Phys. Rev., 51:400–29.

With Douglas Marlow. A precision two crystal X-ray spectrometer of wide applicability with worm wheel drive. An improved precise method of equalizing the spacing of worm wheel teeth. Rev. Sci. Instrum., 8:112–21. Also: A method of removing the errors of tooth spacing in high precision worm gears by lapping (unpublished article, detailed description of the technique).

With J. P. Youtz. The thirty kilowatt continuous input X-ray equipment and high constant voltage generating plant of the Watters Memorial Research Laboratory at the California Institute of Technology. Rev. Sci. Instrum., 8:294–307.

With H. A. Kirkpatrick. A direct spectrum of the structure and shift of the Compton line with helium gas as the scatterer. Phys. Rev., 52:875–83.

Theory of the use of more than two successive X-ray crystal reflections to obtain increased resolving power. Phys. Rev., 52:875–83.

Does the formula for the Rydberg constant require revision? Phys. Rev., 52:1251.

1938

The "Palace of Discovery" at the Paris Exposition of 1937. J. Appl. Phys., 9:5.

An approximate method of cutting short circular cylindrical arcs of large radii of curvature in the milling machine. Rev. Sci. Instrum., 9:329.

With V. L. Bollman and H. H. Bailey. Exploratory study of plural X-ray reflection methods applied to the problem of the diffraction pattern of calcite. Phys. Rev., 54:792.

With F. R. Hirsch, Jr. X-ray evidence on the nature of the surface layers of thin ground quartz crystals secured with the Cauchois spectrograph. Phys. Rev., 54:789.

With H. A. Kirkpatrick. Shape of the modified Compton line for hydrogen and Ceylon graphite scatterers. Phys. Rev., 54:802.

With V. Bollman. Further tests of the validity of X-ray crystal methods of determining e. Phys. Rev., 54:1005.

1939

Our present dilemma regarding the values of the natural constants e, m and h. A new graphical method of representation. Phys. Rev., 56:153.

1940

With P. H. Miller. Tests for the validity of the X-ray crystal method for determining N and e with aluminum, silver and quartz. Phys. Rev., 56:198.

With J. P. Youtz. An X-ray method of determining rates of diffusion in the solid state. J. Appl. Phys., 11:357.

A complete isometric consistency chart for the natural constants, e, m, and h. Phys. Rev., 58:457.

1941

Construction of thermodynamic models for elementary teaching. Am. J. Phys., 9 (4):234–37.

1942

With W. K. H. Panofsky and A. E. S. Green. A precision determination of h/e by means of the short wavelength limit of the continuous X-ray spectrum at 20 kv. Phys. Rev., 62:214.

1946

With E. R. Cohen, W. K. H. Panofsky, and E. Deeds. A determination of the wave-forms and laws of propagation and dissipation of ballistic shock-waves. J. Acoust. Soc. Am., 8:97.

1947

A method of correcting low angle X-ray diffraction curves for the study of small particle sizes. Phys. Rev., 72:83–84.

A solid state interpretation of the structure near the limit of the continuous X-ray spectrum. Phys. Rev., 72:276–83.

With D. A. Lind and E. R. Cohen. A precision method of generating circular cylindrical surfaces of large radius of curvature for use in the curved-crystal spectrometer. Rev. Sci. Instrum., 18:617–26.

A high resolving power, curved-crystal focusing spectrometer for short wavelength X-rays and gamma-rays. Rev. Sci. Instrum., 18:626–38.

1948

With E. R. Cohen. Our knowledge of the atomic constants F, N, m, and h in 1947, and of other constants derivable therefrom. Rev. Mod. Phys., 20:82–108.

With D. A. Lind and B. B. Watson. A precision wavelength and energy measurement of gamma-rays from Au^{198} with a focusing quartz crystal spectrometer. Phys. Rev., 73:1392–94.

Erratum: A solid state interpretation of the structure near the limit of the continuous X-ray spectrum. Phys. Rev., 74:1883.

1949

With B. B. Watson, W. J. West, and D. A. Lind. A precision study of the tungsten K spectrum using the 2-meter focusing curved crystal spectrometer. Phys. Rev., 75:505–12.

Conditions for optimum luminosity and energy resolution in an axial β-ray spectrometer with homogeneous magnetic field. Rev. Sci. Instrum., 20:160–69.

Erratum: Conditions for optimum luminosity and energy resolution in axial β-ray spectrometer with homogeneous magnetic field. Rev. Sci. Instrum., 20:616.

With David A. Lind. Design and performance of a multicellular Geiger counter for gamma radiation. Rev. Sci. Instrum., 20:233–35.

Inappreciable effect of Compton shifted scattering, within a gamma-ray source, on precision wavelength determinations with the focusing crystal spectrometer. Phys. Rev., 75:1266.

With D. A. Lind and B. B. Watson. Precision measurement of the wavelength and spectral profile of the annihilation radiation from Cu^{64} with the two-meter focusing curved crystal spectrometer. Phys. Rev., 75:1226–39.

Recent changes and additions in the consistency diagram of the natural atomic constants. Phys. Rev., 75:1267.

With D. A. Lind, J. Brown, D. Klein and D. Muller. Precision measurements of gamma-rays from I^{131} with the two-meter focusing curved crystal spectrometer. Phys. Rev., 75:1544–45.

Erratum: With E. R. Cohen. Our knowledge of the atomic constants, F, N, m, and h in 1947, and of other constants derivable therefrom. Rev. Mod. Phys., 21(4):651–52.

With D. A. Lind and J. R. Brown. Precision wavelength measurements of the 1.1 and 1.3 Mev lines of Co^{60} with the 2-meter focusing curved crystal spectrometer. Phys. Rev., 76:1838–43.

1950

The "1947 Values" of the atomic constants and the revision of the Faraday constant. Phys. Rev., 77:411.

Point-focus X-ray monochromators for low angle diffraction. Rev. Sci. Instrum., 21:188–89.

With D. A. Lind and W. J. West. X-ray and gamma-ray reflection properties from 500 x-units to nine x-units of unstressed and of bent quartz plates for use in the two-meter curved crystal focusing gamma-ray spectrometer. Phys. Rev., 77:475.

With David A. Lind. Measuring gamma-ray wavelengths. Off. Nav. Res. (U.S.) Res. Rev., 10:10–21.

Erratum: With D. A. Lind and J. W. West. X-ray and gamma-ray reflection properties from 500 x-units to nine x-units of unstressed and of bent quartz plates. Phys. Rev., 78:474.

With E. R. Cohen. Least-squares adjustment of atomic constants as of December 1950. Report to the NRC Committee on constants and conversion factors of physics.

1951

With E. R. Cohen. Non-independent observational equations in the theory of least squares. Phys. Rev., 81:162.

The masses of the negative and positive electrons. Phys. Rev., 81:468.

With E. R. Cohen. Least-squares adjusted values of the atomic constants as of December 1950. Phys. Rev., 82:555.

1952

With E. R. Cohen. Probable values of the physical constants. In: *Lange's Handbook of Chemistry*, ed. N. A. Lange and G. M. Forker, 8th ed. Athens, Ohio: Handbook Publishing.

With E. R. Cohen. Recent advances in our knowledge of the numerical values of the fundamental atomic constants. Am. Sci., 40:447–67.

With W. E. Danielson and L. Shenfil. A point focusing X-ray monochromator for the study of low angle diffraction. J. Appl. Phys., 23:454–65.

With J. N. Harris. A precision Megohm ratio unit for high voltage measurements. Rev. Sci. Instrum., 23:404–13.

With E. R. Cohen. The Rydberg constant and the atomic mass of the electron. Phys. Rev., 88:353–60.

With D. W. Muller, H. C. Hoyt, and D. J. Klein. Precision measurements of nuclear γ-ray wavelengths of Ir^{192}, Ta^{182}, RaTh, Rn, W^{187}, Cs^{137}, Au^{198}, and annihilation radiation. Phys. Rev., 88:775–93.

Improvements in the precision of beta-ray spectroscopy. Phys. Today, 5(12):10–13.

Higher precision in nuclear spectroscopy. Phys. Today, 5:13.

Improvements in the precision of beta-ray spectroscopy. Phys. Today, 5:10.

1953

With B. Henke. Low angle X-ray diffraction with long wavelengths. Phys. Rev., 89:1300.

With H. C. Hoyt and J. J. Murray. Comparison of gamma-ray reflections from the (550) and (310) planes of quartz. Phys. Rev., 90:169.

With E. R. Cohen. The basis for the criterion of least squares. Rev. Mod. Phys., 25:109–13.

With E. R. Cohen. Least-squares adjustment of the atomic constants, 1952. Rev. Mod. Phys., 25:691–708.

With H. C. Hoyt. Gamma radiation following decay of I^{131}. Phys. Rev., 91:1027.

With H. C. Hoyt, P. E. Marmier, and J. J. Murray. The decay of Ta^{183}. Phys. Rev., 92:202.

With G. L. Felt and J. N. Harris. A precision measurement at 24500 volts of the conversion constant, V. Phys. Rev., 92:1160–75.

1954

With E. R. Cohen. Variety of our sources of information on Avogadro's number and other constants. Phys. Rev., 94:1790.

With F. Boehm and P. Marmier. Gamma transitions in W^{182}. Phys. Rev., 95:864.

With P. Snelgrove and J. El-Hussaini. Corrected values of tungsten K-series X-ray wavelengths with the 2-meter curved crystal diffraction spectrometer. Phys. Rev., 95:1203–4.

With P. E. Marmier and D. W. Berriman. New point-focusing monochromator. Rev. Sci. Instrum., 25:1219.

With P. Duwez and D. B. Wittry. Design and development of an electronic X-ray probe for the study of alloys and the structure of metals. Unpublished Technical Report No. 1, Dept. of the Army Contract D. A. -04-495-Ord-463 D/A Project No. 593-08-024. Ord. Project No. %B4-161A. Pasadena, Cal.: California Institute of Technology.

The spectroscopy of nuclear gamma rays by direct crystal diffraction methods. Report to Office of Naval Research, then Atomic Energy Commission. Office of Naval Research, Special Technical Report No. 28, Contract N60NR-244, T. O. IV (NR 017-602) AEC Special Technical Report No. 8, Contract No. AT(04-3)-8. Pasadena, Cal.: California Institute of Technology.

1955

With P. Marmier and F. Boehm. Energy levels of Hf^{177}. Phys. Rev., 97:102–4.

Crystal diffraction spectroscopy of nuclear gamma-rays. In: *Beta and Gamma-Ray Spectroscopy*, ed S. K. Siegbahn, pp. 100–131. Amsterdam: North-Holland Publishing.

With E. R. Cohen. The fundamental constants of atomic physics. In: *Handbuch der Physik*, vol. 35, pp. 1–87. Berlin: Springer-Verlag.

With E. R. Cohen. Physical constants, values of October 1955. In: *Fundamental Formulas of Physics*, ed. Donald H. Menzel, pp. 145a–54a. N.Y.: Dover Publications.

With J. J. Murray, F. Boehm, and P. Marmier. Decays of Ta^{182} and Ta^{183}. Phys. Rev., 95:1007–16.

With E. R. Cohen. Comments on Straumanis' concepts regarding Avogadro's number. Phys. Rev., 98:1128–29.

With B. Henke. Submicroscopic structure determination by long wave-length X-ray diffraction. J. Appl. Phys., 26:903–17.

With J. S. Rollett, T. W. Layton, and E. R. Cohen. Analysis of variance of the 1952 data on the atomic constants and a new adjustment, 1955. Rev. Mod. Phys., 27:363–80.

With D. W. Berriman. Single quartz crystal point-focusing X-ray monochromator. Rev. Sci. Instrum., 26:1048–52.

The spectroscopy of nuclear gamma rays by direct crystal diffraction methods. Ergeb. Exakten Naturwiss., 28:232–301.

With L. L. Baggerly, P. Marmier, and F. Boehm. Decay of Ir^{192}. Phys. Rev., 100:1364–67.

With P. Marmier and F. Boehm. Energy levels of Hf^{177}. Phys. Rev., 97:103–4.

With P. E. Marmier and H. E. Henrikson. Final report on beta-ray spectroscopy. Office of Ordnance Research Contract No. D.A.-04-495-Ord.-444. Dept. of Army Project No. 599-01-004. Ordnance Research and Development Project No. TB2-0001. OOR Project 931, California Institute of Technology. Report prepared at the date that sponsorship of this project was taken over by the US Atomic Energy Commission.

With J. S. Rollett and T. W. Layton. Datatron digital computer program for least-squares analyses of variance. Unpublished US Atomic Energy Commission Special Technical Report No. 18, Contract No. AT(04-3)-63, US AEC. Pasadena, Cal.: California Institute of Technology.

With D. W. Berriman. A single quartz crystal point focusing X-ray monochromator. Unpublished paper read at the National Academy of Sciences, November 3, 1955.

1956

With E. R. Cohen. Standard errors of the residues in a least-squares analysis. Phys. Rev., 101:1641–42.

With F. Boehm and P. Marmier. Gamma transitions in Ta^{181}. Phys. Rev., 103:342–43.

With E. R. Cohen. Need for upward revision of λ_g/λ_s and its consequences. Phys. Rev., 103:1583.

With E. R. Cohen and K. M. Crowe. Pion and muon masses. Phys. Rev., 104:266–67.

With F. Boehm and P. Marmier. Gamma transitions in Ta^{181}. Phys. Rev., 103:342–43.

With E. N. Hatch, F. Boehm, and P. Marmier. Rotational and intrinsic levels in Tm^{169} and Lu^{175}. Phys. Rev., 104:745–52.

With E. R. Cohen. Probable values of the physical constants. In: *Lange's Handbook of Chemistry*, ed. N. A. Lange, 9th ed. Athens, Ohio: Handbook Publishing.

With Robert L. Shacklett. A precision measurement of the L_{II}-L_{III} X-ray energy level difference in some heavy elements and a comparison with the predictions of the Schawalow-Townes theory of the nuclear size effect. Unpublished special technical report No. 23 under Contract No. AT(04-3)-63 with the US Atomic Energy Commission. Pasadena, Cal.: California Institute of Technology.

With H. E. Henrikson. The design, construction and performance of a magnetic focusing, semi-circular, low energy, beta-ray spectrometer. Unpublished special technical report No. 24, Contract AT(04-3)-63 with the US Atomic Energy Commission. Pasadena, Cal.: California Institute of Technology.

1957

With F. Boehm and P. Marmier. Isomer in iridium-193. Phys. Rev., 105:974–76.

With E. N. Hatch and F. Boehm. Rotational spectrum of Tm^{171}. Phys. Rev., 108:113–15.

With R. L. Shacklett. Precision measurement of X-ray fine structure: Effects of nuclear size and quantum electrodynamics. Phys. Rev., 106: 501–12.

Present sources of precise information on the universal physical constants. Nuovo Cimento Suppl., VI(X,1):69–109.

Mathematical analysis of the universal physical constants. Nuovo Cimento Suppl., VI(X,1):110–40.

With E. L. Chupp, A. F. Clark, F. J. Gordon, and H. Mark. Precision determination of the low-lying energy levels of W^{182}, W^{183}, W^{184}, and W^{186}. Phys. Rev., 107:745–50.

Gamma-ray spectroscopy by means of bent crystal diffraction. Proceedings of Rehovoth Conference on Nuclear Structure.

With D. B. Wittry. An electron probe for local analysis by means of X-rays. Interim technical report No. 5, Department of the Army, Contract DA-04-495-Ord.-463, Project No. T.B. 2-0001, Office of Ordnance Research Project No. 1609. Pasadena, Cal.: California Institute of Technology.

1958

Gamma-ray spectroscopy by direct crystal diffraction. Annu. Rev. Nucl. Sci., 8:163–80.

With E. L. Chupp, F. J. Gordon, R. C. Jopson, and H. Mark. Precision determination of some energy levels in Fe^{57}, Zn^{67}, and Tc^{99}. Phys. Rev., 109:6.

With J. J. Merrill. Precision measurement of the LX-ray spectra of uranium and plutonium. Phys. Rev., 110:79–84.

With R. L. Shacklett. Nuclear size estimates from X-ray fine structure measurements. Rev. Mod. Phys., 30:521–27.

With E. R. Cohen. Changes in the 1955 atomic constants occasioned by revision of μ_e/μ_0. Phys. Rev. Lett., 1:8.

With E. L. Chupp, F. J. Gordon, R. C. Jopson, and H. Mark. Precision determination of nuclear energy levels in heavy elements. Phys. Rev., 112:518–31.

With E. L. Chupp, F. J. Gordon, R. C. Jopson, and H. Mark. Precision determination of gamma-rays following (p, p', γ) and (p, n, γ) reactions. Phys. Rev., 112:532–35.

With E. L. Chupp, F. J. Gordon, B. C. Jopson, and H. Mark. K series X-ray wavelengths in rare earth elements. Phys. Rev., 112:1183–86.

With E. L. Chupp and H. Mark. Measurement of high energy gamma-rays with a photographic bent crystal spectrograph. Rev. Sci. Instrum., 29:1153–54.

Present status of precise information on the universal physical constants. Has the time arrived for their adoption to replace our present arbitrary conventional standards? IRE Trans. Instrum., I-7(3 & 4):136–75.

1959

A survey of our present sources of information on the conversion constant, $\Lambda(=\lambda_g/\lambda_s)$ and the absolute wavelengths of X-ray emission lines. Proc. Natl. Acad. Sci. USA, 45(7):1052–80.

With W. E. Dibble. Many-particle cooperative scattering of X-rays in the two-crystal spectrometer. Phys. Rev. Lett., 3(3):131–32.

Status of knowledge of the fundamental constants of physics and chemistry as of January 1959. Ann. Phys., 7:4.

Electronic charge (e), determination of, pp. 774–77; Electronic charge-to-mass, (e/m), pp. 777–78; Electronic charge-to-mass ratio (e/m), determination of, pp. 778–79; Fundamental constants of atomic physics, pp. 319–24; and Gamma-ray spectroscopy, pp. 381–87. In: *Encyclopedic Dictionary of Physics.* N.Y.: Pergamon Press.

1960

Compton effect. In: *McGraw-Hill Encyclopedia of Science and Technology,* vol. 3, pp. 353–59. N.Y.: McGraw-Hill.

With C. J. Gallagher, Jr., W. F. Edwards, and G. Manning. The W^{187} decay scheme and possible vibrational levels in an odd-mass nucleus. Nucl. Phys., 19:18–39.

With J. Everitt. A circular-arc-shaped slit with fixed center and continuously adjustable radius for the analysis of circularly symmetric low-angle X-ray diffraction patterns. Ann. Phys., 11:49–64.

Absence of dispersion properties of space for electromagnetic radiation tested to $\pm 14 \times 10^{-5}$. Comments on a proposal of Softky and Squire. Proc. Natl. Acad. Sci. USA, 47:347–48.

1961

With A. H. Muir and F. Boehm. Nuclear spectroscopy of Ta^{181}. Phys. Rev., 122:1564–73.

With W. F. Edwards and F. Boehm. Decay of Hf^{180}. Phys. Rev., 121:1499–503.

With W. F. Edwards and C. J. Gallagher, Jr. Decay of Se^{75}. Nucl. Phys., 26:649.

With W. F. Edwards and F. Boehm. An intensity calibration of the two-meter curved crystal spectrometer. Nucl. Phys., 6:670–80.

With E. J. Seppi. Nuclear gamma-ray spectroscopy by crystal diffraction. Hilger J., 6(3):1–8.

With J. J. Merrill. Precision measurement of L X-ray wavelengths and line widths for $74 \leq Z \leq 95$ and their interpretation in terms of nuclear perturbations. Ann. Phys., 14:166–228.

With E. J. Seppi, H. Henrikson, and F. Boehm. A germanium bent-crystal monochromator for nuclear spectroscopy. Nucl. Instrum. Methods, 16:17–28.

With E. R. Cohen and A. G. McNish. *International Tables of X-Ray Crystallography* (physical and chemical tables), vol. III. 2.1. Constants and units, elements and their properties. 2.1.1. List of some universal physical constants. (Values corrected to 1961.)

With E. U. Condon and H. Odishaw. Fundamental constants of atomic physics. In: *Handbook of Physics,* pp. 7-143–7-173. N.Y.: McGraw-Hill.

1962

With E. J. Seppi and F. Boehm. Nuclear resonance excitation using a diffraction monochromator. Phys. Rev., 128:2334.

With F. Boehm and R. Brockmeier. Intrinsic quadrupole moments in W^{183}. Proceedings Uppsala Meeting of May 27.

1963

With P. Alexander and F. Boehm. Properties of some states in Dy^{160}. Nucl. Phys., 41:553.

With P. Alexander and F. Boehm. Properties of nuclear energy levels in Tm^{169}. Nucl. Phys., 46:108.

With W. E. Dibble. Design and construction of a Berreman-type point-focusing X-ray monochromator for use in low-angle scattering studies. J. Ultrastruct. Res., 9:419–44.

With E. J. Seppi, H. E. Henrikson, and F. Boehm. Design of a germanium bent-crystal diffraction monochromator and its application in nuclear spectroscopy. J. Sci. Ind. Res. India, 22:29–43.

Optimization of parameters in a Siegbahn-Svartholm-type $\sqrt{2}\,\pi$ double focusing internally converted β-ray spectrometer. Sixth Technical Progress Report, National Science Board Grant P-963. Unpublished.

1964

With E. R. Cohen. Present status of our knowledge of the numerical values of the fundamental physical constants. In: *Proceedings of the Second International Conference on Nuclidic Masses,* ed. Walter H. Johnson, Jr., pp. 152–86. Vienna: Springer-Verlag.

With E. N. Hatch. Concerning bent-crystal spectrometer measurements of KαX-rays from radioactive sources. Z. Phys., 177:337.

With P. Alexander, F. Boehm, and E. Kankeleit. Spin-23/2- isomer of Lu^{177}. Phys. Rev. B, 133:284.

With P. Alexander. Properties of gamma transitions in the decays of Sm^{153} and Gd^{153} into Eu^{153}. Phys. Rev. B, 134:499.

The increasing importance of high precision measurements in physics and physical chemistry; 1963 values of the fundamental constants. Sci. Humanity.

Symposium on crystal diffraction of nuclear gamma rays. The National Technical University, Athens, Greece. Privately circulated report, 316 pp.

A complete list of all gamma-ray energies measured with the Mark I, 2-meter, bent crystal diffraction gamma-ray spectrometer at CIT. Unpublished.

With P. Alexander and H. E. Henrikson. Design and construction of a 35 cm radius $\sqrt{2}\,\pi$ iron-free beta spectrometer. Final report to the National Science Foundation, Grant GP-963.

1965

With E. R. Cohen. Our knowledge of the fundamental constants of physics and chemistry in 1965. Rev. Mod. Phys., 37(4):537–94.

Pilgrims' progress in search of the fundamental constants. Phys. Today, 18(10):26–43.

With R. J. Brockmeier, S. Wahlborn, E. J. Seppi, and F. Boehm. Coriolis coupling between rotational bands in the nucleus W^{183}. Nucl. Phys., 63:102.

With W. F. Edwards, F. Boehm, J. Rogers, and E. J. Seppi. Relative intensities of gamma rays following the decay of Ta^{182} and Ta^{183}. Nucl. Phys., 63:97.

With P. Alexander and R. S. Hager. High-resolution measurements of internal conversion lines in W^{183}. Phys. Rev. B, 139:288.

Where do we go from here in X-rays: a brief review of recent research trends. Unpublished contribution read and distributed on June 22, 1965 at the International Symposium on X-rays at Cornell University, Ithaca, N.Y. 20 pp., 8 figs.

With J. J. Reidy, A. B. Miller, and M. L. Wiedenbeck. The curved crystal spectrometer at the University of Michigan. (A preprint.)

1966

The present key importance of the fine structure constant, α, to a better knowledge of all the fundamental physical constants. Z. Naturforsch. A, 21:70–79.

With E. R. Cohen. A review of recent work in the determination of fundamental physical constants. Nuovo Cimento Suppl., 4(I):839–62.

1967

With E. R. Cohen. The problem of determining most probable values of the fundamental constants of physics. Kosmos.

With H. A. Kirkpatrick and E. R. Cohen. Remeasurement of the conversion constant, Λ. In: *Proceedings of the Third International Conference on Atomic Masses,* pp. 347–82. Winnipeg: Univ. of Manitoba Press.

With H. A. Kirkpatrick. A 42-foot grazing incidence vacuum spectrograph. J. Q. Spectros. Radiat. Trans., 2:715–24.

1968

With E. C. Seltzer. The iron-free magnetic beta-ray spectrometer. Eng. Sci., 31(6):15–18.

With E. R. Cohen. Experiments on atomic constants and the numerical value of the Sommerfield fine structure constant. In: *Proceedings of the Symposium on Physics of One and Two Electron Atoms,* pp. 117–38. Amsterdam: North-Holland Publishing.

Introduction. In: Robert Andrews Millikan, *Electron; Its Isolation, Measurements and the Determination of Some of its Properties.* Ed. J. W. M. DuMond. Chicago: Univ. of Chicago Press.

With E. R. Cohen. The status of the fundamental physical constants in 1968. Unpublished informal progress report to the Joint Commission on Atomic Masses.

1970

The unsuitability of a long-accepted method for the precise normalization of X-ray characteristic wavelengths in fundamental units: The method of comparison spectroscopy using a ruled grating at grazing incidence. Privately circulated communication.

With E. L. Chupp, A. F. Clark, F. J. Gordon and H. Mark. Precision determination of the low-lying energy levels of W^{182}, W^{183}, W^{184}, and W^{186}. Report to US Atomic Energy Commission, contract No. W-7405-eng-48 of the University of California Radiation Laboratory, Livermore Site.

LUIGI GORINI

November 13, 1903 – August 13, 1976

BY JONATHAN BECKWITH
AND
DAN FRAENKEL

LUIGI GORINI, professor in the Department of Microbiology and Molecular Genetics at Harvard Medical School and a member of the National Academy of Sciences, died August 13, 1976. He was born on November 13, 1903 in Milan, Italy. His father was a microbiologist. Luigi obtained his first degree from the University of Pavia in 1925; his thesis (1925) was in organic chemistry, but his interest was in biology. He continued his studies in organic chemistry, but he was to publish only four papers in the next twenty years.

In 1931 the Italian government moved to control the universities by requiring a Fascist oath. Luigi described this period in a speech at Montana State University on February 10, 1970.

> The first uproar was *no* unanimously—we will never do that. But then came second thoughts, the rationalization: we scientists should not be involved in politics, we should not permit that others, worse than us, would take our responsibilities, etc. At the end, we were about one hundred *no's* out of about 10,000 university people. And so we quit. It was not an easy thing to do, not only materially but especially for the spirit. We, the one percent, started a double life, political underground for our soul and professional marginal for our belly. I discovered very quickly that the ability to convey opinions, to convince others, was not a gift that I had, so I did my underground work which may look romantically wonderful in retrospect, but seen from inside was a day by day realization of inefficiency.

The next ten years were spent in Turin in a succession of small pharmaceutical houses where his politics, which were Socialist, were tolerated. The work was research, development, and quality control. In these years he was married and had two children. His son from this marriage, Jan, is now following a career of research in immunology in the Laboratory of Radiation Pathology, Casaccia-Rome, and his daughter, Isa, is now a biochemist in Milan. The external circumstances of his life were relatively comfortable.

When the war came, Luigi refused induction and went partially underground with the assumed name Carlo Cattaneo. Cattaneo was a nineteenth century Italian patriot and opponent of the monarchy who edited a journal of science and politics. Luigi avoided arrest when the police came for him in 1942 and escaped to Milan, where he found work in a very small research institute (Istituto Giuliana Ronzoni) owned by an anti-Fascist industrialist. There he met Annamaria Torriani, who had just finished her studies. She was to be his colleague in the laboratory and in the resistance, and later his wife. They had one son, Daniel, who is now eighteen and a student at Rhode Island School of Design.

In the resistance, Luigi was involved in the collection and distribution of news among several cities. He also carried food, medicines, and documents to the partisans in the mountains above Milan. Although a pacifist and nominally unarmed, one of his occasional duties was to collect money. This meant going to the prospective contributor, taking out a gun, and explaining the advantages of supporting the cause.

When Milan was liberated (April 25, 1945), the Socialist party gave Luigi the task of taking over a property in the mountains at Selvino which had been a summer camp for children of Fascists. The most needy at the time were Jewish children from the liberated concentration camps who had begun to appear in Milan. Luigi and Annamaria decided to use Selvino for them. In the next three years it served as a rehabilitation center for about a thousand children. They were from several countries of origin, and ranged from three-year-olds to teenagers. Selvino was to help rebuild their confidence prior to their emigration to Palestine. Luigi was nominally the administrator, but mainly a friend and counsellor. At the same time he was doing scientific work at the Institute in Milan. In 1976 Luigi and Annamaria were honored by the government of Israel for their work at Selvino, and an account of these activities was placed in the Martyrs and Heroes Archives at Yad-Vashem, Israel.

The last group of children left for Israel in 1948. Meanwhile, Luigi's academic title had been restored, but only at its former level as beginning assistant. Annamaria went to the Pasteur Institute in Paris. Her work there together with Melvin Cohn and Jacques Monod is well known (she is now a professor of biology at Massachusetts Institute of Technology). Luigi joined the laboratory of Claude Fromageot at the Sorbonne as a member of the CNRS (Centre National Recherche Scientifique), and he soon was independent.

Over the next seven years there were seventeen papers published dealing with aspects of bacterial proteolysis and the biochemistry of extracellular enzymes. Much of this work was on the mechanism of protection of various bacterial proteases by ions such as calcium and manganese. He and his coworkers were able to show that the metal ions protected these enzymes against autodigestion by stabilizing particular protein conformations. This work had wide impact in that it provided a strong suggestion that proteins do not have unique folding patterns, but can exist in several different stable states. This work was a continuation of his earlier interests in microbiology, and its quality was recognized early by the award of the Kronauer Prize (1949, University of Paris).

The work on physiology of proteolysis led to the discovery in 1954 of an unusual bacterial growth factor, catechol. Bernard Davis, who was then interested in aromatic biosynthesis, invited Luigi to his Department of Pharmacology at New York University. In 1957, Luigi joined the Department of Bacteriology and Immunology at Harvard Medical School, of which Dr. Davis had become head.

Soon after arriving in New York, Luigi, working together with Werner Maas, made a fundamental discovery in bacterial regulation. It was known at the time that some bacterial enzymes in sugar degradative pathways were inducible. There were also indications of regulation of enzyme synthesis in biosynthetic pathways, since the level of such enzymes was somewhat lower when the end-product was available than when it had to be made. Gorini and Maas showed that if partial starvation of the end-product of the pathway was arranged—they used an arginine-limited chemostat—the rate of synthesis of an enzyme in the arginine pathway became high (derepression). This phenomenon, "bacteria in overdrive," showed that enzyme synthesis in biosynthetic pathways was variable over a wide range, somehow responding to the endogenous level of end-product. This finding had a profound impact on thinking about regulation of gene expression and played a major role in the development of the concept of the repressor. Kenneth Schaffner, who has reviewed the early history of this field, puts it this way:

> Arthur Pardee recalls that the short paper by Gorini and Maas particularly "attracted attention" because it was "simply presented." . . . The demonstration, particularly striking in the case of Gorini's and Maas' experiment, that elimination of the repressing metabolite could result in a rapid and continued rate of constitutive enzyme synthesis, suggested . . . that inducible systems might perhaps be analyzed by a similar mechanism of negative control. . . .*

---

*K. Schaffner, "Logic of Discovery and Justification in Regulatory Genetics," *Studies in the History and Philosophy of Science*, 4 (4) (1974):349–85.

At Harvard the arginine pathway was Luigi's main research for some years. His group was concerned early with sorting out the physiological role of the derepression phenomenon from the other mechanism controlling flow in the pathway, end-product inhibition of the first enzyme. Luigi was interested in whether the system might really function by a combination of induction and repression and eventually established that apparent strain differences in regulation reflected differences in repressor protein only. Luigi and his co-workers continued to publish work on the regulation of the arginine biosynthetic genes until his death.

In 1964 Luigi and his colleagues published the first of a long series of papers on bacterial ribosomes that were to dramatically change the thinking of biologists about the function of the ribosomes. Up until that time, it was thought that all the specificity of translation of the genetic code lay in the interaction between transfer RNA and messenger RNA. Ribosomes were seen as passive templates upon which this process took place. In 1961 Gorini, Gundersen, and Berger noticed the peculiarity that an arginine auxotroph in the presence of a streptomycin-resistant mutation could be restored to prototrophy by the addition of streptomycin to the growth medium. Rather than ignoring this finding as one often does with peculiar observations, Luigi followed it up, and in 1964 he and Eva Kataja presented evidence that streptomycin was altering the specificity of translation via an interaction with the ribosome. (There already existed evidence that streptomycin acted on the ribosome.) From this they suggested that "the ribosomal structure could include the accuracy of the reading of the code during translation."* There quickly followed work in collaboration with Drs. Julian Davies and Walter Gilbert providing direct *in vitro* confirmation of this proposal.

* Luigi Gorini and E. Kataja, "Phenotypic Repair by Streptomycin of Defective Genotypes in *E. coli, Proceedings of the National Academy of Sciences* (USA), 51:487–93.

Luigi proceeded over the next twelve years to develop a new field: the study of factors influencing the fidelity of translation of the genetic code. The influence of ribosomal mutations was extensively studied. Certain mutations to drug resistance, which affected a ribosomal protein, were found to decrease drug-dependent misreading. Other mutations in the same protein caused total dependence on streptomycin for growth in any medium. It appeared that the ribosome was then so distorted as to function usefully only in the presence of an agent causing translational ambiguity. A new type of ribosome mutation, "ram" (ribosomal ambiguity), was discovered which increased misreading even in the absence of antibiotics.

Much work followed on the types of mutations corrected by misreading. While initially it appeared that chain-terminating (nonsense) mutations were the only ones affected, work from Luigi's laboratory subsequently showed that the translation of missense and even frame-shift mutations could be changed by alteration of the ribosome. Further, altered transfer RNA molecules appeared particularly sensitive to ribosomal mutations.

Luigi also had characteristically original ideas about other aspects of antibiotic action, such as the possibility that streptomycin might bind to RNA directly and affect ribosome assembly. In some of his last work, evidence was obtained for a link between mutations affecting the ribosome and mutations in RNA polymerase, suggesting that there may be unexplored levels of interaction between transcription and translation.

All this work, of course, was done with a long succession of collaborators—graduate and medical students, postdoctoral fellows, and other visitors. But Luigi always worked in the laboratory himself. He arrived first in the morning and was not above looking at his colleagues' experiments before they came in themselves. He was blessed with a remarkable vitality. The whole story of ribosomal suppression was discovered when he was in his sixties, and even after his formal retirement at seventy the work continued with fifteen papers. Luigi's science was well recognized. He became an American Cancer Society Professor (1964), received Harvard's Ledlie Prize (1965), and was elected to membership in the National Academy of Sciences (1971).

But it was not only science that he discussed with his colleagues; it was more often politics or literature. He slept little and was extraordinarily well organized. He read the local papers and the *New York Times, The New York Review, The Guardian, Le Monde,* and *Jerusalem Post* weeklies as well as books they mentioned, and that is what he talked about, often indignantly, passionately, always interestingly.

He had an unusually genuine and strong sense of outrage over injustice and inequality. He was particularly concerned about the plight of minority groups in this country and of third world peoples in general. Luigi accepted many invitations to speak at black southern colleges, taking these opportunities to actively oppose the pseudoscientific theories that were used to support racism. For instance, in a talk at Southern University on February 21, 1974, referring to genetic theories of inequality:

> All this nonsense could be disregarded as no more than science fiction in bad taste if it were not the fact that in this way science is dangerously and irresponsibly misused to justify the right to power and wealth for the benefit of only a few racial groups, or families, or individuals, no matter what were the means these groups or their ancestors used to acquire their present dominant position in society.

Luigi was heavily involved in anti-Vietnam War activities, and when Henry Kissinger was awarded the Nobel Prize for Peace in 1973, Luigi organized a petition protesting the award. The petition was sent to the Nobel Committee and received publicity in this country.

His attitudes toward science and the role of scientists in society influenced many around him. This influence is exemplified by a paragraph from the Ph.D. thesis acknowledgement of one of his students, Dirk Elseviers.

> Luigi Gorini directed my work in Boston. His creativity, enthusiasm and energy are a constant stimulus for everybody around him. He has taught me that the satisfaction in doing science lies in doing it and in nothing else. [But] above all that it is of capital importance to keep in touch with reality; our lives are in the hands of politicians and not of Science. I really like him.

And in Luigi's own words, again from his speech at Montana State University:

> My job here tonight is to make you realize that for me, like for hundreds of us scientists, my own scientific interest means a lot intellectually but, morally speaking, science alone does not satisfy entirely my conscience. I will try to be the most unequivocal radical possible and at the same time constructive, so that when I quit, your opinion about me should not be similar to that expressed a long time ago by the fascist Italian police about someone whom I know after his first confrontation with them. He was very happy to be released, for a time at least, but a few years later he discovered by chance the written motivation for letting him out and he was really not satisfied. The police file sounds like the following: "Lonely anarchist; he is not dangerous."

When he "quit," Luigi left behind him a spirit of rigorous scientific curiosity and social conscience which has affected many of those who were close to him.

HONORS AND DISTINCTIONS

ACADEMIC POSITIONS

1946–1949	In charge of Department of Biochemistry, Instituto Scientifico di Chimica e Biochimica Giuliana Ronzoni, Milan, Italy
1949–1951	Attaché de Recherches, Centre National Recherche Scientifique, Laboratoire de Chimie Biologique, Sorbonne, Paris, France
1951–1954	Chargé de Recherches, Centre National Recherche Scientifique, Laboratoire de Chimie Biologique, Sorbonne, Paris, France
1954–1955	Maître de Recherches, Centre National Recherche Scientifique, Laboratoire de Chimie Biologique, Sorbonne, Paris, France
1955–1957	Visiting Researcher, Department of Pharmacology, College of Medicine, New York University, New York
1957–1962	Lecturer, Department of Bacteriology and Immunology, Harvard Medical School, Boston, Massachusetts
1962–1964	American Cancer Society Associate Professor, Department of Bacteriology and Immunology, Harvard Medical School
1964– June 30, 1974	American Cancer Society Professor, Department of Microbiology and Molecular Genetics, Harvard Medical School
July 1, 1974	Professor Emeritus, Department of Microbiology and Molecular Genetics, Harvard Medical School

HONORS

1925	Highest *cum laude* honors awarded by the University of Pavia
1927	Prize for Advancement in Organic Chemistry awarded by the Politecnico of Milan
1949	Prize Kronauer awarded by Faculté des Sciences, Sorbonne, Paris
1963	Elected to the American Academy of Arts and Sciences

1965   Ledlie Prize awarded by Harvard University
1971   Elected to the National Academy of Sciences

PROFESSIONAL AND HONORARY SOCIETIES

American Society for Microbiology
Federation of American Societies for Experimental Biology
Society of General Physiologists
American Society of Biological Chemists
American Association for the Advancement of Science

BIBLIOGRAPHY

1924

Analogia di Costituzione tra il fenantrene ed il 2-N-fenil-α, β-Naftotriazolchinone. Ph.D. thesis, Ist Chimica Generale Universita di Pavia.

With A. Dansi. Intorno all'azione delle sostanze coloranti sulla sensibilita della gelatina-bromuro d'argento. I) Rivista Fotografica Italiana (April): 1–36.

1925

With A. Dansi. Intorno all'azione delle sostanze coloranti sulla sensibilita della gelatina-bromuro d'argento. II) Rivista Fotografica Italiana (June):3–8.

With G. Charier and A. Manfredi. Sul 2-Nofenil [α,β] nafto-1-2-3-triazolchinone. Gazz. Chim. Ital., 56:196–207.

1933

Azionone della trimetilamina su l'esametidiaminoisopropanolo dioduro. Gazz. Chim. Ital., 63:751–56.

1935

With C. Gorini. Ulteriori richerche sulle proteasi degli acidoproteolitici. Rend. R. Ist. Lomb. Sci. Lett., 68:115–25.

1938

Ancora sul sistema proteasico degli acidoproteolitici. Rend. R. Ist. Lomb. Sci. Lett., 72:133–46.

Sulle proteasi degli acidoproteolitici. Enzymologia, 10:192–202.

1946

With A. Torriani. Sulla purificazione della penicillinase da Bacterium Coli. Boll. Soc. Ital. Biol. Sper., 22:1.

1947

With A. Torriani. Biochemistry of *Escherichia coli* and the production of penicillinase. Nature, 160:332–33.

1948

With A. Torriani. Action de la penicilline sur l'activité protéolytique des bactéries acido-protéolytiques. Biochim. Biophys. Acta, 2:226–38.

1949

With Cl. Fromageot. Une protéinase bactérienne (*Micrococcus lysodeikticus*) nécessitant l'ion calcium pour son fonctionnement. C. R. Acad. Sci., 229:559–61.

1950

With Cl. Fromageot. Les facteurs physiologiques conditionnant la présence de protéinase dans les cultures de *Micrococcus lysodeikticus*. Biochim. Biophys. Acta, 5:524–34.

Le rôle du calcium dans l'activité et la stabilité de quelques protéinases bactériennes. Biochim. Biophys. Acta, 6:237–55.

1951

Rôle du calcium dans le systeme trypsine-serumalbumine. Biochim. Biophys. Acta, 7:318–34.

With L. Audrain. Nécessité du calcium dans la croissance de bactéries lorsque la source d'azote est une protéine pure. Biochim. Biophys. Acta, 6:477–86.

With M. Grevier. Le comportement de la protéinase endocellulaire de *Micrococcus lysodeikticus* au cours de la lyse de cet organisme par le lysozyme. Biochim. Biophys. Acta, 7:291–95.

1952

With L. Audrain. Influence du calcium sur la stabilité du complex trypsine-ovomucoide. Biochim. Biophys. Acta, 8:702–3.

With L. Audrain. Action de quelques métaux bivalents sur la sensibilité de la serumalbumine à l'action de la trypsine. Biochim. Biophys. Acta, 9:180–92.

With L. Audrain. Influence du zinc sur la stabilité de la plasmine. Biochim. Biophys. Acta, 9:337–38.

1953

With F. Felix. Influence du manganèse sur la stabilité du lysozyme. I. Influence du manganèse sur la vitesse d'inactivation irrever-

sible du lysozyme par la chaleur. Biochim. Biophys. Acta, 10:128–35.
With L. Audrain. Le complexe ovomucoide-trypsine. Son activité protéolytique et le role de quelques métaux dans la stabilité de ses constituents. Biochim. Biophys. Acta, 10:570–79.
With F. Felix. Sur le mécanisme de protection de la trypsine par Ca^{++} ou Mn^{++}. Biochim. Biophys. Acta, 11:535–42.
With F. Felix and Cl. Fromageot. Influence du manganèse sur la stabilité du lysozyme. II. Role protecteur du manganèse lors de l'hydrolyse du lysozyme par la trypsine. Biochim. Biophys. Acta, 12:283–88.

1954

With J. Labouesse-Mercouroff. Sur les facteurs conditionnant l'activité enzymatique de la carboxypeptidase. Biochim. Biophys. Acta, 13:291–93.
With G. Lanzavecchia. Recherches sur le mécanisme du production d'une protéinase bactérienne. I. Nouvelle technique de détermination d'une protéinase par la coagulation du lait. Biochim. Biophys. Acta, 14:407–14.
With G. Lanzavecchia. Recherches sur le mécanisme de production d'une protéinase bactérienne. II. Mise en evidence d'un zymogène précurseur de la protéinase de *Coccus P*. Biochim. Biophys. Acta, 15:399–410.

1956

With R. Lord. Necessité des orthodiphenols pour la croissance de *Coccus P (Sarcina Sp.)*. Biochim. Biophys. Acta, 19:84–90.
With L. Audrain. Relations entre degré de dénaturation et sensibilité à la trypsine de la serumalbumine. Influence de Ca^{++} et de Mn^{++} et rôle des ponts disulfure. Biochim. Biophys. Acta, 19:289–96.

1957

With W. K. Maas. End-product control for the formation of a biosynthetic enzyme. Fed. Proc. Fed. Am. Soc. Exp. Biol., 16:215.
With W. K. Maas. The potential for the formation of a biosynthetic enzyme in *Escherichia coli*. Biochim. Biophys. Acta, 25:208–9.

1958

With W. K. Maas. Negative feedback control of the formation of biosynthetic enzymes. In: *Physiological Adaptation*, pp. 151–58. Wash., D.C.: American Physiological Society.

With W. K. Maas. Feedback control of the formation of biosynthetic enzymes. In: *A Symposium on the Chemical Basis of Development*, ed. W. D. McElroy and B. Glass, pp. 469–78. Baltimore: Johns Hopkins Univ. Press.

Regulation en retour (feedback control) de la synthèse de l'arginine chez *Escherichia coli*. Bull. Soc. Chim. Biol., 40:1939–52.

1959

With H. L. Ennis. Feedback control of the synthesis of enzyme and end product in arginine biosynthesis in *Escherichia coli*. Fed. Proc. Fed. Am. Soc. Exp. Biol., 18:222.

1960

With H. Kaufman. Selecting bacterial mutants by the penicillin method. Science, 131:604–5.

Antagonism between substrate and repressor in controlling the formation of a biosynthetic enzyme. Proc. Natl. Acad. Sci. USA, 46:682–90.

1961

With H. L. Ennis. Control of arginine biosynthesis in strains of *Escherichia coli* not repressible by arginine. J. Mol. Biol., 3:439–46.

With W. Gundersen. Repressor and modulator, two cellular tools for controlling synthesis of biosynthetic enzymes. In: *Proceedings of the 5th International Congress of Biochemistry*, vol. 1, pp. 155–59. Oxford: Pergamon Press.

With W. Gundersen. Induction by arginine of enzymes of arginine biosynthesis in *Escherichia coli* B. Proc. Natl. Acad. Sci. USA, 47:961–71.

With M. Berger and W. Gundersen. Coordinate repression and genetic sequence of the arginine biosynthetic enzymes in *Escherichia coli*. Communication at the 5th International Congress of Biochemistry, Moscow.

Effect of L-cystine on initiation of anaerobic growth of *Escherichia coli* and *Aerobacter aerogenes*. J. Bacteriol., 82:305–12.

With W. Gundersen and M. Berger. Genetics of regulation of enzyme synthesis in the arginine biosynthetic pathway of *Escherichia coli*. Cold Spring Harbor Symp. Quant. Biol., 26:173–82.

1963

With S. M. Kalman. Control by uracil of carbamyl phosphate synthesis in *Escherichia coli*. Biochim. Biophys. Acta, 69:355–60.

Control by repression of a biochemical pathway. Bacteriol. Rev., 27:182–90.

1964

With E. E. Sercarz. Different contributions of exogenous and endogenous arginine to repressor formation. J. Mol. Biol., 8:254–62.

Conditional streptomycin dependent mutants and control mechanisms. Communication presented at 6th International Congress of Biochemistry, New York.

With E. Kataja. Phenotypic repair by streptomycin of defective genotypes in *E. coli*. Proc. Natl. Acad. Sci. USA, 51:487–93.

With E. B. Horowitz. Coordination between repression and retroinhibition in control of a biosynthetic pathway. In: *Comparative Biochemistry of Arginine and Derivatives* (Ciba Foundation, Study Group No. 19), pp. 64–81. Boston: Little, Brown.

With J. E. Davies and W. Gilbert. Streptomycin suppression and the code. Proc. Natl. Acad. Sci. USA, 51:883–90.

With E. Kataja. Streptomycin-induced oversuppression in *E. coli*. Proc. Natl. Acad. Sci. USA, 51:995–1001.

Streptomycin and the ambiguity of the genetic code. New Sci., 24:776–79.

1965

With J. Yashphe. Phosphorylation of carbamate *in vivo* and *in vitro*. J. Biol. Chem., 240:1681–86.

With E. Kataja. Suppression activated by streptomycin and related antibiotics in drug sensitive strains. Biochem. Biophys. Res. Commun., 18:656–63.

With J. Davies and B. D. Davis. Misreading of RNA codewords induced by aminoglycoside antibiotics. Mol. Pharmacol., 1:93–106.

With W. F. Anderson and L. Breckenridge. Role of ribosomes in streptomycin-activated suppression. Proc. Natl. Acad. Sci. USA, 54:1076–83.

With D. Old. Amino acid changes provoked by streptomycin in a polypeptide synthesized *in vitro*. Science, 150: 1290–92.

1966

Antibiotics and the genetic code. Sci. Am., 214:102–9.

The action of streptomycin on protein synthesis *in vivo*. Bull. N.Y. Acad. Med., 42:633–37.

With J. R. Beckwith. Suppression. Annu. Rev. Microbiol., 20:401–22.

With G. Jacoby and L. Breckenridge. Ribosomal ambiguity. Cold Spring Harbor Symp. Quant. Biol., 31:657–64.

1967

Induction of code ambiguity by aminoglycoside antibiotics. Fed. Proc. Fed. Am. Soc. Exp. Biol., 26:5–8.

With G. A. Jacoby. Genetics of control of the arginine pathway in *Escherichia coli* B and K. J. Mol. Biol., 24:41–50.

With G. A. Jacoby. The effect of streptomycin and other aminoglycoside antibiotics on protein synthesis. In: *Mechanism of Action and Biosynthesis of Antibiotics*, ed. D. Gottlieb and P. Shaw, vol. I, pp. 726–47. Berlin, Heidelberg, and N.Y.: Springer-Verlag.

With R. Rosset and R. A. Zimmermann. Phenotypic masking and streptomycin dependence. Science, 157:1314–17.

Ambiguity in the translation of the genetic code into proteins, induced by aminoglycoside antibiotics. In: *Immunity, Cancer and Chemotherapy*, pp. 167–75. N.Y.: Academic Press.

1968

With J. Davies. The effect of streptomycin on ribosomal function. Curr. Top. Microbiol. Immunol., 44:100–122.

1969

With G. A. Jacoby. A unitary account of the repression mechanism of arginine biosynthesis in *Escherichia coli*. I. The genetic evidence. J. Mol. Biol., 39:73–87.

With O. Karlstrom. A unitary account of the repression mechanism of arginine biosynthesis in *Escherichia coli*. II. Application to the physiological evidence. J. Mol. Biol., 39:89–94.

With R. Rosset. A ribosomal ambiguity mutation. J. Mol. Biol., 39:95–112.

With L. Breckenridge. The dominance of streptomycin sensitivity re-examined. Proc. Natl. Acad. Sci. USA, 62: 979–85.

The contrasting role of *strA* and *ram* gene products in ribosomal functioning. Cold Spring Harbor Symp. Quant. Biol., 34:101–11.

1970

With P. Strigini. Ribosomal mutations affecting efficiency of amber suppression. J. Mol. Biol., 47:517–30.

With L. Breckenridge. Genetic analysis of streptomycin resistance in *Escherichia coli*. Genetics, 65:9–25.

Informational suppression. Annu. Rev. Genet., 4:107–34.

1971

With N. Z. Sarner, M. J. Bissell, and M. DiGirolamo. Mechanism of excretion of a bacterial proteinase. I. Demonstration of two proteolytic enzymes produced by a *Sarcina* strain *(Coccus P)*. J. Bacteriol., 105:3, 1090–98.

With M. J. Bissell and R. Tosi. Mechanism of excretion of a bacterial proteinase. II. Factors controlling accumulation of the extracellular proteinase of a *Sarcina* strain *(Coccus P)*. J. Bacteriol., 105:3, 1099–1109.

With U. Bjare. Drug dependence reversed by a ribosomal ambiguity mutation, *ram*, in *Escherichia coli*. J. Mol. Biol., 57:423–35.

With H. Momose. Genetic analysis of streptomycin dependence in *Escherichia coli*. Genetics, 67:19–38.

With R. A. Zimmermann and R. Rosset. Nature of phenotypic masking exhibited by drug-dependent streptomycin A mutants of *Escherichia coli*. J. Mol. Biol., 57:403–22.

With R. A. Zimmermann and R. T. Garvin. Alteration of a 30s ribosomal protein accompanying the *ram* mutation in *E. coli*. Proc. Natl. Acad. Sci. USA, 68:2263.

Ribosomal discrimination of tRNA's. Nature (London) New Biol., 234:52, 261–64.

1972

With D. K. Biswas. Restriction, de-restriction and mistranslation in missense suppression. Ribosomal discrimination of tRNA's. J. Mol. Biol., 64:119–34.

With P. J. Piggott and M. D. Sklar. Ribosomal alterations controlling alkaline phosphatase isozymes in *E. coli*. J. Bacteriol., 110:291–99.

With J. F. Atkins and D. Elseviers. Low level activity in β-galactosidase frameshift mutants of *E. coli*. Proc. Natl. Acad. Sci. USA, 69:1192–95.

With D. K. Biswas. The attachment site of streptomycin to the 30s ribosomal subunit. Proc. Natl. Acad. Sci. USA, 69:2141–44.

1973

I Ribosomi. In: *Enciclopedia Della Scienza e della Tecnica Mondadori*, ed. Arnaldo Mondadori, pp. 305–12. Milan: Edizioni Scientifiche e Techniche.

With R. T. Garvin and R. Rosset. Ribosomal assembly influenced by growth in the presence of streptomycin. Proc. Natl. Acad. Sci. USA, 70:2762–66.

1974

With D. Elseviers. Direct selection of ribosomal mutants with altered translation efficiency in *E. coli* B. Fed. Proc. Fed. Am. Soc. Exp. Biol., 33:1335.

With R. T. Garvin and D. K. Biswas. The effects of streptomycin or dihydrostreptomycin binding to 16S RNA or to 30S ribosomal subunits. Proc. Natl. Acad. Sci. USA, 71:3814–18.

Streptomycin and misreading of the genetic code. In: *Ribosomes*, ed. P. Lengyel, M. Nomura, and A. Tissieres, pp. 791–803. N.Y.: Cold Spring Harbor Laboratory.

1975

With S. Chakrabarti. Growth of bacteriophages MS2 and T7 on streptomycin-resistant mutants of *Escherichia coli*. J. Bacteriol., 121:670–74.

With D. Elseviers. Misreading and the mode of action of streptomycin. In: *Drug Action and Drug Resistance in Bacteria*, vol. 2, *Aminoglycosidic Antibiotics*, ed. H. Umezawa, pp. 147–75. Tokyo: Univ. of Tokyo Press.

With R. T. Garvin. A new gene for ribosomal restriction in *Escherichia coli*. Mol. Gen. Genet., 137:73–78.

With M. Duncan. A ribonucleoprotein precursor of both the 30S and 50S ribosomal subunits of *E. coli*. Proc. Natl. Acad. Sci. USA, 72:1533–37.

With A. Kikuchi and D. Elseviers. Isolation and characterization of lambda transducing bacteriophages for *argF, argI* and adjacent genes. J. Bacteriol., 122:727–42.

With D. Elseviers. Direct selection of mutants restricting efficiency of suppression and misreading levels in *E. coli* B. Mol. Gen. Genet., 137:277–87.

With S. L. Chakrabarti. A link between streptomycin and rifampicin mutation. Proc. Natl. Acad. Sci. USA, 72:2084–87.

With A. Kikuchi. Similarity of genes *argF* and *argI*. Nature (London), 256:621–24.

1976

With A. Kikuchi. Studies of the DNA carrying genes *valS, argI, pyrB*, and *argF* by electron microscopy and by site specific endonuclease. J. Microsc. Biol. Cell., 27:1–10.

1977

With S. Chakrabarti. Interaction between mutations of ribosomes and RNA polymerase: A pair of *strA* and *rif* mutations individually temperature-insensitive but temperature-sensitive in combination. Proc. Natl. Acad. Sci. USA, 74:1157–61.

PERCY LAVON JULIAN
April 11, 1899–April 19, 1975

BY BERNHARD WITKOP

Deep in the intricate country of the mind
I took a twisting path that led me stumbling
To a wind-racked hill.
Those thickets, briary, tough to break
And swampy sometimes underfoot
Were well behind me now
Lost to sight and for the moment
Lost to mind.
The hill I had reached was high enough
To look on distances that dropped away fold upon fold
Melting far to the Westward into a dim horizon
They beckoned me.
And my feet, so heavy as I had begun to climb the hill
Were now uplifted to lighter pace,
What land is this, I asked, in taking breath,
What lies behind that seventh fold?
Take heart, I told myself,
Go farther on.

DONALD ADAMS
The Seventh Fold

WHENEVER PERCY JULIAN told his friends about his life, and how he had overcome all the obstacles from his beginning as the grandson of a slave, born "at the corner of Jeff Davis Avenue and South Oak Street in Montgomery, Alabama, the Capital in the cradle of the confederacy,"* to scientist, inventor, business leader, humanist, protagonist of human rights, he liked to illustrate this long arduous climb by Donald Adams' *The Seventh Fold*:

> My dear friends, who daily climb uncertain hills in the countries of their minds, hills that have to do with the future of our country and of our children, may I humbly submit to you, the only thing that has enabled me to keep doing the creative work, was the constant determination: Take heart! Go farther on! †

This imperative, *go on!*, characterizes not only his life but his research, where each answer created at least two new questions and led to the exponential growth of science as Percy experienced it in his lifetime. With this growth, he later realized the concomitant responsibility and questions of ethics.

Percy Julian was born on April 11, 1899, the oldest of six children of James Sumner Julian, a railway mail clerk, and his wife, Elizabeth Lena Adams. Since 1976 his birthday has been a holiday for the Village of Oak Park, a fashionable suburb of Chicago where the Julian family has resided since 1950, initially under precarious conditions (the Julian home, the first in the neighborhood to be owned by a black family, was the victim of arsonists on Thanksgiving Day, 1950, and the target of a dynamite bomb on June 12, 1951), and where other famous people, such as Ernest Hemingway and Frank Lloyd Wright, had their residences. Because Percy's father was a federal employee, the family held a higher status than most blacks of that day. This advantage, and the fact that his well-

---

*Percy Julian, "Response," in *Percy Lavon Julian, A Tribute* (Jacksonville, Illinois: MacMurray College, 1972), p. 23.
†*Ibid.*, p. 28.

read father had a great love for mathematics and philosophy, helped him on the way to a formal education.

Clearly, his must have been "a mind forever voyaging through strange seas of thought" (Wordsworth), or "a restless curiosity about things which he cannot understand" (Pascal), but the cultural and, above all, religious tradition in his family provided not only a repository of substantive values, but also a coding device for new ideas and achievements. That "the fear of the Lord is the beginning of all practical wisdom" was taught him, and not in Latin, by his revered paternal great-grandfather.

> My children and my friends all know him as Grandpa Cabe because they've heard me speak about him so many times. My great-grandfather, with the rest of us that day, was singing in the cotton field, where we children, particularly Dr. James Julian, my next brother, and I were sent to my grandfather's farm to work during the summer. We were singing on that day a beautiful spiritual, "There is a balm in Gilead to make the wounded whole. There is a balm in Gilead to heal the sin-sick soul."
>
> "Grandpa Cabe," I asked, "what's a balm in Gilead?"
>
> "Well, Sonny, you see, Gilead was a famous town in Israel for the manufacture of salves to heal wounds and sores," he told me. "And they called these salves balms. Now one day Jeremiah was having a hard time trying to lead his people the right way. Everything was going wrong for Jeremiah, and he cried out in anguish, 'Is there no balm in Gilead?' You see, what he was saying was, 'Ain't there no way out?' I want you to know that, Sonny, because I believe there is always a way out."
>
> It was then that I made my vow—that I would forever fight to keep hope alive because there is always a way out. . . .
>
> His optimism was one of the most pertinent lessons I learned as a youngster. Next to my parents and my grandparents, I owe my eternal optimism to my students and my co-workers, who over the past forty years have worked with me, and to my great-Grandpa Cabe.*

Respect for the dignity of the poor and survival with dignity came naturally to the Julian family as the results of hard work, family pride, love, acceptance, belonging, high moral

---

*Ibid., pp. 24–25.

standards, good parental example, decent food, discipline, respect for authority, and God-centeredness. The major weapon for liberation was faith in education, the door that led from alienation to emancipation.

Percy often compared his fortunate family and his upbringing with the situation today:

> The kind of hope I grew up with is missing in today's ghetto youth because of a breakdown in family life. It has its roots in slavery when often the father of the family was uprooted and sold down the river. The son would grow up and get married and, when he was unable to get a job because there were not jobs for a black man, he would get embarrassed that he could not support his family and walk out thinking, "my mother did it alone and my wife is no better." Well, that went on generation after generation, and it's no better today. There still are no jobs and welfare encourages the man to leave the family. One of the greatest problems facing the country is how to reconcile the young ghetto dweller with the rest of America. We have a large problem of ignorance, lack of opportunity, and divided families. I worry about how we are going to solve it. It's not just trying to persuade people to be nice and understanding. I've been as angry as anyone else. But most people define the end of anger as when you become well-off. I think as we resolve the breakdown of the black family, caused by slavery and continued by welfare, the problem will come closer to its solution.*

Public education for blacks in Alabama stopped at the eighth grade. Traveling on an empty stomach, Percy made the long trip from Montgomery, Alabama to Greencastle, Indiana, where, "because of the meager quality of my early training I was enrolled at DePauw University as a 'sub-freshman' until nearly my senior year in college. On my first day in College," Percy liked to tell, "I remember walking in and a white fellow stuck out his hand and said, 'How are you?—Welcome!' I had never shaken hands with a white boy before and did not know whether I should or not. But you know," he added smilingly, "in the shake of a hand my whole

---

*Quoted in: William Montague Cobb, First Percy L. Julian Memorial Lecture, DePauw University, April 28, 1977.

life was changed, I soon learned to smile and act like I believed they all liked me, whether they wanted to or not."*

He lived in the attic of a fraternity house. His support and tuition came from his earnings as a waiter. Often he worked as a ditchdigger during the day and attended classes in the evening.

Percy often related this early college experience with loving detail. Much later he started writing his memoirs in which the journey to Greencastle and his entry into DePauw forms the first and, alas, last chapter of an autobiography that would never be completed.

Later the entire family moved to Greencastle, and his two brothers, James and Emerson, and each of his three sisters, Mattie, Irma, and Elizabeth, in due turn graduated from DePauw University.

Before he received his A.B. in 1920, he had been elected to Phi Beta Kappa and became the valedictorian. Then his respected teachers informed him there were no opportunities for those of his color, and they could not help. Percy responded by going first to Fisk University, from 1920 to 1922, as an instructor in chemistry and then to Harvard, where as an Austin fellow, he obtained his master of arts in 1923. Through Harvard Fellowships for Studies in Biophysics and Organic Chemistry, he was able to investigate the chemistry of conjugated unsaturated systems with Professor E. P. Kohler. But even Harvard in those days was unable, or unwilling, to offer a Negro a faculty position. To Percy, the realization of this failure was not only discouraging, it was traumatic. Instead, he went to West Virginia State College, at that time an all-black institution, to teach as a professor of chemistry from 1926 to 1927. John W. Davis was president of the College at the time.

Little did Percy know that forty-five years later, on May

---

*Ibid.

12, 1972, he would meet his old "boss," then three times retired, at the dedication of the Percy Lavon Julian Laboratory at MacMurray College in Jacksonville, Illinois. It was a festive occasion that none of the participants would ever forget.

Davis, whom Percy called "a great educator, one of the greatest men I've ever known," had come to the dedication from Englewood, New Jersey, where he headed a fund for the training of Negro lawyers in the South, in honor of his former colleague's greatest moment. Dr. Davis related that at the end of his tenure, West Virginia State College had turned from 100 percent black to 70 percent white—completely and happily integrated. Percy at this point turned to a young assertive black student:

> I am telling you that this is a wonderful time to be living—a day of great opportunity. The country has changed course. Don't nurse your anger, but get together and help make this a really united nation.
>
> You know, I first spoke at MacMurray College in 1948. After my lecture everyone went to the Dunlap Hotel for the night. I was late getting away from the auditorium and by the time I joined the others, the management met me at the entrance. "The others have rooms," they said, "But we don't take coloreds. We have a train reservation for you back to Chicago." But, the Dunlaps and I are old friends now and this time they are giving me a party. I think it's a kind of formal apology.*

Percy Julian's commitment to the integrity of his group remained undiminished, but time and again he gave us reason to admire him for overcoming and sublimating the tension between the particularist and the universalist elements in the value system of a man with such a steep and spectacular career. One of his closest friends, Archibald J. Carey, Jr., judge of the Circuit Court of Cook County in Chicago, for this reason, in a eulogy at his funeral, described him as "the most complete human being I have ever known. A man who made contributions to healing, not only of the body, but of

---

*Remarks on the occasion of the "Tribute," MacMurray College.

our society where he has built bridges between many people and groups." His nineteen honorary degrees, his eighteen academic and civic citations, his twenty-nine involvements as a trustee, chairman, or member of educational, religious, and civic activities amplify and illustrate Judge Carey's statement.

Now comes a "change of venue," to stay within judicial terminology, so unlikely and so unique that Percy Julian was probably the only grandson of a slave who, in his time, not only went to Harvard from Montgomery, Alabama, but on to the former imperial capital of Vienna. This return to the Old World was prompted by a fellowship from the Rockefeller Foundation which he received while on the faculty of Howard University. Percy selected Vienna because the chemistry of natural products fascinated him, and Ernst Späth's research on alkaloids had attracted his attention. But in the back of his mind there must have been other thoughts and associations: the historic tradition of the world's musical capital, the elegance, the proverbial Viennese charm, the opera, and *der Heurige*. Percy never elaborated on his method of selection.

There was of course the memory of that picture in the house of his youth. It showed a valley surrounded by high hills—in the middle of it stood an old man and a little boy. The man was pointing to the mountain and the title of the picture was: *There are people over those mountains*. Percy, in life and in science, was always driven by a holy curiosity to know what is on the other side, in this case, of the Atlantic. We are fortunate to be able to draw upon the personal memories of his closest Viennese friend, Edwin Mosettig, a fellow chemist, slightly younger than Percy, and brother of Erich Mosettig (1898–1962), both from Späth's laboratory.

Percy's arrival in Vienna in the fall of 1929 had elements of the story of the three Magi, he being the black king. He brought gold, in the form of dollars, to impoverished Austria. Instead of myrrh and frankincense, he had large crates shipped to Späth's laboratory on Währingerstrasse 38, the contents of which were marveled at by all the students. The boxes contained treasures of ground glass equipment, elaborate laboratory glassware (mostly made to order), electric stirrers, and other extravagances not known to the average student. Percy's good humor and friendly personality conquered all hearts in no time. His only reservation was toward Edwin Mosettig, later his most intimate friend, because in steady discussions with Percy's predecessor, Stephen Foster Darling from Harvard University, Edwin had adorned his English with an American accent to such an extent that he aroused the suspicion of Percy. Edwin told him that his predecessor had always defined "English as an American dialect."

Percy perfected his German in no time. He even became fluent in Viennese, a talent he used on the occasion of a taxi ride from the airport to his hotel when he revisited Vienna after the war. The taxi driver literally "took Percy for a ride," and first went on a great detour to the Prater. All of a sudden his American fare was heard to ask: "Ja herens, wo samma denn eigentli [Now listen, where are we actually]?" The driver was scared to death and immediately headed for the Hotel Sacher.

His linguistic perfection became known, and he received an invitation for a radio presentation. He chose a reading of poems and thoughts by Anton Wildgans (1881–1932), director of the Burgtheater and noted poet, whose slightly melancholic, socially perceptive and critical writings, and melodious style impressed and attracted Percy. He felt Wildgans' *Grosse Österreich-Rede* addressed the notion that Austria is not a nation of fiddlers and dancers, but a stepchild of history punished by wars, depressions, and unemployment. The sample poem which he read illustrates the other view, the blessings of this country:

ÖSTERREICHISCHES LIED

Wo sich der ewige Schnee
spiegelt im Alpensee,
Sturzbach am Fels zerstäubt,
eingedämmt Werke treibt,

wo in der Berge Herz
dämmert das Eisenerz,
Hammer Gestein zerstampft,
zischend die Schmelzglut dampft,

wo durch der Ebene Gold
silbern der Strom hinrollt,
Ufer von Früchten schwillt,
hügelan Rebe quillt,

Pflügerschweiss, Städtefleiss
hat da die rechte Weis'
was auch Geschick beschied,
immer noch blüht ein Lied.

Österreich heisst das Land!
Da er's mit gnädiger Hand
schuf, und so reichbegabt,
Gott hat es liebgehabt! *

Franz Grillparzer's (1791–1872) ominous prediction, "from humanity to nationality to bestiality," set the fateful stages in the sequence that culminated in the events of World War II. All this struck a familiar chord in Percy, even one decade ahead of the events.

Percy cultivated his musical talents by receiving piano lessons from Edwin Mosettig's mother, a well-known teacher in the Theresienstrasse, where he was treated like a member of the family, participating in family outings, musical soirées, swimming in the Danube, tennis, and even one bold skiing excursion to the Rax Mountains, not to be repeated. Percy felt intimidated by all the proficient skiing experts. However, he practiced his tennis to the point where he defeated his friend Edwin more or less routinely.

The place where Percy "held court" by giving very generous receptions was an elegant apartment in a famous location: an der Strudlhofstiege, later the title of an 800-page

---

*Ludwig Reiners, *Der ewige Brunnen* (München: Verlag-C. F. Beck, 1955), p. 485.

best-selling novel by Heimito von Doderer (1896–1966) describing the social changes in Austria before, during, and after World War I. From his dwelling he could easily walk within minutes to the Boltzmann Gasse where the Chemische Institut was. Equally close was Frau Dr. Neumann's "Mittagstisch" where a select group of friends and prominent people used to partake of an elaborate luncheon à la Viennoise.

His social contacts were preferably with the leading intellectual and literary Jewish families of Vienna, such as the Polgars and the Lederers. Jewish solidarity and loyalty (*ahavath Yisra' el*) probably reminded him of his own minority and their comparable determination to survive.

His first opera was *Die Zauberflöte*. A normal student could only afford a *stehsitz* on the *galerie,* with no view. For music fans this did not matter; they followed the miniaturized score with the help of a flashlight and hardly looked at the stage. But Percy had tickets for an expensive loge (box) and invited Edwin to share it, who in this way *sat* through his first opera. Percy was elegantly dressed in a long black opera coat and homburg. He followed the complicated plot most attentively and was very receptive to all the special effects, such as the three protective graces who descend to the stage held by invisible ropes. "Well done, well done," was his repeated enthusiastic response.

To Edwin he confided many of his innermost thoughts, for instance the traumatic memory of his disappointment at Harvard, where instead of a teaching position he received a citation. Percy, in front of all the students, according to Edwin Mosettig, walked up to the dean, shook his fist and exclaimed: "I do not pray for mercy, I want justice!" This story was told and retold many times with much anger and emotion. Whether this incident really happened that way, and there are doubts, or whether it was a projection of a mind under stress, in the end probably makes little difference.

Percy impressed his Viennese fellow students not only with the spirituals he played on the piano, but also with his passion for hard work and study, his profound chemical knowledge, and his astounding memory. Professor Ernst Späth, a critical, pitiless examiner, a teacher who ignored lazy or untalented students, characterized Percy in these words: "Ein ausserordentlicher Student, wie ich ihn in meiner Laufbahn als Lehrer niemals hatte [An extraordinary student, his like I have not seen before in my career as a teacher]!"

The preparation for the *Rigorosum*, or Ph.D. examination, was done *in clausura* with Edwin Mosettig in the scenic *Wachau*. His thesis was on the alkaloids of *Corydalis cava*, a plant growing in the *Wiener Wald*. This work had a decisive influence on his extensive later studies, all synthetic, on indole alkaloids and tryptophan metabolites.

In the postwar misery, Percy revisited Späth's widow, who was then eking out a marginal existence on a state pension. He managed to provide her with enough precious coal so her body—and her heart—kept warm all through the following winter.

In the sixties he passed Vienna again on the way to Budapest to negotiate some patent matters. He was invited to give an address over Radio Budapest. After a lengthy introduction in Hungarian, Percy's suspicion was aroused. He demanded a literal translation. After much hemming and hawing he guessed from their prevarications that he was announced as one of the leading American Negro scientists, who was still disadvantaged and suppressed by his capitalist fellow countrymen. Percy replied that he had no intention to betray his country and withdrew his talk.

Josef Pikl, another of his long-time Viennese friends and associates, provided this perceptive summary in a personal letter to me:

> The time spent in Austria had a great influence in developing the personality of Julian. For the first time in his life, he was completely at ease, no open or hidden barriers, really an equal among equals. He may have even enjoyed a standing a few notches higher than his friends. In the laboratory at Vienna, he was particularly noticed for his neatness, the cleanliness of his work bench, his ready and contagious laugh, completely uninhibited. All the fifteen other graduate students in the room were his friends. He loved the freedom in Austria so much that a year after his graduation, he returned for the Summer and we spent a few weeks cycling through parts of Carinthia and the bordering area of Yugoslavia. One incident from this time he recited with much glee. When in a remote country village of Austria a boy about 8 years old slowly sneaked up to him and rubbed his hand and then looked to see if the color came off. A group of boys who had never seen a black man, except a chimney sweep, wanted to know if the color rubbed off.

Yet all this happened in the lull before the storm that unleashed the furies of war and genocide.

After he received his Ph.D. in Vienna in September 1931, Percy and his Viennese friend Josef Pikl sailed to America on the *Queen Elizabeth* and started their long-term collaboration at Howard University. Two years later, some unfortunate intrigue forced them to leave and go to DePauw University.

At this juncture the steep career of Percy Julian, the scientist, began. The best account of this period was rendered by Max Tishler, one of his many friends and admirers, when he presented him with the Honor Scroll of the Chicago Chapter of the American Institute of Chemists on November 13, 1964.

> His important research work began at DePauw University, where he was invited in 1933 by the late Dr. W. M. Blanchard, professor and dean of the College of Liberal Arts, to teach the senior courses in organic chemistry. With Prof. Blanchard's aid and counsel, he inaugurated a program

designed to help "bridge the gap between college and university." In place of the usual college senior courses in Qualitative Organic Analyses, Organic Syntheses, Identification of Organic Compounds, or Literature Studies, he boldly attempted a synthesis of these disciplines in the Senior Student's training. Each qualified Senior was given a fundamental research problem. The result was astounding, even to oldsters in such endeavors like Harry Holmes of Oberlin, who became a staunch friend. Thirty beautiful senior theses resulted in a matter of 4 years, and 11 of these led to publications in the *Journal of the American Chemical Society*. What is more significant, most of these publications read more like Doctoral dissertations than expanded senior theses.

At the same time that he was guiding this student work, he was setting a fast pace for his students in his own individual laboratory work. Together with a devoted friend and brilliant fellow-student from Vienna, Dr. Josef Pikl, whom he had invited and assisted in coming to America, he had inaugurated a vigorous program of work on the constitution and syntheses of certain plant alkaloids having an indole nucleus. The first of these undertakings was the total synthesis of the alkaloid, physostigmine, an important drug. In a series of five papers, published in the *Journal of the A.C.S.* with Dr. Pikl, he reported this synthesis.*

The pace of work and the research climate of that time come through in Dr. Pikl's memories:

> Throughout the six years of our collaboration, we made a good team. Percy generated ideas faster than half a dozen people could critically review and test them. He also did most of the writing, did practically all of the analytical work, such as carbon-hydrogen analyses, and determination of active hydrogen with his Grignard machine, and helped with much of the dish-washing chores using a two foot diameter porcelain dish with hot sulfuric acid and nitric acid, unaware of the dangers of this method, outside of acid burns. When we were celebrating some progress or the receipt of a nice letter, we drove out about six miles to the crossing of the Transcontinental Route 40 where there was a small snack restaurant. Usually, however, we stayed up to 11–12 o'clock in the laboratory so that we heard some complaints of burning too much midnight oil! †

---

*Max Tishler, "Percy L. Julian, the Scientist," *The Chemist*, 42(1965):105–6.
† J. Pikl 1977: personal communication.

Tishler continued:

In a sense, this work was the turning point in his early career. In three papers, he had developed step by step the chemistry leading to his synthesis. As the fourth paper, describing the next to the last step, entitled, "The Synthesis of d,l-Eserethole" was about to be posted to the Editor of the *Journal*, there appeared the last of a series of ten papers by Sir Robert Robinson of Oxford on the identical subject. Since the synthesis of eserethole virtually completed, except for the resolution of the optical antipodes, the synthesis of physostigmine, it looked as though Julian would come in "second best," and no chemist likes to see the end goal of his most monumental effort achieved first by another, no matter how different the approaches and how equally novel the chemistry. What was more disturbing than the loss of priority was that Sir Robert's "d,l-eserethole" was quite different from the d,l-eserethole Julian was publishing—different in all its physico-chemical parameters.

Firm in his conviction that the logic of his synthesis left no room for doubt, Julian altered his paper and added the following:

> In a series of ten beautiful papers, Robinson and his co-workers have described syntheses of compounds which they call "d,l-Eserethole," and "d,l-Esermethole." Their "d,l-Eserethole" is not the compound described in this communication as d,l-Eserethole, and the constitution of which can hardly be questioned. We believe that the English authors are in error, that the compound they describe as "d,l-Eserethole" is not the substance, and that we are describing for the first time the real d,l-Eserethole.

Dr. Pikl was quite unhappy, for those were hard depression days in America, and if they were wrong, the sun would not soon shine upon two young, brash neophytes having the audacity to challenge so eminent a scientist. Moreover, in Europe the prospects of a young man were usually irretrievably ruined in such a case. The paper went to press, and by this time chemists on two continents held their breaths and many took sides. Even Prof. Kohler warned him, "I know you realize that you must be right in this cordial polemic or else it might lead to grave doubts concerning the authenticity of your future work." Here is the outcome of this challenge as published in Julian's fifth and last paper on the subject, entitled "The Complete Synthesis of Physostigmine":

> Physostigmine, the principal alkaloid of the Calabar bean, and long used as a drug, has, since its isolation by Jobst and Hesse 70

years ago, been the subject of numerous investigations. The determination of its constitution was rendered particularly difficult since its peculiar chemical structure found no analog in other plant products of known composition.... Shortly after promising experiments in the direction of (its synthesis) were under way (in our laboratories) the work had to be interrupted and could only be resumed recently. In the meantime, the first of a series of ten papers dealing with the synthesis of Physostigmine, by Robinson and his collaborators, appeared and seemingly proved convincingly that the (course) suggested in our formulas could not be realized in practice. Our experiments, nevertheless, were continued. . .led to the successful synthesis of d,l-Eserethole. . . .

To our surprise, our (d,1-Eserethole) exhibited entirely different properties than those of a compound synthesized by Robinson and his co-workers and called "d,1-Eserethole." Likewise were all derivatives different. Inasmuch as our (optically) inactive material subjected to characteristic reactions of Eserethole of natural origin, yielded perfectly analogous results, we expressed the belief that our product was the real constitution. This is now proved conclusively by synthesis of 1-Eserethole, identical with the product of natural origin.

Telegrams of congratulations came from all parts of America, Europe, and Asia. A young chemist had made his mark, and how badly he needed it, for DePauw was hard up for funds. Julian needed a job and a living, and American firms and universities with research facilities were reluctant to hire a man of color in those days.

And then came one of those bits of "accidental chemistry" referred to by Prof. Wittig. In attempts to isolate Geneserin, a companion alkaloid of Physostigmine, from the Calabar bean (*Physostigma venenosum*), Julian had first extracted the oil from this rather lovely bean. The oil had been washed with dilute acid and then with water, and was set aside wet. On examining it some weeks later, glistening small crystals had separated. They were carefully separated from the oil and found to be a hydrate, which upon losing its water, was again soluble in the oil. After careful recrystallization of the minute quantity of dehydrated material, microanalysis showed the formula $C_{29}H_{48}O$. A literature search showed that it was the sterol, stigmasterol, named after the plant *Physostigma venenosum*, from which Windaus and Hauth had separated it 29 years before.

About the time of Julian's isolation of the stigmasterol, Fernholz and Butenandt were publishing the first of their epoch-making papers on the preparation of certain sex hormones from this same stigmasterol which they had now separated from soybean oil. Julian wrote the Glidden Company asking for a 5-gallon sample of soybean oil. Imagine his surprise when a vice president of the Glidden Company called him on the long-distance phone, inviting him for an interview, and telling him he was being considered for a research position in Glidden's Soya Products Division in Chicago. The circumstances surrounding this call are of historical significance:

> The late Mr. W. J. O'Brien, Glidden Vice-President, tells the story that he had been attending a Board meeting of the Institute of Paper Chemistry at Appleton, Wisconsin. Julian was being discussed for a possible position on the research staff there, thanks to Dean Harry Lewis, who had accepted several of Julian's DePauw students for the Doctorate in Paper Chemistry. The hitch, however, was how he might fare in the community in view of an old statute on the Appleton city books that "No Negro should be bedded or boarded in Appleton overnight." After listening to the discussion, O'Brien said to himself, "If he is half as good as they say he is, I can use him at Glidden. I won't say anything about who he is; I'll just hire him. If I ask about it, get consent and he fails, it will be 'We told you so, Billy.'" So O'Brien slipped out to the telephone and called Julian. After the interview, Julian was hired on the spot as Glidden's Assistant Director of Research of the Soya Products Division.

On arriving, in 1936, to take up his duties, Julian found that he had been given the title of Director of Research of the Soya Products Division of Glidden. A new plant for the efficient and near quantitative extraction of oil from soybeans had been built by Electro-Chemie in Hamburg, Germany, and was being erected at the Glidden plant. Julian's fluent German stood him in good stead as he had to consult with the large coterie of German technicians, and he was on "24-hour call." He had every reason to forget forever his stigmasterol in the hectic few years following. Here was a stupendous pioneer effort to exploit every ingredient of the soybean. . . .

In his more than 18 years at Glidden, all these problems were solved and the Soya Products Division became Glidden's most profitable single entity. Soya phosphatides became a large commodity on the market and virtually a monopoly of Glidden, culminating in Julian's development of an oil-free granular product stabilized against rancidity, and widely sold today as "Lecithin Granules," a food supplement. Glidden's soya oil became a preferred product. Durkee's edible emulsifiers opened up a new era in liquid shortening, and Julian found himself one day also Director of Research for the Durkee Famous Foods Division of Glidden, an added job, and importantly soybean meal became an ingredient of nearly all animal feed, poultry feed now containing as much as 35%. One of the most enthusiastic and hard-hitting crews ever to man an industrial laboratory in a young enterprise surrounded him. Names like Levinson, Wilhelm, Engstron, Oberg (now of Carnation Milk), Karpel, Circle, Bain, Malter, Cole, Meyer, Magnani, Iveson, Herness, Ryden, Printy, and others appeared on the more than 100 patents applied for.

O'Brien's protein plant became a reality, with Julian in the early days functioning as engineer, chemist, researcher, and salesman. Today that plant (now owned by the Central Soya Co.) produces about 40 tons daily, and the protein has a world-wide sale. This remains the world's first and largest isolation and production of a relatively pure vegetable protein on a massive scale. And there was no small amount of chemistry involved, the ultimate secret being Julian's laboratory adjustment of the size of the soya protein micelle or molecule to fit particular applications, entailing countless electrophoresis and ultracentrifugal studies.

But though it took Julian almost 4 years before he could return to his stigmasterol, the dogged persistence prevailed. Soybean oil contains only 0.2 of% sterols, of which only 18% is stigmasterol—it would take 1000 pounds of soybean oil to yield 2 pounds of stigmasterol. Obviously, so much precious oil could not be destroyed just for this purpose.

One day a worker in the plant called Julian, as chief "trouble shooter," to counsel on what was to be done with a 100,000 gallon tank of "purified" soybean oil into which water had leaked. "The tank," phoned the worker, "contains a mass of white solid." Remembering his DePauw experience, Julian was there in a matter of minutes, had the whole tank centrifuged, and came out with an oily mass containing about 15% of mixed soya sterols. A modification of this accidental procedure introduced into the oil refining soon found Julian producing 100 pounds of mixed soya sterols daily. This was in 1940, and the value of this daily by-product production, in terms of the sex hormones that might be obtained from it, was then about $10,000 daily, but who could devise a facile industrial process for producing the sterols, for synthesizing the hormones, and who could possibly use so much hormone—as much as 5 to 6 pounds daily?

Julian, however, was soon ozonizing 100 pounds daily of mixed sterol dibromides, the first time that so large an ozonizer had been industrially employed for a potentially dangerously explosive reaction. The result: the female hormone, Progesterone, was put on the American market in bulk for the first time, and other sex hormones soon followed.

If, at this time, Julian had yielded his innate desire to participate personally in research to the administrative duties of being director of research for the Soya Products Division, manager of the Fine Chemical Division, and director of research for the Durkee Famous Food Division, he would have been remembered long for his scientific accomplishments. But these responsibilities did not stop this research chemist; instead, dramatic developments in the steroid field stimulated an even greater power within him. In 1948, Hench and Kendall at the Mayo Clinic made the epochal discovery that cortisone, then called Kendall's Compound E, reversed the symptoms of rheumatoid arthritis, using cortisone synthesized for the first time by Sarett in the Merck Laboratories. Since cortisone is a steroid, Julian reacted quickly. Scarcely had the announcement of the Mayo Clinic been made, when Julian published a new synthesis for *Reichstein's Substance S*, which is also present in the cortex of the adrenal gland and which differs from cortisone in lacking only an oxygen atom in position-11. In contrast to the previous synthesis, Julian's procedure was practical and made Substance S available in commercial quantities. Substance S is still an important commodity, and Julian's process, which starts with 16-dehydropregnenolone, is probably the most widely used for the production of hydrocortisone. It is marked by simplicity and high yields; I have been told that yields of 84% are obtainable.

In a series of patent applications, Julian reported improved syntheses of a wide variety of substituted Substance S compounds, which in turn can be converted microbiologically into the corresponding hydrocortisone derivatives. These include 16-Alkyl, 16-Hydroxy, 6-Alkyl and 6-Halogenated derivatives of Substance S.*

These were times of hectic activities, as a letter from Percy dated September 28, 1949 attests:

As you can no doubt imagine, during the past six months I have worked an average of fourteen to fifteen hours daily including Saturdays and Sundays on partial syntheses of cortical steroids. Most of my other

*Max Tishler, "Percy Julian, the Scientist," *The Chemist*, 42(1965):107–11.

work has received scant attention during this period, a circumstance which I must remedy at the earliest possible moment. Our communication on the synthesis of *Reichstein's Compound S* will appear in the October *Journal*. Gallagher's publication antedates ours as you have noticed from this month's *Journal*. You will also note, however, that he starts with what Fieser would call epipregnanolone (pregnane-3α-ol-20-one) while we begin with the cheap and readily available pregnenolone (5-pregnene-3β-ol-20-one). I presume that he secured his epipregnanolone from the accumulations from urine extracts. Theoretically it gives him an advantage in that he has something of a dress rehearsal for Compound E from desoxycholic acid (which is more closely related to epipregnanolone than to pregnenolone). Nevertheless, I completed just about a month ago a new procedure for preparing epipregnanolone from pregnenolone so that the former substance would be available in quantity, which is not the case at present. Our same synthesis has been applied to Cortisone, although we are not satisfied at the present time with certain phases of this latter synthesis so far as large-scale production is concerned. We have sent out for clinical investigation over six hundred grams of the three compounds, 17α-Hydroxyprogesterone, Reichstein's Compound S, and 4-Pregnene-17α,20β,21-triol-3-one (as well as its 20α isomer). As you can well realize the production of these compounds in these quantities has been no small job, especially when vigorous research was being prosecuted at the same time in order to clear up yields, and so forth, at every step.

Tishler comments:

In the course of his intensive steroid study, much new and valuable chemistry has been evolved, including new compounds and new reactions. Thus, in the synthesis of certain 16-Methyl-11-oxygenated corticoids (in which Merck has been interested) a valuable intermediate, 11-Keto-16-dehydropregnenolone, was first synthesized and patented by Julian. His celebrated 16,17-Epoxy-steroids have found wide use in steroid chemistry. His facile preparation of 21-Iodo-compounds; his reduction of the latter with sodium bisulfite; his chromous chloride dehalogenation of halogenated steroids; his reductive Raney Nickel dehalogenation of steroid bromohydrins, leading to new and widely-used methods of producing 17α-Hydroxy-steroids; his general method for introducing the diacetone side chain into the steroid molecule; his early use of steroid ketals as protected centers within the steroid molecule, leading to his facile synthesis of Reichstein's Substance S; his preparation and study of 4,5-epoxy-steroids and their conversion to 4-Halo-derivatives; his variety of steroids containing the diosphenol structure—these are but some of his "firsts" in the steroid field.*

From his association with Glidden to the presidency of an independent personal venture was a time of work and strain, as a letter dated July 22, 1957 indicates:

> In the meantime—during the critical building years of Julian Laboratories, the last three years—I have had to become a businessman and have had very little time to devote to any researches other than our steroid researches with various clients, particularly with Smith, Kline and French Laboratories. Now that Julian Laboratories have become a success (for your confidential information our accountants have just given me our sales for the first 10 months of our fiscal year ending August 31st, and they show close to 1.5 million dollars), I am again able to turn back to some of the things which have interested me, of course, most of my life. I still am far from being out of the woods. I need more men badly, among them a good plant manager and good production superintendent, several research men, two more Ph.D.'s at least and three or four junior assistants, a new personal research assistant, etc., etc. Incidentally, in this connection, I would appreciate it if you know of any young men who might like to join our organization. As you can probably imagine, we have a very ambitious research program going on in the steroid field, some of which will, no doubt, be published shortly, now that the necessary patents and the necessary protections for our clients have all been cared for. You may also be interested to know that we import from our plantations and our factory in Central America, Dioscorea root, process it into Diosgenin, and into 16-Dehydro-pregnenolone here at Julian Laboratories, and thus have become very competitive, and the field a bit overcrowded, we have enjoyed a very good business, and are looking forward to double our sales for the coming year, now that our raw material supply is adequate. I hope that in the not-too-distant future, you can visit our laboratories here and see our research and production set-up.

Tishler continued:

> His studies on Yohimbine alkaloids include a facile synthesis of the Yohimbine ring skeleton as well as syntheses of Yobyrine, Yobyrone,

*Ibid., pp. 111–12.

Tetrahydroyobyrine and Ketoyobyrine. . . . [He synthesized] for the first time the elusive Oxindole-Acetic Acid. . . . [He devoted much thought] to the study of the metabolism of the amino acid Tryptophan in the animal organism, by synthesizing Oxindole-Alanine and Dioxindole-Alanine, and demonstrating that the latter is not an intermediate in the conversion of Tryptophan to Kynurenine. . . . his monograph on the Chemistry of Indoles, occupying most of Volume 3 of *Heterocyclics*, edited by Elderfield, is a classic reference work for students and investigators in this field. . . .

The words of an eminent chemist complete my portrait of Julian the Scientist: In presenting him for the honorary degree of D.Sc., at the Oberlin Commencement in June [1964], Prof. Luke E. Steiner of Oberlin tendered the following citation:

> In these days in which specialization sometimes seems to dominate, I have the privilege of presenting a man who illustrates the general usefulness of an educated mind. In sequence as chemistry teacher, teacher and researcher, researcher and administrator, and entrepreneur and researcher, Percy Julian joined several careers through his continuing interest in natural materials from plants.
>
> He demonstrated his chemical competence and creative imagination in applied chemistry by securing a number of patents for the making of desired substances from the plant products, but he also kept on publishing in pure chemistry an impressive series of papers on indoles, sterols and steroids, and conjugated systems. Finally, he founded two firms through which he could apply his scientific knowledge, inventive skill, and judgment to recover large quantities of intermediate substances from soya beans and other plants and to make from them hormones and other drugs at low cost. We honor him for his humane objectives.*

The memorial prayer for the dead begins in the Sephardic rite: "A good name is better than precious oil." Percy would have smiled at this attempt to associate his worldly success in Glidden's soybean oil operation with the sum of his qualities that made him a man of virtue, *arete* (excellence, valor, virtue, manliness, the sum of good qualities that make

---

Ibid., p. 112.

character), in the old sense, with an abiding and infectious faith in the old values. His was a concept of life of activity, the Aristotelian concept of eudaemonism, with reason forming the basis of human felicity and little room for hedonism where happiness is pleasure. By dwelling on the experience of his life we enhance our own.

Percy Julian the businessman was lovingly praised and characterized by Benjamin M. Becker, his lawyer and business counselor since 1945:

> It is often said that business is rough, tough, ruthless and heartless. Percy, "the man who never gave up" proved the American dream from obscurity to astounding business greatness, but with a heart. He helped employees with personal and financial problems and solved business problems without resorting to endless litigation; he never had a single lawsuit against his company. Charity knew no bounds in the hearts of Percy and his admirable wife Anna. When a new product had been developed and the marketing and pricing was under consideration, Dr. Julian would say: "Well, let's make it moderate, so that everyone who needs it may get it." When we discussed details with a buyer and Percy had made some over-generous offer or concession, when we were alone, he would smile and say: "Ben, I don't mind making a profit, but I want them to make one too." So his count was moderated by his compassion.*

Percy's dear friend, the great historian and humanist John Hope Franklin, in his tribute at the Visitation (wake) preceding the funeral on April 23, 1975, gave moving expression to his admiration for Percy who in 1973 was honored, together with Anna Julian, for bringing to life the Legal Defense and Educational Fund in Chicago. "His wit and charm and grace made him one of the most 'clubbable' persons it has ever been my pleasure to know. He very much cherished the company of others, and others cherished his company even more, if such was possible."

---

*Benjamin Becker, remarks on the occasion of the Tribute to Percy Julian, MacMurray College, May 12, 1972.

Percy himself described his role as scholar and humanist in his acceptance address when he received the Chicago AIC Honor Scroll. His own words are an eloquent plea that to his friends and colleagues projects and preserves his memory. His body may be gone, but his spirit lives on in these words in which he expresses his apprehension on what Albert Einstein called our age: "Eine Zeit vollkommener Mittel und verworrener Ziele [A time of perfected methods and confused aims]":

> Where should the Scholar live
> In solitude or in society?
> In the green stillness of the country,
> Where he can hear the heart of Nature beat,
> Or in the dark grey town
> Where he can hear and feel?
> I'll make the answer for him
> And say: In the dark grey town!
>
> H. W. Longfellow

Almost forgotten and seldom quoted today, this prophetic little poem strikes deep at the heart of the devoted scholar's worries in this age of megaton bombs, short-sighted specialists, panacea thinking, status-quo paralysis, and philosophical void. If Longfellow in his day feared that the obsession of the scholar with his particular discipline might make him deaf to the anguished cries of humanity for direction and purpose, he most certainly would be appalled at the detached clichés of over-specialization and lack of universal concern so pronouncedly characteristic of the "educated" men of our times.

If there were a time when we thought that our system of liberal arts education would guarantee us the safeguard of future generations, trained in the broad requirements for citizenship in a great democracy, our dreams seem to have been shattered. There is no shadow of a doubt that the overpowering motivation—and perhaps the creeping paralysis—in our education today is the *development* of marketable skills. It is indeed doubtful if such an over-emphasis in an educational system can develop that scholar who "can hear and feel that throbbing heart of man." . . .

Scientific research projects, some good and some poor, are being spawned and supported by ample funds in nearly every college and university, large and small. I think the end result will be good for our nation. My prime concern here is that the scientist, particularly the chemist, recognizes the magnitude of the responsibility resting upon his shoulders when the nation entrusts so much of its wealth in his hands. Shall we become, for example, so deeply immersed in a sea of 'sense reality' that we sap the vitality of scholarly probing in the deeper well-springs of human destiny? Is it not our mission, particularly as teachers and even as members of industrial groups, to encourage, participate in where possible, indeed to give of ourselves and our energies something toward creative imagination in the world of ideas concerning the Whole Man, man searching for that symphony of ideas about himself and human destiny, without which all our efforts are but feeble ripples upon a turbulent sea of world confusion? . . .

Dr. Robert Hutchins warns us that the grave problems facing humanity cannot be entrusted to men of fractional culture (scientists). Indeed, he calls this fractional culture, pseudo-culture in essence. Father Theodore Hesburgh of Notre Dame, in a *Saturday Review* article entitled, "Science Is Amoral; Need Scientists Be Amoral Too?," seriously poses the question whether "science and technology are getting out of hand,"

> Historians of tomorrow may well ask why scientists did not join the human race in our time when the opportunities were so great and the means at hand so magnificent.

What does all this mean to you and me of the world of chemistry? To begin with, I cannot, and I hope you cannot, accept the blank statement that "Science is Amoral." While this may be said of its methodology and specific aims at a given time, Science is something more than methodologies, symbolisms, and technological devices; it is vastly more than the creation of mere things; computers and mechanical robots are only incidental by-products of its spirit of inquiry. Science, like all man's noble endeavors, involves the whole personality of those who pursue it. To say flatly that Science is amoral is to separate this man-made discipline from man himself and from the destiny of man. . . .

The challenge to us in the great debate with Humanists is clear. Too many of us have been satisfied to seek Truth only through the medium of certain facets of our discipline. We should have been the strong right arm of the humanist, but for the most part, we have not carved a basic social philosophy out of our endeavors. And yet where would one find more appropriate experience for such a philosophy than ours, where we live amidst the incomparable beauty of Nature's truth, Nature's objectivity, Nature's solemn and honest justice, Nature's grand nobility and bigness where no smallness can prevail in either mind or matter, Nature's understanding and tolerance where even the lowliest creation—whether it be the bee or the lilies of the field—performs its functions with dignity and glory, Nature's understanding and delicate balance, where on the one hand microorganisms can bring about the most dreaded disease, and on the other, bequeath to us the wonders of penicillin and aureomycin. The plea of Father Hesburgh that more of us should join the human race has some justification in fact. We must give more of our understanding to those who struggle to reinstate the majesty of the human will in the conduct of man, even in the utilization of our own hewn-out Truth.

Unless we, who know better than most world citizens the horror of the mushroom cloud that hangs ominously over us, become active Humanists in word and in deed, we may well condemn our world to awake some day never to view again the "green stillness of the country where we can hear the heart of Nature beat," but instead to crawl about and gasp for breath on limited terrain, surrounded by lakes and seas of molten lava, representing the remnants of that which once we knew as Mother Earth. Then may we in sad humility remember the words of the prophet:

Behold this beautiful land which the Lord, thy God hath given thee! *

I AM DIRECTLY and personally indebted to Mrs. Anna J. Julian, Dr. Julian's widow; to Joan Bowman, his long-time secretary; to Dr. Josef Pikl; to Dr. Edwin Mosettig, Vienna; to Judge Archibald J. Carey; and to Dr. Max Tishler, Wesleyan University, for giving their thoughts, memories, records, and devotion to this obituary. Too many of Percy's close friends and collaborators contributed indirectly, and only lack of space, but not lack of gratitude, prevents individual mention. The first Percy L. Julian Memorial Lecture was delivered by William Montague Cobb, the distinguished educator, anthropologist, author, and humanitarian, at DePauw University on April 28, 1977, under the title, "Onward and Upward." The second Percy L. Julian Memorial Lecture, "The Humanist as a Chemist," was given by B. Witkop on May 4, 1978.

* Percy L. Julian, "The Chemist as Scholar and Humanist," *The Chemist*, 42:101–4.

The magnificent portrait of "Grandpa Cabe" is part of Percy Julian's "Response" to the tributes paid to him by educators and scientists on the occasion of the dedication of the Percy Lavon Julian Laboratory at MacMurray College, May 12–13, 1972.

"Percy L. Julian, the Scientist," was the address delivered by Max Tishler when Percy Julian received the Honor Scroll of the Chicago AIC Chapter, November 13, 1964, in Chicago (see *The Chemist*, 42[1965]:105–13). In the same March issue is Percy Julian's response, "The Chemist as Scholar and Humanist." (pp. 101–4).

W. Montague Cobb set a monument to his lifelong friend in *Medical History*, 63(1971):143–50;162 references.

HONORS AND DISTINCTIONS

HONORARY DEGREES

D.Sc., DePauw University, 1947
D.Sc., Fisk University, November 1947
D.Sc., West Virginia State College, 1948
D.Sc., Northeastern University, Boston, October 1948
D.Sc., Morgan State College, Baltimore, June 1950
D.Sc., Howard University, Washington, D.C., June 1951
D.Sc., Northwestern University, Evanston, June 1951
D.Sc., Lincoln University, Philadelphia, April 1954
D.Sc., Roosevelt University, Chicago, September 1961
D.Sc., Virginia State College, Petersburg, May 1962
D.Sc., Morehouse College, Atlanta, Georgia, June 4, 1963
D.Sc., Oberlin College, Oberlin, Ohio, June 1964
LL.D., Lafayette College, Easton, Pennsylvania, September 1968
L.H.D., MacMurray College, Jacksonville, Illinois, June 1969
D.Sc., Indiana University, Bloomington, Indiana, June 1969
D.Sc., Michigan State University, East Lansing, Michigan, June 1972
LL.D., Atlanta University, Atlanta, Georgia, May 1973
LL.D., Illinois State University, Normal-Bloomington, Illinois, May 1974
D.Sc., Lincoln University of Missouri, Jefferson City, May 10, 1975 (posthumously)

ACADEMIC AND CIVIC HONORS

Spingarn Medal Award, National Association for the Advancement of Colored People (NAACP), June 27, 1947
Distinguished Service Award for 1949–50, Phi Beta Kappa Association of Chicago Area, December 1949
"Chicagoan of the Year" Award, *The Chicago Sun-Times* and Junior Chamber of Commerce, January 1950
The Coveted "Old Gold Goblet" Award, DePauw University, 1951 (For Distinguished Service as an Alumnus, given to only one alumnus annually)
Centennial Distinguished Citizen Award, Centennial Convocation, Northwestern University, Evanston, Illinois, December 2, 1951
Distinguished Merit Award for 1950, Decalogue Society of Lawyers, Chicago, March 3, 1951

Social Action Churchmanship Award of the Congregational Christian Churches of New Haven Conference, 1954

Jesuit Centennial Award as One of One Hundred Outstanding Chicagoans, December 12, 1957

Layman of the Year Award, Church Federation of Greater Chicago, April 23, 1964

Annual Silver Plaque Award, National Conference of Christians and Jews, Chicago, May 27, 1965

Founder's Day Award, Loyola University, Chicago, October 31, 1967

Merit Award of the Chicago Technical Societies Council, Chicago, November 14, 1967

Chemical Pioneer Award, American Institute of Chemists, Atlanta, May 11, 1968

Citation from the Mennonite Hospital, Bloomington, Illinois for Outstanding Contributions and Services to Mankind, January 24, 1970

Elected as a Laureate in the Lincoln Academy, Springfield, Illinois, May 20, 1972

MacMurray College's Chemistry Building named the Percy Lavon Julian Hall of Chemistry, May 13, 1972 (Jacksonville, Illinois)

Coppin State College's Percy L. Julian Science Classroom Building dedicated May 3, 1968 (Baltimore, Maryland)

Illinois State University, Normal, Illinois, Percy Julian Hall dedicated October 26, 1975

LEARNED SOCIETIES

Fellow, American Institute of Chemists
Fellow, Chemical Society of London
Fellow, New York Academy of Science
Member, American Chemical Society
Laureate, Lincoln Academy, Springfield, Illinois, May 20, 1972
Member, American Association for the Advancement of Science
Honorary Member, Illinois State Academy of Sciences, elected April 19, 1975
Member, National Academy of Sciences

EDUCATIONAL, RELIGIOUS, AND CIVIC ACTIVITIES

Member, Board of Trustees, DePauw University, Greencastle, Indiana

Member, Board of Trustees, Roosevelt University, Chicago, Illinois
Member, Board of Directors, Chicago Theological Seminary
Member, Board of Trustees, Southern Union College, Wadley, Alabama
Member, Board of Governors, International House, University of Chicago
Member, Phi Beta Kappa Associates
Member, Board of Directors, NAACP Legal Defense and Educational Fund
Vice President, Business Advisory Council of the Chicago Urban League
Chairman, Commonwealth Edison Environmental Advisory Council
Co-Chairman, National Negro Business and Professional Committee of the Legal Defense and Educational Fund
Emeritus Member, Executive Committee of the Board of Trustees, Howard University, Washington, D.C.
Emeritus Member, Board of Trustees, Fisk University, Nashville, Tennessee
Past Member, Board of Regents, State of Illinois Colleges and Universities
Extramural Counselor, National Institute of Arthritis and Metabolic Diseases, National Institutes of Health, Bethesda, Maryland
Past Member, Board of Directors, Fund for the Republic, Center for the Study of Democratic Institutions
Retired Member, Executive Board, Chicago Chapter, National Conference of Christians and Jews
Past President, Phi Beta Kappa Association of Greater Chicago
Past Director, Mental Health Association of Greater Chicago
Past Member, Illinois Advisory Committee, Commission on Civil Rights
Past Chairman of the Council for Social Action, Congregational Christian Churches of America (Now United Church of Christ)
Retired Deacon and Retired Trustee, First Congregational Church of Oak Park
Past Member, Board of Public Welfare Commissioners of the State of Illinois
Past Director, Provident Hospital, Chicago
Past Director, The Mandel Clinic, Chicago

Past Director, The Chicago Urban League
Past Secretary, Troop 8, Boy Scouts of America, Oak Park
Past Member, Midwest Regional Advisory Committee of the Institute of International Education
Century Member, Thatcher Woods Council, Boy Scouts of America

BIOGRAPHICAL SKETCHES

"The Man Who Wouldn't Give Up," *Reader's Digest,* August 1946
"In the Shake of a Hand," *Milwaukee Journal,* August 1947
"Slavery's Grandchildren," *Coronet,* January 1948
"The House that Joyce Built," *Fortune,* May 1949
"The Man Who Wouldn't Give Up," *Advance Magazine,* December 1952
"Julian Aids Mankind," *Chicago Tribune,* 6 January 1963
"Chemist with a Cause," *The Rotarian,* June 1963
"Eminent Scientist and Public Servant," *Advance Magazine,* January 1958
"Percy L. Julian's Fight for His Life," *Ebony Magazine,* March 1975

SCHOOLS NAMED FOR DR. JULIAN

P. L. Julian School, Phoenix, Arizona
Percy L. Julian School, Marrero, Louisiana
Percy Julian High School, 10330 South Elizabeth Street, Chicago, Illinois 60649

BIBLIOGRAPHY

1931

With E. Späth. Neue Corydalis-Alkaloide: dTetrahydro-copisin, d-Canadin and Hydrohydrastinin. Ber. Dtsch. Chem. Ges. 64:1131–37.

1932

With W. Passler. Thermal interconversion of mixed benzoins. J. Am. Chem. Soc., 54:4756.

1933

With J. Pikl. Studies in the indole series. I. Synthesis of alpha-benzylindoles. J. Am. Chem. Soc., 55:2105–10.

1934

On the progenitors of certain plant alkaloids and the mechanism of their formation in the plant structure. Proc. Indiana Acad. Sci., 43:122–25.

With J. Pikl and D. Boggess. Studies in the indole series. II. The alkylation of 1-Methyl-3-formyloxindole and a synthesis of the basic ring structure of physostigmine. J. Am. Chem. Soc., 56:1797–1801.

With A. Magnani. Addition to the conjugated systems in the anthracene series. I. The action of phenylmagnesium bromide on methyleneanthrone. J. Am. Chem. Soc., 56:2174–77.

1935

With J. Pikl. Studies in the indole series. III. On the synthesis of physostigmine. J. Am. Chem. Soc., 57:539–44.

With J. Pikl. Studies in the indole series. IV. The synthesis of d,l-eserethole. J. Am. Chem. Soc., 57:563–66.

With J. Pikl. Studies in the indole series. V. The complete synthesis of physostigmine (eserine). J. Am. Chem. Soc., 57:755–57.

With J. Pikl and F. E. Wantz. Studies in the indole series. VI. On the synthesis of oxytryptophan and further studies of 3-alkylation of oxindoles. J. Am. Chem. Soc., 57:2026–29.

With W. Cole. Additions to conjugated systems in the anthracene series. II. The behavior of certain anthranols. J. Am. Chem. Soc., 57:1607–11.

With W. Cole and T. F. Wood. Additions to conjugated systems in the anthracene series. III. Factors influencing the mode and extent of reactions of the Gringnard reagent with ketones. J. Am. Chem. Soc., 57:2508–13.

With W. J. Gist. The action of the Grignard reagent on certain fuchsones. J. Am. Chem. Soc., 57:2030–32.

With B. M. Sturgis. Homoamines and homoacids. J. Am. Chem. Soc., 57:1126–28.

1936

With J. Pikl. Studies in the indole series. VII. The course of the Fischer reaction with ketones of the type $R\text{-}CH_2\text{-}CO\text{-}CH_3$. *Alpha*-propyl and *alpha*-homoveratryl indole. Proc. Indiana Acad. Sci., 45:145–50.

1938

With J. P. and R. Dawson. The constituents of *Ceanothus americanus*. I. Ceanothic acid. J. Am. Chem. Soc., 60:77–79.

With J. J. Oliver, R. H. Kimball, A. B. Pike, and G. D. Jefferson. α-Phenylacetoacetonitrile. Org. Synth., 18:66; Collect. vol. II. (1943): 487–89.

With J. J. Oliver. Methyl benzyl ketone. Org. Synth., 18:54; Collect. vol. II. (1943): 391–93.

1943

The effect of heat on protein. The Baker's Digest (August). Also in: Chem. Abstr., 37:5741.

1945

With E. W. Meyer, A. Magnani, and W. Cole. Studies in the indole series. IX. The reactions of *alpha*-halogenated and *alpha*-Hydroxy ketones with arylamines. Part 1. J. Am. Chem. Soc., 67:1203–11.

With W. Cole and G. Diemer. Conjugated systems in the anthracene series. IV. Transannular anthranol peroxide. J. Am. Chem. Soc., 67:1721–23.

With W. Cole. Sterols. I. A study of the 22-ketosteroids. J. Am. Chem. Soc., 67:1369–75.

With W. Cole and E. W. Meyer. Conjugated systems. V. A 1,7-shift of hydrogen of alkylidene anthrones into vinyl anthranols. J. Am. Chem. Soc., 67:1724–27.

With W. Cole, E. W. Meyer, and R. A. Herness. Sterols. II. Unsaturation at the C_{22}-position and the behavior of C_{20}-isomeric carbinols. J. Am. Chem. Soc., 67:1375–81.

With W. Cole, A. Magnani, and E. W. Meyer. Sterols. III. A method for the dehalogenation of steroids. J. Am. Chem. Soc., 67: 1728–30.

1948

With J. Pikl, A. Magnani, and W. J. Karpel. Studies in the indole series. VIII. Yohimbine (Part 1). The mechanism of dehydrogenation of yohimbine and related compounds. J. Am. Chem. Soc., 70:174–79.

With W. J. Karpel, A. Magnani, and E. W. Meyer. Studies in the indole series. X. Yohimbine (Part 2). The synthesis of yobyrine, yobyrone and tetrahydroyobyrine. J. Am. Chem. Soc., 70: 180–83.

With E. W. Meyer and H. C. Printy. Sterols. IV. Δ^{20}-Pregnenes from bisnorsteroid acids. J. Am. Chem. Soc., 70:887–92.

With A. Magnani, E. W. Meyer, and W. Cole. Sterols. V. The i-cholesterylamines. J. Am. Chem. Soc., 70:1834–37.

With W. J. Karpel, A. Magnani, and B. W. Meyer. The synthesis of ketoyobyrine. J. Am. Chem. Soc., 70:2834.

With E. W. Meyer and H. C. Printy. Sterols. VI. 16-Methyltestosterone. J. Am. Chem. Soc., 70:3872–75.

1949

With E. W. Meyer and I. Ryden. Sterols. VII. 17α-Hydroxysteroids. J. Am. Chem. Soc., 71:756.

With W. Cole, G. Diemer, and J. G. Schafer. Conjugated systems. VI. 1,5-Anionotropic shifts in the anthracene series. J. Am. Chem. Soc., 71:2058–61.

With W. Cole and R. Schroeder. Conjugated systems. VII. A resonance hybrid to which a triarylmethyl and a biarylnitrogen are contributing structures. J. Am. Chem. Soc., 71:2368–70.

With H. C. Printy. Studies in the indole series. XI. The reduction of certain oxindoles with $LiAlH_4$. J. Am. Chem. Soc., 71:3206–7.

With A. Magnani. Studies in the indole series. XII. Yohimbine (Part 3). A novel synthesis of the yohimbine ring structure. J. Am. Chem. Soc., 71:3207–10.

With E. W. Meyer, W. J. Karpel, and I. Ryden. Sterols. VIII. 17α-Hydroxyprogesterone and 17α-Hydroxy-11-desoxycorticosterone. J. Am. Chem. Soc., 71:3574.

1950

With W. J. Karpel. Sterols. IX. The selective halogenation and dehydrohalogenation of certain steroids (Part 1). J. Am. Chem. Soc., 72:362–66.
With E. W. Meyer and I. Ryden. Sterols. X. 17α-Hydroxyprogesterone. J. Am. Chem. Soc., 72:367–70.
With E. W. Meyer, W. J. Karpel, and I. Ryden Waller. Sterols. XI. 17α-Hydroxy-11-desoxycorticosterone (Reichstein's Substance "S"). J. Am. Chem. Soc., 72:5145–47.

1951

With E. W. Meyer, W. J. Karpel, and W. Cole. Sterols. XII. The partial synthesis of 4-Pregnene-17α,20,21-triol-3-ones and Reichstein's Substance "E." J. Am. Chem. Soc., 73:1982–85.
With W. Cole, E. W. Meyer, A. Magnani, W. J. Karpel, H. C. Printy, and I. Ryden Waller. Sterols. XIII. Chemistry of the adrenal cortex steroids. Recent Prog. Horm. Res., 6:195–214.

1952

With E. W. Meyer and H. C. Printy. The chemistry of indoles. In: *Heterocyclic Compounds,* ed. R. C. Elderfield, vol. 3, pp. 1–274. N.Y.: John Wiley & Sons.

1953

With H. C. Printy. Studies in the indole series. XIII. Oxindole-3-propionic acid. J. Am. Chem. Soc., 75:5301–5.
With H. C. Printy, Roger Ketcham, and Robert Doone. Studies in the indole series. XIV. Oxindole-3-acetic acid. J. Am. Chem. Soc., 75:5305–9.

1954

With W. Cole. Sterols. XIV. Reduction of epoxy ketones by chromous salts. J. Org. Chem., 19:131–38.
With W. Cole, E. W. Meyer, and B. M. Regan. Sterols. XV. Cortisone and analogs (Part 1). 16α-Hydroxy and 16α,17α-epoxy analogs of cortisone. J. Am. Chem. Soc., 77:4601–4.

1956

With C. C. Cochrane, A. Magnani, and W. J. Karpel. Sterols. XVI. Cortisone and analogs (Part 2). 17α,21-Dihydroxy-4-pregnene-3,12,20-trione. J. Am. Chem. Soc., 78:3153–58.

With H. C. Printy and E. E. Dailey. Studies in the indole series. XV. Dioxindole-3-propionic acid. J. Am. Chem. Soc., 78:3501–3.

With E. E. Dailey, H. C. Printy, H. L. Cohen, and S. Hamashige. Studies in the indole series. XVI. Oxindole-3-alanine and dioxindole-3-alanine. J. Am. Chem. Soc., 78:3503–8.

1969

With L. Bauer, C. L. Bell, and R. E. Hewitson. Mechanism of the reaction of 2ξ,6β-dibromocholest-4-en-3-one with potassium acetate. J. Am. Chem. Soc., 91:1690–96.

PATENTS

1940

U.S. 2,218,971. With E. W. Meyer and N. C. Krause. Recovery of Sterols. Granted October 22. (C.A. 35: 1072 [1941])

1941

U.S. 2,238,329. With A. G. Engstrom. Process for the Production of a Derived Vegetable Protein. Granted April 15. (C.A. 35: 4881 [1941])

U.S. 2,246,466. With B. T. Malter. Process of Preparing Vegetable Protein. Granted June 17. (C.A. 35: 6112 [1941])

U.S. 2,249,002. With A. G. Engstrom. Preparation of Vegetable Phosphatides. Granted July 15. (C.A. 35: 6825 [1941])

U.S. 2,249,003. With E. B. Oberg. A Protein-Urea Complex. Granted July 15. (C.A. 35: 6701 [1941])

1942

U.S. 2,273,045. With J. Wayne Cole. Process for the Recovering of Sterols. Granted February 17. (C.A. 36: 3692 [1942])

U.S. 2,273,046. With J. Wayne Cole. Process for Recovering Sterols. Granted February 17. (C.A. 36: 3692 [1942])

U.S. 2,281,584. With E. B. Oberg. Preparation of a Soybean Plastic with Waterproofing Characteristics. Granted May 5. (C.A. 36: 5917 [1942])

U.S. 2,296,284. With J. Wayne Cole. Method of Preparing Material Having the Physiological Activity of the Corpus Luteum Hormone. Granted September 22. (C.A. 37: 1230 [1943])

U.S. 2,304,099. With B. T. Malter. Process for Isolating Vegetable Proteins. Granted December 8. (C.A. 37: 2844 [1943])

U.S. 2,304,100. With J. Wayne Cole and P. J. Carr. Preparation of Tertiary Carbonols of the Cyclopentanophenanthrene Series. Granted December 8. (C.A. 37: 2889 [1943])

U.S. 2,304,101. With J. Wayne Cole. Acyl Chlorides and Ketones Derived Therefrom in the Cyclopentanophenanthrene Series. Granted December 8. (C.A. 37: 2889 [1943])

U.S. 2,304,102. With A. G. Engstrom and E. B. Oberg. A Protein Composition for Paints and Paint Clears. Granted December 8. (C.A. 37: 2849 [1943])

1944

U.S. 2,341,557. With J. Wayne Cole. Process of Preparing Ketones of the Cyclopentanohydrophenanthrene Series. Granted February 14. (C.A. 38: 4387 [1944])

U.S. 2,342,147. With J. Wayne Cole. The Preparation of Etio-Cholenic Acid Derivatives. Granted February 22. (C.A. 38: 4620 [1944])

U.S. 2,355,081. With E. W. Meyer. Preparation of an Oil-Soluble Phosphatide Composition. Granted August 8. (C.A. 38: 6585 [1944])

U.S. 2,363,794. With E. B. Oberg and B. T. Malter. Protein Composition of Matter Resistant to Formaldehyde Coagulation. Granted November 28. (C.A. 39: 3098 [1945])

1945

U.S. 2,373,686. With E. W. Meyer and H. T. Iveson. Methylation of the Phospholipid, Cephalin. Granted April 17. (C.A. 39: 3093 [1945])

U.S. 2,373,687. With E. W. Meyer and H. T. Iveson. The Alteration and Control of Viscosity of Chocolate via Phospholipids. Granted April 17. (C.A. 39: 3093 [1945])

U.S. 2,374,681. With E. W. Meyer. Increasing the Oil Solubility of Phospholipids. Granted May 1. (C.A. 39: 3379 [1945])

U.S. 2,374,682. With E. W. Meyer. Oil Phosphatide Composition for High Pressure Lubrication. Granted May 1. (C.A. 39: 3660 [1945])

U.S. 2,374,683. With J. Wayne Cole, A. Magnani, and H. E. Conde. Dehalogenation of Halogenated Steroids. Granted May 1. (C.A. 40: 1636 [1946])

U.S. 2,381,407. With A. Levinson and A. G. Engstrom. Conversion of Soybean Globulin into an Egg Albumin-Like Protein. Granted August 7. (C.A. 39: 5004 [1945])

1946

U.S. 2,391,462. With E. W. Meyer. Effecting Phospholipid Solubility by Acid Treatment. Granted December 25. (C.A. 40: 3283 [1946])

U.S. 2,392,390. With H. T. Iveson. Refining Vegetable Oils. Granted January 8. (C.A. 40: 2326 [1946])

U.S. 2,394,551. With J. W. Cole. Unsaturated Ketones of the Cyclopentanophenanthrene Series. Granted February 12. (C.A. 40: 2593 [1946])

U.S. 2,400,120. With E. W. Meyer. New Quarternary Compounds from Phospholipids. Granted May 14. (C.A. 40: 5398 [1946])

U.S. 2,400,123. With A. Levinson and B. T. Malter. Process for the Canning of Soybeans and Product. Granted May 14. (C.A. 41: 5234 [1947])

1947

U.S. 2,428,368. With J. W. Cole and E. W. Meyer. Amines of the i-Steroid Series. Granted October 7. (C.A. 42: 624 [1948])

1948

U.S. 2,430,467. With J. W. Cole, A. Magnani, and E. W. Meyer. The Preparation of 3-Amino-Derivatives of Steroids. Granted November 11. (C.A. 42: 1974 [1948])

U.S. 2,433,848. With J. W. Cole, A. Magnani, and H. E. Conde. Procedure for the Preparation of Progesterone. Granted January 6. (C.A. 42: 1710 [1948])

U.S. 2,446,538. With J. W. Cole, A. Magnani, and E. W. Meyer. Method for Preparing 3-Amino-Steroids from i-Steroids. Granted August 10. (C.A. 42: 8218 [1948])

1949

U.S. 2,464,236. With W. J. Karpel and J. W. Armstrong. Oxidation of Soya Sitosteryl Acetate Dibromide. Granted March 14. (C.A. 43: 9538 [1949])

U.S. 2,484,833. With J. W. Cole, A. Magnani, and E. W. Meyer. 6-Alkoxy-i-androstene-17-ols. Granted October 18. (C.A. 44: 5549 [1950])

1950

U.S. 2,531,441. With J. W. Cole, E. W. Meyer, and A. Magnani. Rearrangement of Steroid Oximes. Granted November 28. (C.A. 45: 2988 [1951])

1951

U.S. 2,561,378. With H. C. Printy and E. W. Meyer. Steroid Dimethylamines and Their Quaternary Halides. Granted July 24. (C.A. 46: 1598 [1952])

U.S. 2,562,194. With E. W. Meyer and H. C. Printy. Steroid Mannich Amines. Granted July 31. (C.A. 46: 1598 [1952])

U.S. 2,566,336. With E. W. Meyer, J. W. Cole, and A. Magnani. Steroidal Ketones Containing Amino Groups. Granted September 4. (C.A. 46: 5096 [1952])

1952

U.S. 2,582,258. With E. W. Meyer, R. Schroeder, and A. Magnani. Preparation and Degradation of Steroid Amines. Granted January 15. (C.A. 46: 7596 [1952])

U.S. 2,588,391. With E. W. Meyer and H. C. Printy. 16-Alkyl-Steroids and Process of Preparing. Granted March 11. (C.A. 46: 9127 [1952])

U.S. 2,588,392. With S. J. Circle and R. T. MacDonald. Process of Improving Alkali-Soluble Acid-Precipitable Vegetable Protein. Granted March 11. (C.A. 46: 5225 [1952])

U.S. 2,606,911. With E. W. Meyer. Preparation of Etio-Steroid Acids. Granted August 12. (C.A. 47: 3353 [1953])

1953

U.S. 2,629,662. With H. T. Iveson and M. L. McClelland. The Hydroxylation of Phospholipids. Granted February 24. (C.A. 47: 5141 [1953])

U.S. 2,648,662. With E. W. Meyer and I. Ryden. Preparation of 3,20-Diketo-17a-Hydroxy-Steroids. Granted August 11. (C.A. 48:7651 [1954])

U.S. 2,648,663. With E. W. Meyer and I. Ryden. Granted August 11. (C.A. 48: 7650 [1954])

U.S. 2,662,904. With E. W. Meyer and I. Ryden. Preparation of 17a-Hydroxy-Steroids. Granted December 15. (C.A. 48: 12817 [1954])

1954

U.S. 2,667,498. With W. J. Karpel. Selective Dehalogenation of Certain Halogenated Ketones. Granted January 26. (C.A. 48: 5232 [1954])

U.S. 2,670,359. With E. W. Meyer. Hofmann Degradation of Steroid Quaternary Ammonium Salts. Granted February 23. (C.A. 48: 4829 [1954])

U.S. 2,671,794. With W. J. Karpel. Procedure for the Preparation of Δ^{16}-20-Keto-Pregnanes. Granted March 9. (C.A. 49: 4034 [1955])

U.S. 2,686,181. With E. W. Meyer and I. Ryden. Preparation of 16,17-Oxido-5-Pregnenes. Granted August 10. (C.A. 49: 15986 [1955])

Swiss 328,265. With E. W. Meyer and I. Ryden. 16,17-Epoxy-Δ^5-Steroids. Granted August 10.

U.S. 2,690,971. With H. T. Iveson and Sol B. Radlove. Edible Shortening Agent Containing Hydroxy-Acyl Groups. Granted October 5. (C.A. 49: 1271 [1955])

U.S. 2,696,490. With W. J. Karpel. Preparation of Steroids of the C_{19} Series. Granted December 7. (C.A. 49: 15987 [1955])

1955

U.S. 2,705,233. 16,17-Oxido-pregnan-3a-ol-11,20-dione. Granted March 29. (C.A. 50: 5790 [1956])

U.S. 2,705,238. With H. C. Printy and E. W. Meyer. Steroid Dimethylamines and Their Quaternary Halides. Granted March 29. (C.A. 50: 5794 [1956])

U.S. 2,724,649. With H. T. Iveson and M. L. McClelland. Improved Margarine. Granted November 22. (C.A. 50: 3673 [1956])

1956

British 736,818. Stereospecific Reduction of 3-Keto-Δ^4-Steroids. (C.A. 50: 7888 [1956])

Mexican 62,981. Preparation of 3-Keto-Steroids Having Cis Junction of Rings A and B.

U.S. 2,752,339. With J. W. Cole. Preparation of Cortisone. Granted June 26. (C.A. 51: 2081 [1957])

British 736,818. Reduction of 3-Keto-Steroids to 3a-Hydroxy-Steroids.

U.S. 2,752,376. With H. T. Iveson and S. B. Radlove. Hydroxylation of Vegetable Oils. Granted June 26. (C.A. 50: 13482 [1956])

U.S. 2,752,378. With H. T. Iveson. Separating Sterols from Vegetable Oils by Hydration. Granted June 26. (C.A. 50: 13482 [1956])

U.S. 2,773,771. With H. T. Iveson and S. B. Radlove. Synergistic Compositions of Matter Comprising the Alcohol-Soluble Moiety of Vegetable Phospholipids. Granted December 11. (C.A. 51: 4599 [1957])

U.S. 2,773,867. With J. C. Klein. Process of Dehalogenating Steroids. Granted December 11. (C.A. 51: 7447 [1957])

British 748,914. Improvements in or Relating to Preparation of 21-Halo-Steroids. Granted May 16. (C.A. 51: 2077 [1957])

1957

U.S. 2,789,989. With W. J. Karpel. Preparation of 21-Bromo- and 21-Iodo-Steroids. Granted April 23. (C.A. 51: 12161 [1957])

British 778,334. Stereospecific Chlorination of Δ^5-Steroids. Granted July 3. (C.A. 52: 2106 [1958]). Also Mexican 62,944.

U.S. 2,816,108. With E. W. Meyer, I. Ryden, and W. J. Karpel. Method for Introducing a 21-Hydroxy Group into 17-Oxygenated Steroids. Granted December 10. (C.A. 52: 8225 [1958])

1958

U.S. 2,820,030. With E. W. Meyer, I. Ryden, and W. J. Karpel. Certain 16,17-Oxido-Steroids of the C_{21}-Series. Granted January 14. (C.A. 52: 10231 [1958])

U.S. 2,849,318. With H. T. Iveson. Separation of the Constituents of Vegetable Phospholipids. Granted August 26. (C.A. 53: 1582 [1959])

1959

U.S. 2,876,237. With J. W. Cole and G. H. Diemer. 5,7-Pregnadiene-3-ol-one, Esters Thereof and Related Compounds. Granted March 3. (C.A. 53: 13208 [1959])

U.S. 2,881,159. With S. J. Circle and R. W. Whitney. Process for Isolating Soya Protein. Granted April 7. (C.A. 53: 14381 [1959])

U.S. 2,885,398. With H. C. Printy. 4,5-Epoxy-Derivatives of 17a-Alkyltestosterones. Granted May 5. (C.A. 53: 22096 [1959])

U.S. 2,887,478. With J. W. Cole, E. W. Meyer, and W. J. Karpel. A Novel Method of Preparing Androstendione and Similar Compounds from 16-Dehydropregnenolone. Granted May 19. (C.A. 53: 20142 [1959])

U.S. 2,891,974. With H. C. Printy. Substituted 2,5-Androstadienes. Granted June 23. (C.A. 54: 1622 [1960])

U.S. 2,891,975. With H. C. Printy. 2,5-Pregnadiene Derivatives. Granted June 23. (C.A. 54: 1624 [1960])

U.S. 2,900,399. With H. C. Printy. Androstan-3,17-diol-4-one Derivatives. Granted August 18. (C.A. 54: 1622 [1960])

U.S. 2,910,487. With V. Georgian and H. C. Printy. Process for the Preparation of 2-Acetoxy-Steroids. Granted October 27. (C.A. 54: 2444 [1960])

1960

Australian 227,519. Process for Epimerizing 11β-Bromo-Steroids. Granted April 1. (C.A. 54: 19772 [1960])

U.S. 2,933,510. With H. C. Printy. 3-Keto-4-Halo-$\Delta^{4,5}$-Steroids. Granted April 19. (C.A. 54: 17482 [1960])

U.S. 2,947,76. With A. Magnani and C. C. Cochrane. Preparation of the 12-Keto-Isomer of Cortisone. Granted August 2. (C.A. 55: 7492 [1961])

U.S. 2,940,991. With A. Magnani. Method for Epimerizing 11-Bromo-Steroids. Granted June 14. (C.A. 54: 19772 [1960]). Also Canadian 630,065.

French 1,254,408. With A. Magnani. Procedure for the Preparation of Steroidal Compounds Utilized for the Obtention of Corticoid Hormones. Granted June 14. (C.A. 54: 19772 [1960])

British 846,045. 11,12-Epoxy-Steroids. Granted August 24. (C.A. 55: 10508 [1961])

U.S. 2,962,421. With D. W. Johnson. Process for Removing Sulfur Dioxide from Aqueous Liquors. Granted November 29. (C.A. 55: 7725 [1961])

1961

U.S. 2,944,052. With A. Magnani. Novel Epoxy-Pregnanes. Granted July 5. (C.A. 55: 1710 [1961])

British 873,633. Improvements in or Relating to Process and Intermediates for Preparing Steroid Compounds. Granted July 26. (C.A. 56: 4838 [1961])

Canadian 630,071. With A. Magnani. 11,12-Epoxy-Steroids and Method of Preparation. Granted October 31.

Canadian 614,085. Liquid Shortening.

U.S. 3,013,026. With A. Magnani and V. Georgian. Process for the Preparation of 3-Keto-Δ^4-20-Alkyl-Amino-Steroids. Granted December 12. (C.A. 56: 8810 [1962])

1962

U.S. 3,019,220. Isolation of Sapogenine. Granted January 30. (C.A. 56: 1440 [1961]). Also Guatemalan 938; Mexican 67,028.

U.S. 3,030,389. With E. Huang and A. Magnani. Process for the Preparation of 16-Alkylpregnenes. Granted April 17. (C.A. 57: 11278 [1962])

British 1,009,802. With E. Huang and A. Magnani. Improvements in or Relating to Novel Process for the Preparation of 16-Alkylpregnenes. Granted April 17. (C.A. 57: 11278 [1962])

British 1,009,803. With E. Huang and A. Magnani. 5,6-Dichloro-16a-Methyl-pregnanolones. Granted April 17. (C.A. 57: 11278 [1962])

U.S. 3,052,694. With A. Magnani. 12-Alkyl-12-Hydroxyprogesterone Derivatives. Granted September 4.

1963

Canadian 662,612. Substituted 2,5-Dien-4-one-Steroid Derivatives. Granted May 7. (C.A. 54: 1622 [1960])

U.S. 3,055,918. With J. W. Cole. The Reduction of an Epoxy Group such as Alpha to a Keto Group. Granted September 25.

1964

U.S. 3,149,132. With A. Magnani. 16-Amino-methyl-17-alkyltestosterone Derivatives. Granted September 15. (C.A. 61: 14751 [1964]). Also South-African 63/4204.

Australian 229,846. Improvements in or Relating to 11,12-Epoxypregnane Derivatives and the Preparation Thereof. Granted October 20.

British 1,031,080. Improvements in or Relating to 16-Amino-methyl-17-alkyltestosterone and Isotestosterone Derivatives. (C.A. 62: 9205 [1965])

U.S. 3,153,061. With E. Huang and A. Magnani. 17-Substituted-2,5-pregnadiene Derivatives. Granted October 13.

U.S. 3,153,646. With A. Magnani. process for the Production of $11\beta,12\beta$-Epoxypregnan-3,20-dione. Granted October 20.

1965

U.S. 3,187,025. With A. Magnani, J. M. Hill and T. C. Aschner. Process for Preparing Compound "S." Granted June 1. (C.A. 63: 10036 [1965])

Netherlands 64/06303. 3-Keto-$\Delta^{4,5}$-Steroids.

Netherlands 64/06306. Corticosteroids.

1966

U.S. 3,231,568. With J. M. Hill. Processes and Intermediates for Preparing 16a-Methyl-Corticoids. Granted January 25. (C.A. 64: 9802 [1966])

U.S. 3,274,178. With A. Magnani. 16a-Hydroxy-cortexolone and Derivatives. Granted September 20.

German 1,293,158. With J. M. Hill. Verfahren zur Herstellung von 16a-Methyl-3β,17a-dihydroxy-$\Delta^{5,6}$-pregnen-20-on und dessen 3-Acetat. Granted January 25. (C.A. 64: 9802 [1966])

British 1,059,643. Process for preparing 5-Pregnene-3β,17α,21-triol-20-one 21-acylates. Also Mexican 83,878; Canadian 787,914; French 1,406,988; German 1,235,907.

British 1,060,354. Process for Preparing 3-Keto-$\Delta^{4,5}$-Steroids. Also French 1,403,946; Mexican 83,686.

British 1,087,899. With J. M. Hill. Process for Preparing 16α-Methyl-3p,17α-Dihydroxy-Δ^5-pregnen-20-one. Granted January 25. (C.A. 64: 9802 [1966])

1970

German 2,018,730. Verfahren zur Einführung einer olefinischen Doppelbindung in ein Steroid durch Reduktion einer Oxidogrupp.

1973

U.S. 3,711,611. Composition of Matter with Low Cholesterol Content and Containing Wool Grease Alcohols as Major Component and Method. Granted January 18. Also Belgian 788,507; British 1,350,355.

U.S. 3,759,899. Process for Introducing a Delta 5,6-Double Bond into a Steroid. Granted September 18.

U.S. 3,761,469. Process for the Manufacture of Steroid Chlorohydrins. Granted September 25.

1974

U.S. 3,784,598. Process for Conversion of a 3-Hydroxy-5,6-Oxido Group of a Steroid into a Δ^4-3-Oxo-Group. Granted January 8.

U.S. 3,821,121. Preparation of Wool Wax Alcohol of Low Cholesterol Content Useful as Dispersing and Emulsifying Agent. Granted June 28.

KARL FRIEDRICH MEYER

May 19, 1884–April 27, 1974

BY ALBERT D. SABIN*

K F MEYER (henceforth "KF," as he was affectionately called by his colleagues) was an outstanding bacteriologist, experimental pathologist, virologist, epidemiologist, ecologist, brilliant and inspiring teacher, and a prototype of the scientist in the service of society. In the tradition of Pasteur and Koch, his scientific studies invariably involved the acquisition of knowledge for the understanding and solution of important practical problems in the field of human and animal diseases. In 1951, when KF was sixty-seven years young, the American Public Health Association presented him a Lasker Award with the following citation that aptly expressed the esteem of his colleagues and summarized his major contributions to science and public health:

Brilliant scientist, dynamic teacher, inspired humanitarian. His influence now extends over two generations of students of medicine, biology,

---

*In writing this biographical memoir, I tried whenever possible to let K. F. Meyer talk for himself in his own colorful, inimitable manner. I am indebted to the director of the Bancroft Library of the University of California, Berkeley, for permission to quote from Dr. Meyer's oral history memoir entitled *Medical Research and Public Health* (Berkeley: University of California, 1976), a transcript of a 1961–1962 unedited tape-recorded oral interview by Edna Tartaul Daniel, Regional Oral History Office, The Bancroft Library. This oral history was also the source of much of my information that is not available elsewhere. Since Dr. Meyer continued to be too busy to read this transcript, I corrected the spelling of some of the names and checked the dates of certain events.

and the allièd health sciences. His research and leadership have benefited all classes of people for four decades. . . .

Among his accomplishments is a major share of responsibility for the control of botulism, and for a classification and international identification center for the clostridia; for our recognition that plague is sylvatic, not merely rat-borne; for understanding of the broad spectrum of brucellosis rather than restricted goat-borne Malta-fever; for the concept of ornithosis rather than psittacosis; for elucidating the role of the arthropod vector in western equine encephalomyelitis; for showing that western ticks are also responsible for relapsing fever; for studying the dinoflagellate causing mussel poisoning; for increasing our knowledge of leptospirosis; for valuable assistance with investigations of Q fever.

No ivory tower recluse, Karl Meyer has responded promptly and gratis to calls for help from physicians, scientists, health officers, farmers, fishermen, canners, the Military and the United States Government.

Inherent in his research is its application. To both he has applied himself with boundless energy and humanitarian generosity, to the great good of mankind.

KF continued his important work and enjoyment of life in his inimitable manner until a brief illness ended his life only twenty-two days before his ninetieth birthday.

FAMILY BACKGROUND AND EARLY LIFE IN SWITZERLAND

KF was born in Basel, Switzerland, the son of Theodor and Sophie (Lichtenhahn) Meyer zum Pfeil van Büren. Both parents were members of old, upper-middle-class Basel families, and KF noted that he traced his family tree back to the fourteenth century. His father was a relatively affluent merchant who imported fine cigars from Cuba and Indonesia for sale throughout Central Europe. His father's hobbies included reading, hunting, fencing, and long walks in the Swiss Alps. His mother taught in elementary school before her marriage, and did much to develop KF's intellectual curiosity in his pre-school years. KF had two sisters, both younger than he. His early years were spent in a large, well-appointed old house overlooking the Rhine River, just off the principal Basel Cathedral Square.

KF attended a private elementary Evangelische Volkschule of the Swiss Zwingli reformed church. After four years of elementary school, he entered Gymnasium where languages (Latin, Greek, classical German, French, and English), history, mathematics, and, to a lesser extent, the sciences were the main components of the curriculum. KF's special interest in the natural sciences led him to spend the last two years in the Realgymnasium where there was greater emphasis on and better teaching of the sciences, especially chemistry, physics, and biology. According to KF's own recollection, he was a pain in the neck to his teachers and a "bête noir," full of mischief and tricks in the classroom right up to the end of his Realgymnasium days. His lifelong impatience with what he regarded as "nonsense," illogical, or factually unproven was already fully developed in his late Gymnasium years, and he apparently never let his teachers get away with what he regarded as questionable statements. Despite this and his propensity for neglecting homework, he graduated second in his Realgymnasium class in 1902 when he was eighteen years old.

KF recalled that physically he was in "fantastic shape" during those years. He fenced, rode horseback, rowed on the Rhine River, and walked a lot. He did not share his father's love for hunting. KF was very popular with his classmates and he put on school plays such as Molière's *Le Malade Imaginaire* and Rostand's *Cyrano de Bergerac*. His extracurricular reading during those days included mostly adventure books, the *Illustrated London Times*, the Swiss daily newspapers, with their "superb editorials," and the German encyclopedia *Conversations Lexicone*.

UNIVERSITY EDUCATION

KF's university education included one-half year (1902) in Basel, two years (1903, 1904) in Zürich, one year (1905) in Munich, and about two and one-half years (1906–1908) of course and thesis work in Bern. At Basel, he was tremendously attracted to zoology, more to the abnormal than to the normal, and was particularly fascinated by the newly emerging protozoology with the recent discoveries of the malarial parasites and the flagellated trypanosomes. KF's recollections of Professor Friedrich Zschokke, the "topnotch" zoology teacher in Switzerland at the time, included all those attributes that later characterized KF's own teaching methods—the "fantastically" prepared and orderly presented lectures followed by dissections and gross and microscopic demonstrations in the laboratory, the Saturday field trips that ended in vivid discussions over steins of beer in an outdoor beer garden. "Bon vivant" KF first joined the Helvetia Fencing Club, where the rapier fencing was too much of a bloody affair for him, and, ultimately, the extensive alcohol consumption also became too much. He then switched to one of the oldest color fraternities, the Zofingia. The independent KF's dislike of being pushed around by the older members of the Zofingia corps, and the heavy beer-drinking and all-night parties, strongly disapproved by his father, led to the decision to move away from Basel.

His move to the University of Zürich was influenced not only by his desire to "get away from the house," but also by the fact that there were many more good departments in Zürich, especially the great departments of comparative anatomy and chemistry. Although his great interest was in zoology, he also worked hard in botany, chemistry, and physics, in which he had to pass examinations for admission to the subsequent studies he wished to pursue. KF recalled that his later career was determined by the recommendation of his professor of comparative anatomy that he continue his studies with Heinrich Zangger, a professor of comparative physiology and pathology at the Veterinary School. KF described Zangger as a "perfectly fabulous individual from the standpoint of what he knew in chemistry and the way he looked at life."* Zangger treated KF as if he were a graduate student and gave him a corner in his laboratory where he could work in his spare time.

KF accepted Zangger's recommendation that he enroll in the Veterinary School where he could learn a great deal about animals. KF also studied human anatomy, physiology, and biochemistry in the medical section of the University. After two years at the University of Zürich, KF passed his examinations with "flying colors." Zangger then steered him to the University of Munich and continued to have a most important influence on KF's career and general outlook on life. KF later said about Zangger: "In my life, he was *the* man." Zangger's concern about human beings and what happened in society, evidenced by his subsequent activities in forensic medicine, in industrial hygiene in the rapidly evolving Swiss chemical industry, and in preventive medicine in industry, led KF to say: "This gave me my social consciousness which I always try to hammer home—social consciousness. You are part of the society and you have to make your contribution."†

KF spent his year in Munich working in the laboratory of Professor Friedrich von Müller in the University's Department of Medicine and in the pathological institute of Hermann Dürck. During the first weeks in Munich, KF again indulged in a great deal of heavy drinking and carousing, often without a stop from Friday night to Monday morning.

Medical Research and Public Health, p. 31.
†*Ibid.*, p. 39.

He soon realized that this was no good and changed his entire way of living. Thereafter, he would leave Friday evening for skiing in the mountains and also enjoyed the superb theatres and concerts in Munich. He was more attracted to the theatre than to music and was especially moved by Ibsen's plays portraying "the dark side of Europe at that time."

Upon completion of his studies in Munich, KF, again on Professor Zangger's advice, went to Bern to complete various required courses at the Veterinary School. But he wanted more than stereotyped lecture and laboratory courses. He wanted to do something by himself as he had done during all of his student days. He always had a little corner where he could work. KF asked the great pathologist, Paul Langerhans, who discovered the "islets of Langerhans," for a few feet of space in his laboratory, saying that he had his own microtome, his own paraffin oven, etc., but was turned away. A few days later he watched Langerhans perform an autopsy on a baby with a tumor of the jaw. KF suspected that the tumor was a teratoma and, when Langerhans was not looking, "snatched" a piece of the tumor; within forty-eight hours KF found liver cells in the stained sections of the tumor. Langerhans confirmed KF's diagnosis and was so impressed by the beautifully stained sections that he offered to help him. Langerhans recommended KF to Professor Wilhelm Kolle, a former pupil and assistant of Robert Koch, at the Institute for Infectious Diseases in Bern. It is here that KF did his work on his thesis that dealt with an interesting intestinal, paratuberculosis infection in cattle. The thesis, completed in 1908, was sent for approval to the veterinary faculty in Zürich, where he originally enrolled as a regular student in the Veterinary School. Thus, although the graduate work was done in Bern, KF received his doctorate in veterinary medicine from Zürich in 1909.

During his period in Bern, KF apparently travelled to other centers of learning and accumulated experiences that greatly influenced his subsequent career. In his acceptance of the Water Reed Medal of 1956 (*American Journal of Tropical Medicine and Hygiene,* 6:341, 1957), KF recalled the opportunity he had of studying the illustrated monograph of Battista Grassi showing the complete life cycle of the human malarial parasite in *Anopheles* and of seeing Grassi's original preparations during a holiday visit in Rome. Also impressed on KF's memory were conversations with Dr. George Nuttall, Professor of Biology at Cambridge University in 1906, recalled at the acceptance ceremony:

> Professor Nuttall planted ideas in my mind that were decisive as a basis for understanding many tropical diseases. He made it clear that topography, climate, vegetation, and other environmental factors determine whether an area will be likely to sustain the malarial parasite. When I was learning what was known about the factors that cause trypanosomiasis to flourish—about the tsetse fly, trees, shade, proximity to water and cattle and wild game—Professor Nuttall intimated that animals might well serve as reservoir hosts of the parasite. He foresaw many of the relationships between animal and man bridged by an insect vector. That this interplay was profoundly involved in the development and public health of Africa was amply emphasized. The implications of conversations with this able scientist haunted me during the next fifty years. They haunt me still.

CHOICE OF CAREER

The choice was between going into practice and into an academic career. For KF, veterinary practice had no appeal because it was against his nature to ask a fee for services rendered. On completion of his thesis, Professor Kolle advised KF to embark on an academic career, and while he offered him a laboratory, he told him he could not pay him anything. The first step at that time in an academic career was to become a "privat dozent" at the university. Unfortunately the income for such a post was unpredictable, since it came from the modest fees paid by students who might be attracted to the dozent's lectures. The opportunities for ultimately getting a professorship at one of the five Swiss universities were very slim. So when KF, at age twenty-four, told his father that he had chosen an academic career, he recalls his father telling him: "Do you think I'm going to feed you until you're fifty-six?"* In the end, Professor Kolle offered to find a job for KF, and several weeks later informed him of an opening for a pathologist at a big new institute in South Africa under Arnold Theiler (later Sir Arnold Theiler, the father of Nobel Laureate Max Theiler), a Swiss who wished to have a Swiss for this post. The salary was 600 pounds sterling ($3,000—a lot of money at the time), free round-trip transportation, and a contract for three years. Kolle, who had worked in South Africa with Robert Koch, told KF that scientifically it was a "fantastic" opportunity because (as KF recalled it) "you can look under the microscope at any blood sample and find a new parasite." KF accepted; his father outfitted him for the trip and even arranged for the best British tailor to make his clothing as he passed through London on his way to South Africa. Thus was KF's career launched at twenty-four years of age.

SOUTH AFRICA (1908–1910)

A magnificent new Institute, just outside of Pretoria, had been built for Arnold Theiler because of his important contributions to the understanding and control of livestock diseases in the preceding twenty years, and was opened only a few months before KF's arrival. The Institute had a large operating budget by the standards of the time (about $200,000), and much experimental work was in progress

*Ibid., p. 41.

there on the nature, transmission, and prevention of diseases of cattle and horses that were of great economic importance to South Africa, such as rinderpest, African horse sickness, East Coast fever, red-water (Texas) fever, bovine pleuropneumonia, anthrax, glanders, and other obscure parasitic and bacterial infections.

The official title of KF's new post was pathologist, Transvaal Department of Agriculture, Onderstepoort, Union of South Africa. His duties included making rabies vaccine, doing autopsies on the hundreds of large animals that were used in experiments or were brought to the Institute by farmers, and diagnostic work involving hundreds of blood smears. This routine work, full of challenges to KF's inquisitive and prepared mind, occupied most of his regular workday from 7 a.m. to 5:30 p.m. He then went horseback riding in the hilly country around the Institute, had his dinner at the hostelry where the unmarried Institute staff members took their meals, and then invariably returned to the laboratory to work until midnight on problems he wished to elucidate.

His routine responsibility for the contagious bovine pleuropneumonia vaccine led him to carry out classic studies on the pathologic anatomy of the disease, which were published in 1909. He also discovered a strain of pleuropneumonia organism that produced arthritis in cattle. (About thirty years later I accidentally discovered a mouse pleuropneumonia strain that produced an experimental arthritis in mice similar to human rheumatoid arthritis.)

The challenging, unsolved problems of African East Coast fever, which had been under study at the Institute for many years, and had previously brought both Robert Koch and Wilhelm Kolle (KF's mentor in Bern) to East and South Africa, soon engaged KF's interest. His work resulted in an important elucidation of the life cycle of *Piroplasma (Theileria) parvum,* which was present in large numbers in the erythrocytes of cattle suffering from the disease. The mystery was that the blood of these diseased cattle failed to transmit the disease to susceptible cattle, although it was already established that certain blood-sucking ticks were effective transmitters of the infection. KF soon demonstrated that while as much as one liter of blood was not infectious, suspensions of the spleen and lymph nodes transmitted the disease. The explanation emerged from a study of the life cycle of the parasite carried out by KF and Institute entomologists. In his 1956 Walter Reed Medal acceptance speech (mentioned earlier), KF described these studies as follows:

> A study of the life cycle of the protozoan disclosed that asexual and sexual multiplication, manifestations of which were seen by Koch and described as Koch's granules, takes place in the cytoplasm of the lymphocytes and endothelial cells. This stage terminates in the formation of gametocytes, and it is these that invade the erythrocytes. In its erythrocytic phase in the mammalian host the parasite cannot multiply further. In time it degenerates in the blood and organs or even when transferred to another susceptible bovine host. However, when, through a blood meal, the parasite is taken into the intestinal tract of *Rhipicephalus appendiculatus* or other ticks capable of transmitting the parasite the gametocyte transforms to zygote, ookinete and finally into sporoblasts. The sporoblast, when introduced into a new host with the saliva of the tick, initiates infection.

The relations between Arnold Theiler and KF were difficult from the beginning. KF recalled that Theiler "was a typical Lucerne squarehead, and a Lucerne squarehead cannot get along very well with a Basel squarehead."* KF's work on the transmission of East Coast fever to susceptible cattle by means of lymph node and spleen suspensions first led Theiler to accuse KF of failing to guard against intercurrent infection by ticks. And when KF repeated his work in more cattle during Theiler's absence from the country, and then showed Theiler a short article he prepared for publication,

Ibid., p. 46.

Theiler said: "Have one thing understood; anything which is done in the institute, *I* have done. *I* wrote this paper."* KF said he did not see it that way, and published this work under his own name in 1909 both in the *Zeitschrift für Infektionskrankheiten* and in the *Journal of Comparative Pathology and Therapeutics*. After that encounter, Theiler and KF did not talk to each other and their only contact was by written communications. KF continued to work until close to the end of his contract in 1910, but it is no exaggeration to conclude that KF and Theiler hated each other, each committing unfriendly acts against the other. In later years KF admitted that while "Theiler made a lot of mistakes . . . he helped a lot in elucidating causes for East Coast fever; he developed the dipping procedure for getting rid of the ticks; and some immunization procedures which were pretty good."† Nevertheless, KF recalled that when Sir Arnold Theiler met him nineteen years later at a meeting in Switzerland, he politely and respectfully addressed him as "Herr Kollege," invited him to lunch, and in response to a question on botulism at the meeting Sir Arnold deferred to his "honorable colleague Meyer."‡

When KF decided to leave South Africa in 1910, he returned to Basel with the resolution to "behave himself" and, now that he had saved enough money to be independent for a while, to work in Kolle's laboratory in Bern again. He recalls, however, that when he walked through the main street in Basel, some of his friends said to him "Are *you* back *again*?" and that "this was just like a stilletto."§ He got to feeling that he no longer fit very well in Switzerland. During this feeling

---

*Ibid., p. 50.
†*Ibid.*, p. 53.
‡I must admit to a certain amount of personal feelings as I write these words because I came to know Sir Arnold's son Max and his work on yellow fever quite well in the 1930's and was the first to recommend Max Theiler for a Nobel Prize in 1947, which he finally received in 1951.
§*Ibid.*, p. 60.

of depression he was invited by an ambassador to Austria, whose wife and daughter KF had met and entertained in South Africa, to spend two weeks with them in a castle. KF had a fine time and opportunities for serious discussions with the ambassador who believed that the United States was the country of the future and that KF should go there. But how? The ambassador happened to have an honorary Doctor of Laws from the University of Pennsylvania and eight weeks later informed KF that there was a position for an assistant professor of pathology and bacteriology at the University of Pennsylvania's School of Veterinary Medicine and that they would like to have a European. The salary was only $1,800, but KF accepted.

UNIVERSITY OF PENNSYLVANIA SCHOOL OF VETERINARY MEDICINE (1910–1913)

KF's mentor in Philadelphia was Dr. Richard M. Pearce, professor of pathology at the University of Pennsylvania School of Medicine. He also met other important faculty members who made him feel welcome, and he quickly became a member of the Philadelphia Pathological Society and a participant in the meetings of the Interurban Clinical Club. Despite these auspicious beginnings, KF soon became very unhappy with the poor preparation and background of the students he had to teach. When he became openly critical of his students, the rumor reached him that faculty reaction to his criticism was: "Don't these foreigners make you sick?"* KF determined to make them even sicker and at the next examination flunked 70 percent of the class. The provost of the University told him: "We don't do things like this around here, because we need the tuition fee."† KF's outspoken criticisms also ruffled feathers at the Philadelphia Patho-

*Ibid., p. 63.
†Ibid.

logical Society. At one of the meetings of the society after a lecture on the mechanism of immunity in streptococcic infections by John Kolmer, professor of immunology, which was loudly applauded by the audience, KF dissected the presentation with a sharp knife. He felt a chill in the audience, which remained perfectly silent after he finished. The chairman of the meeting, Dr. Richard Pearce, who was KF's mentor, on the way out told him: "You know, we don't do things like this.* When KF reacted to this blow by saying he was only doing what should be done at such meetings, Pearce advised him not to talk any more at these meetings until he was asked to talk. Three months later he was asked to talk on some interesting studies he just carried out on sporotrichosis.

KF got a feeling of the basic fairness of his American mentor when Dr. Pearce helped him become a member of the American Association of Pathologists and Bacteriologists only five months after his arrival in the United States and took him to the 1911 national meeting in Chicago to present a paper on the life cycles of blood parasites in South Africa. The appreciation of these studies publicly expressed by Frederick Novy, the great American microbiologist of the University of Michigan, was salve for KF's bruised ego. When Novy and the University of Michigan's distinguished pathologist Alfred S. Warthin then invited him to spend the long Easter weekend with them at Ann Arbor on his way back to Philadelphia, KF felt that he was at last appreciated in the United States, and by men whose scientific work and philosophy he could admire. Despite the Easter holiday, KF and his hosts spent much time in the laboratories, where KF also met Paul de Kruif and Victor Vaughan, the pioneering professor of hygiene. Many years later, KF credited Novy's account of his studies on plague in kindling his own subsequent lifelong

*Ibid., p. 64.

interest in this infection. Many years later, KF remarked: "I must say these three days in Ann Arbor restored my confidence that this is a country where something is going on. This is worth staying around for."* The warm and stimulating experience at Ann Arbor, where, in KF's words, he "was promptly accepted as being somebody," led him later to express his feelings about Philadelphia in the following perceptive words:

> Well, perhaps they recognized the background of my training, but they did not like the way I made use of it. I was too darned critical; I had too sharp a tongue, and I never cloaked anything in a lot of praises when I knew perfectly that the work which was done was a five-cent kind of hash piece. That they didn't like.†

Based on my own familiarity with KF in later years, he did not change, but his colleagues adapted themselves to this aspect of KF's character, because his "darned critical" comments were invariably well founded. Apparently this was also the case in Philadelphia, because he was promoted to full professor in 1911, when he was only twenty-seven years old, and was also appointed director of the Laboratory and Experimental Farm of the Pennsylvania Livestock Sanitary Board—with an increase in salary from $1,800 to $4,000. The diagnostic work and research on animal diseases that KF carried out during the two years at this Laboratory resulted in publications on glanders, biliary fever in dogs, contagious abortion of cattle, paratuberculous enteritis of cattle in America, epizootic abortion in mares, and coccidiosis in chickens. In his review on filterable viruses, he referred to his studies on the possible viral cause of equine encephalitis, work that he brilliantly resumed seventeen years later in California.

*Ibid., p. 68.
†Ibid., p. 66.

During the Philadelphia period, KF also met Dr. Theobald Smith, then professor of comparative pathology at Harvard, at a meeting in Boston where both presented papers on *Bacillus abortus* (later called Brucella on KF's initiative), the cause of infectious abortion of cattle. After the meeting Theobald Smith invited him to the laboratory and home to dinner. The whole experience left an indelible impression that KF later described as follows:

> I went to the laboratory and here this gentleman unrolled before me one of the most fantastic stories in science. The philosophies which he expounded later on tremendously influenced my way of thinking. One remark I will not forget: He said, "You know, one must always get these infections either human or animal, into small laboratory animals. Then we can study them, because it's too expensive to study them in larger animals. Besides with this present desire to control, to eradicate, they frequently eradicate a disease before we understand it." Only too true.*

Despite his meetings with leading bacteriologists and pathologists who appreciated his work, KF was basically disappointed in his post at Pennsylvania and even considered returning to Europe. Early in 1913, Dr. Richard Pearce told KF that he did not fit into the set-up in Philadelphia and advised him to go west to California. Dr. Pearce had just come back from Berkeley where he learned that there would soon be an opening in the Department of Pathology at the Medical School and that the University of California had just received a large gift from Mrs. Hooper to establish an Institute for Medical Research that could become the Rockefeller Institute of the West. KF recalls that Simon Flexner told him: "If you go to California, you will disappear in the Pacific Ocean, because the intelligentsia of the United States lives within a hundred miles from New York."† After considerable hag-

*Ibid., p. 70.
†Ibid., p. 74.

gling with Dr. Frederick P. Gay, who was the head of the Department of Pathology and Bacteriology at Berkeley, KF accepted an appointment as associate professor of bacteriology and protozoology at a salary of $3,000 per annum, with the understanding that he would be promoted to full professor the following year.

After acceptance of this appointment, KF married Mary Elizabeth Lindsay, whom he met during his popular man-about-town activities in Philadelphia, and went off to Europe for several months before going to California in October.

CALIFORNIA (1913–1974)

It was in California that KF finally, despite many tribulations, was able to fulfill his life's goals and find his gratifications from students who inspired him with their eagerness to learn, from fighting battles that he sometimes lost but more often won, and from a citizenry who appreciated his concern for their welfare and his well-directed studies for the solution of some of their serious problems. California also supplied him ample opportunities for enjoying the many nonprofessional aspects of life that were always also very important to KF.

KF's early years in California were devoted largely to the development of his own distinctive teaching programs; their excellence soon won KF a reputation as an exacting, demanding, unique, but brilliant and enchanting teacher. He soon had 286 students in microbiology with laboratory space for only sixty-five, and he remembered that the Bunsen burner was kept burning from 8 a.m. to 10 p.m. He constantly insisted that things be done right or not at all, and his students never forgot him—and their numbers grew over the years. When Dr. David R. Goddard, Home Secretary of the Academy, wrote me in 1978 about my agreement to write KF's story for the Academy's *Biographical Memoirs,* he did not fail to mention that as an undergraduate student at Berkeley he had "the good fortune in taking a course in animal pathology from Dr. Meyer." Dr. Dorothy M. Horstmann, professor of epidemiology and pediatrics at the Yale University School of Medicine, who took the bacteriology course from Dr. Meyer while she was a second-year medical student in California, wrote me: "The lectures started on Fridays at 1 p.m. and ended anytime between 4 and 6 p.m. But he was always interesting to listen to—and gave scholarly yet colorful lectures. Their main impact for me was due to his tremendous knowledge of pathology and pathogenesis. It was this that stimulated my interest in infectious diseases, and directed my course from then on. I owe Dr. Meyer a great deal!" Dr. Edward B. Shaw, emeritus professor of pediatrics at the University of California, San Francisco, wrote me: "I started to work with him about 1918 and got a great deal of my medical education from him as a preceptor. He was always so generous; he put my name on publications when I was still a medical student.... You know well that I could go on and on about all he has meant to me and to many others." One of KF's later students and co-workers on brucellosis, Sanford S. Elberg (subsequently professor of immunology and medical microbiology at the School of Public Health and dean, Graduate Studies Division, University of California at Berkeley), described in vivid language (*American Society of Microbiology News*, 40, September 1974) the unique qualities of KF as a teacher. Elberg said that KF "was a walking encyclopaedia of information about theory and practice of bacteriology in those days and withal a master of showmanship and sense of drama, and a great platform speaker.... The material in the course over the weeks gradually began to take shape in student minds as a dynamic entity that seemed to unfold in an orderly way. Occasionally the session ended with a burst of applause and students would flock to the lecture bench to ask him questions and follow him to his tiny office. . . . K. F. Meyer was one of the very greatest teachers, especially for large classes, in the history of the University of California and on that score alone is one of the University's immortals."*

KF's own recollections were that "the relationship with the students was perfectly marvelous, the echo from them was unbelievable; it was perfect."† Julius Schachter (now professor of epidemiology and acting director of the Hooper Foundation) became his last student in 1960, when KF was seventy-six, and then continued as his co-worker for the remaining fourteen years of KF's life. Schachter, who shares the affection and dedication of KF's earlier students, provided an insight on what it was like to work with KF (*Bull. Schweiz. Akad. Med. Wiss.*, 33: 187–99, 1977):

> Meyer was never easy on graduate students, and I suspect that I was fortunate in coming along when he had mellowed. Our modus operandi for differing experimental approaches was simple. Meyer always let me do the experiments my way—as long as I also did them his way. Successful experiments had to be repeated again and again. . . . During the years when I was a student of Meyer's I could receive phone calls at all hours of the night from him informing me that one of my animals looked sick and I better get up to the laboratory and do something about it. . . . Not only would Meyer call the staff at home about a problem, but if you worked at the Hooper Foundation it was impossible to go to a meeting and be out of Karl Meyer's reach. . . . I remember one instance in the early 1960's when I was in New Orleans on the second day of a five-day meeting. I was paged at breakfast to receive a telegram which said: "Had discussions with Albert Sabin yesterday. He had some interesting ideas. Meet him in Cincinnati tomorrow." Of course I went. . . . Meyer was a man of dignity and courtesy. Even when I was a lowly graduate student he always introduced me as his "colleague." . . . All of us have had our lives enriched by his presence. . . . What we regret is that we have no more like him.

Lucille Foster (B.A. in bacteriology, University of Cali-

---

*Ibid., p. 374–75.
†Ibid., p. 76.

fornia at Berkeley, 1932), who was KF's senior laboratory assistant until his death in 1974, affectionately recalled: "When he was young, we were all scared to death of him. He really yelled. He mellowed considerably as he grew older. . . . He was a very fair boss. He never stayed angry."*

In 1914 George F. Whipple (later Nobel Laureate in medicine) came from Johns Hopkins to become the first director of the George Williams Hooper Foundation for Medical Research with laboratories in San Francisco. On recommendation of Dr. Richard Pearce (KF's critical Philadelphia mentor), Whipple invited KF to join the Hooper Foundation as associate professor of tropical medicine in charge of the section on infectious diseases and immunology. KF accepted and in January 1915 moved from Berkeley to San Francisco and then commuted to Berkeley three or four times a week for teaching. The Hooper Foundation was the research center for the medical school. KF's appointment at the Hooper provided him more time and better facilities for research.

He was public health conscious from the beginning and quickly became involved in San Francisco and California State Health Department activities. All his subsequent studies on typhoid, brucellosis, botulism, plague, ornithosis, and equine and human encephalomyelitis stemmed directly from his involvement with the public health activities in California. KF served as director of the Hooper Foundation for Medical Research for thirty years, from 1924 to 1954, but continued to work for another twenty years.

At the same time he organized the Departments of Bacteriology at the Medical School in San Francisco and in the College of Letters and Science at Berkeley, and was chairman of both from 1924 to 1948. Thereafter until his "retirement"

---

*Ibid., p. 387.

at age seventy in 1954, he was professor of experimental pathology.

BOTULISM

KF's involvement in research on botulism in 1919 was largely in response to the serious threat to the billion-dollar canning industry in California. This highly fatal disease first aroused special public and professional concern during the eighteenth century in Germany after a number of human outbreaks of so-called blood sausage (Latin *botulus*) poisoning. For a long time, human botulism was believed to be associated with uncooked, inadequately cured, contaminated meats and other foodstuffs containing animal protein. Although eleven fatal cases of typical botulism occurred among twelve persons who ate a wax-bean salad in Germany in 1904, it was an outbreak of botulism in California involving twelve persons who consumed a string-bean salad at a sorority party at Stanford University in November 1913 that focused attention on canned vegetables as a possible source of this neurotoxin. The disease at Stanford was diagnosed as botulism by Dr. Ray Lyman Wilbur, who saw some of the botulism patients in Germany in 1904, even though the preserved string beans in the Stanford sorority salad were known to have been boiled for one hour on three successive days as was then recommended by the U.S. Department of Agriculture. Although it had been established by then that human botulism followed the ingestion of a highly fatal neurotoxin that was formed in food in which *Clostridium botulinum* had multiplied, the conditions that led to the appearance of this neurotoxin in preserved boiled food were still poorly understood. Following the 1913 Stanford outbreak, Dr. Wilbur, president of Stanford University, induced Dr. Ernest Dickson to study this problem. Dr. Dickson soon found that *C. botulinum* spores could not be sterilized by the recommended procedure for home canning. By 1919, commercial food processing had become a big industry in the United States, and especially so in California. During the ten-year period from 1910 to 1919 there were forty-eight botulism outbreaks attributed to home processed food and fourteen to commercially processed food. The number of cases in the United States was never very large (only 957 reported deaths during the entire seventy-one-year period of 1899 to 1969—E. J. Gangarosa et al., *American Journal of Epidemiology*, 93: 93, 1971), but the panic and impact of one small outbreak could be enormous.

It was just such an event in 1919 that forced the California canning industry and the National Canners Association to seek help. Between August and November 1919, there were twenty-eight cases of botulism with seventeen deaths in Ohio, Michigan, and Montana, all of which were traced to the ingestion of olives canned in California. The California canning industry was faced with a possible embargo on their olives. KF, who had no previous experience with botulism but already had a reputation as a bacteriologist concerned with public health, and Dr. Dickson, who had been working on the problem at Stanford University for a number of years, were asked for advice on what to do. KF told the canning industry executives that based on Dickson's work, asparagus, corn, spinach, and string beans—not only olives—were apt to cause trouble. He frankly told them that nobody could tell the industry what to do to avoid trouble on the basis of existing knowledge. He believed that only a comprehensive research program involving studies in the field where the vegetables and fruits are harvested, in the factories where they are processed, and of the special factors in outbreaks of human botulism might provide the knowledge for a truly scientific rather than empirical technology for the canning industry. Such a research program would undoubtedly cost a lot more money than they ever spent before. KF later recalled that if they would have objected to the size of his proposed budget he was prepared to tell them: "No money, no research, no salvation of the canning industry."*

The canning industry was wise enough to settle for new knowledge and provided the money KF requested. A program was then developed for collaborative studies at the Hooper Foundation of the University of California and at Stanford University. Dickson was to continue with the toxin studies, including heat resistance, at Stanford University. KF reserved for himself and associates at the Hooper the epidemiologic investigations, the determination of where the organism was in nature, the studies on the metabolism of the various strains, the heat penetration for various products in the cans, and the like.

KF recalled that this kind of industrial research at a university was regarded by some faculty members as a "prostitution of science." KF could not see why studies on the behavior of a microorganism under artificial conditions in test tubes in the laboratory constituted "appropriate" science, while studies on the behavior of bacteria in cans or in nature, or the acquisition of new knowledge required for the understanding and control of practically important industrial processes, did not constitute a scientific activity that was appropriate for a university. He was deeply hurt by this criticism, especially since Pasteur's contributions to industrial fermentations were generally regarded as great science.

The methodical basic approach to the problem by KF and his co-workers is reflected in the titles of the numerous publications (especially in the *Journal of Infectious Diseases*) that appeared from 1922 to 1924:

1. An experimental study of the methods available for the enrichment, demonstration, and isolation of *B. botulinus*

---

*Ibid., p. 99.

in specimens of soil and its products, in suspected food, and in clinical and in necropsy material.

2. The distribution of the spores of *B. botulinus* in California, in the United States, in the Territory of Alaska, in the Dominion of Canada, in Belgium, Denmark, England, the Netherlands, and Switzerland, and in the Hawaiian Islands and China. It was during the course of these global studies that it became apparent that the dusty, dry soil of California at harvest time forced *B. botulinus* into the resting spore state and thus everything that became contaminated with the dust contained large numbers of spores.

3. Some observations on the pathogenicity of *B. botulinus*.

4. The heat resistance of the spores of *B. botulinus* and allied anaerobes.

5. Toxin production and signs of spoilage in commercially canned vegetables and fruits inoculated with detoxified spores of *B. botulinus*.

6. Effect of glucose on biochemical activities, including growth and toxin production of *B. botulinus*. Studies on metabolism of anaerobic bacteria.

7. Studies on serologic classification of *B. botulinus*.

8. Occurrence of *B. botulinus* in human and animal excreta.

9. Effect of direct sunlight, diffuse daylight, and heat on potency of botulinus toxin in culture media and vegetable products.

10. The epidemiology of botulism.

From these and other fundamental studies in subsequent years, and from the analysis of special processing problems related to specific foods such as spinach, fish, and the like, emerged a body of knowledge that provided a scientific basis for protective measures against botulism. Writing on "The

Rise and Fall of Botulism" in the May 1973 issue of *California Medicine*, KF noted (pp. 63–64):

> Scientifically established sterilization standards replaced former procedures as the result of experiments exposing the spores of 107 different strains of *C. botulinum* (Types A and B) to five different heating temperatures and demonstrating that thermal destruction of the most resistant pathogens required a four-minute exposure at 248°F and 330 minutes at 212°F. The time and temperature essential for the destruction of heat-resistant spores were calculated from the heat-penetration and thermal-time slopes. The [botulism] commission recommended that olives and spinach be processed under pressure in retorts. The regulations merely coped with an emergency—without specifying the type and means of operating of equipment nor insisting on rigid, continuous inspection of the packing and processing procedures. Therefore unsterilized, commercially packed food continued to cause botulism.

KF soon discovered that merely having a body of knowledge for proper regulations was not enough; without continued inspection and control, botulism problems would not be eliminated. Since KF was not one to be satisfied merely with the acquisition of knowledge but was concerned with its proper utilization, he was involved for many years in establishing methods of inspection and control. Botulism did not disappear from the United States, but home processed foods were responsible for most of the outbreaks. During the twenty-year period from 1910 to 1929, commercially processed foods accounted for 32 percent of the 125 outbreaks of known source, but for only 3.3 percent of the 305 outbreaks of known source during the subsequent thirty years (1930–1959). The necessity for ongoing laboratory activities—not only for surveillance but also for studies of emerging new problems—resulted in the establishment of an ongoing Laboratory for Research in the Canning Industries at the University of California, of which KF was the director from 1926 to 1930. KF remained a consultant to the canning industry for the remainder of his life.

BRUCELLOSIS

Brucellosis is now recognized as a worldwide infection and disease of many different species of animals that is transmissible to human beings, in whom, depending on the species and strain of the microorganism, the infection is either inapparent, mild and unrecognized, or severe. In 1887 David Bruce isolated a bacterium he called *Micrococcus melitensis* from the spleen of a patient who died of Malta Fever, a disease that affected many British military and naval personnel on Malta. Shortly thereafter it was also recognized in North Africa, South Africa, and the United States. In 1905 Zammit of the British Mediterranean Fever Commission, searching for the cause of this human disease, accidentally found this bacterium in goat milk. When consumption of raw goat's milk was stopped, the disease quickly declined in the British personnel—but not in the native population that continued to drink raw goat's milk. In 1897 Bang isolated an organism, *Bacillus abortus bovinus,* from cattle with infectious, epizootic abortion, an organism whose relationship to *M. melitensis* in goats was discovered only later.

It was in this context that KF's interest in this zoonosis was first aroused in South Africa in 1908 and 1909, when he isolated *M. melitensis* from a human illness. When KF moved to Philadelphia he was soon involved in studies on contagious abortion in cattle (first publication in 1912), which at that time was an important problem in the dairy industry, and in etiologic studies on epizootic abortion of mares (publication in 1913). In 1911, KF first met Theobald Smith at a meeting in Boston, where both presented papers on *Bacillus abortus bovinus.* It was after this meeting that Theobald Smith showed KF how he accidentally (in guinea pigs used to test for tubercle bacilli in milk) discovered that *B. abortus* was eliminated in cow's milk and suggested to KF the possibility of a relationship between the *"Micrococcus melitensis"* of goats and *B. abor-*

tus of cattle. Soon after KF's arrival in California and his early association with the San Francisco Milk Commission, he learned of Dr. E. C. Fleischner's finding (to use KF's own words) "this abortion organism in the certified, high-class milk of San Francisco, and we then became interested to find out if it was transmissible to man."* After several years (1915–1918) of hard work, they failed to demonstrate any illness attributable to this organism among infants and children who drank such contaminated milk. This was the beginning of the ultimate realization that the bovine abortion organism was not very virulent for human beings and especially for infants and children. At about this time, Alice Evans showed a close biologic relationship between the melitensis organisms of goats and the abortion organisms of cattle (first published in 1918). The studies by KF and his student E. B. Shaw (later professor of pediatrics at the University of California in San Francisco) on the morphologic, cultural, and biochemical characteristics of *B. abortus* and *B. melitensis* led them to establish the new genus of *Brucella* for these and related organisms (first publication in 1920).

After his all-absorbing involvement in studies on botulism, KF left the field of brucellosis in 1920 for about seven years. His later activities were very largely concerned with the practical problems of eradication of *B. abortus* from cattle in the United States, including vaccination of calves with the live, attenuated strain 19 of *B. abortus* isolated in the United States by Buck in 1923. In 1951 the first of a series of studies on immunization against brucella infection by Elberg, KF, and associates was published—studies that were continued in considerable depth by Sanford Elberg and his associates in subsequent years.

*Ibid., p. 127.

WESTERN EQUINE ENCEPHALITIS

KF's work on Western equine encephalitis was a real trailblazer not only because of the isolation of a totally new kind of virus, but because the methods used soon led to the discovery of similar viruses as the causative agents of certain types of human encephalitis in different parts of the world as part of a complex ecological cycle involving mosquito transmission from inapparently infected hosts. KF recalled his involvement in the following words:

> In July of 1930 a large number of horses were reported dying in the San Joaquin Valley from botulism. Well, the moment that word is mentioned I have to investigate, and I had my theoretical reservations because in summertime you couldn't have botulism, there would not be an adequate amount of moisture in the feed to permit [C.] botulinus to grow and produce its toxin.*

Dr. J. C. Geiger, who was sent by KF to a ranch where the disease was occurring, reported that the horses were partly paralyzed, and when they were still able to get around, they walked in circles. The two horse heads Geiger brought back were highly contaminated and were suitable only for microscopic examination, which revealed lesions that convinced KF that they died of encephalitis and not of botulism. KF went out into the field, carried out autopsies by careful aseptic methods, and inoculated brain suspensions in horses and rabbits, and nothing happened. KF later recalled:

> By that time, it was the latter part of October and the number of cases became less and less, and I was afraid this would begin to disappear with no solution. . . . My failure to isolate this agent [the hypothetical virus] out of the brain was perhaps attributable to the fact that I used only the brains of dead horses. . . . I said we must get a horse which has the first signs of

---

*Ibid., p. 213.

it. [Such a horse was located, but they telephoned KF that the farmer said] "I won't sell the horse, and if you ever do anything to the horse, I shoot you." . . . I went down and I had a $20 bill in my pocket. This was a depression year and I was sure they would be glad to get rid of the horse for $20. [KF was warned not to talk to the farmer, and he said:] "I'm not going to talk to him. I'm going to talk to his wife." I said, "Look here, this horse is going to die anyhow, and when it's dead you haven't anything. It just goes to the rendering plant and you get a couple of dollars. On the other hand, you see, you could contribute to the knowledge of what this is and perhaps to its prevention." "Well," she said, "My husband is just irate about this." I said, "Yes, I can readily understand, but look here, suppose I trust you, and I give you $20 and the next morning you will find in the backyard the horse without a head?" "How are you going to do this?" "Look here, about nine o'clock at night when it is dark, I'll be over here behind some bushes . . . [where] I can see the window of your house. When your husband is sound asleep you lift up the shade." . . . I had a syringe with strychnine, I had a good sharp knife, and I sat around there and smoked a pipe, and sure enough about twenty minutes past nine the shade went up. Within about two minutes I was over the fence and in another two minutes the strychnine was under the skin of the horse and in another two or three minutes, the horse went down, and in another five minutes the head was off.

It was a heavy head, but I threw it over the fence and wrapped it up in burlap and we vanished as fast as we could to the most remote corner on the other side of the town of Merced where Haring [C. M. Haring, Chief, Division of Veterinary Science, College of Agriculture, University of California at Berkeley] had located an old abandoned chicken coop, and there with the help of flashlights I did a careful dissection of the brain and wrapped it up so it was not contaminated, etc. This was all done and we were about ready to go home by midnight. We drove back, and I tell you, naturally, I was fantastically excited. . . .

We got back to the lab about six o'clock in the morning. I immediately got busy and made a suspension of the brain material. I was over in Berkeley about 9:30 and by ten o'clock I had made two inoculations. I inoculated the suspension directly into the eye of a horse and another part of the suspension I put into the brain of the horse. . . . The rest of the brain was prepared by Miss [Beatrice] Howitt, who was with me and who was very, very good, and we had agreed that instead of merely using rabbits we would use mice, we would use guinea pigs, and we would even use monkeys and we would put the material directly into the brain. This gave us the virus.*

Such a "microbe hunter" was Karl F. Meyer! The description of the disease and the isolation and identification of this virus were reported (without the dramatic episodes described above) by Meyer, Haring, and Howitt in the August 28, 1931 issue of *Science*. Using similar procedures, the virus of human St. Louis encephalitis was isolated in 1933 by Ralph Muckenfuss et al. in monkeys and by Leslie Webster and G. L. Fite in mice; and the virus of human Japanese B encephalitis was isolated in 1934 in monkeys and in 1935 in mice. When KF studied the epidemiology of the equine encephalitis in California in 1930, he was struck by a concurrent increase in cases of "poliomyelitis" from rural areas that were admitted to the Kern County Hospital, and he noted that clinically these cases had the manifestations of encephalitis rather than poliomyelitis. Studies in subsequent years proved that the virus of Western equine encephalitis caused encephalitis in human beings. When KF mapped the horse encephalitis cases in 1930, he "began to see one crazy thing, that most of the cases were in an irrigated area. The moment you went in the foothills, no cases,"† and this led him to suspect mosquito transmission. When an epidemic of human encephalitis hit St. Louis in 1933, KF went there, among other things, to study the distribution of the cases and found that all the cases lived in the outlying suburban areas where "the mosquitoes were perfectly scandalous."‡ After a few additional personal studies with this virus, KF became deeply involved in wide-ranging studies on psittacosis and sylvatic plague, and left the job of working out the intricate ecological cycle and proof of

Ibid., pp. 215–17.
†*Ibid.*, p. 218.
‡*Ibid.*, p. 219.

mosquito transmission of the Western equine encephalitis and St. Louis encephalitis viruses to Dr. William McD. Hammon and entomologist Dr. William C. Reeves, whom he brought to the Hooper Foundation laboratories. KF later had this to say about their work:

> These two [each of whom in turn later became Dean of the School of Public Health of the University of California at Berkeley] have filled out the complete story and have shown that the infection is doubtless originally picked up by one species of mosquitoes, namely, culex tarsalis, early in spring and probably from migratory birds. This culex [Culex] tarsalis prefers to feed on birds and frequently brings it to human habitations by feeding on chickens. . . . Then they showed beautifully that in the chickens for four or five days this virus circulates in the blood in sufficient concentration to give the mosquito a chance to get infected; therefore, gradually during the summer there is an enormous build-up of infected mosquitoes and then [when the numbers are large enough] it naturally slops over to human beings and to horses. The cycle is, therefore a bird-mosquito cycle which has operated probably in this state [California] since time immemorial, but it never came to light until man began to irrigate and created vegetation and humidity adequate to build up an enormous mosquito population. Man, together with his work-horse, had the misfortune of being susceptible. The bird population is susceptible, yes, but they never get sick. Their infection is not apparent.*

PSITTACOSIS—ORNITHOSIS
LYMPHOGRANULOMA VENEREUM

The cause of psittacosis, a human infectious disease resulting from contact with parrots, was isolated from parrots and patients in 1930 and erroneously identified as a virus for many years. It was later shown to be a very small, obligately parasitic, intracellular bacterium. The information at the time led to the assumption that diseased parrots were the only source of the infectious agent. KF's work with this new animal source of human disease began with the death of three el-

―――――
*Ibid., p. 221.

derly ladies within a period of five to ten days in December 1930, after they had all been at a home in Grass Valley, California. It was an involvement that continued for more than forty years. Since the diagnosis was "typhoid pneumonia," an older name for psittacosis, KF asked the state health officer to look for a sick or dead parrot. The health officer telephoned back that evening to say that there was a healthy parakeet hanging in a cage over the table where the dead ladies had gathered for coffee, that another parakeet in that cage had died and was buried, and that the husband in this household was now in the hospital with the same illness. KF asked for blood and sputum from the patient, for the live parakeet, and if possible the carcass of the dead one. The specimens arrived at ten o'clock that night, the sputum and blood were promptly inoculated into animals, and the psittacosis agents were isolated. KF then showed that rice birds (finches) that were put into a clean jar with the live parakeet died of psittacosis, thus, "proving conclusively what had not been known until that time, that parakeets were really shedding the virus in the droppings."*

But KF was not a bench-bound microbiologist. He wanted to know where these parakeets came from. He learned from the hospitalized husband, just before he died of psittacosis, that he had bought the pair of parakeets from an itinerant peddler called Meyer. The highway patrol located this man and brought him to KF for an interview. The peddler at first said that the parakeets came from Japan, but when more human cases began to be reported from other parts of the state where the same peddler had sold parakeets, KF grilled him again and discovered that he got them from Los Angeles where thousands of parakeets were being bred by poor people who were trying to make a living during the depression.

*Ibid., p. 150.

Just about that time, cases of psittacosis began to be reported from Los Angeles. KF pursued the problem to Los Angeles and within about a month he had evidence that practically every one of the aviaries contained locally bred psittacosis-infected parakeets, that other birds in the aviaries acquired the infection, and that more and more exposed people were getting the disease. His request that the health department put an embargo on the export of these birds was resisted for a long time. The birds continued to be exported to other states, and soon there were many psittacosis cases that were traced to the birds imported from California. Among these cases happened to be Senator Borah's wife. The senator "raised cain" with the Public Health Service and convinced President Hoover to put an interstate embargo on the export of parakeets.

KF's concern for the people who were losing money as a result of this embargo led him to offer to establish certified psittacosis-free aviaries in California by testing 10 to 20 percent of the breeding stock that would be sacrificed for isolation of the psittacosis agent by mouse inoculation. The Public Health Service agreed, and soon this became the main activity in this field at the Hooper Foundation. By 1934, 25,000 to 30,000 parakeets had been tested, and about 185 aviaries were found to be free of psittacosis. In the 1930's the Hooper Foundation laboratory was the only place in the United States where psittacosis work was being done on a large scale. Amidst all of this activity the first scientific publication by KF and his devoted co-worker, Bernice Eddie, appeared in 1933, reporting on spontaneous psittacosis infections of the canary and butterfly finch. KF became severely ill with psittacosis, and he wrote it up as an infection in a laboratory worker in a publication that appeared in 1936.

It became apparent in the subsequent work that the national reservoir of psittacosis was not just in parrots, and in sick parrots at that, as was assumed when KF began his field and laboratory investigations. The discovery of the extensive reservoir in extrapsittacine birds brought forth the term "ornithosis" to describe the psittacosis infections in these birds. Published reports of KF and Eddie implicated pigeons (1942), chickens (1942), ducks (1952), turkeys (1953), and pheasants (1956). As a rule the infections in these birds were inapparent, although occasional epizootics by virulent strains brought heavy direct and indirect losses to poultry raising and processing industries. The inapparent infections in these birds, however, constituted reservoirs of occasional serious, even fatal, occupational hazards for human beings. The turkey ornithosis agent was considerably more virulent for human beings, and turkey ranching and processing procedures presented special problems for investigation by KF and his co-workers.

Other investigators found infectious agents in a great variety of mammals (e.g., sheep, goat, cattle, cat, mouse, hamster, guinea pig) that are biologically and antigenically related to the agents of psittacosis and ornithosis, but these turned out to be of very low virulence and almost never seen in human infections. However, the strictly human agent that is responsible for the veneral disease called lymphogranuloma venereum was shown in 1938 to be another member of this group of obligately parasitic, intracellular, very small bacteria. Subsequently J. W. Moulder and KF created the genus *Bedsonia*. The name honored S. P. Bedson, who with J. O. W. Bland first described the developmental cycle of the psittacosis "virus" in 1932 and subsequently made important fundamental contributions to our understanding of the nature of this agent. In subsequent years, the genus *Chlamydia* replaced *Bedsonia* to accommodate the biologically related agents of human trachoma and inclusion conjunctivitis, and in 1970 KF published a paper on antigens in *Chlamydia psit-*

taci. From 1966 to 1975, there appeared a whole series of publications by Julius Schachter (currently acting director of the Hooper Foundation), KF et al., elucidating the nature of the agent of lymphogranuloma venereum and other *Chlamydia* organisms and their role in human disease.

James H. Steele, in his biographical notes on K. F. Meyer (checked by KF just before his death) published in the supplement to the May 1974 issue of the *Journal of Infectious Diseases*, noted (p. 57):

> With the advent of broad-spectrum antibiotics (i.e., tetracycline), psittacosis was no longer the dangerous disease it had been, although it was a serious occupational disease among turkey producers and processors from 1948 to 1961. It could, however, be controlled by tetracyclines in turkey feed, and the disease in humans could be abated by treatment with tetracyclines. K. F. was to have an important role in all of these developments. Today public health and animal health officials ask what happened to psittacosis and ornithosis; all one can say is that these diseases are no longer the problems they were 20 years ago, thanks to the work of K. F., his colleagues, and other investigators influenced by him, who worked out the epidemiology of the disease and developed control procedures.

PLAGUE

In a chapter on plague KF said: "For centuries the Black Death found a highly susceptible population living in poverty, congestion and ignorance in Europe and took an appalling toll, justifying all of its somber aliases and the awe in which it has always been held."*

A Swiss, Alexander Yersin, discovered the plague bacillus in 1894. The role of rats and rat fleas was already known at the beginning of the twentieth century. At the end of the nineteenth century and during the early years of the twentieth, extensive epidemics were occurring in India, and

---

Bacterial and Mycotic Infections of Man, ed. R. J. Dubos and J. G. Hirsch, 4th ed. (Philadelphia: J. B. Lippincott, 1965), p. 664.

plague was being disseminated by rat-infested ships to seaports around the world, including San Francisco. Evidence that rodents, other than rats, were infected was found in Mongolia (1895), India (1898), South Africa (1906–1908), and California (1908). When KF arrived in California in 1913, he found Dr. George McCoy in the U.S. Public Health Service laboratory in San Francisco "engaged in methodically unravelling the complex interplay between wild rodents and commensal rats." In 1915 the Public Health Service announced that plague had been eradicated from California.

In 1919 KF was asked to advise on an outbreak of pneumonic plague (which can spread from man to man when a rodent–flea-transmitted human infection involves the lungs) affecting thirteen persons, including two physicians, that suddenly appeared in Oakland, California. An epidemiologic study traced these cases to a primary case of bubonic plague in a person who had been hunting in the Berkeley hills. The question that led KF to begin laboratory work on plague was one of pure curiosity—why were there so many pneumonic cases? Was it possible that there may be special pneumotropic strains of the plague bacillus? The work that he began in 1919 continued for the remainder of his life. In the special May 1974 issue of the *Journal of Infectious Diseases*, published in honor of his ninetieth birthday and devoted entirely to plague, KF was the first author or coauthor of ten of the twelve original communications.

KF did not publish anything on plague from 1919 to 1925—that was the period of intensive work on botulism. Another outbreak of thirty-one cases of pneumonic plague in the Mexican quarter of Los Angeles in 1924 got KF to work on plague again. He went to Los Angeles, accompanied the survey crews in their search for possible sources of infection, and was there when the first infected rat was found under a staircase leading up to a grocery store in the Mexican quarter.

He attended autopsies on the fatal cases, obtained a lot of cultures, and became intensely interested "in how this thing established itself in Los Angeles." His studies showed that the rat infection could not have come from the port. However, rats in the areas around Los Angeles were found to have ground squirrel fleas on them, and KF visualized an infection chain from ground squirrels to rats to humans, and from humans with lung involvement to other humans. These observations became the basis for the extensive subsequent field and laboratory work on wild rodents and their fleas that revealed a reservoir of plague bacillus infection in squirrels and chipmunks—the beginning of his more extensive studies on "sylvatic plague" in California. After a while, KF realized that the best place to look for plague bacilli was not in the organs of wild rodents, but in the fleas that were combed from them. The survey crews then found sylvatic plague in the states of Oregon, Washington, Montana, and Nevada. KF recalled: "Without asking for it, we realized that plague suddenly was all over the landscape,"* although only rare sporadic cases were occurring in human beings.

About 1940, when many military installations were being established in California, there was concern about plague and KF was again asked for advice. After his advice on how to get rid of the ground squirrels and their fleas proved successful, KF made the important discovery that plague infection was widespread in all sorts of field mice and their fleas. He later recalled:

> Well, this threw an entirely different light on the whole question, namely, that you were dealing here with a very mobile, migratory species of animal which easily could slop it over miles. Furthermore, the average resistance of these field voles was very high. It didn't kill, as it did in rats, 80 to 90 percent of them. Sometimes it only killed 20 percent. It looked to

---

*Medical Research and Public Health, p. 181.

me, and I hypothecated, that the persistence of plague in certain areas is entirely conditioned by the amount of resistance in the wild rodents. If they are resistant they can maintain infected fleas, because if all the rodents would die naturally with it, infection would get wiped out, as happened with rats. But with these wild rodents there is always a possibility that an infected flea will get a meal and during the wintertime maintain the infection and then start it all up in the springtime, which was always the case here.*

He was then helped by Air Force crews that gathered material for him from widespread areas, and "practically every day, there would be an icebox coming in with bottles full of fleas," all of which were ground up and inoculated into guinea pigs. At that time about 50 percent of the Hooper Foundation funds were spent on the laboratory work with plague. Most of the work was done by graduate students working for their Ph.D.'s. Miss Bernice Eddie worked along with them, often till midnight and on Saturdays and Sundays because of her great interest in the work. All of this plague work was done in a special isolation building that was built after 1936 with funds KF obtained from the Rosenberg Foundation, because there were fears about work with the "Black Death" bacteria on the San Francisco campus. It was in this building that KF had a big room with a "mouse village" where he scattered infected fleas in two sections—in one the mice were receiving sulfanilamide in their diet and in the other, only the regular diet. All mice on the regular diet died, while all on the sulfanilamide diet remained well.

During World War II it was evident that American military personnel would have to operate in areas of the world where plague was a potential threat. Accordingly, KF and his associates began to work on immunity and effective vaccination against plague. Except for sulfadiazine, the highly effec-

*Ibid., p. 183.

tive therapeutic antibiotics (streptomycin, tetracycline, chloramphenicol) did not become available till later. Special aspects of the metabolism, physiology, and antigens of the plague bacillus had to be studied. Animal models for reliable potency testing and serologic tests that would measure the immune response in humans had to be developed. While all this was going on, there was a request to produce twenty-six million doses of the best vaccine that could be prepared for use in the military forces—and mass production of the vaccine could be carried out only in the special plague isolation building of the Hooper Foundation. A formalin-killed vaccine, which had to be given in multiple doses every six months, was developed and produced. For whatever reasons (because multiple control procedures were used), KF and McCoy reported in 1964 that no cases of plague occurred among the U.S. Armed Forces, although they operated in areas in which small numbers of cases were occurring in the native population and also in some members of the British Armed Forces. KF and his associates continued work on immunization against plague for many years, as the reports in the May 1974 issue of the *Journal of Infectious Diseases* testify. While there is no place for immunization of the general population in the worldwide vigilance against plague, a practically useful, effective method of immunization could be a valuable component in the total strategy for the protection of persons who may be at special risk during limited periods of time.

K. F. MEYER, THE PERSON

To have known KF was an unforgettable, enriching experience. Julius Schachter (now acting director of the Hooper Foundation) said in a recent article:*

*Bulletin der Schweizerischen Akademie der Medizinischen Wissenschaften, 33 (1977): 187.

The enthusiasm and application that Meyer showed in his professional career were also expressed in a great appetite for life's pleasures. In the spring he seemed to get reports straight from the farms on the progress of the first asparagus of the season. He would later discuss with great gusto the quality of the year's crop. Similar enthusiasm was shown for a recently discovered restaurant, wildflower display, or a new film that did a better job of showing the texture of redwood bark or the colors of the wild flowers.

I personally recall with great pleasure the many good times we had together. I remember especially the gourmet dinners we had at his "Family Club" in San Francisco, and the time he gave me a package of luscious asparagus and special sauce to take home to Cincinnati. I shall also long remember the experiences we shared in a night on the town in Istanbul (escorted by a Turkish police officer) during the 1954 International Congress of Tropical Medicine. J. B. de C. M. Saunders and Edward B. Shaw, colleagues and friends over many decades, concluded their March 1976 University of California "In Memoriam" as follows:

> Science and friends alike will miss his rugged personality, his directness, his genius, his bonhomie, his love of company and conversation, and his graciousness. He was an accomplished photographer, fascinated by radio in its early days, loved good conversation, good company, and good wine. Those who knew him at close hand rejoiced in his friendship. His lifelong devoted support was a priceless boon to those who had worked with him—the "hand on the shoulder" for many years.
>
> Karl Meyer married Mary Elizabeth Lindsay at Philadelphia in 1913 and to this union was born his only daughter, Charlotte (Mrs. Bartley P. Cardon). The first Mrs. Meyer died [in 1958] following a prolonged illness in which her husband gave her every care and attention. In 1960, he married Marion Lewis, a happy and blissful union of which "God hath no better praise."

KF's marriage to Marion Lewis—by all accounts a delightful person—brought him great happiness during the last fourteen years of his life. She wrote me: "The last fourteen years of his life were, indeed, the happiest of all of mine. He was a warm, passionate, affectionate man; perhaps one could simply say we were two fortunate people who were blessed with the privilege of sharing in a perfect union. Humbly, I am glad it was me!"

KF's deep concern for the course of human events in the world scene is reflected in the quotation with which he concluded his "Acceptance of the Walter Reed Medal" in 1956 (*American Journal of Tropical Medicine and Hygiene,* 6:341, 1957). The quotation was from comments made by Dr. Hans Zinsser in 1935 at the Second International Congress for Microbiology in London:

> And may some political Leeuwenhoek discover a microscope by which he can see and define the little animalculae of enmity and hatred and savagery, so that at last, in International Congresses assembled, wise men may sit in peaceful assembly planning research into the virulence of human stupidity and consider measures of active immunization, chlorination and delousing for international politics as we do this for infectious disease.

HONORS AND DISTINCTIONS

DEGREES

A.B., University of Zurich, 1905
D.V.M., University of Zurich, 1909
Ph.D., University of Zurich, 1924

HONORARY DEGREES

M.D., College of Medical Evangelists, Los Angeles, 1936
Dr. Med., h.c., University of Zurich, 1937
LL.D., University of Southern California, 1946
D.V.M., h.c., University of Zurich, 1949
Dr. Med., h.c., University of Basel, 1952
D.V.M., h.c., Tierärztliche Hochschule, Hanover, 1953
LL.D., h.c., University of California, 1958
D. Sc., University of Ohio, 1958
D. Sc., University of Pennsylvania, 1959

PROFESSIONAL APPOINTMENTS

Pathologist, Transvaal Department of Agriculture, Onderstepoort, Union of South Africa, 1908–1910
Assistant Professor of Pathology and Bacteriology, School of Veterinary Medicine, University of Pennsylvania, 1910–1911
Professor of Pathology and Bacteriology, School of Veterinary Medicine, University of Pennsylvania, 1911–1913
Director, Laboratory and Experimental Farm, Pennsylvania Livestock Sanitary Board, Philadelphia, 1911–1913

University of California:
   Associate Professor of Bacteriology and Protozoology, 1913–1914
   Professor of Bacteriology and Protozoology, 1914–1915
   Associate Professor of Tropical Medicine, George Williams Hooper Foundation for Medical Research, 1915–1924
   Acting Director, George Williams Hooper Foundation for Medical Research, 1921–1924
   Director, George Williams Hooper Foundation for Medical Research, 1924–1954
   Professor of Bacteriology, 1924–1948
   Director, Laboratory for Research in the Canning Industries, 1926–1930

Director, Public Health Curricula, 1936-1939
Professor of Experimental Pathology, 1948-1954
Director Emeritus, George Williams Hooper Foundation for Medical Research, 1954-1974
Professor Emeritus of Experimental Pathology, 1954-1974

CONSULTANCIES

Consultant in Bacteriology, Board of Public Health, State of California
General Consultant, Board of Public Health, State of California, 1948-1974
Consultant on Public Health, Southern Pacific Railway, 1920-1974
Chief Consultant, California State Department of Public Health, 1927-1947
Consultant in Bacteriology, Department of Health, City and County of San Francisco, 1935-1945
Consultant to the Board of Health, Chicago, 1939-1950
Consultant on Epidemic Diseases, Secretary of War, 1942-1945, 1948
Consultant to Department of Clinical Laboratories, Mount Zion Hospital, San Francisco
Consultant on Tropical Medicine, Secretary of War, 1942
Consulting Bacteriologist, Langley Porter Clinic, San Francisco
Consultant, Office of The Surgeon General, Medical Research and Development Board (appointed 1951-1974)
Member, National Advisory Health Council, 1940-1950
Member, Study Section on Microbiology and Immunology, Grants Division, United States Public Health Service
Scientific Advisory Board of Consultants to the Armed Forces Institute of Pathology, 1952-1974
Consultant to the Communicable Disease Center, United States Public Health Service, Atlanta, Georgia, 1949-1974
Senior Civilian Consultant on Clinical Pathology (appointed by The Surgeon General, 1953-1974)

COMMITTEES, BOARDS, COMMISSIONS

National Research Council, various committees
Committee on Sylvatic Plague, American Public Health Association

World's Fair Advisory Commission, 1939
Commission on Virus Research, National Foundation for Infantile Paralysis, 1938–1948
Commission on Epidemics and Public Health, National Foundation for Infantile Paralysis, 1938–1948
National Advisory Health Council, National Institutes of Health, United States Public Health Service, 1941–1945; 1946–1974
Commission on Tropical Diseases, 1942–1945
Respiratory Disease Advisory Council, California Board of Public Health, 1943
Army Epidemiological Board, 1946–1948
Commission on Immunization, Committee on Plague, Armed Forces Epidemiological Board, 1949–1974
Board of Trustees, Langley Porter Clinic, 1945–1974
Committee on Medical Research and Therapy, American Trudeau Society, Medical Section of the National Tuberculosis Association, 1953–1954
Committee on Social Research, National Tuberculosis Association, 1952–1974
Expert Advisory Panel on Plague, World Health Organization, 1949–1974
Expert Advisory Panel on Zoonoses, World Health Organization, 1952–1974
Temporary Advisor, Technical Discussion Group, World Health Organization, 1954–1974
Inter-American Society of Microbiology Committee, Society of American Bacteriologists, 1952–1974
Advisory Committee, Armed Forces Medical Library, 1952–1974
Medical Advisory Committee, Research Foundation
Committee on Army Medical Library, National Research Council, 1952–1974
Chairman, Standing Committee on Public Health and Medical Science, 9th Pacific Science Congress, 1957; 10th Pacific Science Congress, 1961

MEMBERSHIPS

Society of American Bacteriologists (Council; Vice President, 1934; President, 1935)

American Public Health Association, Western Branch (Council; President, 1942)
American Association of Immunologists, (Council; President, 1940)
American Society of Tropical Medicine (Charter Member, 1918; Vice President, 1937)
Northern California Public Health Association (2nd Vice President, 1930)
American Academy of Tropical Medicine (Charter Member; Council, 1945–1948)
American Association of Medical Milk Commissioners (President, 1929)
American Association of Pathologists and Bacteriologists, 1911–1974
American Veterinary Medical Association, 1911–1974
Pathological Society of Philadelphia, 1911–1974
Society for Experimental Biology and Medicine, 1915–1974
American Society for Experimental Pathology
American Therapeutic Society, 1924–1926
Société Helvétique des Sciences Naturelles, 1924–1974
American Epidemiological Society, 1936–1974
Asociacion Fronteriza Mexico Estadounidense de Salubridad Publica (Charter Member)
Inter-American Society for Microbiology
National Society for Medical Research
California Academy of Medicine
Institute of Food Technologists
California Academy of Sciences
New York Academy of Sciences, 1939–1974
National Academy of Sciences, 1940–1974
American Academy of Arts and Sciences
American Philatelic Society
Sigma Xi
Delta Omega
Phi Sigma
Alpha Omega Alpha

HONORARY MEMBERSHIPS

Los Angeles Surgical Society, 1922
National Association of Sanitarians, Inc., 1939–1974

Sigma Kappa Theta, 1940–1974
Swiss Academy of Medical Sciences
Alumni Association, College of Medical Evangelists, Los Angeles
San Francisco County Medical Society, 1951–1974
American Trudeau Society, Medical Section, National Tuberculosis Association, 1953–1974
Harvey Society, 1939–1974
Institute of American Poultry Industries
International Epidemiological Association
American Society for Microbiology
Infectious Diseases Society

FELLOWSHIPS

American Association for the Advancement of Science, 1920–1974
American Academy of Arts and Sciences, 1935–1974
American Public Health Association, 1935–1974
National Academy of Sciences, 1940–1974
Associate Fellow, Academy of Pediatrics, 1941–1974
New York Academy of Sciences, 1941–1974

HONORARY FELLOWSHIPS

American Board of Veterinary Public Health, 1953 (Awarded at the XV International Veterinary Congress, Stockholm, Sweden)

AWARDS AND HONORS

Sedgwick Memorial Medal, 1946
James D. Bruce Medal (Preventive Medicine), 1949
Officier, l'Ordre de la Santé Publique, 1946
U. S. Certificate of Merit (Conduct in Aid of the War Effort, World War II), 1948
Certificate of Appreciation, Bureau of Medicine and Surgery, United States Navy
Tribute, National Canners' Association (Prevention of botulism and development of canning techniques), 1939
Annual Prize, Outdoor Life (Conservation of natural resources), 1931
Honors, American Academy of Tuberculosis Physicians (for promoting scientific medicine and public health), 1950

Lasker Award, Albert and Mary Lasker Foundation at the meeting of the American Public Health Association, 1951
Humanitarian Award, Variety Clubs International, 1953
Borden Award, Association of American Medical Colleges, 1954
Walter Reed Medal, American Society for Tropical Medicine and Hygiene, 1956
Howard L. Ricketts Award, University of Chicago, 1960
Forty-Niners Service Award for the outstanding services to the Canning and Allied Industry, 1961
Jessie Stevenson Kovalenko Medal, National Academy of Sciences (for outstanding contributions to Medical Science as an investigator, teacher, and administrator over a period of half a century), 1961
Award of the "Animal Care Panel," 1961
XII International Veterinary Congress Prize, American Veterinary Medical Association, 1964
The 1964 Special Award, "The Goldheaded Cane," known as "The Karl F. Meyer Award," presented by the Conference of Public Health Veterinarians, Atlanta, 1964
The 1970 Bristol Award for Distinguished Achievement in Infectious Diseases, Infectious Diseases Society of America, 1970
Certificate of Recognition, American Public Health Association, 1972
Certificate of Appreciation for Patriotic Civilian Service, in recognition of years of devoted service as a consultant to the staff of the Surgeon General, Department of the Army, Washington, D.C., 1973
Certificate of Commendation in recognition of services as President of the American Association of Immunologists from 1941 to 1942, 1973
Selected as one of the subjects in a biographical film series "Leaders in American Medicine" made for the Medical Audiovisual Center, National Library of Medicine, Atlanta, Georgia, 1973. The film has been deposited as audiovisual history and will be available as an educational medium
Canners' League Hall of Fame Document, by the Canners' League of California, Sacramento, 1974

SELECTED BIBLIOGRAPHY*

1908

Über die durch säurefeste Bakterien hervorgerufene diffuse Hypertrophie der Darmschleimhaut des Rindes. (Enteritis hypertrophica bovis specifica.) Arb. Inst. Erforschung Infektionskrankheiten Bern Laborator. Schweizer Serum-und Impfinstitutes, 2: 47–153 + 3 plts.

1909

Notes on the pathological anatomy of pleuro-pneumonia contagiosa bovum. In: *Transvaal Department of Agriculture. The Veterinary Bacteriological Laboratories*, pp. 135–64 + 7 plts. Pretoria: Government Printing and Stationery Office.

Zur Übertragung von afrikanischem Küstenfieber auf gesunde Tiere durch intraperitoneale Verimpfung von Milzen und Milzstücken kranker Tiere. Z. Infektionskrankheiten, 6 (5): 374–79.

Preliminary note on the transmission of East Coast fever to cattle by intraperitoneal inoculation of the spleen or portions of the spleen of a sick animal. J. Comp. Pathol. Ther., 22 (3): 213–17.

1911

Beiträge zur Genese und Bedeutung der Kochschen Plasmakugeln in der Pathogenese des afrikanischen Küstenfiebers. Zentralbl. Bakteriol., Abt. I., Orig., 57 (5): 415–32 + 3 plts.

1913

The conjunctival reaction for glanders. (Ophthalmic test.) J. Infect. Dis., 12 (2): 170–90; Am. Vet. Rev., 43: 233–51.

The specific paratuberculous enteritis of cattle in America. J. Med. Res., 29 (2) [n.s., 24 (2)]: 147–89.

With F. Boerner. Studies on the etiology of epizootic abortion in mares. J. Med. Res., 29 (2) [n.s., 24 (2)]: 325–66.

---

*A complete bibliography of the works of Karl F. Meyer is available from the Archives of the National Academy of Sciences.

1914

Zur chronischen, paratuberkulösen Darmentzundung des Rindes. Schweizer Arch. Tierheilkd., 56 (8/9): 393–403.

Filterable viruses. Am. Vet. Rev., 46 (2): 132–44; 46 (3): 264–80.

1915

The relation of animal to human sporotrichosis: Studies on American sporotrichosis. III. J. Am. Med. Assoc., 65 (7): 579–85.

Epizootic lymphangitis and sporotrichosis: Studies on American sporotrichosis. II. Am. J. Trop. Dis. Prev. Med., 3 (3): 144–63.

The etiology of "symptomatic anthrax" in swine: "Specific gas-phlegmon of hogs." J. Infect. Dis., 17 (3): 458–96.

With J. A. Aird. Various sporotricha differentiated by the fermentation of carbohydrates. Studies on American sporotrichosis. I. J. Infect. Dis., 16 (3): 399–409.

1916

With S. H. Hurwitz. Studies on the blood proteins. I. The serum globulins in bacterial infection and immunity. J. Exp. Med., 24 (5): 515–46.

Notes on the occurrence of equine sporotrichosis in Montana and the "blastomycotic" form of *Sporotrichum schencki-beurmanni*. Proc. Soc. Exp. Biol. Med., 14: 23–24.

With J. Traum and C. L. Roadhouse. The *Bacillus enteritidis* as the cause of infectious diarrhea in calves. J. Am. Vet. Med. Assoc., 2 (1): 17–35.

1917

With E. C. Fleischner. Observations on the presence of the *Bacillus abortus bovinus* in certified milk. Preliminary notes. Am. J. Dis. Child., 14: 157–73.

The intracutaneous 'typhoidin' reaction. III. The relation of cutaneous hypersensitiveness to experimental immunity and infection. J. Infect. Dis., 20 (4): 424–41.

1918

With E. C. Fleischner. The bearing of cutaneous hypersensitiveness on the pathogenicity of the *Bacillus abortus bovinus.* Am. J. Dis. Child., 16: 268–73.

With S. H. Hurwitz and L. Taussig. Studies on the blood proteins. III. Albumin-globulin ratio in antitoxic immunity. J. Infect. Dis., 22 (1): 1–27.

1919

With E. C. Fleischner and E. B. Shaw. A résumé of some experimental studies on cutaneous hypersensitiveness. Am. J. Dis. Child., 18: 577–90.

With E. C. Fleischner and E. B. Shaw. The pathogenicity of *Bacterium melitensis* for guinea pigs. Proc. Soc. Exp. Biol. Med., 16: 152–56.

With L. E. McRoberts, J. E. Stockel, H. E. Brown, and J. Wollenberg. A review of our knowledge concerning the etiology of influenza: With notes on the bacterial flora of respiratory cultures of influenza patients in San Francisco, and the value of prophylactic vaccination with *B. influenzae* vaccine. Calif. State J. Med., 17: 216–48.

1920

With M. L. Feusier. Principles in serologic grouping of *B. abortus* and *B. melitensis:* Correlation between absorption and agglutination tests. Studies on the genus Brucella nov. gen. II. J. Infect. Dis., 27 (3): 185–206.

With E. C. Fleischner. Preliminary observations on the pathogenicity for monkeys of the *Bacillus abortus bovinus.* Trans. Am. Pediatr. Soc., 32: 141–56.

With N. M. Neilson. Irregular typhoid strains and the infections caused by them. J. Infect. Dis., 27 (1): 46–71.

With E. B. Shaw. A comparison of the morphologic, cultural and biochemical characteristics of *B. abortus* and *B. melitensis:* Studies of the genus Brucella nov. gen. I. J. Infect. Dis., 27 (3): 173–84.

1921

With C. R. Christiansen and N. M. Neilson. Do "carrier" strains differ from strains isolated from ordinary typhoid cases? Experimental typhoid-paratyphoid carriers. III. J. Infect. Dis., 28 (4): 394–407.

With E. C. Fleischner, M. Vecki, and E. B. Shaw. The pathogenicity of *B. abortus* and *B. melitensis* for monkeys: Studies on the genus Brucella nov. gen. III. J. Infect. Dis., 29 (6): 663–98.

Experimental typhoid-paratyphoid carriers. J. Infect. Dis., 28 (5): 381–83.

Some suggestions concerning the bacteriological diagnosis of human botulism. Public Health Rpt., 36 (23): 1313–17.

With N. M. Neilson and M. L. Feusier. A comparative study of the infections produced by intravenous injections of typhoid, paratyphoid A and B bacilli in normal and immunized rabbits: Experimental typhoid-paratyphoid carriers. IV. J. Infect. Dis., 28 (4): 408–55.

The bacteriostatic and germicidal properties of bile: Experimental typhoid-paratyphoid carriers. VII. J. Infect. Dis., 28 (4): 542–87.

1922

With G. E. Coleman. Some observations on the pathogenicity of *B. botulinus*. X. J. Infect. Dis., 31 (6): 622–29.

With B. J. Dubovsky. An experimental study of the methods available for the enrichment, demonstration and isolation of *B. botulinus* in specimens of soil and its products, in suspected food, in clinical and in necropsy material. I. J. Infect. Dis., 31:501–40.

With J. R. Esty. The heat resistance of the spores of *B. botulinus* and allied anacrobes. XI. J. Infect. Dis., 31:650–63.

With E. B. Shaw and E. C. Fleischner. The pathogenicity of *B. melitensis* and *B. abortus* for guinea-pigs. Studies of the genus Brucella nov. gen. IV. J. Infect. Dis., 31 (2):159–97.

1923

With P. Schoenholz. Studies on serologic classification of *B. botulinus*. 1. Preparation of antiserum. J. Infect. Dis., 32 (6):417–20.

With P. Schoenholz and J. R. Esty. Toxin production and signs of spoilage in commercially canned vegetables and fruits inoculated with detoxified spores of *B. botulinus*. XII. J. Infect. Dis., 33 (4):289–327.

1924

With C. C. Dozier and E. Wagner. Effect of glucose on biochemical activities, including growth and toxin production of *B. botulinus*. Studies on metabolism of anaerobic bacteria. II. J. Infect. Dis., 34 (1):85–102.

With E. J. Easton. Occurrence of *Bacillus botulinus* in human and animal excreta. XXI. J. Infect. Dis., 35 (2):207–12.

With P. Schoenholz. Effect of direct sunlight, diffuse daylight and heat on potency of botulinus toxin in culture mediums and vegetable products. XXIV. J. Infect. Dis., 35 (4):361–89. .

1925

With P. Schoenholz. Studies on the serologic classification of *B. botulinus*. II. Agglutination. J. Immunol., 10 (1):1–53.

1926

With A. Batchelder. Local immunization of guinea pigs to cutaneous infection with a pasturella isolated from wild rats. Proc. Soc. Exp. Biol. Med., 23 (8):730–34.

Selective mediums in the diagnosis of rodent plague. Plague studies 1. J. Infect. Dis. 39 (5):370–85.

A disease in wild rats caused by *Pasteurella muricida*, n. sp. Plague studies 2. J. Infect. Dis., 39 (5):386–412.

With E. W. Sommer and H. Sommer. The purification of botulinum toxin. J. Infect. Dis., 39 (5):345–50.

1928

With J. C. Geiger. Experimental food poisoning in white mice with heat stabile paratyphoid poisons. Proc. Soc. Exp. Biol. Med., 26 (2):91–93.

With J. B. Gunnison. Susceptibility of *Macacus rhesus* monkeys to botulinum toxin type B, C and D. Proc. Soc. Exp. Biol. Med., 26 (2):89–90.

With J. B. Gunnison. *Cl. botulinum* type D sp. n. Proc. Soc. Exp. Biol. Med., 26 (2):88–89.

With H. Sommer and P. Schoenholz. Mussel poisoning. J. Prev. Med., 2 (5):365–94.

1929

With H. L. Averill. Cutaneous immunization against *B. aertrycke* in the guinea-pig J. Infect. Dis., 44 (6):495–502.
Further studies on the pathogenicity of *Br. abortus* and *Br. melitensis* for monkeys. Proc. Soc. Exp. Biol. Med., 27 (3):222–24.
With J. B. Gunnison. European strains of *Cl. botulinum*. XXXVI. J. Infect. Dis., 45 (2):96–105.
South African cultures of *Clostridium botulinum* and *parabotulinum*. XXXVII: With a description of *Cl. botulinum* type D, n. sp. J. Infect. Dis., 45 (2):106–18.

1930

With J. B. Gunnison. Susceptibility of monkeys, goats and small animals to oral administration of botulinum toxin, types B, C and D. J. Infect. Dis., 46 (4):335–40.
With B. Howitt. The convalescent serum therapy in poliomyelitis. Calif. State Dep. Public Health, Wkly. Bull., 9 (22):85–86.
With C. E. Zobell. The metabolism of the Brucella group in synthetic media. Science, 72 (1859):176.
Metabolism studies on the Brucella group. II. The fermentation of monosaccharides. Proc. Soc. Exp. Biol. Med., 28 (2):160–62.

1931

With C. M. Haring and B. Howitt. The etiology of epizootic encephalomyelitis of horses in the San Joaquin Valley, 1930. Science, 74 (1913):227–28.

1932

With R. A. Stewart. Isolation of *Coccidioides immitis* (Stiles) from the soil. Proc. Soc. Exp. Biol. Med., 29 (8):937–38.
With C. E. Zobell. Metabolism studies on the Brucella group. V. The production of hydrogen sulphide. J. Infect. Dis., 51:91–98.
Metabolism studies on the Brucella group. VI. Nitrate and nitrite reduction. J. Infect. Dis., 51:99–108.

1933

With B. Eddie. Spontaneous psittacosis infections of the canary and butterfly finch. Proc. Soc. Exp. Biol. Med., 30 (4):481–82.
Latent psittacosis infections in mice. Proc. Soc. Exp. Biol. Med., 30 (4):483–84.
Latent psittacosis infections in shell parakeets. Proc. Soc. Exp. Biol. Med., 30 (4):484–88.

1934

With B. F. Howitt. Tests for cross-immunity between the virus of Borna disease and that of equine encephalomyelitis. J. Infect. Dis., 54:364–67.
With O. Larsell and C. M. Haring. Histological changes in the central nervous system following equine encephalomyelitis. Am. J. Pathol., 10 (3):361–74.
Virus diseases of animals transmissible to man. Ann. Intern. Med., 8 (5):552–69.
The common cold. Calif. West. Med., 41 (6):361–65.
With B. Eddie. Psittacosis in the native Australian budgerigars. Proc. Soc. Exp. Biol. Med., 31 (8):917–20.
Latent psittacosis and Salmonella psittacosis infection in South American parrotlets and conures. Science, 79 (2059):546-48.
With F. Wood, C. M. Haring, and B. Howitt. Susceptibility of nonimmune, hyperimmunized horses and goats to Eastern, Western and Argentine virus of equine encephalomyelitis. Proc. Soc. Exp. Biol. Med., 32 (1):56–58.

1935

With B. Eddie. The problem of caprine brucella infections in the United States. J. Am. Vet. Med. Assoc., 86 (3):286–303.
With B. Eddie and L. Foster. Cytology of psittacosis virus in the sparrow (Zonotrichia). Proc. Soc. Exp. Biol. Med., 32 (9):1656–58.
With C. M. Wheeler and W. B. Herms. A new tick vector of relapsing fever in California. Proc. Soc. Exp. Biol. Med., 32 (8):1290–92.

1936

With J. B. Gunnison and J. R. Cummings. *Clostridium botulinum* type E. Proc. Soc. Exp. Biol. Med., 35 (2):278–80.

Latent infections. J. Bacteriol., 31 (2):109–35.

The therapeutic use of convalescent serum in poliomyelitis. Calif. West. Med., 44 (4):254.

1937

With A. S. Lazarus and B. Eddie. Propagation of variola virus in the developing egg. Proc. Soc. Exp. Biol. Med., 36 (1):7–8.

Ultrafiltration of psittacosis virus. Proc. Soc. Exp. Biol. Med., 36 (4):437–38.

With C. L. Connor, F. S. Smyth, and B. Eddie. Chronic relapsing latent meningeal plague. Arch. Intern. Med., 59 (6):967–80.

With H. Sommer, and the assistance of R. Stohler, N. Sharma, K. Jenkins, H. Mueller, W. F. Whedon, and R. J. Silverberg. Paralytic shell-fish poisoning. Arch. Pathol., 24 (5):560–98.

1938

With B. Eddie. Persistence of sylvatic plague. Proc. Soc. Exp. Biol. Med., 38 (3):333–34.

With B. Eddie and B. Anderson-Stewart. Canine, murine and human leptospirosis in California. Proc. Soc. Exp. Biol. Med., 38 (1):17–19.

1939

With S. S. Elberg. The nutritional requirements of *Clostridium parabotulinum*, A. J. Bacteriol., 37 (4):429–45.

The extracellular proteolytic system of *Clostridium parabotulinum*. J. Bacteriol., 37 (5):541–65.

With J. C. Geiger, A. B. Crowley, and B. U. Eddie. Administrative problems in connection with psittacosis and the importation of Australian parrots. J. Am. Med. Assoc., 113 (16):1479–81.

With A. S. Lazarus. The virus of psittacosis. I. Propagation and developmental cycle in the egg membrane, purification and concentration. J. Bacteriol., 38 (2):121–51.

The virus of psittacosis. II. Centrifugation, filtration and measurement of particle size. J. Bacteriol., 38 (2):153–69.

The virus of psittacosis. III. Serological investigations. J. Bacteriol., 38 (2):171–98.
With B. Eddie. The value of the complement fixation test in the diagnosis of psittacosis. J. Infect. Dis., 65 (3):225–33.
Psittacosis in importations of psittacine birds from the South American and Australian continent. J. Infect. Dis., 65 (3):234–41.
With B. Eddie and H. Yanamura. Complement-fixation test with tissue-culture antigens as aid in recognizing latent avian psittacosis (ornithosis). Proc. Soc. Exp. Biol. Med., 41 (1):173–76.
With B. Stewart-Anderson and B. Eddie. Epidemiology of leptospirosis. Am. J. Public Health, 29 (4):347–53.
Canine leptospirosis in the United States. J. Am. Vet. Med. Assoc., 95 (753):710–29.

1940

The host-parasite relationship in the heterogeneous infection chains. Harvey Lect., 35:91–134.
With J. G. Molner. Jaundice in Detroit. Am. J. Public Health, 30 (5):509–15.

1941

With B. Eddie. Laboratory infections due to Brucella. J. Infect. Dis., 68 (1):24–32.
With H. Y. Yanamura. Studies on the virus of psittacosis cultivated in vitro. J. Infect. Dis., 68 (1):1–15.

1942

The known and the unknown in plague. Am. J. Trop. Med., 22 (1):9–36.
The ecology of plague. Medicine, 21 (2):143–74.
The ecology of psittacosis and ornithosis. Medicine, 21 (2):175–206.
With B. Eddie. Spontaneous ornithosis (psittacosis) in chickens the cause of a human infection. Proc. Soc. Exp. Biol. Med., 49 (4):522–25.
With B. Eddie and H. Y. Yanamura. Ornithosis (psittacosis) in pigeons and its relation to human pneumonitis. Proc. Soc. Exp. Biol. Med., 49 (4):609–15.
Active immunization to the *Microbacterium multiforme psittacosis* in parrakeets and ricebirds. J. Immunol., 44 (3): 211–17.

With H. Y. Yanamura. Active immunity to the *Microbacterium multiforme psittacosis* in the mouse. J. Immunol., 44 (3):195–209.

1943

With E. Jawetz. Avirulent strains of *Pasteurella pestis*. J. Infect. Dis., 73:124–43.

With R. Holdenried, A. L. Burroughs, and E. Jawetz. Sylvatic plague studies. IV. Inapparent, latent sylvatic plague in ground squirrels in central California. J. Infect. Dis., 73:144–57.

1944

With E. Jawetz. The behavior of virulent and avirulent *P. pestis* in normal and immune experimental animals. J. Infect. Dis., 74 (1):1–13.

Experimental infection of the chick embryo with virulent and avirulent *Pasteurella pestis*. Am. J. Pathol., 20 (3):457–69.

Studies on plague immunity in experimental animals. I. Protective and antitoxic antibodies in the serum of actively immunized animals. J. Immunol., 49 (1):1–14.

Studies on plague immunity in experimental animals. II. Some factors of the immunity mechanism in bubonic plague. J. Immunol., 49 (1):15–30.

With W. A. Sawyer, M. D. Eaton, J. H. Bauer, P. Putnam, and F. F. Schwentker. Jaundice in army personnel in the western region of the United States and its relation to vaccination against yellow fever. (Part I) Am. J. Hyg., 39 (3):337–430; (Part II, III, and IV) Calif. West. Med., 40 (1):35–107.

1945

With A. L. Burroughs, R. Holdenried, and D. S. Longanecker. A field study of latent tularemia in rodents with a list of all known naturally infected vertebrates. J. Infect. Dis., 76 (2):115–19.

1947

With E. E. Baker, H. Sommer, L. E. Foster, and E. Meyer. Antigenic structure of *Pasteurella pestis* and the isolation of a crystalline antigen. Proc. Soc. Exp. Biol. Med., 64:139–41.

With B. Eddie. The knowledge of human virus infections of animal origin. J. Am. Med. Assoc., 133 (12):822–28.

With S. F. Quan, L. E. Foster, and A. Larson. Streptomycin in experimental plague. Proc. Soc. Exp. Biol. Med., 66:528–32.

1948

With G. F. Hoessly and A. Larson. Mechanism of immunity in plague infections. Science, 108:681.
With S. F. Quan and A. Larson. Prophylactic immunization and specific therapy of experimental pneumonic plague. Am. Rev. Tuberc., 57 (4):312–21.
With L. E. Foster, E. E. Baker, H. Sommer, and A. Larson. Experimental appraisal of antiplague vaccination with dead virulent and living avirulent plague bacilli. *Proceedings, Fourth International Congress on Tropical Medicine and Malaria*, Washington, D.C., vol. 1, pp. 264–74. Wash., D.C.: U.S. Govt. Print. Off.

1949

With K. T. Brunner. Streptomycin in the treatment of leptospira carriers. Experiments with hamsters and dogs. Proc. Soc. Exp. Biol. Med., 70 (3):450–52.

1950

With K. T. Brunner. Effect of aureomycin on *Leptospira canicola* and *Leptospira icterohaemorrhagiae in vitro* and experimental carrier studies. Am. J. Vet. Res., 11 (38):89–90.
Immunization of hamsters and dogs against experimental leptospirosis. J. Immunol., 64 (5):365–72.
With H. Karrer and B. Eddie. The complement fixation inhibition test and its application to the diagnosis of ornithosis in chickens and in ducks. I. Principles and technique of the test. J. Infect. Dis., 87 (1):13–36.
The complement fixation inhibition test and its application to the diagnosis of ornithosis in chickens and in ducks. II. Confirmation of the specificity and epidemiological application of the test. J. Infect. Dis., 87 (1):24–36.
With G. P. Manire. The toxins of the psittacosis-lymphogranuloma group of agents. I. The toxicity of various members of the psittacosis-lymphogranuloma venereum group. J. Infect. Dis., 86 (3):226–32.
The toxins of the psittacosis-lymphogranuloma group of agents. II.

effect of aureomycin and penicillin upon the toxins of psittacosis viruses. J. Infect. Dis., 86 (3):233–40.

The toxins of the psittacosis-lymphogranuloma group of agents. III. Differentiation of strains by the toxin neutralization test. J. Infect. Dis., 86 (3):241–50.

Global strategy in preventive medicine (James D. Bruce Memorial Lecture in Preventive Medicine, presented at the thirty-first annual session of the American College of Physicians, Boston, Mass.). Ann. Intl. Med., 33 (2):275–91.

With S. F. Quan and T. H. Chen. Protective action of antibiotics against the toxin of *Pasteurella pestis* in mice. Proc. Soc. Exp. Biol. Med., 75 (2): 548–49.

With S. F. Quan and B. Eddie. Attempts to cure parakeet psittacosis carriers with aureomycin and penicillin. J. Infect. Dis., 86 (2):132–35.

1951

With S. Elberg, M. Herzberg, P. Schneider, and S. J. Silverman. Studies on the immunization of guinea pigs and mice to brucella infection by means of the "native antigen." J. Immunol., 67 (1):1–13.

1952

With E. E. Baker, H. Sommer, L. E. Foster, and E. Meyer. Studies on immunization against plague. I. The isolation and characterization of the soluble antigen of *Pasteurella pestis*. J. Immunol., 68 (2):131–45.

With T. H. Chen and S. F. Quan. Studies on immunization against plague. II. The complement-fixation test. J. Immunol., 68 (2):147–58.

Historical notes on disinfected mail. J. Nerv. Ment. Dis., 116 (6):523–54.

With B. Eddie. Reservoirs of the psittacosis agent. Acta Tropica, 9 (3):204–15.

Human pneumonitis viruses and their classification. Archiv Gesamte Virusforsch., 4 (5):579–90.

With S. F. Quan, F. R. McCrumb, and A. Larson. Effective treatment of plague. Ann. N.Y. Acad. Sci., 55 (6):1228–74.

With M. S. Silverman, S. S. Elberg, and L. Foster. Studies on immunization against plague III. Quantitative serological studies on an immunizing antigen of *Pasteurella pestis*. J. Immunol., 68 (6):609–20.

1953

With M. Herzberg and S. S. Elberg. Immunization against brucella infection. II. Effectiveness of a streptomycin-dependent strain of *Brucella melitensis*. J. Bacteriol., 66 (5):600–605.

With F. R. McCrumb, Jr. and A. Larson. The chemotherapy of experimental plague in the primate host. J. Infect. Dis., 92:273–87.

Recent studies on the immunity response to administration of different plague vaccines. Bull. WHO, 9 (5):619–36.

With B. Eddie. Characteristics of a psittacosis viral agent isolated from a turkey. Proc. Soc. Exp. Biol. Med., 83:99–101.

With D. L. Walker, L. E. Foster, T. H. Chen, and A. Larson. Studies on immunization against plague. V. Multiplication and persistence of virulent and avirulent *Pasteurella pestis* in mice and guinea pigs. J. Immunol., 70 (3):245–52.

1954

With T. H. Chen. Studies on immunization against plague. VII. A hemagglutination test with the protein fraction of *Pasteurella pestis:* A serologic comparison of virulent and avirulent strains with observations on the structure of the bacterial cells and its relationship to infection and immunity. J. Immunol., 72 (4):282–98.

With E. Englesberg, T. H. Chen, J. B. Levy, and L. E. Foster. Virulence in *Pasteurella pestis*. Science, 119 (3091):413–14.

1955

With T. H. Chen. Studies on immunization against plague. X. Specific precipitation of *Pasteurella pestis* antigens and antibodies in gels. J. Immunol., 74 (6):501–7.

Studies on immunization against plague. XI. A study of the immunogenicity and toxicity of eleven avirulent variants of virulent strains of *Pasteurella pestis*. J. Infect. Dis., 96 (2): 145–51.

With N. J. Ehrenkranz. Studies on immunization against plague. VIII. Study of three immunizing preparations in protecting primates against pneumonic plague. J. Infect. Dis., 96 (2): 138–44.

With G. F. Hoessly, D. L. Walker, and A. Larson. Experimental bubonic plague in monkeys. I. Study of the development of the disease and the peripheral circulatory failure. Acta Tropica, 12 (3): 240–51.

With F. R. McCrumb, Jr., S. Mercier, T. H. Chen, and K. Goodnero. Studies on the antibody patterns in pneumonic plague patients. J. Infect. Dis., 96 (1): 88–94.

With F. E. Payne, A. Larson, D. L. Walker, and L. Foster. Studies on immunization against plague. IX. The effect of cortisone on mouse resistance to attenuated strains of *Pasturella pestis*. J. Infect. Dis., 96 (2): 168–73.

With S. F. Quan and A. G. McManus. Comparisons of sulfisoxazole with sulfadiazine, and thiocymetin with chloramphenicol, in chemotherapy of experimental plague in mice. Am. J. Trop. Med. Hyg., 4 (6): 1028–36.

1956

With N. V. Bhagavan and T. H. Chen. Further studies of antigenic structure of *Pasteurella pestis* in gels. Proc. Soc. Exp. Biol. Med., 91 (3): 353–56.

With T. T. Crocker, and T. H. Chen. Electron microscopic study of the extracellular materials of *Pasteurella pestis*. J. Bacteriol., 72 (6): 851–57.

With M. Schär. Studies on immunization against plague. XV. The pathophysiologic action of the toxin of *Pasteurella pestis* in experimental animals. Schweiz. Z. Allg. Pathol. Bakteriol., 19 (1): 51–70.

1957

Acceptance of the Walter Reed Medal. Am. J. Trop. Med. Hyg., 6 (2): 341–46.

1958

With S. Elberg. Caprine immunization against brucellosis. A summary of experiments on the isolation, properties and behaviour of a vaccine strain. Bull. WHO, 19: 711–24.

With M. L. Spivack, L. Foster, A. Larson, T. H. Chen, and E. E. Baker. The immune response of the guinea pig to the antigens of *Pasteurella pestis*. J. Immunol., 80 (2): 132–41.

1960

With B. Eddie. Feather mites and ornithosis. Science, 132 (3422): 300.

1961

With T. H. Chen and L. E. Foster. Experimental comparison of the immunogenicity of antigens in the residue of ultrasonated avirulent *Pasteurella pestis* with a vaccine prepared with killed virulent whole organisms. J. Immunol., 87 (1): 64–71.
With R. L. Doherty, J. G. Carley, P. E. Lee, and B. Eddie. The effect of chlortetracycline on Australian parrots naturally infected with psittacosis. Med. J. Aust., 2 (4): 134–47.
Pneumonic plague. Bacteriol. Rev., 25 (3): 249–61.

1962

With B. Eddie, F. L. Lambrecht, and D. P. Furman. Isolation of ornithosis bedsoniae from mites collected in turkey quarters and from chicken lice. J. Infect. Dis., 110: 231–37.
Antimicrobial therapy and prophylactic immunization in the control of psittacosis or bedsonia infection in show birds. Schweiz. Med. Wochenschr. 92: 59–76.
With B. Eddie. Immunity against some bedsonia in man resulting from infection and in animals from infection or vaccination. Ann. N.Y. Acad. Sci., 98: 288–313.

1964

With P. Arnstein and D. H. Cohen. Medication of pigeons with chlortetracycline in feed. J. Am. Vet. Med. Assoc., 145 (9): 921–24.
With T. H. Chen and A. Larson. Studies on immunization against plague. XVII. Experimental studies on the effectiveness of aluminum-hydroxide-adsorbed formalin-killed *Pasteurella pestis*. J. Immunol., 93 (4): 663–76.

1965

With T. H. Chen. Susceptibility of the langur monkey (*Semnopithecus entellus*) to experimental plague: Pathology and immunity. J. Infect. Dis., 115: 456–64.

With D. McNeill. *Pasteurella pestis* antibody patterns in sera of plague-convalescent and vaccinated persons determined by immunoelectrophoresis and passive hemagglutination. J. Immunol., 94 (5): 778–84.

1966

With B. Eddie, W. J. L. Sladen, and B. K. Sladen. Serologic studies and isolation of *Bedsonia* agents from northern fur seals on the Pribilof Islands. Am. J. Epidemiol., 84 (2): 405–9.

With J. Schachter, M. G. Barnes, J. P. Jones, Jr., and E. P. Engleman. Isolation of bedsoniae from the joints of patients with Reiter's syndrome. Proc. Soc. Exp. Biol. Med., 122: 283–85.

1967

With J. Schachter and L. Rose. The venereal nature of inclusion conjunctivitis. Am. J. Epidemiol., 85 (3): 445–52.

1968

With J. Schachter, P. Arnstein, C. R. Dawson, L. Hanna, and P. Thygeson. Human follicular conjunctivitis caused by infection with a psittacosis agent. Proc. Soc. Exp. Biol. Med., 127: 292–95.

1969

With P. Arnstein, W. G. Buchanan, and B. Eddie. Chlortetracycline chemotherapy for nectar-feeding psittacine birds. J. Am. Vet. Med. Assoc., 154 (2): 190–91.

Lymphogranuloma venereum. II. Characterization of some recently isolated strains. J. Bacteriol., 99 (3): 636–38.

With J. Schachter and H. B. Ostler. Human infection with the agent of feline pneumonitis. Lancet: 1063–65.

With J. Schachter, D. E. Smith, C. R. Dawson, et al. Lymphogranuloma venereum. I. Comparison of the Frei test, complement fixation test, and isolation of the agent. J. Infect. Dis., 120 (3): 372–75.

1970

Effectiveness of live or killed plague vaccines in man. Bull. WHO, 42: 653–66.

With J. Banks, B. Eddie, and J. Schachter. Plaque formation by *Chlamydia* in L cells. Infect. Immunol., 1 (3): 259–62.

With J. Banks, B. Eddie, M. Sung, N. Sugg, and J. Schachter. Plaque reduction technique for demonstrating neutralizing antibodies for *Chlamydia*. Infect. Immunol., 2 (4): 443–47.

1971

With E. J. Gangarosa, J. A. Donadio, R. W. Armstrong, et al. Botulism in the United States, 1899–1969. Am. J. Epidemiol., 93 (2): 93–101.

With J. Schachter and M. Sung. Potential danger of Q fever in a university hospital environment. J. Infect. Dis., 123 (3): 301–4.

1973

With R. J. Gilbert, J. Schachter, and E. P. Engleman. Antibiotic therapy in experimental bedsonial arthritis. Arthritis Rheum., 16 (1) 30–33.

With A. F. Hallett and M. Isaacson. Pathogenicity and immunogenic efficacy of a live attenuated plague vaccine in vervet monkeys. Infect. Immun., 8 (6): 876–81.

The rise and fall of botulism. Calif. Med., 118 (5): 63–64.

With D. E. Smith, P. G. James, J. Schachter, and E. P. Engleman. Experimental bedsonial arthritis. Arthritis Rheum., 16 (1): 21–29.

1974

With D. C. Cavanaugh, B. L. Elisberg, C. H. Llewellyn, et al. Plague immunization. V. Indirect evidence for the efficacy of plague vaccine. J. Infect. Dis., 129: S37–S40.

With T. H. Chen. Susceptibility and immune response to experimental plague in two species of langurs and in African green (grivet) monkeys. J. Infect. Dis., 129: S46–S52.

Susceptibility and antibody response of *Rattus* species to experimental plague. J. Infect. Dis., 129: S62–S71.

With T. H. Chen and L. E. Foster. Comparison of the immune response to three different *Yersinia pestis* vaccines in guinea pigs and langurs. J. Infect. Dis., 129: S53–S61.

With J. D. Marshall, Jr., P. J. Bartelloni, D. C. Cavanaugh, and P. J. Kadull. Plague immunization. II. Relation of adverse clinical reactions to multiple immunizations with killed vaccine. J. Infect. Dis., 129: S19–S25.

With J. D. Marshall, Jr., D. C. Cavanaugh, and P. J. Bartelloni. Plague immunization. III. Serologic response to multiple inoculations of vaccine. J. Infect. Dis., 129: S26–S29.

With D. C. Cavanaugh, P. J. Bartelloni, and J. D. Marshall, Jr. Plague immunization. I. Past and present trends. J. Infect. Dis., 129: S13–S18.

With G. Smith, L. E. Foster, J. D. Marshall, Jr., and D. C. Cavanaugh. Plague immunization. IV. Clinical reactions and serologic response to inoculations of Haffkine and freeze-dried plague vaccine. J. Infect. Dis., 129: S30–S36.

With J. A. Hightower and F. R. McCrumb. Plague immunization. VI. Vaccination with the fraction 1 antigen of *Yersinia pestis*. J. Infect. Dis., 129: S41–S45.

With G. Smith, L. Foster, M. Brookman, and M. Sung. Live, attenuated *Yersinia pestis* vaccine: Virulent in nonhuman primates, harmless to guinea pigs. J. Infect. Dis., 129: S85–S120.

With J. Schachter, J. Banks, N. Sugg, M. Sung, and J. Storz. Serotyping of *Chlamydia* I. Isolates of ovine origin. Infect. Immun., 9 (1): 92–94.

1975

With J. Schachter, E. C. Hill, E. B. King, V. R. Coleman, and P. Jones. Chlamydial infection in women with cervical dysplasia. Am. J. Obstet. Gynecol., 123: 753–57.

With J. Schachter, J. Banks, N. Sugg, M. Sung, and J. Storz. Serotyping of *Chlamydia:* Isolates of bovine origin. Infect. Immun., 11: 904–7.

With J. Schachter, L. Hanna, E. C. Hill, et al. Are chlamydial infections the most prevalent venereal disease? J. Am. Med. Assoc., 231: 1252–55.

George Scatchard

GEORGE SCATCHARD

March 19, 1892–December 10, 1973

BY JOHN T. EDSALL AND WALTER H. STOCKMAYER

GEORGE SCATCHARD'S many scientific contributions dealt almost entirely with the physical chemistry of solutions; with solutions in equilibrium and solutions undergoing change with time. The range of his studies was wide and deep, extending from the simplest mixtures of nonpolar molecules to systems containing highly polar molecules and ions, and to macromolecules, especially proteins. His involvement with proteins, at a time when most physical chemists avoided such complicated substances, stemmed initially from his close personal and scientific friendship with Edwin J. Cohn, whose laboratory at Harvard Medical School was close to Scatchard's own laboratory at Massachusetts Institute of Technology.

Many of Scatchard's papers are difficult reading for most chemists, for he commonly wrote in a highly condensed style, in which each sentence and equation carried nearly its maximum possible load of meaning. Yet he could write and talk with great simplicity and directness. His work on proteins brought him into touch with many biochemists and clinicians, and he took a deep interest in their problems. His advice and insight were crucial to a good many scientific papers on which his name never appeared.

He was born in Oneonta, New York on March 19, 1892,

the second son and the fourth child of Elmer Ellsworth and Fanny Lavinia Harmer Scatchard. In an autobiographical sketch he wrote:

> Oneonta was a village of about ten thousand, on the Susquehanna in the northern foothills of the Catskills, about twenty miles south of the much better known Cooperstown. It was the largest village for fifty miles in any direction. Its most important industry was the shops of the Delaware and Hudson Railroad. It was also the site of the Oneonta Normal School which had about one boy student to ten girls in my time. It had an excellent High School Department when I was ready for it.
>
> ... I was an avid reader often for the almost mechanical pleasure of reading.... Except for reading I had the normal childhood of a small town boy—hiking, bird watching, swimming, skating, coasting and later bicycling. I helped organize and played on the "Oneonta Juniors" basketball team and later on the Oneonta Normal School team. I was manager then and officiated more than I played ... I was a very shy child. My shyness was cured only when I worked in my brother's drugstore during my high school years. I still remember the agony of waiting on a customer at the beginning, but it could not last. At first I opened the store in the morning, swept and mopped the floor and snaked the hundred and fifty pound cakes of ice from the sidewalk to the icebox behind the store. On ice-cream days I fetched the cream about three blocks from the creamery, added the sugar and flavoring and turned the crank of the five gallon freezer. Later I graduated from the early morning and menial work. My brother had the theory that in the evenings when our neighbors from the hardware and clothing stores had gone home, we should do no work not directly connected with waiting on trade. My reading branched out into drug journals, the pharmacopeia, materia medica and prescriptions—the latter with difficulty. Most physicians had terrible handwriting and prescriptions were written with English or Latin abbreviations.... I did make myself into a good practical pharmacist, and managed the store when my brother was absent.*

Following graduation from high school, Scatchard entered Amherst College, from which he graduated in 1913 with the highest marks in his class. From the beginning his

---

*G. Scatchard, "Autobiographical Note," *Equilibrium in Solutions and Surface and Colloid Chemistry* (Cambridge: Harvard Univ. Press, 1976), pp. xix-xx.

major interest was evidently in chemistry, and the background he had acquired while working in the drugstore undoubtedly influenced this choice. He records in his autobiographical notes that one of his teachers, Professor Howard W. Doughty, ". . . was one of the first people in the country, and probably in the world, to use simple physical chemistry in analytical chemistry." Scatchard assisted him in the laboratory. Doughty, although a Johns Hopkins graduate, advised Scatchard to go to Columbia for graduate work, and as Scatchard notes, "neither of us thought of any subject for my thesis other than synthetic organic chemistry." He entered the Columbia graduate school and did his thesis with Marston T. Bogert.

Edwin J. Cohn, who later became Scatchard's intimate friend and close scientific associate, was a contemporary as an undergraduate at Amherst. In his Cohn Memorial Lecture (1969, pp. 39–40), Scatchard included a passage that illuminates the character of both men:

> I did not like Cohn as an undergraduate. We were as different as our backgrounds. My family had to sacrifice to send me to college, though I earned most of my expenses working during the summer. Cohn had no financial problems. If he did not have the best of everything he had the most expensive, when his family did not know that that was not the best, which was seldom. He was an esthete. I regarded him as one of the flower children of my generation, less like those of the present than like those of an earlier generation caricaturized by W. S. Gilbert in *Patience*. . . . Cohn even fraternized with some of the faculty. I would approve of that now, but I did not then.

Scatchard's Ph.D. thesis at Columbia, submitted in 1916, dealt with 2-uraminobenzoic acid, benzoylene urea, quinazolines, and related compounds. It naturally reflected the interests of his thesis director, Professor Bogert, and was very different in character from Scatchard's later work. It did involve a study of the use of dinitrobenzoylene urea as an indicator in the pH range between 6 and 8, and this to some extent foreshadowed Scatchard's future interests in physical chemistry.

In 1917 and 1918 Scatchard was teaching organic chemistry, mostly as a laboratory assistant, and doing a little war research at Columbia under the direction of Professor W. K. Lewis of MIT. When the United States entered the First World War he proposed to leave and join the army, but Bogert and Lewis persuaded him to stay, on the ground that his work was important. Finally, he was drafted. Through the recommendations of Bogert and Lewis, he received a commission as first lieutenant in the Sanitary Corps, the only place where a chemist could be commissioned before the days of the Chemical Warfare Service. Shortly thereafter he was sent to France, where he accepted the opportunity of working with Victor Grignard, who was at the Sorbonne in the Laboratory of Georges Urbain, since Grignard's own laboratory at Nancy had been occupied by the Germans. With Grignard and G. Rivat, Scatchard developed a rapid and sensitive method for the detection of small quantities of mustard gas in air, a matter of urgent importance for troops in the field. In the course of the work Scatchard suffered burns of the throat with mustard gas and phosgene and was incapacitated for several weeks.

Early in 1919 he was about to return to the United States, but because of the acute shortage of medical officers he was assigned, along with a dentist, to be responsible for the medical care of fifteen hundred men who were unfit for further duty and were being transferred from St. Aignan to Brest. When he pointed out his lack of medical training they said, "You can read a clinical thermometer, can't you? You're better than nobody. If they don't have you they'll have nobody." Then he was urgently called back from Brest to Paris, where his oldest sister died of meningitis. Eventually he sailed for home on the *Orizaba,* and finally arrived in New York on his twenty-seventh birthday, March 19, 1919.

He applied for and received one of the first group of National Research Council Fellowships, but gave it up to return to Amherst as a teacher of chemistry on the invitation of Alexander Meiklejohn, president of Amherst, who had embarked on his brief but highly significant career of educational reform there. Scatchard wrote: "They were exciting years for a young teacher there [in Amherst]. Meiklejohn believed that to teach well one must be learning. He also believed that chemistry and physics are so simple that to learn about them a man must do research. He brought me to Amherst to prove that research in the physical sciences could be done in a small liberal arts college with the right atmosphere."* It was indeed at Amherst that Scatchard produced the first three papers that contained his own ideas. However, in 1923 the sharp disagreements between Meiklejohn and the Amherst trustees came to a head, and Meiklejohn resigned. Scatchard, an ardent Meiklejohn supporter, resigned also. He was rewarded the National Research Council Fellowship and went to the Massachusetts Institute of Technology to work with Duncan A. MacInnes in electrochemistry. In gratitude to the National Research Council, he later undertook, with three colleagues and a student, the arduous work of tabulating the densities and thermal expansions of aqueous electrolyte solutions for the *International Critical Tables*.

A year after going to MIT, Scatchard was appointed to the teaching staff. He was associated with the Institute for the rest of his life, becoming associate professor of chemistry in 1928, professor in 1937, and professor emeritus in 1957. His activity in research, however, continued to the end of his life, and a number of his important contributions appeared in the decade after 1960.

The years at MIT, from his arrival there until the Second World War, were a time of steady development of Scatchard's

---

*Scatchard, "Autobiographical Note," p. xxiv.

theoretical and experimental studies on solutions. In the following section we trace the progress and the character of these fundamental studies. The range of his scientific interests, however, extended beyond that of most members of the Chemistry Department at MIT. This was primarily due to the influence of Edwin Cohn.* We have seen that Scatchard and Cohn had not been congenial as undergraduates at Amherst. Of the close friendship that developed from 1923 on, Scatchard spoke on two occasions: first in an address on Cohn's scientific work, when Cohn received the Theodore W. Richards Medal in 1948; and then twenty-one years later in his Cohn Memorial Lecture (1969). On the latter occasion he wrote:

> Soon after I came to MIT in 1923, Cohn and I attended a reception of the Science Club of Amherst College for Niels Bohr. We stayed with a mutual friend and drove back to Cambridge together. I was surprised to find that he thought more like me than anybody I had ever met. His thoughts were more developed and polished than mine, but there was little other difference. From that day we became close friends and frequent collaborators although we never published a paper together.
>
> It is difficult to realize how customs have changed since that time. When I came to MIT, I was the only one who called himself a physical chemist in the area, perhaps in the country, who would listen to a physician or even a physiologist talking science. Cohn is probably responsible for my doing so.

Cohn's field of research was the physical chemistry of proteins. Scatchard became deeply concerned with these macromolecules and developed his thinking about solutions to encompass their special properties, as well as those of simpler molecules and ions. We speak later of his work in that area; here we simply note the importance of the relation between these two very different men. Cohn was a driving,

---

*See J. T. Edsall, "Edwin Joseph Cohn (1892–1953)," in *Biographical Memoirs* (Wash., D.C.: National Academy of Sciences, 1961), 35:47–83.

aggressive, dynamic organizer, with an excellent capacity for perceiving important scientific problems and arousing the enthusiasm of his associates, while maintaining rigorous standards of work in the laboratory. Scatchard was quieter; he never operated with a large group of people in his laboratory; in his thinking about the fundamentals of the chemistry of solutions he went deeper than Cohn, and his critical judgment was more rigorous and searching, with a far greater command of basic theoretical chemistry. In their complementary relation the two men were stronger than either could have been alone.

In 1928 Scatchard married Willian Watson Beaumont, always called Billie by him and their friends. He had known her since 1916, when he was a graduate student at Columbia and she was taking a degree there in education, in preparation for her career as a teacher of music. She was born and brought up in Montana and had taken two degrees in music at the University of Montana before coming east. She taught music in New York for some ten years before their marriage, and thereafter joined the Department of Music in Smith College, Northampton, Massachusetts, about a hundred miles from Cambridge. They lived in Cambridge in an apartment on Memorial Drive, overlooking the Charles River, near Harvard Square. Because of the demands of her work, she was away for just over half the week during the academic year. Each Sunday evening she took the train to Northampton, returning on the following Thursday afternoon. That evening she would go down to MIT to conduct the women's chorus there. On Saturday evenings throughout the concert season, she and George almost invariably attended the concert of the Boston Symphony Orchestra. Then, on the following evening, she returned again to Smith. This cycle was repeated, throughout the academic year, until her retirement from Smith in 1957. During George's year abroad as a Guggenheim Fellow in 1931–32, they attended several musical festivals together. He shared her deep love of music, and their life together was congenial and harmonious, in spite of the circumstances that obliged her to spend so much time away from Cambridge.

The coming of the Second World War brought urgent new demands into George Scatchard's life. He led a triple life. He was acting director of the Physical Chemistry Laboratory at MIT and had to keep the department running in a period of great stress. He was scientific advisor in the Manhattan Project to Harold Urey at Columbia, where he did important work on the thermodynamics of the fluorocarbon systems that were needed for the separation of uranium isotopes by diffusion; he commuted weekly to New York to take part in this work. He devoted even more of his time to the work on the blood plasma fractionation project, headed by Edwin Cohn, which grew into a major enterprise, involving dozens of chemists, biochemists, and clinicians, and seven major pharmaceutical firms that produced for the armed forces the serum albumin, gamma globulin, and other products of plasma fractionation that were used in medicine and surgery. Scatchard served as an advisor on almost every aspect of the program; he was particularly concerned with serum albumin, with its osmotic action, important in the treatment of shock, and with its capacity to bind rather tightly all sorts of small molecules and ions. This led him into important researches in his own laboratory that continued long after the war; of these we speak later, in the discussion of his work on proteins.

In 1946, when the war was over, he served for six months as scientific advisor to General Lucius D. Clay, deputy military governor of the Office of Military Government in Berlin. In those chaotic days there was much confusion and conflict in dealing with the problems of a defeated and divided Germany, with four powers occupying different parts of the country. Scatchard dealt with many problems involving German science and scientists, and had some battles with the Russian members of the quadripartite committee during his first days in Berlin concerning the treatment of German scientists. After that things were calmer. He returned to the United States, to his research and teaching at MIT, at the end of 1946.

Not long after this he became a scientific consultant to the Oak Ridge National Laboratory, and for many years he and Mrs. Scatchard stayed at Oak Ridge for about six weeks each summer. He collaborated closely during those years with K. A. Kraus and J. S. Johnson, and extended his treatment of the thermodynamic properties of solutions containing charged macromolecules to a rigorous treatment of sedimentation in the ultracentrifuge. Later his collaboration with them, and with Y. C. Yu and R. M. Rush, involved studies of mixed electrolyte solutions containing many components, a subject with which he was closely concerned during the last years of his research at MIT.

He retained his mental alertness to the end of his life, but his physical energy declined gradually during his final five years. In 1970 he fell and broke his hip, and had to remain several months in a nursing home. He was then able to return to the apartment in Cambridge, but did not regain his previous energy and vitality. With Mrs. Scatchard's devoted care, his life remained pleasant and comfortable; he enjoyed seeing his friends and talking with them about science and the world in general, but he was easily fatigued and usually did not attempt to rise from his chair when visitors arrived. In December 1973, after dental surgery that required general anesthesia, he suffered a fatal heart attack and stroke.

RESEARCH ON NONELECTROLYTE SOLUTIONS

Because of the breadth and diversity of Scatchard's research work, a purely chronological account of it would lack coherence. As we have seen, he was interested in systems aqueous and nonaqueous, electrolytes and nonelectrolytes, small molecules and macromolecules, and colloidal systems where surface forces were important. Moreover, though he was concerned mainly with equilibria, he did not neglect reaction rates. Usually he would work simultaneously in several different areas, frequently with fruitful overlap between them. The divisions chosen in our description of his scientific contributions are thus certainly arbitrary and in some ways artificial.

At Amherst College, his first independent work dealt with the hydrolysis rates and vapor pressures of concentrated aqueous sucrose solutions. Assuming that mole fractions were the most fundamental units of concentration and that in sugar solutions the various hydrated species could be treated as ideal solutes with activities equal to their mole fractions, Scatchard estimated the hydration of dissolved sucrose from both the rate and equilibrium data, with satisfactory agreement between the two methods. Years later, in referring to the ideal law for the entropy of mixing, on which the above treatment fundamentally rests, he remarked drily that most attempts to justify it in physical terms were "more entertaining than convincing."

In 1931 Scatchard published what he later considered to be his first important paper, a definitive theoretical discussion of the thermodynamics of nonelectrolyte solutions. In common with other contemporary treatments, he assumed that the entropy of mixing was ideal, so that the deviations of real solutions from the ideal laws were to be related to the enthalpy changes on isothermal mixing. Such solutions had been dubbed "regular" by Joel Hildebrand. The difference among the several existing theories lay in the interpretation of the mixing enthalpy. Thus Hildebrand (largely on the basis of solubilities and other data) and Heitler (from a lattice model) regarded this quantity as a quadratic function of the composition expressed as mole fraction; Irving Langmuir preferred "surface fractions," involving estimated molecular surface areas; while Scatchard, like his predecessor J. J. van Laar, argued that a quadratic expression in the volume fractions was most suitable. Moreover, Scatchard gave the simplest and most successful formula for predicting the magnitude of the mixing enthalpy, based on what he called the "cohesive energy density" (a piece of nomenclature which has survived). Unlike its rivals, Scatchard's expression can be completely evaluated numerically from the properties (vapor pressures and densities) of the pure components, and it thus constituted a genuinely predictive theory, which he showed in the same paper to give a rather good account of the existing data for many binary nonpolar solutions. Later, in the course of demonstrating further applications of the theory in several papers with W. J. Hamer, Scatchard introduced the notion of the excess free energy, defined simply as the difference between real and ideal free energies. Today the use of excess functions provides the most commonly used procedure for characterizing the thermodynamic properties of solutions.

In the foregoing paragraph we make no attempt to describe the methodology used by Scatchard in arriving at his theory, and indeed he did not present this completely. Like essentially all physical chemists of his generation, he did not use the formal methods of statistical mechanics, but relied on more intuitive arguments. The applications of statistical thermodynamics to solutions began a few years later in England, when R. H. Fowler, E. A. Guggenheim, and their followers studied lattice models and thus defined more sharply the fundamental basis of Scatchard's and related theories. Scatchard followed these and later developments with great interest, but did not again attempt a complete theory. His mastery of the classical thermodynamics of Gibbs was, however, brought out in an important paper in 1937. In this article he showed how experimental data obtained under constant pressure conditions should be converted to a constant-volume basis for more rigorous confrontation with theory.

During the same period, Scatchard and his collaborators, including Hamer, S. E. Wood, H. H. Gilmann, C. L. Raymond, and J. E. Mochel, constructed an accurate "equilibrium still" for the measurement of vapor pressure and composition over a range of temperatures, and produced data of then unrivalled accuracy and precision for a number of binary liquid mixtures. These results revealed complexities of thermodynamic behavior not encompassed by the earlier theory. There was, of course, strong evidence of hydrogen bonding in chloroform-ethanol. The benzene-cyclohexane system was not "regular," despite the nonpolar nature of both components, revealing a distinct positive excess entropy even at constant volume. Solutions of methanol with carbon tetrachloride and benzene were more complex still; in the latter case, the excess entropy was positive at low concentrations of methanol, but became negative at higher methanol content.

About 1950 a new equilibrium still was built and was used to investigate H_2O-H_2O_2 mixtures (then of practical interest) and also the ternary system benzene-carbon tetrachloride-methanol, for which data on the three parent binary combinations had already been obtained. At about the same time Scatchard developed a simple calorimeter to obtain heats of mixing more accurate than those derived from temperature coefficients of vapor pressures. A few years later, the final work on nonelectrolytes in his laboratory involved construction by F. G. Satkiewicz and G. M. Wilson of yet another apparatus for studying vapor-liquid equilibrium, and its use for several polar systems. Wilson found a simple and remarkably successful two-parameter equation for correlating these results,* but neither Scatchard nor anyone else has offered a complete derivation of it.

Today the simple 1931 theory still finds useful practical applications, thanks in large part to its further systematic development by Hildebrand and his students in terms of the "solubility parameter," which is the square root of the cohesive energy density. From a purely theoretical standpoint, however, it now has mainly historical interest.

INTERACTIONS OF IONS, DIPOLAR IONS, AND UNCHARGED MOLECULES

Scatchard promptly assimilated the Debye-Hückel theory of interionic attraction when it appeared in 1923.† Not long after joining the MIT faculty he initiated a comprehensive study of the freezing points of aqueous salt solutions, including salt mixtures. The results of these studies, which also involved mixed solvents (water-alcohol, water-dioxane), appeared in ten papers from 1932 to 1936. The principal collaborator in this work was S. S. Prentiss; P. T. Jones and M. A. Benedict were also involved. The experimental technique was the most precise yet devised for such measurements, and the calculation of osmotic and activity coefficients from the data followed the general approach of G. N. Lewis and his associates, but with certain refinements.

The freezing-point data in dilute solution amply confirmed the validity of the Debye-Hückel limiting law; in addition, the measurements on solutions of salt mixtures gave strong support to J. N. Brönsted's "principle of specific ion interactions" and to a corollary commonly known as Harned's

*G. M. Wilson, *Journal of the American Chemical Society*, 86 (1964):127–30.

†Concerning Peter J. W. Debye, whose work profoundly influenced Scatchard, see M. Davies, *Biographical Memoirs*, (London: Royal Society, 1970), 16:175–232; J. W. Williams, *Biographical Memoirs*, (Wash., D.C.: National Academy of Sciences, 1975), 46:23–68.

rule. Scatchard presented the Brönsted principle in his graduate course on solutions, with a characteristic humorous twist. In his *Equilibrium in Solutions* (published posthumously in 1976) he remarked, "The theory may be stated very simply, and it is reminiscent of the famous chapter in a natural history of Ireland: '*The Snakes of Ireland*. There are no snakes in Ireland.' The principle is that the electrostatic forces are so strong that ions with charges of like sign never approach close enough for their short-range, non-electrostatic specific interactions to become appreciable" (p. 143). The students naturally remembered this quotation with pleasure. In one memorable Christmas skit, the student who played Scatchard (disguised as King Lear) received a gift from Ireland which wriggled out of its container and caused him to exclaim "Gad! Brönsted must be wrong!"

Scatchard also recognized the importance of the salting-out effect, which involves the interaction of ions with uncharged molecules in aqueous solutions. The solubility (S) in water of a molecule containing nonpolar groups generally decreases as the concentration of salt (C_s) increases, according to the equation:

$$-\log(S/S_0) = K_s C_s$$

Here S_0 is the solubility of the nonelectrolyte in the absence of salt, and K_s is the salting-out coefficient. Debye interpreted salting out in terms of the preferential attraction of the highly polar water molecules around the ion, the less polar solute molecules being "squeezed out," so that their solubility diminished. In special cases, as with highly polar solutes, and with certain anions such as iodide or thiocyanate, K_s becomes negative and the solute is actually "salted in."

As was well known, proteins are also salted out at high salt concentrations, and the salting-out coefficients are much larger than for small compounds. Scatchard was well aware of this, through his discussions with Cohn, and he incorporated such interactions into his thinking from an early stage in his career.

In the middle thirties, Scatchard turned to more concentrated electrolyte solutions; in a notable review in 1936 he combined the Debye theories of ion interaction and salting-out with his own treatment of nonelectrolytes (to deal with the "specific interactions") and, with the aid of a single disposable parameter chosen to match the data for sodium chloride, produced an impressive fit of the data for all alkali halides up to concentrations of the order of 6M. At the same time, he initiated a new experimental program of measuring the activities of concentrated solutions of nonvolatile solutes (both electrolyte and nonelectrolyte) by the isopiestic method of R. A. Robinson.

The Debye-Hückel limiting law, however, was soon again to intrude on Scatchard's thoughts. T. Shedlovsky and D. A. MacInnes reported that dilute aqueous solutions of lanthanum chloride, as measured by "concentration cells with transference," displayed serious disagreement with the limiting law. A new and still more precise freezing-point apparatus was thereupon designed and built in Scatchard's laboratory by B. Vonnegut and D. W. Beaumont. Their measurements were finished in 1942 and gave results for lanthanum chloride which strongly supported the Debye-Hückel theory. Scatchard held off publication until well after Shedlovsky had discovered a computational error in the emf (electromotive force) data, bringing the disagreement to an end.

In 1949 another defense of Debye and Hückel was called for after A. R. Olson and T. R. Simonson at Berkeley had presented extensive measurements of salt effects on rates of second-order reactions (and also some equilibria) involving two ions with charges of like sign. They showed (in amplification of some earlier work by V. K. LaMer) that under most experimental conditions the concentration of oppositely charged ions, rather than the ionic strength, was the important controlling variable. On this basis some chemists questioned the entire Debye-Hückel theory. Scatchard again responded to the challenge, showing by numerous calculations based on the modern extended theories of J. G. Kirkwood and of J. E. Mayer and J. D. Poirier that the essential Debye-Hückel model of charged hard spheres in a dielectric continuum (now often called the "primitive model" of electrolyte solutions) could account for all the results, but that for solutions of highly charged ion species one should, of course, not expect the ionic-strength principle or the limiting law to hold except at very low concentrations. This work appeared in a symposium at the National Bureau of Standards (1953).

STUDIES ON AMINO ACIDS AND PROTEINS

Scatchard and Cohn, from about 1924 on, constantly discussed the relation of the Debye-Hückel theory and the salting-out effect to the behavior of proteins, especially the solubility of proteins in salt solutions. Addition of small amounts of salt greatly increases the solubility of many proteins in water. This was, at least qualitatively, to be expected of molecules like proteins, with their electrically charged groups, in the light of the Debye-Hückel theory. At much higher concentrations of salts such as ammonium sulfate, proteins had long been known to be salted out, the protein concentration dropping very rapidly as the salt concentration increased.

E. Q. Adams in 1915 and Niels Bjerrum in 1923, with a much greater array of evidence, had concluded that aliphatic amino acids, even at their isoelectric points, bear positive and negative charges, separated by substantial distances; that is, an isoelectric α-amino acid has the formula $^+H_3N \cdot CHR \cdot COO^-$, not $H_2N \cdot CHR \cdot COOH$, as nearly all chemists had supposed earlier. The centers of positive and negative charge, separated by about 3Å, should give rise to a large dipole moment of about 15 Debye units. Isoelectric proteins, with many positive and negative charges, should possess much higher moments than this. They might therefore be expected to interact with ions of salts, at least qualitatively, as if they were ions, even though the net charge on the protein (or amino acid) was zero; that is, the molecule was a so-called zwitterion, or dipolar ion. The nature of such interactions gave rise to intense discussion in Cohn's laboratory; and Scatchard took a most active part in the seminars there. The mathematical problems of calculating interactions between ions and dipolar ions were formidable, and taxed even Scatchard's very considerable mathematical powers. Fortunately a brilliant younger associate at the Massachusetts Institute of Technology, John G. Kirkwood, became involved in the discussions. Scatchard and Kirkwood undertook a joint theoretical research during the year 1931–32, when they and Cohn were on leave of absence in Europe. Their calculations involved a "dumbbell" model of a zwitterion, composed of two charged spheres, one positive and one negative, separated by a thin rigid connection. It soon became apparent that the activity coefficient of any such model, in the lower limit near zero ionic strength, would be a linear function of the first power of the ionic strength, not of the square root, as in the case of an ion carrying a net charge. Scatchard, in his autobiography, described a discussion with Debye in Leipzig. "When I introduced Kirkwood to Debye, he (Debye) was apparently very busy and did not invite us into his office. He asked what we were working on. I said we were correcting Bjerrum's statement that molecules with widely separated charges behave like two independent ions even in the limiting law. Debye said, 'Bjerrum must be right.' I said, 'Do you forget that at infinite dilution the ion atmosphere is at an infinite distance?' Debye said, 'That's right. Bjerrum must be wrong.' "*

The resulting paper appeared, in German, in the *Physikalische Zeitschrift* in 1932. Its fundamental conclusions were qualitatively sound, but the model was still inadequate for describing such molecules as amino acids. It was Kirkwood who carried the problem much further, by calculations on spherical and ellipsoidal models with charges appropriately placed. These provided an excellent basis of comparison with the experimental data obtained in Cohn's laboratory on amino acids and peptides; the correspondence of theory and experiment was impressive. Kirkwood went on to a brilliant career at Cornell, California Institute of Technology, and Yale—a career tragically cut short by his death from cancer at the age of fifty-two. Scatchard's relation with Kirkwood was second only to that with Cohn in its combination of personal friendship and closely shared scientific interests. Scatchard's brief memoir (1960) is at present the best account we have of Kirkwood's career.

Scatchard's freezing point studies on ethanol, glycine, sodium chloride, and their mixtures demonstrated both the "salting in" of glycine by the salt, due to electrostatic interactions, and the salting out of ethanol and the repulsive interactions between ethanol and glycine, due to the nonpolar portion of the ethanol molecule and its interaction with the positive and negative charges on the glycine dipolar ion. Related studies of solubilities of amino acids, in media containing salts and ethanol, were proceeding at the same time in Cohn's laboratory. The solubility studies were more comprehensive in scope, but Scatchard's measurements had the advantage of being carried out at very low concentrations of the solute molecules and ions, where the interaction

*Scatchard, "Autobiographical Note," p. xxviii.

coefficients could be determined with less ambiguity of interpretation.

OSMOTIC PRESSURE OF PROTEINS AND BINDING OF IONS AND OTHER LIGANDS

Scatchard's interest in proteins had certainly begun before 1925, as a result of his constant interchange of ideas with Cohn. It was the blood plasma fractionation program in the Second World War, however, that drew him to study proteins in his own laboratory; these studies continued for the rest of his career in research.

His major concern was with serum (plasma) albumin, which plays the major role in maintaining osmotic equilibrium between the plasma and the cells and tissues with which it is in contact. It was therefore a matter of great practical concern, and also of fundamental scientific interest, to determine accurately the osmotic pressure of albumin solutions under varied conditions.

Several investigators, notably S. P. L. Sörensen in Copenhagen and G. S. Adair in Cambridge, England, had made excellent use of osmotic pressure to determine the molecular weights of proteins. Scatchard's work was distinctive in extending the measurements over a wide range of both pH and salt and protein concentration, and in avoiding the use of buffers other than the albumin itself. This permitted the evaluation of thermodynamic interaction coefficients between the albumin molecules, over a wide range of positive and negative net charge, and between the albumin and the ions of the salt (sodium chloride). The experimental work (reported in 1946) was done in collaboration with A. C. Batchelder and A. Brown. In an immediately preceding paper, Scatchard developed the thermodynamic theory of osmotic pressure with a degree of rigor never previously attained; the paper makes difficult reading, even for most of the specialists in the field, but it is fundamental. Scatchard, Batchelder, and Brown determined the molecular weight of bovine serum albumin as 69,000, and they characterized the protein-protein and protein-salt interactions in great detail.

Perhaps the most striking finding to emerge from their study was the selective tendency of albumin to bind anions, such as chloride, even when the albumin molecule carried a net negative charge, which would tend to repel anions and attract cations. They found no evidence that sodium ions were bound. These observations led to Scatchard's long series of researches on ion binding by albumin. One approach, demonstrated in his work with E. S. Black (1949), was to add salts to an isoionic solution of albumin—that is, to a solution initially containing only water, albumin, hydrogen, and hydroxyl ions. The mean net charge on the isoionic albumin is close to zero. If a salt is added, the albumin selectively binds the anion, thus acquiring a negative net charge. This in turn causes the ionized carboxylic groups in the albumin to bind more protons by electrostatic attraction, thus removing H^+ ions from the solution and thereby raising the pH. The greater the anion binding, the greater the upward shift in pH. The measurements indicated that, for instance, binding of anions increased in the order chloride < iodide < thiocyanate.

Most of the further studies of ion binding involved electromotive force measurements. The first major studies, with I. H. Scheinberg and S. H. Armstrong, Jr. (1948), dealt with the binding of chloride and thiocyanate ions. Later Scatchard devoted much effort to the development of ion-exchanger electrodes. His reasons were well stated in a later paper:

> Ion exchangers have advantages in the electrochemical study of protein solutions because their pores are too small to admit protein molecules and because they repel ions of the same sign. Therefore, even in the presence of protein, a cation exchanger membrane behaves as a small-cation elec-

trode and an anion exchanger membrane as a small-anion electrode in the same sense that a glass membrane may behave as a hydrogen electrode.

Some advantages are that there is no oxidation or reduction at these membranes, they are not limited to ions for which there are reversible true electrodes, and the combination of a cation and an anion exchanger permits the measurement of the free energy of transfer of the salt. [Scatchard, Coleman, and Shen 1957, p. 12.]

The paper by Scatchard, Wu, and Shen (1959) reported the most accurate and comprehensive studies on ion binding by albumin by studies of pH and electrical potentials of anion-exchanger electrodes, and in more concentrated solutions by osmotic pressure measurements. They inferred from this work three classes of anion-binding sites on the albumin: a single site in the first class showing very strong binding; eight in the second class, with weaker binding; and eighteen in the third class, with still weaker binding. The ratio of the association constants, for both chloride and iodide, for the three classes, was given by the relation: $K_1 = 24K_2 = 720K_3$.

The special features of the serum albumin molecule that give it this remarkable tendency to bind all sorts of anions were still obscure, and remain obscure today. Serum albumin is unique among proteins in this respect.

Scatchard's studies on ion binding led him to an equation of extreme simplicity for plotting binding data to evaluate the number of binding sites and the association constants involved. The simplest case arises when there are n equivalent and independent sites in a macromolecule for the binding of a given ligand. In this case the data can be described by a single association constant k. If n and k are both initially unknown, the problem is to evaluate them as accurately as possible from the data. Assuming that electrostatic interactions between the charged protein and the anion could be neglected, Scatchard concluded that the best plot of the data, which would give the most appropriate relative weight to the various measurements of amount of ligand bound ($\bar{v}$), corresponded to the form:

$$\bar{v}/c = k(n-\bar{v})$$

where k is the intrinsic association constant, and c is the concentration of free ligand. If the basic assumptions hold, the plot of $\bar{v}/c$ as ordinate against $\bar{v}$ as abscissa is a straight line of negative slope; the intercept on the abscissa gives n, that on the ordinate gives kn. This equation, which Scatchard first employed in a discussion on "The Attractions of Proteins for Small Molecules and Ions" (1949) has proved enormously useful, and such "Scatchard plots" appear in dozens of papers every year.

Such plots may deviate greatly from linearity if binding at one site affects binding at others, or if there are different classes of binding sites with inherently different affinities for the ligand. Scatchard considered in his discussion how such factors modify the representation of the data, and how to derive information about the nature of the system from plots of the above variables in more complicated cases. Further work by others has shown that Scatchard plots for proteins that undergo important conformational changes during ligand binding (allosteric transitions) may assume quite unusual shapes.*

---

*The Michaelis-Menten equation for the rate of an enzyme-catalyzed reaction is mathematically equivalent to the equation for the binding of a ligand at a set of identical and independent binding sites. This is discussed in detail by J. T. Edsall and J. Wyman (*Biophysical Chemistry*, vol. I, pp. 620–23 [New York: Academic Press, 1958]). The initial rate (v) of the enzyme-catalyzed reaction corresponds to $\bar{v}$, the maximum velocity (V_{max}) to n, and the reciprocal of the Michaelis constant (K_M^{-1}) to k. The equivalent of the Scatchard plot, in enzyme kinetics, was apparently first proposed by Barnet Woolf of Cambridge University, and published in J. B. S. Haldane and K. G. Stern (*Allgemeine Chemie der Enzyme* [Dresden and Leipzig, 1932], p. 119). We take this information from M. Dixon and E. C. Webb (*Enzymes*, 2d edition [Academic Press, 1964], p. 69). Later G. S. Eadie (*J. Biol. Chem.*, 146

One of us (J. T. E.) is indebted to Scatchard for another valuable method of calculating binding constants for molecules or ions with n initially equivalent binding sites, with interactions between them. Here n is a known quantity, and the problem is to determine the n successive binding constants. Examples are ions such as Ca^{++} or Zn^{++}, with four binding sites for such ligands as ammonia or imidazole, and hemoglobin with its four heme groups, binding oxygen or carbon monoxide. Scatchard's proposal was to plot a quantity $Q = \bar{\nu}/(n-\bar{\nu})c$ (or $\log Q$) as a function of the bound ligand, $\bar{\nu}$, which varies from 0 to n as the concentration (c) of free ligand increases. It is readily shown that the limiting value of Q as $\bar{\nu}$ approaches zero equals K_1/n, where K_1 is the first association constant; and the limiting value of Q as $c \to \infty$ is nK_n, where K_n is the n'th association constant. Knowledge of these limiting K values is an important first step in calculating the other association constants. The method demands high accuracy in determining the values of $\bar{\nu}$, in the neighborhood of $\bar{\nu} = 0$ and $\bar{\nu} = n$. The plot of $\log Q$ against $\bar{\nu}$ also reveals immediately whether the interactions between the binding sites are cooperative, with a curve that rises as $\bar{\nu}$ increases, or anticooperative, with a descending curve. Equivalent and independent groups give a horizontal straight line. On Scatchard's suggestion this plot was first used by Edsall et al.,*

[1942]:85) also independently derived and used the equation. Thus what we may call the "Woolf plot" anticipated the Scatchard plot by seventeen years. Scatchard was almost certainly unaware of this. It is interesting to note that the enzyme chemists have made very little use of this method of plotting their data, whereas the workers on equilibrium binding have employed the Scatchard plot in hundreds of papers.

An important discussion on the various forms assumed by the Scatchard plot, for independent sites, interacting sites, and mixed interacting and noninteracting sites, is given by A. A. Schreier and P. R. Schimmel (*Journal of Molecular Biology*, 86 [1974]:601–20) in a study of the binding of manganese ions to transfer RNA.

*J. T. Edsall, G. Felsenfeld, D. S. Goodman, and F. R. N. Gurd, *Journal of the American Chemical Society*, 76 (1954):3054. See also J. T. Edsall and J. Wyman, *Biophysical Chemistry*, vol. I (New York: Academic Press, 1958), pp. 629–35.

who were studying the binding of imidazole to Zn^{++} and Ca^{++} ions. A number of authors used it later. Since Scatchard was not listed as an author on any of these papers, we take this opportunity to note this valuable contribution.

COLLABORATIVE WORK AT THE OAK RIDGE NATIONAL LABORATORY

Scatchard's collaboration with J. S. Johnson, Jr. and K. A. Kraus at Oak Ridge began in 1950 and continued every summer for some fifteen years, during the summer periods when Scatchard was free to leave MIT. It included elaborate calculations of the distribution of charged polymers at equilibrium in a centrifugal field, the use of interference optics in such studies, and studies on silicotungstic acid in the ultracentrifuge and by light scattering. Later, with Johnson, R. M. Rush, and Y. C. Wu, he undertook extensive studies of the osmotic activity coefficients of salt mixtures. These papers show Scatchard's almost unparalleled grasp of the complexities of the thermodynamic interactions in multicomponent systems. They furnish outstanding examples of the interpretation of such complex systems in terms of simpler systems, where only one or two solute components at a time are considered.

Scatchard's last student at MIT, H. F. Gibbard, Jr., studied the vapor-liquid equilibrium of synthetic seawater solutions from 20 to 100°C, and made detailed studies of liquid-vapor equilibrium in aqueous lithium and sodium chloride solutions, over a wide range of composition and temperature.

Dr. J. S. Johnson, Jr. of Oak Ridge has provided illuminating comments on Scatchard's role as a consultant there. He wrote that his scientific group "particularly benefited, because of several common interests—ultracentrifugation, ion exchange, thermodynamics of solutions—[and because] he has a trait oddly rare, in my experience, in consultants

... he discusses with you your problems, rather than his. ... His patience in explicating his ideas to us has been immense. Once one understands what he is about, intriguing subtleties frequently become apparent in his style. There are other occasions, particularly in his MIT lecture notes, when he has produced about the only worthwhile discussion of many topics. And there is no ally I'd rather have in a scientific controversy" (quoted from I. H. Scheinberg's introduction to Scatchards' *Equilibrium in Solutions* [1976]).

SCATCHARD AS THINKER, TEACHER, AND CRITIC

George Scatchard was a master of the science of thermodynamics. In his insight into the thermodynamic relations of systems containing many components, he was directly in the line of descent from Willard Gibbs. He resembled Gibbs also in his resolutely brief and austere presentation of his results. It was often not easy to follow the path by which he traveled from basic principles to final results, but those who made the effort could always verify the fact that the path was there, and that it provided a firm footing for the traveler. Moreover, deeply though he valued the elegance and rigor of pure thermodynamics, he was always concerned with the nature of molecules and their interactions. In his published work he made scarcely any use of the formal relations of modern statistical mechanics. Throughout his career, however, he was concerned to understand what he called, in one of his semi-popular lectures (1950), "the social behavior of molecules." His interests ranged from the monatomic gases to the large proteins, and his contributions to our understanding of their interactions were fruitful all along the line.

His standards of work were high, and he could be a severe critic. Charles Tanford has described this aspect of his character well:

He did not necessarily expect others to match his own precision of thought or experiment, but he expected them to try their best. When he detected gross confusion or misconceptions, and especially when they masqueraded behind a facade of glib showmanship, he could be merciless. He will not be forgotten by anyone who presented seminars at the Harvard–MIT Physical Chemistry Colloquium when he was present. There was a perpetual frown on his face, deepening at each point where the speaker was glossing over theoretical or experimental difficulties. At the end of the seminar there was relief when he asked an innocuous question, and (depending on the personality of the speaker) either anger or a silent resolve never to err again when he rose to expose a fallacy. There are undoubtedly some who remember George Scatchard with less than affection as the result of such an encounter, but there are many more who are grateful for his example and for the effect it had of raising their own standards of what is and is not a valid piece of scientific research."*

He was involved in polemics on several occasions, when he felt it necessary to criticize sloppy work and thinking in published papers or books. For many years at MIT he taught a course in surface and colloid chemistry. In his Kendall Award Address (1962; published, 1973), "Half a Century as a Part-time Colloid Chemist," he contrasted ". . . the unionists—Einstein and Svedberg for example—who held that a colloid particle is a macromolecule, like an ordinary macromolecule only more so, as opposed to the isolationists like (Wolfgang) Ostwald who claimed that the world of neglected dimensions was subject only to its own laws." In his early days, as he said in the same article: "The textbooks on colloid chemistry . . . seemed mostly cook book or nonsense." In his own class notes on his course, posthumously published in 1976, he presented the subject in solid and rigorous fashion. The major part of the same book, *Equilibrium in Solutions*, was written for his graduate course at MIT. As one of us (W. H. S.) has written in the introduction to that book:

---

*From an (unsigned) obituary in *Nature*, 248 (1974):367.

It conveys, in the same compressed style that makes his major papers difficult, Scatchard's methodology in dealing with solutions of any degree of complexity, from noble gas mixtures to multicomponent electrolyte or protein systems. It is this breadth and the continuous subtle interplay between strict thermodynamic reasoning and intuitive molecular interpretation which are unique. Although the modern student of solutions will not find the extensive statistical-mechanical developments of the past two decades, he will find in Scatchard's chapters many guides and examples of procedures that are still viable and valuable. It is not irrelevant (or irreverent) to suggest a qualitative parallel with the papers of Gibbs, and indeed this suggestion has already been made by others. [Cambridge, Mass.: Harvard Univ. Press, 1976, p. xvii–xviii.]

In the early 1920's he submitted a paper on the activities of hydrochloric acid in solutions, by electromotive force measurements. Merle Randall in Berkeley, who reviewed this manuscript, wrote that his own freezing point measurements on this system made all other measurements obsolete, and asked that he should be permitted to discuss his measurements before anyone else. At this point, Scatchard notes in his autobiographical sketch, "I fought." Later, in 1925, at an American Chemical Society meeting in Pasadena, he met Professor William Bray of Berkeley, who said: "Scatchard, you don't look nearly as belligerent as I expected."* Bray had seen all the correspondence; he and Scatchard soon became very good friends.

Many years later (1950) Scatchard reviewed the well-known treatise on *Thermodynamics* by E. A. Guggenheim, a book with a strongly individual flavor. In his searching review Scatchard remarked that the book might well be subtitled *Pride and Prejudice*. Guggenheim, who dearly loved an argument, duly noted the comment in the preface to the second edition, and invited his readers to judge for themselves.

Although Scatchard could thus be a formidable critic, there were many workers, especially biochemists and clinical

*Scatchard, "Autobiographical Note," p. xxvi.

investigators, who found him most approachable and helpful when they came to him to discuss their problems. In personal discussions he learned to gauge the level of scientific understanding of those who came to see him, and he spent countless hours in helping to disentangle their problems and to suggest fruitful lines of approach. His formulation of the "Scatchard plot" for analyzing the binding of small molecules to proteins grew out of such discussions with the protein chemists. He was well aware of the practical importance of such phenomena, as in the stabilization of serum albumin against heat denaturation by addition of certain fatty acid anions to the solution, which permitted the solution to be heated so as to destroy the virus of serum hepatitis. For many years after World War II he worked closely with the Commission on Plasma Fractionation to help insure the quality and safety of serum albumin preparations for clinical use, and was always vigilant and helpful as an adviser.

As a teacher in undergraduate courses, Scatchard was somewhat baffling to many of the students. He did make serious efforts to present basic material simply, but many points that were elementary to him were not easily grasped by most undergraduates, and they often lost the thread of his thinking at a rather early stage. Indeed some students used to refer to the time of his lectures as the "mystery hour." This was in contrast to his capacity for patient and careful explanation when he was talking to individuals. In the give-and-take of mutual discussion he would gradually discover the difficulties that were troubling his interlocutor, and clear them away, step by step. Almost anyone who came to him with a real desire for clarification of some difficult point would leave with a better understanding than when he came.

HONORS AND AWARDS

Scatchard received the honorary degree of Sc.D. from his college, Amherst, in 1948. He was elected to the National

Academy of Sciences in 1946, and was a Fellow of the American Academy of Arts and Sciences. The award that he most valued was probably the Theodore Richards Medal of the American Chemical Society, which he received in 1954. His long concern with systems of colloidal dimensions was recognized by the Kendall Award in Colloid Science (1962).

IN THE WRITING of this memoir, Mrs. Scatchard was most helpful in commenting on earlier drafts of this biography, and in supplying photographs and other unpublished material. She died in 1976. We are indebted to Dr. I. H. Scheinberg for his personal recollections of George Scatchard, many of them embodied in his introduction to Scatchard's *Equilibrium in Solutions* (1976), which also includes the recollections of several other colleagues who were closely associated with Scatchard, the present authors among them. We thank the Harvard University Press for permission to quote some passages from this introduction, and also to include extensive quotations from Scatchard's autobiographical note in the same volume.

BIBLIOGRAPHY

1916

With M. T. Bogert. Researches on quinazolines. XXXIII. A new and sensitive indicator for acidimetry and alkalimetry, and for the determination of hydrogen-ion concentrations between the limits of 6 and 8 on the Sörensen scale. J. Am. Chem. Soc., 38:1606–15.

2-Uraminobenzoic acid, benzoylene urea and some of their derivatives: and the use of dinitrobenzoylene urea as an indicator. Dissertation, Columbia University, pp. 1–37. Easton, Penn.: Eschenbach Printing.

1919

With A. Smith and H. Eastlock. The transition of dry ammonium chloride. J. Am. Chem. Soc., 41:1961–69.

With M. T. Bogert. Researches on quinazolines. XXXIV. The synthesis of certain nitro and amino benzoylene ureas and some compounds related thereto. J. Am. Chem. Soc., 41:2052–68.

1920

With V. Grignard and G. Rivat. Sur le Sulfure d'Éthyle β-β'-Bi-iodé et son Application à la Détection et au Dosage de l'Ypérite. Ann. Chim. (9e serie), 15:5–18.

1921

The speed of reaction in concentrated solutions and the mechanism of the inversion of sucrose. I. J. Am. Chem. Soc., 46:2387–2406.

The hydration of sucrose in water solution as calculated from vapor-pressure measurements. J. Am. Chem. Soc., 43:2406–18.

1923

The speed of reaction in concentrated solution and the mechanism of the inversion of sucrose. II. J. Am. Chem. Soc., 45:1580–92.

Electromotive-force measurements with a saturated potassium chloride bridge or with concentration cells with a liquid junction. J. Am. Chem. Soc., 45:1716–23.

1924

The influence of gelatin on transference numbers. J. Am. Chem. Soc., 46:2353–57.

1925

The activities of strong electrolytes. I. The activity of hydrochloric acid derived from the electromotive force of hydrogen-silver-chloride cells. J. Am. Chem. Soc., 47:641–48.

The activities of strong electrolytes. II. A revision of the activity coefficients of potassium, sodium, and lithium chlorides, and potassium hydroxide. J. Am. Chem. Soc., 47:648–61.

The activities of strong electrolytes. III. The use of the flowing junction to study the liquid-junction potential between dilute hydrochloric acid and saturated potassium chloride solutions; and the revision of some single-electrode potentials. J. Am. Chem. Soc., 47:696–709.

The activity of strong electrolytes. IV. The application of the Debye-Hückel equation to alcoholic solutions. J. Am. Chem. Soc., 47:2098–2111.

1926

Electromotive-force measurements in aqueous solutions of hydrochloric acid containing sucrose. J. Am. Chem. Soc., 48:2026–35.

The unimolecularity of the inversion process. J. Am. Chem. Soc., 48:2259–63.

The Milner and Debye theories of strong electrolytes. Philos. Mag., 2:577–86.

1927

A revision of some activities in water-alcohol mixtures. J. Am. Chem. Soc., 49:217–18.

The interaction of electrolytes with non-electrolytes. Chem. Rev., 3:383–402.

Mixed solutions of electrolytes and non-electrolytes. Trans. Faraday Soc., 23:454–62.

1928

With J. A. Beattie, B. T. Brooks, L. J. Gillespie, W. C. Schumb, and R. F. Tefft. Density (specific gravity) and thermal expansion (under atmospheric pressure) of aqueous solutions of inorganic substances and of strong electrolytes. *International Critical Tables,* 3:51–111.

1929

The Moore Laboratory of Chemistry, Amherst College. Nucleus, Dec.

1930

The rate of reaction in a changing environment. J. Am. Chem. Soc., 52:52–61.
With R. F. Tefft. Some electromotive force measuremens with calcium chloride solutions. J. Am. Chem. Soc., 52:2265–71.
With R. F. Tefft. Electromotive force measurements on cells containing zinc chloride. The activity coefficients of the chlorides of the bivalent metals. J. Am. Chem. Soc., 52:2272–81.
Note on the equation of state explicit in the volume. Proc. Natl. Acad. Sci. USA, 16:811–13.

1931

With T. F. Buehrer. An effect of the breadth of junction on the electromotive force of a simple concentration cell. J. Am. Chem. Soc., 53:574–78.
Equilibria in non-electrolyte solutions in relation to the vapor pressures and densities of the components. Chem. Rev., 8:321–33.
Thermal expansion and the Debye-Hückel heat of dilution. J. Am. Chem. Soc., 53:2037–39.
Interatomic forces in binary alloys. J. Am. Chem. Soc., 53:3186–88.

1932

Die Anwendung der Debyeschen Elektrolyttheorie auf konzentrierte Lösungen. Physik. Z., 33:22–32.
Statistical mechanics and reaction rates in liquid solutions. Chem. Rev., 10:229–40.
With J. G. Kirkwood. Das Verhalten von Zwitterionen und von

mehrwertigen Ionen mit weit entfernten Ladungen in Elektrolytlösungen. Physik. Z., 33:297–300.
With P. T. Jones and S. S. Prentiss. The freezing points of aqueous solutions. I. A freezing point apparatus. J. Am. Chem. Soc., 54:2676–90.
With P. T. Jones and S. S. Prentiss. The freezing points of aqueous solutions. II. Potassium, sodium, and lithium nitrates. J. Am. Chem. Soc., 54:2690–95.
With S. S. Prentiss. The freezing points of aqueous solutions. III. Ammonium chloride, bromide, iodide, nitrate, and sulfate. J. Am. Chem. Soc., 54:2696–2705.
The effect of the forces between solvent molecules on the properties of electrolyte solutions. Chemistry at the Centenary Meeting, Brit. Assoc., 1931, pp. 70–72.
Ligevaegt i Blandiger af Ikke-Elektrolyter. Kem. Maanedsbl. (Copenhagen), 13:77–78(A).

1933

The coming of age of the interionic-attraction theory. Chem. Rev., 13:7–27.
With S. S. Prentiss. An objective study of dilute aqueous solutions of uni-univalent electrolytes. Chem. Rev., 13:139–46.
With S. S. Prentiss. The freezing points of aqueous solutions. IV. Potassium, sodium and lithium chlorides and bromides. J. Am. Chem. Soc., 55:4355–62.

1934

With S. S. Prentiss and P. T. Jones. The freezing points of aqueous solutions. V. Potassium, sodium and lithium chlorates and perchlorates. J. Am. Chem. Soc., 56:805–7.
With S. S. Prentiss. The freezing points of aqueous solutions. VI. Potassium, sodium and lithium formates and acetates. J. Am. Chem. Soc., 56:807–11.
Non-electrolyte solutions. J. Am. Chem. Soc., 56:995–96.
With S. S. Prentiss. Freezing points of aqueous solutions. VII. Ethyl alcohol, glycine and their mixtures. J. Am. Chem. Soc., 56:1486–92.
With S. S. Prentiss. Freezing points of aqueous solutions. VIII.

Mixtures of sodium chloride with glycine and ethyl alcohol. J. Am. Chem. Soc., 56:2314–19.

With S. S. Prentiss. The freezing points of aqueous solutions. IX. Mixtures of the reciprocal salt pair: Potassium nitrate-lithium chloride. J. Am. Chem. Soc., 56:2320–26.

1935

With W. J. Hamer. The application of equations for the chemical potentials to partially miscible solutions. J. Am. Chem. Soc., 57:1805–9.

With W. J. Hamer. The application of equations for the chemical potentials to equilibria between solid solution and liquid solution. J. Am. Chem. Soc., 57:1809–11.

1936

With Marjorie A. Benedict. The freezing points of aqueous solutions. X. Dioxane and its mixtures with lithium, sodium and potassium chlorides. J. Am. Chem. Soc., 58:837–42.

Concentrated solutions of strong electrolytes. Chem. Rev., 19:309–27.

1937

Change of volume on mixing and the equations for non-electrolyte mixtures. Trans. Faraday Soc., 33:160–66.

Book review: *Ions in Solution* by R. W. Gurney. J. Am. Chem. Soc., 59:2751.

1938

With C. L. Raymond and H. H. Gilmann. Vapor-liquid equilibrium. I. Apparatus for the study of systems with volatile components. J. Am. Chem. Soc., 60:1275–78.

With C. L. Raymond. Vapor-liquid equilibrium. II. Chloroform-ethanol mixtures at 35, 45, and 55°. J. Am. Chem. Soc., 60:1278–87.

With W. J. Hamer and S. E. Wood. Isotonic solutions. I. The chemical potential of water in aqueous solutions of sodium chloride, potassium chloride, sulfuric acid, sucrose, urea and glycerol at 25°. J. Am. Chem. Soc., 60:3061–70.

1939

Symposium on intermolecular action: Introduction; Discussion. J. Phys. Chem., 43:1–3; 281–96.

With S. E. Wood and J. M. Mochel. Vapor-liquid equilibrium. III. Benzene-cyclohexane mixtures. J. Phys. Chem., 43:119–30.

The nature of the critical complex and the effect of changing medium on the rate of reaction. J. Chem. Phys., 7:657–63.

With S. E. Wood and J. M. Mochel. Vapor-liquid equilibrium. IV. Carbon tetrachloride-cyclohexane mixtures. J. Am. Chem. Soc., 61:3206–10.

1940

With S. E. Wood and J. M. Mochel. Vapor-liquid equilibrium. V. Carbon tetrachloride-benzene mixtures. J. Am. Chem. Soc., 62:712–16.

The effect of solvents on reaction rates (discussion of paper by Laidler and Eyring). Ann. N.Y. Acad. Sci., 39:341–44.

The calculation of the compositions of phases in equilibrium. J. Am. Chem. Soc., 62:2426–29.

1941

The sorting of mixed solvents by ions. J. Chem. Phys., 9:34–41.

1942

With L. F. Epstein. The calculation of the thermodynamic properties and the association of electrolyte solutions. Chem. Rev., 30:211–26.

Equilibrium thermodynamics and biological chemistry. Science, 95:27–32.

1943

Book review: *Elementary Physical Chemistry* by H. S. Taylor and H. A. Taylor. Chem. Eng. News, 21:196, 198.

Constants of the Debye-Hückel theory. J. Am. Chem. Soc., 65:1249.

Thermodynamics and simple electrostatic theory, pp. 20–74; Solubility of amino acids, peptides, and related substances in water and organic solvents, pp. 177–95; Interactions in protein solutions calculated from electromotive force and osmotic measurements, pp. 619–22. In: *Proteins, Amino Acids and Peptides,* ed. E. J. Cohn and J. T. Edsall. N.Y.: Reinhold Publishing.

1944

With S. T. Gibson, L. M. Woodruff, A. C. Batchelder, and A. Brown. Chemical, clinical, and immunological studies on the products of human plasma fractionation. IV. A study of the thermal stability of human serum albumin. J. Clin. Invest., 23:445–53.

With A. C. Batchelder and A. Brown. Chemical, clinical, and immunological studies on the products of human plasma fractionation. VI. The osmotic pressure of plasma and of serum albumin. J. Clin. Invest., 23:458–64.

With J. L. Oncley, J. W. Williams, and A. Brown. Size distribution in gelatin solutions. Preliminary report. J. Am. Chem. Soc., 66:1980–81.

Book review: *The Physical Chemistry of Electrolytic Solutions* by H. S. Harned and B. B. Owen. J. Am. Chem. Soc., 66:1043.

Louis John Gillespie (1886–1941). Proc. Am. Acad. Arts Sci., 75:164.

1945

With L. E. Strong, W. L. Hughes, Jr., J. N. Ashworth, and A. H. Sparrow. Chemical, clinical, and immunological studies on the products of human plasma fractionation. XXVI. The properties of solutions of human serum albumin of low salt content. J. Clin. Invest., 24:671–79.

1946

With S. E. Wood and J. M. Mochel. Vapor-liquid equilibrium. VI. Benzene-methanol mixtures. J. Am. Chem. Soc., 68:1957–60.

With S. E. Wood and J. M. Mochel. Vapor-liquid equilibrium. VII. Carbon tetrachloride-methanol mixtures. J. Am. Chem. Soc., 68:1960–63.

Physical chemistry of protein solutions. I. Derivation of the equations for the osmotic pressure. J. Am. Chem. Soc., 68:2315–19.

With A. C. Batchelder and A. Brown. Preparation and properties of serum and plasma proteins. VI. Osmotic equilibria in solutions of serum albumin and sodium chloride. J. Am. Chem. Soc., 68:2320–29.

With A. C. Batchelder, A. Brown, and Mary Zosa. Preparation and properties of serum and plasma proteins. VII. Osmotic equilibrium in concentrated solutions of serum albumin. J. Am. Chem. Soc., 68:2610–12.

1947

With J. L. Oncley and A. Brown. Physical-chemical characteristics of certain of the proteins of normal human plasma. J. Phys. Colloid Chem., 51:184–98.

With L. F. Epstein, J. Warburton, Jr., and P. J. Cody. Thermodynamic properties of saturated liquid and vapor of ammonia-water mixtures. Refrig. Eng., 53:413–21.

1948

Book review: *Thermodynamics for Chemists* by S. Glasstone. J. Am. Chem. Soc., 70:886.

With S. S. Gellis, J. R. Neefe, J. Stokes, Jr., L. E. Strong, and C. A. Janeway. Chemical, clinical, and immunological studies on the products of human plasma fractionation. XXXVI. Inactivation of the virus of homologous serum hepatitis in solutions of normal human serum albumin by means of heat. J. Clin. Invest., 27:239–44.

The scientific work of Edwin Joseph Cohn (address on Cohn's receiving the Richards Medal). Nucleus, 25:263–76.

1949

With Elizabeth S. Black. The effect of salts on the isoionic and isoelectric points of proteins. J. Phys. Colloid Chem., 53:88–99.

Equilibrium in non-electrolyte mixtures. Chem. Rev., 44:7–35.

Book review: *Outlines of Physical Chemistry* by F. Daniels. J. Chem. Ed., 26:120.

The attractions of proteins for small molecules and ions. Ann. N.Y. Acad. Sci., 51:660–72.

1950

With I. H. Scheinberg and S. H. Armstrong, Jr. Physical chemistry of protein solutions. IV. The combination of human serum albumin with chloride ion. J. Am. Chem. Soc., 72:535–40.

With I. H. Scheinberg and S. H. Armstrong, Jr. Physical chemistry of protein solutions. V. The combination of human serum albumin with thiocyanate ion. J. Am. Chem. Soc., 72:540–46.

Book review: *Thermodynamics. An Advanced Treatment for Chemists and Physicists* by E. A. Guggenheim. J. Chem. Ed., 27:291.

The social behavior of molecules. Am. Sci., 38:437–42.

1951

The colloid osmotic pressure of serum. Science, 113:201–2.

Molecular interactions in protein solutions (Sigma Xi lecture). In: *Science in Progress*, ed. G. A. Baitsell, pp. 239–66. New Haven, Conn.: Yale Univ. Press.

1952

With G. M. Kavanagh and L. B. Ticknor. Vapor-liquid equilibrium. VIII. Hydrogen peroxide–water mixtures. J. Am. Chem. Soc., 74:3715–20.

With L. B. Ticknor, J. R. Goates, and E. R. McCartney. Heats of mixing in some non-electrolyte solutions. J. Am. Chem. Soc., 74:3721–24.

With L. B. Ticknor. Vapor-liquid equilibrium. IV. The methanol-carbon tetrachloride-benzene system. J. Am. Chem. Soc., 74:3724–29.

Solutions of nonelectrolytes. Ann. Rev. Phys. Chem., 3:259–74.

Some physical chemical aspects of "plasma extenders." Ann. N.Y. Acad. Sci., 55:455–64.

Molecular interactions in protein solutions. Am. Sci., 40:61–83.

Some electrochemical properties of ion exchange membranes. Nucleus, 30:76–79.

1953

Ion exchanger electrodes. J. Am. Chem. Soc., 75:2883–87.

Equilibria and reaction rates in dilute electrolyte solutions. Natl. Bur. Stand. (U.S.) Circ., 524:185–92.

With R. A. Westlund, Jr. Equilibrium of solid α-silver-zinc alloys with zinc vapor. J. Am. Chem. Soc., 75:4189–93.

1954

Transport of ions across charged membranes. In: *Ion Transport Across Membranes*, ed. H. T. Clarke, pp. 128–43. N.Y.: Academic Press.

With W. L. Hughes, Jr., F. R. N. Gurd, and P. E. Wilcox. The interaction of proteins with small molecules and ions. In: *Chemical Specificity in Biological Interactions*, ed. F. R. N. Gurd, pp. 193–219. N.Y.: Academic Press.

With A. Gee and Jeanette Weeks. Physical chemistry of protein solutions. VI. The osmotic pressures of mixtures of human serum albumin and gamma-globulins in aqueous sodium chloride. J. Phys. Chem., 58:783–87.

With A. Brown, R. M. Bridgforth, Jeanette Weeks, and A. Gee. A precision modification of the Hepp type osmometer. Mimeographed, Dept. of Chemistry, MIT (undated).

With R. G. Breckenridge. Isotonic solutions. II. The chemical potential of water in aqueous solutions of potassium and sodium phosphates and arsenates at 25°C. J. Phys. Chem., 58:596–602; corr. 59:1234 (1955).

With J. S. Johnson and K. A. Kraus. Distribution of charged polymers at equilibrium in a centrifugal field. J. Phys. Chem., 58:1034–39.

Some aspects of the physical chemistry of protein solutions (Richards' Medal address). Nucleus, 31:211–17.

1955

Transport of ions across charged membranes. In: *Electrochemistry in Biology and Medicine*, ed. T. Shedlovsky, pp. 18–32. N.Y.: J. Wiley and Sons.

1956

Book review: *Electrolyte Solutions. The Measurement and Interpretation of Conductance, Chemical Potential and Diffusion* by R. A. Robinson and R. H. Stokes. J. Colloid Sci., 11:289–91.

With R. H. Boyd. The equilibrium of alpha-silver-cadmium alloys with cadmium vapor. J. Am. Chem. Soc., 78:3889–93.

General introduction of discussions of membrane phenomena. Discuss. Faraday Soc., 21:27–30.

With F. Helfferich. The effect of stirring on cells with cation exchanger membranes. Discuss. Faraday Soc., 21:70–82.

1957

Book review: *The Molecular Theory of Solutions* by I. Prigogine. Chem. Eng. News (Sept. 30), p. 84.

With J. S. Coleman and Amy L. Shen. Physical chemistry of protein solutions. VII. The binding of some small anions to serum albumin. J. Am. Chem. Soc., 79:12–20.

1959

The interpretation of activity and osmotic coefficients. In: *The Structure of Electrolytic Solutions*, ed. W. J. Hamer, pp. 9–18. N.Y.: J. Wiley and Sons.
With B. A. Soldano, R. W. Stoughton, and R. J. Fox. A high temperature isopiestic unit. In: *The Structure of Electrolytic Solutions*, ed. W. J. Hamer, pp. 224–35. N.Y.: J. Wiley and Sons.
With J. S. Johnson and K. A. Kraus. The use of interference optics in equilibrium ultracentrifugations of charged systems. J. Phys. Chem., 63:787–93.
With Judith Bregman. Physical chemistry of protein solutions. VIII. The effect of temperature on the light scattering of serum albumin solutions. J. Am. Chem. Soc., 81:6095–6100.
With S. Zaromb. Physical chemistry of protein solutions. IX. A light scattering study of the binding of trichloroacetate ion to serum albumin. J. Am. Chem. Soc., 81:6100–6104.
With Y. V. Wu and Amy L. Shen. Physical chemistry of protein solutions. X. The binding of small anions by serum albumin. J. Am. Chem. Soc., 81:6104–9.

1960

John Gamble Kirkwood, 1907–1959. J. Chem. Phys., 33:1279–81.
With B. Vonnegut and D. W. Beaumont. New type of freezing-point apparatus. Freezing points of dilute lanthanum chloride solutions. J. Chem. Phys., 33:1292–98.
With J. S. Johnson and K. A. Kraus. Activity coefficients of silicotungstic acid; ultracentrifugation and light scattering. J. Phys. Chem., 64:1867–73.
Osmotic coefficients and activity coefficients in mixed electrolyte solutions. J. Am. Chem. Soc., 83:2636–42.

1961

With N. J. Anderson. The determination of the equilibrium water content of ion exchange resins. J. Phys. Chem., 65:1536–39.
Book review: *Electrolytic Dissociation* by C. B. Monk. J. Am. Chem. Soc., 83:5043.

With R. M. Rush. Molal volumes and refractive index increments of $BaCl_2$-HCl solutions. Mixture rules. J. Phys. Chem., 65:2240–42.

1962

With T. P. Lin. The equilibrium of alpha-silver-zinc-cadmium alloys with zinc and cadmium vapors. J. Am. Chem. Soc., 84:28–34.

With J. Pigliacampi. Physical chemistry of protein solutions. XI. The osmotic pressures of serum albumin, carbonylhemoglobin and their mixtures in aqueous sodium chloride at 25°. J. Am. Chem. Soc., 84:127–34.

The Gibbs adsorption isotherm. J. Phys. Chem., 66:618–20.

Book review: *States of Matter* by E. A. Moelwyn-Hughes. J. Am. Chem. Soc., 84:1518.

Book review: *Thermodynamics* by G. N. Lewis and M. Randall. J. Am. Chem. Soc., 84:3791.

1963

Solutions of electrolytes. Ann. Rev. Phys. Chem., 14:161–76.

Basic equilibrium equations. In: *Ultracentrifugal Analysis in Theory and Experiment*, ed. J. W. Williams, pp. 105–17. N.Y.: Academic Press.

1964

With G. M. Wilson and F. G. Satkiewicz. Vapor-liquid equilibrium. X. An apparatus for static equilibrium measurements. J. Am. Chem. Soc., 86:125–27.

With F. G. Satkiewicz. Vapor-liquid equilibrium. XII. The system ethanol-cyclohexane from 5 to 65°. J. Am. Chem. Soc., 86:130–33.

With G. M. Wilson. Vapor-liquid equilibrium. XIII. The system water-butyl glycol from 5 to 85°. J. Am. Chem. Soc., 86:133–37.

With D. H. Freeman. Electrokinetic behavior of ion-exchange resin. Science, 144:411–12.

The effect of dielectric constant difference on hyperfiltration of salt solutions. J. Phys. Chem., 68:1056–61.

With W. T. Yap. The physical chemistry of protein solutions. XII. The effects of temperature and hydroxide ion on the binding of small anions to human serum albumin. J. Am. Chem. Soc., 86:3434–38.

1965

With D. H. Freeman. Volumetric studies of ion-exchange resin particles using microscopy. J. Phys. Chem., 69:70–74.

The computation of the activity coefficients of small ions from the Loeb, Overbeek and Wiersema tables. Z. Phys. Chem., 228:354–63.

1966

The osmotic pressure, light scattering and ultracentrifuge equilibrium of polyelectrolyte solutions. In: *Chemical Physics of Ionic Solutions*, ed. B. E. Conway and R. G. Barradas, pp. 347–60. N.Y.: J. Wiley and Sons.

Water; a review. Fed. Proc., 25:954–57.

Remarks on osmotic pressure. Fed. Proc., 25:1115–17.

With W. H. Orttung. The electromotive forces of NH_4Br and KBr concentration cells. Are the abnormalities in the freezing points of ammonium salts due to surface effects? J. Colloid Sci., 22:12–18.

With S. Y. Tyree, Jr., R. L. Angstadt, F. C. Hentz, Jr., and R. L. Yoest. The osmotic coefficients and other related properties of aqueous 12-tungstosilicic acid ($H_4W_{12}SiO_{40}$) at 25°. J. Phys. Chem., 70:3917–21.

1968

The excess free energy and related properties of solutions containing electrolytes. J. Am. Chem. Soc., 90:3124–27; corr. (1969)91:90.

With Y. C. Wu and R. M. Rush. Osmotic and activity coefficients for binary mixtures of sodium chloride, sodium sulfate, magnesium sulfate, and magnesium chloride in water at 25°. I. Isopiestic measurements on the four systems with common ions. J. Phys. Chem., 72:4048–53.

1969

Edwin J. Cohn Lecture: Edwin J. Cohn and protein chemistry. Vox Sanguinis, 17:37–44.

With Y. C. Wu and R. M. Rush. Osmotic and activity coefficients for binary mixtures of sodium chloride, sodium sulfate, magnesium sulfate, and magnesium chloride in water at 25°. II. Isopiestic and electromotive force measurements on the two systems without common ions. J. Phys. Chem., 73:2047–53.

1970

With R. M. Rush and J. S. Johnson. Osmotic and activity coefficients for binary mixtures of sodium chloride, sodium sulfate, magnesium sulfate, and magnesium chloride in water at 25°. III. Treatment with ions as components. J. Phys. Chem., 74:3786.

1972

With H. F. Gibbard, Jr. The vapor-liquid equilibria of synthetic seawater solutions from 25–100°C. J. Chem. Eng. Data, 17: 498–501.

1973

With H. F. Gibbard, Jr. Liquid-vapor equilibrium of aqueous lithium chloride, from 25° to 100°C and from 1.0 to 18.5 molal, and related properties. J. Chem. Eng. Data, 18:293–97.

Half a century as a part-time colloid chemist (Kendall Award address, 1962). In: *Twenty Years of Colloid and Surface Chemistry: The Kendall Award Addresses*, ed. K. J. Mysels, C. M. Samour, and J. M. Hollister, pp. 101–6. Wash., D.C.: American Chemical Society.

1974

With H. F. Gibbard, Jr., R. A. Rousseau, and J. L. Creek. The liquid-vapor equilibrium of aqueous sodium chloride from 298 to 373K and from 1 to 6 mol kg^{-1}, and related properties. J. Chem. Eng. Data, 19:281.

1976

Equilibrium in Solutions (pp. 1–208) *and Surface and Colloid Chemistry* (pp. 209–79). Introduction by I. H. Scheinberg, pp. vii–xviii, and "Autobiographical note" by George Scatchard, pp. xix–xxxiv. Cambridge, Mass.: Harvard Univ. Press.

THEODORE SHEDLOVSKY
October 29, 1898–November 5, 1976

BY RAYMOND M. FUOSS

IN APRIL 1953, at the one hundred and third meeting of the Electrochemical Society, Theodore Shedlovsky opened a symposium on Electrochemistry in Biology and Medicine with the following introduction:

Electrochemistry is concerned with the electrical properties and behavior of substances and with the transformation of chemical energy into electrical energy or vice versa. It is related to biology and medicine in two ways. First, it provides powerful laboratory methods and tools for the study of biologically important substances, such as viruses, hormones, enzymes and other proteins, and also for the determination in biological environments of such factors as acidity, oxidation-reduction, ionic mobility, activity and diffusion, dielectric constant and dipole moments. Second, living organisms and in fact all living cells are complicated electrochemical systems capable of transforming chemical energy and ionic transport into electrical signals. With appropriate apparatus the neurophysiologist may examine such electrical signals to learn what he can about the functions of nerve and muscle. The medical clinician, armed with a substantial background of correlated, empirical knowledge, observes the electrical signals from the heart or from the brain and thus is aided in arriving at a diagnosis. Living matter or a living cell is not a mere assembly of chemical compounds. It is an oriented, dynamic system of complex materials in constant interaction with its environment, a complex chemical laboratory manufacturing many compounds no chemist has yet been able to synthesize, and electrochemical in many if not perhaps all of its functions. Between the inside and the outside of a living cell there exists normally an electrical potential usually of about a tenth of a volt. It is true of plant cells as well as cells of mammals, birds, or fishes. This is the so-called "resting" potential. In certain cells like nerve cells, this potential may be quickly altered and restored again, giving rise to electric "action potentials" in response to various stimuli. In nerve, this happens within a few milliseconds and is in the nature of electric transients. The theory of the fundamental electrochemical mechanism underlying these bio-electric phenomena is now an active subject of research.

Development of precise electrochemical methods and their application to biochemical problems were Shedlovsky's life work at the Rockefeller Institute for Medical Research (since 1965, The Rockefeller University). In 1926, W. J. V. Osterhout invited Duncan A. MacInnes (then professor of chemistry at the Massachusetts Institute of Technology) to come to Rockefeller and organize a research group to work on the physical chemistry of electrolytic solutions. MacInnes accepted; his first appointee (1927) was Shedlovsky, who had been one of his graduate students at MIT. Lewis G. Longsworth joined the group in 1928, first as a fellow of the National Research Council; he subsequently became a member of the Rockefeller staff. Within five or six years, the triumvirate of MacInnes, Shedlovsky, and Longsworth created at Rockefeller one of the world's outstanding centers of electrolyte research. Their classical contributions included work on thermodynamic properties of electrolytic solutions, conductance, diffusion, and electrophoresis. Shedlovsky chose conductance as his special field of interest and by the mid-1930's was generally recognized as an authority on the subject. In addition to his work on inorganic electrolytes, he collaborated with a number of bio-oriented colleagues on work with biochemical systems. His tangible contributions to science are characterized by ingenuity in design of experiments and apparatus, precision in execution, and clarity of thinking and presentation. Equally valuable, however, were his intangible contributions: he served as an interpreter between the physical chemist and the biochemist, bringing to each field ideas from the other. He also had an uncanny instinct for bringing together people who had problems with people who had ideas and suggestions.

Shedlovsky had many interests besides science. He was fluent in Russian, German, and French (his elementary schooling was in Paris). He was an expert chess player, phenomenally good in rapid transit play, and had given checkmate to masters. An ardent music lover, he established and directed The Rockefeller University Concerts, which have been held monthly in Caspary Auditorium every year since 1958. In 1965, he founded the Rockefeller Children's School for children aged three to seven whose parents are members of the faculty, staff, and student body of the University. In 1975, in recognition of his contributions to science and to the life at Rockefeller, he was awarded the honorary degree of Doctor of Science. In the citation at commencement, Professor Vincent P. Dole said:

> Professor Theodore Shedlovsky combines many rare qualities. In his scientific work he is distinguished as an electrochemist.... There is much to admire in his scientific achievements, and yet they are not the only reason why we honor him today. As a person, Ted Shedlovsky represents something even rarer than master electrochemist—he is a special person who makes the world around him richer. He has launched conferences, started and guided our remarkable concert series, created a school for University children and counseled many of us. No wonder he has so many friends.

As background for a review of Shedlovsky's career of a half century at Rockefeller, an introductory discussion of electrolytes and electrochemistry is in order. Electrolytic solutions are systems in which the electric current is carried by ions; ions are molecules (monatomic or polyatomic) that are electrically charged. The simplest example is a solution of salt in water: the current is carried by hydrated sodium ions (sodium atoms that have lost an electron and are therefore positively charged) and chloride ions (chlorine atoms that have gained an electron and are negatively charged). The ions of biochemical electrolytes are much more complicated: a protein is a polyamide, a long sequence of condensed α-amino acids,

$$\ldots -NH \cdot CHR' \cdot CO - NH \cdot CHR'' \cdot CO - NH \cdot CHR''' \cdot CO - \ldots,$$

where the units containing the R groups are selected by biosynthesis from about twenty amino acids whose general formula is $H_2N \cdot CHR \cdot CO_2H$. Some of the R groups are ionogenic; for example, glutamic acid $HO_2C(CH_2)_2CH(NH_2)CO_2H$, where R = $-(CH_2)_2CO_2H$, contains a terminal carboxyl group that generates the negative carboxyl ion $-CO_2^-$; or lysine $H_2N(CH_2)_4CH(NH_2)CO_2H$, which forms the positive ammonium ion $-(CH_2)_4NH_3^+$. Therefore, depending on the relative number of positive and negative ionogenic R's in the protein and on the pH (a measure of the hydrogen ion concentration) of the buffer (serum, for example) in which the protein is dissolved, the protein may have either a net positive or negative charge. Such charged macromolecules are called polyelectrolytes; proteins and the two types of nucleic acids (ribonucleic acid [RNA] and deoxyribonucleic acid [DNA]) are the most important categories of biochemical polyelectrolytes. (We shall be concerned here only with the properties of electrolytic solutions, usually aqueous, and exclude as irrelevant fused salts and certain solids, which also carry the electric current by ionic transport.)

The properties of electrolytic solutions depend on the chemical structure and composition of the electrolyte and on its concentration. The velocity v, imparted to an ion by a given electrical potential across two electrodes immersed in the solution, is proportional to the charge on the ion because the force driving the ion is Xze, field strength times net charge ze (e = unit charge). The velocity $v = Xze/f$ is less the larger the ion because the friction coefficient f increases with increasing size of the moving particle. The electrophoretic velocity of a polyelectrolyte ion is a measure of its charge and size; and also of its shape, because the friction coefficient for an ellipsoid, for example, is greater than for a sphere of equal volume. A protein molecule in acid solution (pH < 7) has a net positive charge; in basic solutions (pH > 7), the positive $-NH_3^+$ ions are converted into neutral amino-groups, and the neutral carboxyl groups become negative $-CO_2^-$ groups. Consequently, there is a value of pH at which the mobility becomes zero (net charge equals zero); that value (the isoelectric point) is characteristic for the protein.

Solutions of different electrolytes at the same concentration show different electrical conductivities. Aqueous solutions of electrolytes are classified traditionally as "strong" and "weak"; for a given stoichiometric concentration, the latter are much poorer conductors, because only part of the solute is present as ions. For example, acetic acid in water exists mostly as hydrated neutral $CH_3CO_2H \cdot H_2O$ molecules, and only a small fraction dissociates into conducting acetate $CH_3CO_2^-$ and hydronium H_3O^+ ions. Determination of the dissociation constants of biochemical acids is an electrochemical problem. The strong electrolytes exist as ions in water; salt water contains no neutral NaCl molecules, but only sodium Na^+ and chloride Cl^- ions. Measurement of the dependence of conducting ability of electrolytes in general on concentration and its theoretical description form a major chapter of electrochemistry. Shedlovsky's contributions, as shown by the titles listed in the bibliography, are on conductance, dissociation constants, and electrophoresis.

In principle, the experimental determination of the conductivity of an electrolytic solution is simple: one measures the resistance R_x between a pair of electrodes immersed in the solution by means of a bridge circuit, and calculates the specific conductance σ (the reciprocal of the resistance of a cube of solution one centimeter on a side) by dividing the cell constant k by R_x, $\sigma = k/R_x$. (The cell constant for parallel plate electrodes of area A placed at a distance d [with $d^2 \ll A$] is $k = d/A$.) The classical method used dipping electrodes for the cell and the Kohlrausch slide wire for the bridge: precision of several percent in σ can be easily obtained, and with care a precision of 0.1–0.2% was attainable. Shedlovsky set a precision of 0.01–0.02% as his goal. In 1930 he published two papers: "A Screened Bridge for the Measurement of Electrolytic Conductance," and "A Conductivity Cell for Eliminating Electrode Effects in Measurements of Electrolytic Conductance." Using this bridge, he and his co-workers determined the conductance of a wide variety of electrolytes to the desired precision; extrapolation of the data to evaluate limiting conductance (*vide infra*) was made using the Shedlovsky 1931 equation.

The screened bridge made possible for the first time measurements of electrolytic conductances by alternating current to one part in 100,000 (0.001%); using it, the experimenter has complete confidence in the electrical data, and the precision in equivalent conductance $\Lambda = 1000\sigma/c$ becomes the precision in concentration c (about 0.01%) and in temperature control (σ varies by about 2% per degree, so thermostatting the solution to $\pm 0.005°$ fixes Λ to 0.01%). The necessity of screening the bridge is a consequence of using audio-frequency alternating current in measuring electrolytic conductance; it must be used because direct current would produce irreversible electrochemical reactions at the electrodes, thereby introducing errors of unknown magnitude. (Direct current can be used only with a few electrolytes for which reversible electrodes can be made; for example, silver-silver chloride electrodes for chloride solutions.) The Wheatstone bridge may be pictured as follows: imagine four points A, B, C, and D connected by resistances $R_{AB}, R_{BC}, R_{CD},$ and R_{DA}. Let $R_{AB} = R_{BC}$. If direct current is fed in at A and C, and R_{DC} (a calibrated rheostat) is varied, the voltage across B and D will go through zero when R_{DC} equals the unknown resistance R_{DA}. But if alternating current is applied across A and C, the condition for zero voltage across B and D is $Z_{AB}/Z_{BC} = Z_{AD}/Z_{DC}$, where Z_{AB} is the impedance between the terminals A and B, etc. Impedance is made up of resistive, capacitative, and inductive elements; the last two play no role in direct current circuitry. Suppose the conductance cell is connected to the terminals A and D. Electrically, it acts as a resistance and capacity in parallel, with capacity paths to ground. There exist in the other three arms of the bridge distributed capacity to ground and resistance-capacity paths among the three elements. Consequently, at zero voltage across B and D, the resistance component of Z_{CD} in general does not equal the resistance of the electrolyte in the cell connected to A and D. Shedlovsky made a theoretical analysis of the rather complicated circuits just described, which led to a bridge design in which the ratio arms AB and BC were symmetrically shielded; the measuring rheostat connected across C and D, and the various lead wires were also screened. All shields were connected to ground (earth point E). Then a Wagner ground was added, which permits the operator to bring points B and D to the potential of E. At final balance, the voltage across B and D is zero and both B and D are at ground potential: under these conditions, the resistance component of Z_{DC} exactly equals the resistance of the electrolyte in the cell. Screening brought two additional advantages: first, effects of stray currents from other electrical equipment in the laboratory were avoided; and second, bridge balance became independent of the position of the operator (for an unscreened bridge, the electrical capacity between the elements of the bridge and the body of the operator also is a path for stray currents to ground).

Shedlovsky also designed a conductance cell that eliminated errors inherent in the dipping electrodes. Cell constants are usually determined by measuring the resistance R of a cell containing a standardizing solution of known specific conductance σ_s; $k = R\sigma_s$. For dipping electrodes, somewhat different values ($\pm 1\%$) were found for a given cell when different calibrating solutions were used; obviously, such cells could not deliver data reliable to $\pm 0.01\%$. Shedlovsky showed that the variation in apparent cell constant with resistance was caused by a series capacity-resistance circuit, which shunted the resistance of the solution between the electrodes. The capacity was the insulation surrounding the lead wires to the electrodes; the resistance was that of the solution between the immersed insulation and the electrodes. This circuit is electrically equivalent to a resistance in series with the electrolytic resistance plus a parallel capacitance. By placing the electrodes in a capsule attached to the container for the solution, the leads to the electrodes do not pass through the solution, and the impedance of the shunt becomes so high that its effect becomes negligible. The value of k for cells so constructed is completely independent of the resistance of the calibrating solution. The principle of this design of conductance cell was universally adopted by other workers in the field of conductance. Several of the conductance cells used by Shedlovsky are in the collection of instruments and apparatus on display in Caspary Hall at Rockefeller.

Conductance measurements are made in order to determine parameters that are characteristic of a given electrolyte. One of these is Λ_0, the limiting equivalent conductance, which is proportional to the velocity of the ions at infinite dilution. The observed equivalent conductance Λ of strong electrolytes decreases with increasing concentration because the long-range electrostatic forces between the ions reduce their mobility. In order to obtain Λ_0, the experimenter measures conductance at a series of concentrations and then extrapolates to zero concentration. Shedlovsky introduced in 1932 a method of extrapolation that has since been widely used. Kohlrausch (1900) found empirically that at low concentrations the observed values of $\Lambda(c)$ approached linearity on a $\Lambda - c^{1/2}$ plot; Debye and Hückel (1923) gave a theoretical explanation of this behavior. Onsager (1927) succeeded in calculating the value of the coefficient S in the equation

$$\Lambda_{LT} = \Lambda_0 - Sc^{1/2} \qquad (1)$$

for the limiting tangent to the Kohlrausch plot. The coefficient S was derived by theoretical treatment of the long-range interionic forces; it is the sum of two terms: $\alpha\Lambda_0$, the relaxation field effect, and β, the electrophoretic coefficient. At non-zero concentrations,

$$\Lambda(c) = \Lambda_0 - Sc^{1/2} + F(c), \qquad (2)$$

that is, the observed conductance curve was concave-up, above the limiting tangent. For very dilute solutions (<0.01 normal for 1-1 salts in water), $F(c)$ appeared to approach linearity in concentration, and the equation

$$\Lambda = \Lambda_0 - Sc^{1/2} + Ac \qquad (3)$$

was used to extrapolate observed conductances to zero concentration. But working at such low concentrations involved many experimental difficulties, and some uncertainty in the absolute value of Λ_0 resulted. Shedlovsky rearranged equation (2) to the form

$$\Lambda_0 = (\Lambda + \beta c^{1/2})/(1-\alpha c^{1/2}) - Bc = \Lambda_0' - Bc \qquad (4)$$

and showed that Λ_0', which contains the observed equivalent conductance Λ and the theoretically predictable terms $\alpha c^{1/2}$ and $\beta c^{1/2}$, was linear in concentration up to about 0.1 normal for 1-1 salts in water (about 6% by weight for sodium chloride). The conductance of a number of 1-1 electrolytes (potassium chloride, sodium chloride, hydrochloric acid, potassium nitrate, silver nitrate, and lithium chloride [1932]) was measured over the concentration range 0.00003–0.10 normal to a precision of about 0.02%. The values of limiting conductances obtained using equation (4) for the data over the entire concentration range agreed exactly with those obtained using equation (3) over the lower range ($0.00003 \le c \le 0.01$); this result showed that it was not necessary to measure conductances at extreme dilutions in order to obtain reliable values of Λ_0. It is sufficient to cover the approximate range $0.005 \le c \le 0.10$, thereby avoiding all the experimental difficulties that beset work with highly dilute salt solutions.

The term $F(c)$ in equation (2) represents the deviation of the observed conductance curve from the limiting tangent, $\Lambda_{LT} = \Lambda_0 - Sc^{1/2}$. Derivation of the functional form of $F(c)$ is a much more difficult problem for the theoretician than prediction of the value of S, because it involves the integration of a set of nonlinear differential equations; however, Onsager (1927) showed that the leading terms of $F(c)$ should be of order $c \log c$ and c. Shedlovsky (1934) measured the conductances of magnesium, calcium, strontium, and barium chlorides over the concentration range $0.0002 \le c \le 0.1$ normal.

Using the data at lower concentrations and equation (4), he obtained values of Λ_0 for the four 2-1 salts. He then demonstrated the existence of the $c \log c$ term by showing that a plot of $(\Lambda_0' - \Lambda_0)/c$ against $\log c$ for the whole set of data approached linearity below about 0.01 normal, thereby establishing the functional form

$$\Lambda = (\Lambda_0 - \beta c^{1/2})/(1 + \alpha c^{1/2}) - Bc + Dc \log c + \ldots \quad (5)$$

predicted by Onsager. Furthermore, the sequence of his empirical values for the coefficients D confirmed the theoretical expectation that D should decrease with increasing size of the cation.

Equations (4) and (5) are valid for strong electrolytes; the corresponding conductance curves lie above the limiting tangent on a $\Lambda - c^{1/2}$ plot. But for many electrolytes, the observed conductance curve lies below the limiting tangent: examples are carboxylic acids and amines in water, or salts in solvents of lower dielectric constant. After an expository introduction, Shedlovsky's many contributions to the field of weak electrolytes will next be reviewed.

Specific conductance is defined as the ratio of current density i to field strength X; current density is the total charge carried per second across the area of one square centimeter perpendicular to the direction of the field:

$$\sigma = i/X = \Sigma_i n_i e_i v_i / X, \quad (6)$$

where n_i is the number per unit volume of ions of species i carrying a charge e_i and moving with a velocity v_i cm/sec. Therefore, equivalent conductance $\Lambda = 10^3 \sigma/c$ is given by

$$\Lambda = A \, \Sigma_i n_i e_i u_i / c, \quad (7)$$

where $u_i = v_i/X$ is the velocity for unit field (one volt/cm) and A is a known constant of proportionality. For strong electrolytes at low concentrations, all the solute is assumed to contribute to transport of charge; for 1-1 electrolytes, the number of cations (or anions) per unit volume is simply $n_i = Nc/1000$, where N is Avogadro's number and c is equivalents of salt per liter. Hence, Λ is proportional to $\Sigma_i u_i$. As mentioned above, the electrostatic forces between the ions reduce their mobility from u_i^0, the value for an isolated ion, by an amount proportional to the square root of concentration; the corresponding conductance function is equation (2). But not all the solute is present as ions in the case of weak electrolytes. Acetic acid, for example, in aqueous solution can rearrange to an ion pair

$$[CH_3CO_2H \cdot H_2O \rightleftarrows H_3O^+ \cdot CH_3CO_2^-],$$

which dissociates into the free hydronium ions and acetate ions that carry the electric current. Denote by γ the fraction of solute that is dissociated; then $\gamma = n_i/(Nc/1000)$ and the concentration c_i of free ions is $c\gamma$. Equation (7) becomes:

$$\Lambda = A'\gamma\Sigma_i u_i = \gamma(\lambda_1 + \lambda_2), \qquad (8)$$

where λ_1 and λ_2 are the single ion conductances of cation and anion respectively; $\lambda_i = \mathcal{F} u_i$, where $\mathcal{F}$ is the Faraday equivalent. The retarding effects on mobility of the interionic forces is proportional to $(c\gamma)^{1/2}$; for low concentrations, the conductance equation, therefore, is

$$\Lambda = \gamma[\Lambda_0 - S(c\gamma)^{1/2}]. \qquad (9)$$

The law of mass action for the postulated equilibrium between neutral molecules and free ions,

$$AB \rightleftarrows A^+ + B^-, \tag{10}$$

relates γ and the stoichiometric concentration c by the equation

$$K = c\gamma^2 f^2/(1-\gamma), \tag{11}$$

where K is the dissociation constant of AB and f is the ionic activity coefficient. For low concentrations, the latter may be approximated by the Debye-Hückel limiting law

$$-\ln f = C(c\gamma)^{1/2}, \tag{12}$$

where C is a known coefficient that depends on dielectric constant and temperature. Equations (9), (11), and (12) can be solved for the two parameters Λ_0 and K, which are characteristics of the electrolyte AB, given a set of conductance data. Equation (9) is the Fuoss-Kraus conductance function (1933); it uses the limiting law (1) as an approximation for the interionic effects on mobility. This approximation is valid only below ionic concentrations $c_i \approx 0.001$ normal. Shedlovsky (1938) discovered that conductance data for 1-1 salts could be reproduced to high precision by the equation

$$\Lambda = \Lambda_0 - \Lambda S c^{1/2}/\Lambda_0 \tag{13}$$

up to concentrations as high as $c_i \approx 0.01$, ten times as far as (1) was usable. Equation (13) rearranges to

$$1/\Lambda = 1/\Lambda_0 + (S/\Lambda_0^2)c^{1/2}. \tag{14}$$

For incompletely dissociated electrolytes ($c_i = c\gamma$), (14) becomes

$$\Lambda = \gamma\Lambda_0/[1 + (S/\Lambda_0)(c\gamma)^{1/2}], \tag{15}$$

which is a quadratic in $\gamma^{1/2}$, in contrast to (9), which is a cubic. The system of equations (15), (11), and (12) is therefore much easier to solve for Λ_0 and K than the system (9), (11), and (12), and is usable over a much wider range of ionic concentrations. It was used by Shedlovsky and by many others to derive values of limiting conductance and dissociation constants for a wide variety of electrolytes.

The above method derives Λ_0 and K for a given electrolyte from conductance data on that electrolyte. It is based on the semi-empirical equation (13) and on the value of S that was calculated for the primitive model (rigid charged spheres of diameter a in a continuum, which is described electrostatically by the dielectric constant of the pure solvent and hydrodynamically by the viscosity). MacInnes and Shedlòvsky (1931) devised a method of obtaining Λ_0 and K that is independent of model and, therefore, does not depend on any theoretical treatment of interionic forces. It is based on the Kohlrausch law of independent mobility (i.e., additivity of equivalent conductances). For a completely dissociated electrolyte, $\gamma = 1$ and $\Lambda = \Lambda_0[1 - G(c)]$, where $G(c)$ represents the total effect of interionic forces on mobilities. For a weak electrolyte (for example, acetic acid), the equivalent conductances of a mole of the *electrolyte* at concentration c is $\Lambda(c) = \gamma \Lambda_0[1 - G(c\gamma)]$; the equivalent conductance Λ' of a mole of a hypothetical completely dissociated acetic acid *at the ionic concentration $c\gamma$* would be

$$\Lambda'(HAc) = \Lambda_0[1 - G(c\gamma)]. \tag{16}$$

Therefore, $\gamma = \Lambda'(HAc)/\Lambda(c)$; the unknown factor $\Lambda_0[1 - G(c\gamma)]$ divides out. Now $\Lambda'(HAc)$ cannot be determined directly, but, by use of the additivity rule,

$$\Lambda'(HAc) = \Lambda(HCl, c\gamma) - \Lambda(NaCl, c\gamma) + \Lambda(NaAc, c\gamma), \tag{17}$$

where the symbols $\Lambda(AB,c\gamma)$ represent the equivalent conductances of the completely dissociated electrolytes AB at stoichiometric concentrations $c\gamma$. In other words, one can synthesize numerical values of $\Lambda'(HAc)$ by interpolation from conductance data on hydrochloric acid, sodium chloride, and sodium acetate, and then calculate γ. A plot of the logarithm of $c\gamma^2/(1-\gamma)$ against $(c\gamma)^{1/2}$ was found to be linear up to 0.01 normal solutions of acetic acid, with the theoretical slope C of (12); values of K calculated by (11) averaged to 1.753×10^{-4}. This result was in perfect agreement with the value reported by Harned and Owen (1930), who had used an entirely different method to determine the dissociation constant of acetic acid (e.m.f. measurements on cells without liquid junction). Later (1935), the same method was used to determine the first dissociation constant of carbonic acid from conductance data on potassium bicarbonate, potassium chloride, and hydrochloric acid. (Carbonic acid, H_2CO_3, is the weak acid formed from water and carbon dioxide, one of the end products of metabolic oxidation.)

The two methods described above for determining dissociation constants of weak electrolytes (based on equations [15] and [17]) were applied to a variety of systems that can serve as physicochemical models for biochemical systems. Very roughly described, the latter are assemblies of cells containing aqueous solutions and suspensions inside nonaqueous membranes; a study of the behavior of electrolytes in nonaqueous media therefore became part of the research program at Rockefeller. Water has a high dielectric constant ($D = 78.35$); most organic liquids have very much lower constants. Guaiacol ($o\text{-}CH_3O \cdot C_6H_4 \cdot OH$) has a dielectric constant of 11.8; for water-saturated guaiacol, $D = 14.3$. Shedlovsky and Uhlig (1934) measured the conductance in guaiacol and in water-saturated guaiacol of the sodium and potassium salts of guaiacol (which show typical strong electrolyte behavior in water). The conductance curves closely resembled those of weak electrolytes in water, and could be reproduced by equation (15); the only conclusion possible was that part of the salts ($Na^+ \cdot Gc^-$ and $K^+ \cdot Gc^-$) in solution were non-conducting. No neutral molecule can form from alkali cation and guaiacolate anion; instead, the non-conducting species consisted of ion pairs, anion and cation held together by the electrostatic force between ions of opposite charge, which is about seven times as great in guaiacol as in water. (According to Coulomb's law, the force varies inversely as D.) The dissociation constant for the ion pair $Na^+ \cdot Gc^-$ in wet guaiacol was found to be 4.3×10^{-5}, about a quarter of that of acetic acid in water. These results showed that the concentration of free ions in organic media of low dielectric constant is much less than the stoichiometric concentration of salt; one infers that most of the alkali ions in biological membranes are paired with the anionic sites in proteins and nucleic acids. The dissociation of carboxylic acids is also strongly dependent on the dielectric constant of the medium, as was shown by a comprehensive study of acetic acid in water-alcohol mixtures (water-methanol, Shedlovsky and Kay, 1956; water-ethanol, Spivey and Shedlovsky, 1967; water-propanol, Goffredi and Shedlovsky, 1967). It was shown (1962) that the dissociation constant of acetic acid in the mixtures is controlled by a set of simultaneous competing reactions,

$$HA + H_2O \rightleftarrows H_2O \cdot HA \rightleftarrows H_3O^+ \cdot A^- \rightleftarrows H_3O^+ + A^- \quad (18)$$

$$HA + ROH \rightleftarrows ROH \cdot HA \rightleftarrows RH_2O^+ \cdot A^- \rightleftarrows RH_2O^+ + A^-, \quad (19)$$

where A denotes the acetyl group (CH_3CO_2) and R the alkyl group of the alcohol. A (neutral) molecule of acetic acid is solvated by a molecule of water or alcohol; by electron rearrangement, an ion pair forms, and then the latter dissociates into free cation and acetate ion. The numerical values of the equilibrium constants that describe reaction (19) are quite different, depending on whether R is methyl, ethyl, or propyl, and therefore, the overall dissociation constant

$$K = [A^-][H_3O^+ + RH_2O^+]f^2/[HA] \qquad (20)$$

for acetic acid is solvent-dependent. These systems present a classical example of the specific nature of short-range interactions between electrolytes and solvent molecules; the specificity is reminiscent (although far from a perfect analog) of the selectivity at the active sites on enzyme molecules.

In living cells are found potential differences as high as 100 millivolts across the cell membrane; they cannot be electrostatic in nature because electric current will flow for relatively long periods of time in a circuit established between the cell fluid and the surrounding liquid. Neither can their origin be in coupled oxidation-reduction reactions such as those that generate a voltage across the two electrodes of conventional electrochemical cells, because in the latter electrons must flow, and living cells (composed of water, salts, and organic compounds) obviously lack the purely metallic components that are essential for transport of electron currents. Shedlovsky proposed that bioelectric potentials were produced by coupled acid-base reactions in which protons carry the electric current. The model was described at a symposium at the National Bureau of Standards during its Semicentennial in 1951. The first comment in the discussion that followed Shedlovsky's presentation was made by W. F. K. Wynne Jones, who said: "Mr. Chairman, I think we have listened to a very brilliant exposition of a brilliant idea, and I would only wish that Brønsted were here today to listen to Shedlovsky." The *proto*chemical cell of biochemical systems can best be explained by reviewing the *electro*chemical cell of the inorganic world, which consists of metallic electrodes (which are reversible to electrons) immersed in electrolytic solutions. A familiar example of the latter is the cell

$$Pt, H_2 | H_3O^+, Cl^-, H_2O | AgCl, Ag.$$

At the anode, hydrogen is oxidized to hydrogen ions and electrons are released to flow through the load in the external metallic circuit to the cathode where they reduce silver ions to metallic silver; the current in the solution is carried by the hydrogen and chloride ions. The cell reaction is

$$\tfrac{1}{2}H_2 + H_2O + Ag^+ = Ag + H_3O^+.$$

Shedlovsky's protochemical cell consists of a glass tube, closed at the bottom by a thin glass membrane that is coated on the inside with a layer of barium laurate and lauric acid. The tube was filled with a solution of barium chloride and hydrochloric acid and dipped into a vessel containing the same solution. Silver-silver chloride electrodes were immersed in the tube and in the vessel: potentials were measured across the latter electrodes. The glass membrane and the laurate-lauric acid coating are reversible to protons (which are carried in the solution by interchange with water molecules: $H^+ + H_2O \rightarrow H_2O + H^+$). The two protodes (a term coined by Shedlovsky to contrast with "electrodes," the entrance and exit for electrons in the *electro*chemical cell) are electrically connected through the solutions, the silver electrodes and the measuring circuit connecting the latter. The effective cell is

$$glass, H_2O | H_3O^+, Ba^{++}Cl^-, H_2O | BaL_2, HL$$

where L is an abbreviation for the laurate ion. The cell reaction is

$$H_3O^+ + L^- = HL + H_2O,$$

which is an acid-base reaction in the Brønsted-Lowry sense. The protodes of biochemical systems are the inner and outer surfaces of the cell membranes, which are chemically different but both reversible to protons; protons flow through the membranes much like they flow through the glass-laurate interface in the Shedlovsky protochemical cell.

A quotation from a paper given at a symposium sponsored by the New York Academy of Sciences in 1943 is presented as preface to a review of Shedlovsky's work on biochemical materials:

> The usual operational criteria for the purity of inorganic and organic materials, which are not megamolecular as are proteins, are constancy of density, refractive index, optical rotation, melting point, boiling point, dielectric constant, electrical conductance, solubility, analytical data, etc., after redistillation, recrystallization, or preparation by different methods. Unfortunately, most of these operations are not available for proteins. These are very labile substances, and the procedures which can be used without fear of profoundly altering them are indeed limited. Also, analytical data on proteins are of relatively little use in most cases for establishing purity, and laboratory synthesis has as yet not been possible. Among the various physicochemical procedures which are applicable to the study of proteins there are a few which provide the most satisfactory criteria we have for estimating the degree of purity. These are electrophoretic analysis, observations in the analytical ultracentrifuge, and the determination of solubility curves in suitable solvents. Proteins form salts with both acids and bases, and, except at the isoelectric point, appear as ions with a net electric charge. Their electrical mobilities depend largely on the pH and on the salt composition of the solution at a fixed temperature. Two different proteins may have identical mobilities in a given solvent, but the probability of the mobilities remaining similar at other values of pH is much smaller. The ultracentrifuge determines sedimentation constants, which depend on the size and shape of the molecules. Here again, two different proteins may happen to have similar sedimentation constants under certain conditions. Determinations of solubility curves involve analogous considerations. However, the likelihood of two different substances behaving alike in all

three respects, that is, electrophoresis, sedimentation and solubility, can probably be ruled out in the present state of our knowledge.

The identification and isolation in pure form of metakentrin, a gonadotrophic hormone, from extracts of the anterior lobe of the pituitary gland was accomplished by physicochemical methods (*Science*, 1940; *Endocrinology*, 1942). The electrophoretic pattern of the protein solution showed three peaks, indicating the presence of three components, only one of which was found to be biologically active. By plotting mobility against pH, their isoelectric points were determined. The active component with isoelectric point at pH 7.45 was isolated by precipitating it from solution by addition of ammonium sulfate at this value of pH; it was then purified by repeatedly dissolving and reprecipitating. Purity was established by showing that the solubility was independent of the ratio of amount of solid protein to volume of saturated solution.

The Forssman antigens are defined as substances that have the common property of evoking cell hemolysis when injected into rabbits, and are widely distributed in nature. The chemical composition and the physical and immunological properties of the Forssman antigen produced by pneumococci were studied at Rockefeller (*Journal of Biological Chemistry*, 1943). The antigen ("F substance") was found to be a lipocarbohydrate constituted from a polysaccharide moiety to which a lipid is bound in firm chemical union. The extracts from the pneumococcus cultures also contained a soluble nitrogenous dextrorotatory carbohydrate ("C-polysaccharide"); this carbohydrate was common to the four types of pneumococcus used as source of the antigen. It was possible to separate the F-substance into lipid and a carbohydrate by rather drastic treatment: the F-polysaccharide was quite similar to the C-polysaccharide in chemical composition and properties. Both polysaccharides precipitate in C-antiserum in dilutions of 1:2 million. But the slightly greater carbon content (45.12% vs 44.01%) of the F-polysaccharide and its lower content of reducing sugars (42.8% vs 50.6%) suggested that the polysaccharide moiety of the F-substance was indeed the C-polysaccharide, but separation from the lipid involved some chemical damage to the molecule. Electrophoresis showed that the two polysaccharides really were different: the mobilities at pH = 7.85 of the C- and F-polysaccharides are 2.2×10^{-5} and 1.7×10^{-5} cm/sec/volt/cm, respectively. But the peaks (both ascending and descending) in the electrophoresis patterns for the F-compound were sharp and symmetrical, while the peaks for the C-compound were broad and asymmetric (especially the descending one). The latter pattern is characteristic for a mixture of polyelectrolytes distributed around an average value, while a sharp peak is obtained for substances that have a definite molecular weight. This observation confirmed the idea that the polysaccharide part of the F-substance was somewhat degraded by the separation from the lipid.

Electrophoresis was the tool used to follow the formation of proteolytic enzymes in cultures of Type A streptococcus (*Journal of Experimental Medicine*, 1951). The precursor of the proteinase has an isoelectric point at pH = 7.35, and the enzyme at pH = 8.42. In a buffer solution at pH = 7.35 (where the net charge on the precursor is zero), the molecules of the precursor will remain stationary in the electrophoresis cell while the enzyme, which carries a positive charge, will move in the electric field. Consequently, the rate of the reaction (precursor → enzyme) can be followed by taking samples from a reacting system, adding iodoacetic acid or ethanol as inhibitor to the sample to stop the reaction, and then running the electric current until the enzyme peak has moved away from the precursor peak. The area under the peak is proportional to the concentration of enzyme; hence, the observer can follow the rate of the biochemical reaction.

Immunology has its origins in Jenner's observation that inoculation with vaccine obtained from the vesicles of a calf infected with vaccinia (cowpox) produced immunity to smallpox. The vaccine is chemically a most complicated mixture; identification and isolation of its components have been the research field for laboratories the world over.

In addition to the immunizing antigens in the vaccine, a variety of other antigens has been found, their presence having been indicated by the variety of antibodies found in the sera of animals following vaccination. The antigens L (heat-labile) and S (heat-stable) were studied intensively at Rockefeller; again, electrophoretic data furnished essential information that permitted isolation and purification of the antigen from the multitude of other substances in the vaccine. By separating through isodielectric precipitation a substance that gave a single peak in the electrophoresis pattern but possessed *both* L- and S-activities, it was found that *both* L- and S-immunological activities reside in a *single* protein molecule. The pure LS-antigen, after heating in solution at 70° for one-half hour, no longer precipitated with L-antibody but did so with S-antibody. On treatment of LS-antigen with chymotrypsin (a proteolytic enzyme), the product precipitated with L-antibody but not with S-antibody. In other words, one could selectively destroy either the L-activity or the S-activity, starting with a molecule that possessed both activities. The LS-protein, the soluble double antigen of vaccinia, is homogeneous electrophoretically and in the ultracentrifuge. It is characterized by the following properties: isoelectric point at pH = 4.8, specific volume at 4° is 0.72 cc/gm, diffusion coefficient 1.50×10^{-7}, sedimentation constant 6.35 Svedberg at 20°, molecular weight 214,000, axial ratio 1:20. These results provide a complete physicochemical description of the protein.

Theodore Shedlovsky was born in St. Petersburg (now Leningrad) on October 29, 1898. He began living in the United States in 1908, and became a citizen in 1927. He received the degree of Bachelor of Science in 1918 and the degree of Doctor of Philosophy in 1925 from the Massachusetts Institute of Technology, where he was an assistant in physical chemistry from 1918 to 1921. He joined the Rockefeller Institute for Medical Research (which became The Rockefeller University in 1965) as a research assistant in 1927 and spent the rest of his life at Rockefeller, holding posts of research associate (1928–1944), associate member (1944–1956), and member and professor (1956–1969). He became Professor Emeritus in 1969 but did not retire from activity at Rockefeller until about two years before his death. In recognition of his many services to science and to Rockefeller, the University conferred on him an honorary degree of Doctor of Science in 1975.

Dr. Shedlovsky was elected to membership in the National Academy of Sciences in 1953. He was also a member of the New York Academy of Sciences (vice-president, 1942–1960), the American Chemical Society, the Harvey Society, the Electrochemical Society, the Biophysical Society, and the American Association for the Advancement of Science.

Shedlovsky is survived by his first wife (née Gladys Lillian Danielson) and their son Richard, who is executive director of the Hebrew Hospital for Chronic Sick (Bronx, New York); his widow (née Beatrice Paul), their daughter Alexandra Shedlovsky Dove, who is a research biochemist at the University of Wisconsin, and their son Julian, who is an administrative officer at the National Center for Atmospheric Research at Boulder, Colorado; and his brother, Dr. Leo Shedlovsky, who is also a physical chemist, now retired. There are eight grandchildren: Richard's Joan and Ellen; Alexandra's William, Patrick, and Susanne; and Julian's Erica, Paul, and Sarah.

REFERENCES

Debye, P., and Hückel, E. Theory of electrolytes. II. The limiting law of electrical conductivity. Phys. Z., 24(1923):305–25.

Fuoss, R. M., and Kraus, C. A. Properties of electrolytic solutions. II. The evaluations of Λ_o and K for incompletely dissociated electrolytes. J. Am. Chem. Soc., 55(1933):476–88.

Harned, H. S., and Owen, B. B. Thermodynamic properties of weak acids and bases in salt solutions, and an exact method of determining their dissociation constants. J. Am. Chem. Soc., 52(1930):5079–91.

Kohlrausch, F., and Maltby, M. E. Das elektrische Leitvermögen wässriger Lösungen von Alkali-Chloriden und Nitraten. Wiss. Abh. Phys. Tech. Reichsanst., 3(1900):155–228.

Onsager, L. Report on a revision of the conductivity theory. Phys. Z., 26(1926):388–92. Also in: Trans. Faraday Soc., 23(1927):341–49.

BIBLIOGRAPHY

1924

With D. A. MacInnes. The intensities of reflection of the characteristic rays of palladium from fluorite. Phys. Rev., 23:290.

1926

With D. A. MacInnes. The relative intensities of reflection of X-rays from the principal atomic planes of fluorite. Phys. Rev., 27:130–37.

1929

With D. A. MacInnes and I. A. Copperthwaite. The conductance and transference number of the chloride ion in mixtures of sodium and potassium chloride. J. Am. Chem. Soc., 51:2671–76.

1930

A screened bridge for the measurement of electrolytic conductance. I. Theory of capacity errors. II. Description of the bridge. J. Am. Chem. Soc., 52:1793–1805.

A conductivity cell for eliminating electrode effects in measurements of electrolytic conductance. J. Am. Chem. Soc., 52:1806–11.

1931

With D. A. MacInnes. The ionization constant of acetic acid. J. Am. Chem. Soc., 53:2419–20.

1932

An equation for electrolytic conductance. J. Am. Chem. Soc., 54:1405–11.

The electrolytic conductivity of some uni-univalent electrolytes in water at 25°. J. Am. Chem. Soc., 54:1411–28.

With D. A. MacInnes. The determination of the ionization constant of acetic acid, at 25°, from conductance measurements. J. Am. Chem. Soc., 54:1429–38.

With D. A. MacInnes and L. G. Longsworth. The limiting equivalent conductances of several univalent ions in water at 25°. J. Am. Chem. Soc., 54:2758–62.

With D. A. MacInnes and L. G. Longsworth. Limiting mobilities of some monovalent ions and the dissociation constant of acetic acid at 25°. Nature, 130:774–75.

1933

With D. A. MacInnes and L. G. Longsworth. The conductance of aqueous solutions of electrolytes and the interionic attraction theory. Chem. Rev., 13:29–46.

1934

With H. H. Uhlig. On guaiacol solutions. I. The electrical conductivity of sodium and potassium guaiacolates in guaiacol. J. Gen. Physiol., 17:549–61.

With H. H. Uhlig. On guaiacol solutions. II. The distribution of sodium and potassium guaiacolates between guaiacol and water. J. Gen. Physiol., 17:563–76.

With A. S. Brown and D. A. MacInnes. The conductance of aqueous electrolytes. Trans. Electrochem. Soc., 66:165–78.

With A. S. Brown. The electrolytic conductivity of alkaline earth chlorides in water at 25°. J. Am. Chem. Soc., 56:1066–71.

1935

With D. A. MacInnes. The first ionization constant of carbonic acid, 0 to 38°, from conductance measurements. J. Am. Chem. Soc., 57:1705–10.

1936

With J. Sendroy, Jr., and D. Belcher. The validity of determinations of the pH of whole blood at thirty-eight degrees with the glass electrode. J. Biol. Chem., 115:529–42.

With D. A. MacInnes. The determination of activity coefficients from the potentials of concentration cells with transference. II. Hydrochloric acid at 25°. J. Am. Chem. Soc., 58:1970–72.

Distribution of electrolytes between non-miscible solvents. Cold Spring Harbor Symp. Quant. Biol., 4:27–33.

1937

With D. A. MacInnes. The determination of activity coefficients from the potentials of concentration cells with transference. III.

Potassium chloride. IV. Calcium chloride. J. Am. Chem. Soc., 59:503–6.

1938

With D. A. MacInnes and D. Belcher. The meaning and standardization of the pH scale. J. Am. Chem. Soc., 60:1094–99.

The computation of ionization constants and limiting conductance values from conductivity measurements. J. Franklin Inst., 225:739–43.

With L. C. Craig, R. G. Gould, Jr., and W. A. Jacobs. The ergot alkaloids. XIV. The positions of the double bond and the carboxyl group in lysergic acid and its isomer. The structure of the alkaloid. J. Biol. Chem., 125:289–98.

With J. E. Smadel and E. G. Pickels. Ultracentrifugation studies on the elementary bodies of vaccine virus. II. The influence of sucrose, glycerol and urea solutions on the physical nature of vaccine virus. J. Exp. Med., 68:607–27.

An equation for transferance numbers. J. Chem. Phys., 6:845–46.

1939

With D. A. MacInnes. The determination of activity from the potentials of concentration cells with transference. V. Lanthanum chloride at 25°. J. Am. Chem. Soc., 61:200–3.

With S. H. Maron. Determination of the ionization constant of aci-nitroethane. J. Am. Chem. Soc., 61:753–54.

With L. G. Longsworth and D. A. MacInnes. Electrophoretic patterns of normal and pathological human blood serum and plasma. J. Exp. Med., 70:399–413.

1940

With A. Rothen, R. O. Greep, H. B. van Dyke, and B. F. Chow. The isolation in pure form of the interstitial cell-stimulating (luteinizing) hormone of the anterior lobe of the pituitary gland. Science, 92:178–80.

With J. E. Smadel. Electrophoretic studies on elementary bodies of vaccinia. J. Exp. Med., 72:511–21.

With J. E. Smadel, E. G. Pickels, and T. M. Rivers. Observations on mixtures of elementary bodies of vaccinia and coated collodion particles by means of ultracentrifugation and electrophoresis. J. Exp. Med., 72:523–29.

1942

With J. Scudder. A comparison of erythrocyte sedimentation rates and electrophoretic patterns of normal and pathological human blood. J. Exp. Med., 75:119–26.

With J. E. Smadel. The LS-antigen of vaccinia. II. Isolation of a single substance containing both L- and S-activity. J. Exp. Med., 75:165–78.

With J. E. Smadel. Antigens and vaccinia. Ann. N.Y. Acad. Sci., 43:35–46.

With B. F. Chow, H. B. van Dyke, R. O. Greep, and A. Rothen. Gonadotropins of the swine pituitary. II. Preparation, and biological and physico-chemical characterization of a protein apparently identical with metakentrin (ICSH). Endocrinology, 30:650–56.

1943

The electrical conductivity of sodium and potassium guaiacolates in guaiacol. J. Gen. Physiol., 26:287–92.

Criteria of purity of proteins. Ann. N.Y. Acad. Sci., 43:259–72.

With A. Rothen and J. E. Smadel. The LS-antigen of vaccinia. III. Physical-chemical properties of LS-antigen and some of its degradation properties. J. Exp. Med., 77:155–64.

With J. E. Smadel and C. L. Hoagland. The LS-antigen of vaccinia. IV. Chemical analysis of LS and the effect of chymotrypsin on LS. J. Exp. Med., 77:165–71.

With W. F. Goebel, G. I. Lavin, and M. H. Adams. The heterophile antigen of pneumococcus. J. Biol. Chem., 148:1–15.

With W. W. Beckman, A. Hiller, and R. M. Archibald. The occurrence in urine of a protein soluble in trichloroacetic acid. J. Biol. Chem., 148:247–48.

1946

Conductometry. In: *Physical Methods of Organic Chemistry*, ed. A. Weissberger, vol. 2, pp. 1011–50. N.Y.: Interscience Publishers.

1949

Conductometry. In: *Physical Methods of Organic Chemistry*, ed. A. Weissberger, vol. 1, pp. 1651–83. N.Y.: Interscience Publishers.

With R. M. Fuoss. Extrapolation of conductance data for weak electrolytes. J. Am. Chem. Soc., 71:1496.

1950

With D. A. MacInnes and L. G. Longsworth. Macroscopic space charge in electrolytes during electrolysis. J. Chem. Phys., 18:333–34.

Activity coefficients of $LaCl_3$, $CaCl_2$, KCl, NaCl and HCl. J. Am. Chem. Soc., 72:3680–82.

With H. B. van Dyke and S. Y. P'an. Follicle-stimulating hormones of the anterior pituitary of the sheep and the hog. Endocrinology, 46:563–73.

1951

With S. D. Elliott. An electrophoretic study of a streptococcal proteinase and its precursor. J. Exp. Med., 94:363–72.

Electromotive force from proton transfer reactions. National Bureau of Standards Circular 524:281–88.

Protochemical cells. Science, 113:561–62.

1952

Electromotive force from proton transfer reactions: a model for bioelectric phenomena. Cold Spring Harbor Symp. Quant. Biol., 17:97–102.

1953

With W. J. V. Osterhout. Surface active properties of an extract of the sperm of *Nereis limbata*. Biol. Bull., 105:383–84.

1954

The glass electrode in water-methanol solutions. Science, 119:585.

1956

With Robert L. Kay. Ionization constants of acetic acid in water-methanol mixtures at 25° from conductance measurements. J. Phys. Chem., 60:151–55.

With W. Goebel and G. T. Barry. Colicine K. I. The production of colicine K in media maintained at constant pH. J. Exp. Med., 103:577–88.

1959

Conductance and pH measurements in methanol-water mixtures. In: *Structure of Electrolytic Solutions*, ed. W. J. Hamer, pp. 268–80. N.Y.: John Wiley and Sons.

1960

Conductometry. In: *Organic Chemistry—Physical Methods*, ed. A. Weissberger, vol. 1, pp. 3011–48. N.Y.: Interscience Publishers.

1962

The behavior of carboxylic acids in mixed solvents. In: *Electrolytes*, ed. B. Pesce, pp. 146–51. N.Y.: Pergamon Press.

1967

With H. O. Spivey. Studies in electrolytic conductance in alcohol-water mixtures. I. Hydrochloric acid, sodium chloride, and sodium acetate at 0°, 25° and 35° in ethanol-water mixtures. J. Phys. Chem., 71:2165–71.

With H. O. Spivey. Studies in electrolytic conductance in alcohol-water mixtures. II. The ionization constant of acetic acid in ethanol-water mixtures at 0°, 25°, and 35°. J. Phys. Chem., 71:2171–75.

With M. Goffredi. Studies of electrolytic conductance in alcohol-water mixtures. III. Sodium chloride in 1-propanol-water mixtures at 15°, 25°, and 35°. J. Phys. Chem., 71:2176–81.

With M. Goffredi. Studies of electrolytic conductance in alcohol-water mixtures. IV. Hydrochloric acid in 1-propanol-water mixtures at 15°, 25°, and 35°. J. Phys. Chem., 71:2176–81.

With M. Goffredi. Studies of electrolytic conductance in alcohol-water mixtures. V. The ionization constant of acetic acid in 1-propanol-water mixtures at 15°, 25° and 35°. J. Phys. Chem., 71:4436–42.

1971

With Leo Shedlovsky. Conductometry. In: *Techniques of Chemistry*, ed. B. W. Rossiter, pp. 163–204. N.Y.: Wiley-Interscience.

VESTO MELVIN SLIPHER
November 11, 1875–November 8, 1969

BY WILLIAM GRAVES HOYT

VESTO MELVIN SLIPHER, a pioneer in the field of astronomical spectroscopy during his long career at the Lowell Observatory at Flagstaff, Arizona, probably made more fundamental discoveries than any other observational astronomer of the twentieth century.[1]

He is best known for his discovery in 1913 of the extraordinary radial velocities of the spiral nebulae, as revealed by the enormous "red shifts" of the absorption lines in their spectra.[2] This discovery provided the first evidence for the now widely held theory of an expanding universe,[3] and it was a prerequisite to Edwin P. Hubble's discovery sixteen years later of the relationship between the radial velocities of nebulae and their distances, which has enabled astronomers to gauge the approximate age and dimensions of the known universe.[4]

In the course of this work, Slipher also discovered that the spiral nebulae are rotating,[5] carried out fruitful investigations of the relative motion and distribution of nebulae and globular star clusters,[6] demonstrated the existence of gas and dust in interstellar space, and found that certain nebulae shine only by the reflected light of nearby stars.[7]

He also made innovative spectrographic studies of the rotation periods of the planets,[8] planetary atmospheres,[9] comets,[10] the solar corona,[11] "peculiar" deep space objects,[12] lightning,[13] the eclipsed moon,[14] the light of the night sky, aurorae, and the zodiacal light.[15] His contributions include his careful planning and effective supervision of the Lowell Observatory's search for Percival Lowell's postulated trans-Neptunian "planet X," which led in 1930 to the discovery of the ninth planet, Pluto, by Clyde W. Tombaugh.[16]

Slipher's productive career spanned nearly forty years, with his most important discoveries coming in the second decade of the century when astronomers were hotly debating the great question of the nature and extent of the universe.[17] It is one of the larger ironies in the history of astronomy that while Slipher's work on nebulae, star clusters, and the interstellar medium bore directly on this problem, his results were not immediately applied to its solution by contemporary theoretical astronomers and astrophysicists.

The reasons for this are many and involve, among other things, a preference by astronomers of the day for other observations, in conflict with Slipher's, that were later found to be erroneous.[18] This, in turn, may reflect the aura of skepticism that then surrounded the work of the Lowell Observatory as a result of the much-publicized ideas of its controversial founder-director, Percival Lowell.[19] Perhaps Slipher's personality was a factor, too. In sharp contrast to his ebullient, impulsive employer, Slipher was a reserved, reticent, cautious man who shunned the public eye and rarely even attended astronomical meetings, often sending his papers for others to read.[20] He consistently postponed publication of his discoveries until he had confirmed them to his own satisfaction, and some of his results were published by others to whom he communicated them in his correspondence. Such distinguished astronomers and astrophysicists as Sir Arthur Stanley Eddington, Knut Lundmark, Gustaf Strömberg, Harlow Shapley, and Hubble were among the beneficiaries of this largesse.[21]

Slipher's published papers number just over one hundred, many of them appearing only as abstracts. They are typically terse, factual accounts of his observations and their results, usually unencumbered by any interpretive discussion.[22] Such speculation as Slipher permitted himself he confined largely to his letters to close and trusted friends in astronomy.[23]

DETAILS OF LIFE AND CAREER

Vesto Melvin Slipher, who was almost always referred to as "V. M.," was born on a farm in Mulberry, Indiana on November 11, 1875 to Daniel Clark and Hannah App Slipher. A younger brother, Earl C. Slipher (1883–1964), also became an astronomer and for a time was one of the leading authorities on the subjects of the planet Mars and planetary photography. Both brothers spent their entire careers at the Lowell Observatory.[24]

Little is known of Slipher's childhood and youth. Certainly life on the family farm helped him develop the strong, vigorous constitution that later stood him in good stead for the more strenuous aspects of observational astronomy. Henry L. Giclas, who worked with Slipher for twenty-three years, remembers that Slipher in his sixties could climb effortlessly on the 12,661-foot San Francisco Peaks north of Flagstaff where the observatory maintained a mountain station in the late 1920's and early 1930's. "V. M. Slipher, thirty-five years my senior, was always ahead of us 'boys' climbing the mountain—we puffing and panting and he, disgusted, waiting for us to catch up," he has recalled.[25] Arthur Adel, also a Lowell astronomer in the 1930's, has noted that "V. M. at age sixty-five could chop wood with the best of them."[26] Slipher sometimes emphasized the necessity for robust health to younger men who sought his advice on a career in astronomy.[27] His bucolic background, incidentally, came in handy during his early years at Lowell Observatory.

For while Lowell lived, Slipher was in charge of the Observatory's cow, Venus, and her progeny and was responsible for Lowell's vegetable garden whenever Lowell himself was not in residence at Flagstaff.[28]

Slipher graduated from high school in Frankfort, Indiana and then taught briefly at a country school north of that city. On September 20, 1897, at age twenty-one, he entered Indiana University at Bloomington. On June 19, 1901 he received an A.B. degree in mechanics and astronomy. He was granted an A.M. degree on June 24, 1903 and the Ph.D. degree on June 23, 1909, also by Indiana. His dissertation was a short paper on "The Spectrum of Mars," which had been published the previous year in the *Astrophysical Journal*.[29]

Slipher's professors at Indiana included John A. Miller, who in 1906 became director of Sproul Observatory at Swarthmore College, Pennsylvania, and Wilbur A. Cogshall, an assistant at Lowell Observatory in 1896 and 1897, thereafter associated with Indiana and its Kirkwood Observatory for more than forty years. Slipher later credited Miller with turning his interest to astronomy,[30] and both Miller and Cogshall remained among Slipher's closest confidants through their long lives.[31]

It was Cogshall who persuaded a reluctant Percival Lowell to bring Slipher to the Lowell Observatory in 1901 for what Lowell clearly intended to be a limited stay.[32] "As regards Mr. Slipher," Lowell wrote to Cogshall in July 1901, "I shall be happy to have him come when he is ready. I have decided, however, that I shall not want another permanent assistant and take him only because I promised to do so and for the term suggested. What it was escapes my memory."[33]

Slipher's "term" turned out to be fifty-three years. He was an assistant at the Observatory until 1915 when he was made assistant director under Lowell. At Lowell's death on November 12, 1916, he became acting director, and he was named director in 1926, serving in that capacity until his retirement in 1954 at the age of seventy-nine. In his later years, he lived quietly in Flagstaff, occasionally taking an interest in astronomical and observatory affairs, but carrying on no further formal research. He died on November 8, 1969, three days before his ninety-fourth birthday.[34] In his will, he provided a fund with which the National Academy of Sciences and the Northern Arizona University Foundation in Flagstaff annually distribute grants and scholarships to science students and for science programs.[35]

On January 1, 1904 Slipher married Emma Rosalie Munger at Frankfort, and brought her to Flagstaff. The couple set up a home at the Observatory atop Mars Hill, on the western edge of the city. They had two children, Marcia Frances (Mrs. K. J. Nicholson) and David Clark Slipher.[36] Slipher was active in community and business affairs, particularly in the years after Lowell's death. He became a member and then chairman of the school board and was instrumental in establishing Flagstaff's first high school. He also participated in the founding of the Northern Arizona Society for Science and Art and its Museum of Northern Arizona, one of the major interdisciplinary research centers of the Southwest, and was a long-time member of its board of directors.[37] As a businessman, Slipher acquired extensive ranch property around Flagstaff, operated a retail furniture store for a time, managed many rental properties, and was a founder of a community hotel (the Hotel Monte Vista) for which he served as board chairman for many years.[38]

EARLY PLANETARY STUDIES

Slipher arrived in Flagstaff on August 10, 1901. Shortly thereafter a fine three-prism spectrograph, made by John A. Brashear of the Allegheny Observatory at Pittsburgh, Pennsylvania, was delivered to the Observatory. Lowell had ordered this instrument the previous year for use "in the matter of Venus' rotation,"[39] and Slipher's first task was to mount it on the Lowell 24-inch refracting telescope, adjust it properly, and then learn its use.[40]

Initially, Slipher encountered many difficulties with the spectrograph. Lowell, from his Boston office, patiently forwarded advice on adjustments and observing techniques.[41] By mid-1902 Slipher had resolved his problems and produced spectrograms of Mars, Jupiter, and Saturn which Lowell thought were good enough to send to several eminent scientists as evidence of the excellence of both his new instrument and his new assistant. Slipher had, in fact, spectrographically confirmed the visually known periods of the planets, as Lowell proclaimed to the Washington, D.C. meeting of the American Association for the Advancement of Science in December.[42]

Slipher's own research interests, however, concerned the determination of radial velocities of stars and the discovery of spectroscopic binary stars by measuring Doppler shifts of the Fraunhofer lines in their spectra resulting from the differential motion of their components in the line of sight. Lowell encouraged this interest, although he set a firm policy that the planetary work of the Observatory must have first priority. Slipher faithfully adhered to this policy, and he pursued his own work only when time and circumstances permitted. It is notable, however, that his first formal publication was a 1902 paper in the *Astronomical Journal* on the variable velocity of the star ζ [zeta] Herculis.[43]

In the fall of 1902, Lowell assigned Slipher two projects; the first involved what came to be known as the "velocity-shift" method for determining constituents of planetary atmospheres.[44] Lowell was anxious for Slipher to apply his new method to determine whether water vapor and oxygen were present in the atmosphere of Mars, and Slipher did, in

1904 and 1905, undertake such observations. They were not successful, however, because the absorption lines he sought are in the near infrared region of the spectrum, i.e., above 6900 Ångstroms, and photographic plates sensitive in this range were simply not available at this time.[45] The method, although theoretically sound, did not in fact prove viable until 1963 when astronomers at the Mount Wilson Observatory, with the 100-inch Hooker reflector, used it to detect slight traces of water vapor and oxygen on Mars.[46] Slipher, in 1908, claimed the spectrographic detection of Martian water vapor and oxygen on other grounds,[47] but his finding was disputed.[48] Although his conclusion was seemingly confirmed by several later observers,[49] it has not been accepted by modern astronomers. This work, nevertheless, turned Slipher's attention to the near infrared of the spectrum where he would soon make some significant discoveries.

Slipher's second assignment concerned the rotation period of Venus, which had long been assumed to be about 23+ hours on the basis of vague shadings on the planet's cloud-shrouded disk, reported as early as 1666 by Giovanni Domenico Cassini. In 1890, however, astronomer Giovanni Virginio Schiaparelli, discoverer of the so-called "canals" of Mars which so intrigued Lowell, concluded that Venus had a much longer rotation period and rotated only once in 225 days, the period of its revolution around the sun.[50] This conclusion was widely disputed, but in 1896 Lowell announced that he had confirmed it from observations of streak-like markings on the planet's "surface."[51] In 1900 Aristarch A. Belopolsky, of Russia's Pulkowa Observatory, reported spectrographic observations that again favored Cassini's short period.[52] It was to counter Belopolsky's finding that Lowell had ordered the Brashear spectrograph. In giving Slipher the assignment, he warned that "the sentence of Belopolsky is indeed a hard nut to crack."[53]

Slipher began work on the problem in November 1902, and by March 1903 he had obtained a series of spectrograms that Lowell claimed confirmed Schiaparelli's and his own conclusions.[54] But the cautious Slipher reported only that they showed "no evidence that Venus has a short period of rotation," and that "so fast a spin as 24 hours could not have escaped detection."[55] Slipher, among others, made similar observations in subsequent years with essentially the same result.[56] His conclusion remained the best available estimate of the situation until the early 1960's, when radar observations revealed that the planet's spin is very slow indeed—243 days and in a retrograde direction.[57]

In 1903 Slipher began a spectrographic investigation of the giant outer planets—first Uranus and Neptune and then Jupiter and Saturn—in the then unexplored infrared region of the spectrum. In this work he experimented with chemical dyes and plate baths to make his plates sensitive farther into the red, and these efforts were quite successful. By 1907 he had obtained a series of spectrograms of the outer planets that revealed strong spectral bands neither he nor anyone else could immediately identify.[58] Not until 1931, with the work of Rupert Wildt, was it found that a few of these bands were due to methane and ammonia in the atmospheres of the planets.[59] Slipher subsequently worked with Lowell astronomer Arthur Adel to confirm this finding and extend it to the rest of the unidentified bands in Slipher's early spectra.[60]

At Lowell's direction, Slipher undertook several other spectrographic studies of the planets. Between 1905 and 1907, and again in 1924, he sought to detect chlorophyll on Mars with a negative result that has stood the test of subsequent observations, both by terrestrial observers and the 1976 Viking spacecraft's examination of the surface of Mars itself.[61]

In 1911 Slipher became the first to spectrographically

determine a rotation period for Uranus of 10.75 hours,[62] a result ultimately confirmed both photometrically and spectrographically and not questioned until 1975, when observers using more sophisticated equipment tentatively suggested a period of 25±4 hours.[63] The rotation period of Neptune, too, was a concern. In 1912 and 1913 he sought to determine the length of the Neptunian "day" spectrographically at Flagstaff,[64] and in 1921 he made another attempt, using the 100-inch Hooker reflector on Mount Wilson. His results, he determined, were inconclusive.[65]

INTERSTELLAR GAS AND DUST

Throughout these years, Slipher continued his work on spectroscopic binary stars. "With regard to yourself, by all means make your star measures for velocity—whenever there is no pressing planetary work—and good luck to you in the result," Lowell had written him in 1904.[66] Slipher had, from time to time, published observations of stars with variable radial velocities, and by 1909 this work had led him to a major discovery.

In 1904 astronomer J. F. Hartmann had noted that the conspicuous H and K calcium lines in the spectrum of the binary star δ [delta] Orionis remained sharp and stationary, while other spectral lines were blurred or broadened by the differential velocity of the components in the line of sight. He thought that this might indicate light absorption by a calcium vapor cloud between the earth and the star, but both his observation and his suggestion remained obscure, and Hartmann did not pursue the work.[67] In 1908 the Dutch theoretical astronomer J. C. Kapteyn independently suggested that interstellar space contained vast quantities of gas and predicted that this gas should produce what he called "space lines" that "would not share in that part of the radial motion which is due to the motion of the stars themselves...."[68] That same year Slipher discovered sharp, stationary calcium lines in the otherwise blurred spectrum of the star β [beta] Scorpii, and over the ensuing year he found the same phenomenon in the spectra of a number of both double and single stars, not only in Scorpio, but in Perseus and Orion as well. From this he concluded that interstellar gas exists in widely separated regions of space, notably "in and near branches of the Milky Way," and produces "selective absorption of light in space." He also suggested that the stationary H and K calcium lines were "the 'space lines' which Kapteyn's researches had led him to predict."[69]

These conclusions brought Slipher congratulatory letters from many eminent astronomers, including Hartmann and Kapteyn.[70] Yet his findings were largely ignored in astronomy for nearly two decades, despite the pertinence of interstellar absorption of light to the so-called "great debate" ten years later over the size of a universe then measured by the intensity of light alone.[71] Further observations by John S. Plaskett in the early 1920's and the theoretical work by Eddington in 1926 eventually showed the validity of Slipher's earlier work.[72] Plaskett considered Slipher's 1909 discovery "the most suggestive and penetrating early contribution to the problem...."[73]

In December 1912, Slipher also demonstrated the existence of dust, or "pulverulent matter," in interstellar space with his discovery that the nebula in the Pleiades near the star Merope was shining solely by reflected starlight.[74] In 1916 he made similar observations of the nebula near the star ρ[rho] Ophiuchi, obtaining a similar result,[75] and in later years he and others added nebulosities in other regions of space to the new class of reflection nebulae.[76]

OBSERVATIONS OF SPIRAL NEBULAE

For a brief time, Slipher considered his Pleiades discovery his most significant work, for he believed that it provided the solution to the long-standing problem of the spiral nebulae.[77] For three centuries astronomers had observed and speculated about these numerous, but faint, diffuse objects, yet almost nothing about them was then known. Some believed that they were vast aggregations of stars beyond the Milky Way, "island universes" as suggested by philosopher Immanuel Kant in 1755. Others felt they might be embryonic planetary systems in early stages of evolution and thus analogs of the primordial solar system. The problem was not resolved until the third decade of this century, and Slipher's discoveries played a part in its resolution.

Slipher turned his attention to the spiral nebulae in 1909 at the behest of Percival Lowell, who thought that if such objects were indeed incipient solar systems, they might show spectrographic similarities to the solar system itself. Early in 1909 he asked Slipher to observe what were then only classified as "green" and "white" nebulae, the latter group containing the enigmatic spirals, and to compare the spectra of their "outer parts" with his spectra of the giant outer planets.[78]

Slipher approached this assignment pessimistically. Because of their faintness, the spirals were difficult to observe spectrographically; the few such observations that had been attempted up to this time had been generally unproductive, even with telescopes larger and considered more suitable for the work than Lowell's 24-inch refractor. "I do not see much hope in getting the spectrum of a white nebula," he pointed out to Lowell, "because the high ratio of focal-length to aperture of the 24-inch gives a very faint image of a nebula.... It would seem the undertaking would have to await the [40-inch] reflector."[79] (The Lowell 40-inch reflector would not be fully operational for another year, and even then Slipher had to carry on his nebular work with the smaller refractor. Lowell assigned the new instrument to what he considered to be more promising work—observations of Mars and his trans-Neptunian planet search.[80])

Despite his pessimism, Slipher went to work on the problem, seeking advice from spectroscopists Edward A. Fath of the Lick Observatory and Edwin B. Frost of Yerkes Observatory, and experimenting with various instrumental and photographic techniques.[81] He soon realized that focal lengths and apertures, or the degree of dispersion his prisms provided, were not particularly germane to the problem—the key factor was the speed of the spectrograph's camera lens. By November 1910, he had devised a single-prism spectrograph "from equipment on hand,"[82] which, he advised Lowell, "requires only about a hundredth part of the exposure required by the three-prism arrangement."[83] Early in December he obtained a spectrogram of the Great Nebula in Andromeda which, he wrote, "seems to me to show faintly peculiarities not commented upon" by earlier workers in the field. "These earlier observations were made with large reflecting telescopes and the idea seems to go undisputed that a long focus telescope and of course a refractor is unsuitable for such work. But I convinced myself that I knew of no reason why the focus-to-aperture ratio had the slightest part to play in spectrum work on extended objects, and this plate proves the proposition completely to my mind."[84]

Through 1911 and 1912 Slipher continued to experiment with faster lenses and with observation techniques whenever the regular work of the Observatory gave him the opportunity and access to the 24-inch telescope. In September 1912, his spectrograph now equipped with a commercial Voigtlander f 2.5 lens, which "gave something like 200 times the speed of the usual three-prism spectrograph,"[85] he again turned his attention to Andromeda.

On September 17, in an exposure of more than six hours, Slipher obtained a plate of the Andromeda nebula that recorded enough detail to encourage him to try specifically to measure the radial velocity of the nebula, an observational feat that astronomers of the day generally considered beyond practical achievement.[86] At this time the radial velocities of some 1200 bright stars and a few bright planetary nebulae had been measured and all found to be moving at speeds on the order of tens of kilometers per second (km/sec). No radial velocities were known for nebulae, but no one expected that they would be appreciably different.[87]

Although encouraged, Slipher was still not confident. "If I succeed in getting any spectra worth while," he wrote Lowell in October, "I might try to measure them for velocity.... But of course there is no rush as I do not know if it is possible to get such spectrograms."[88]

Slipher now made two spectrograms of Andromeda with exposures extending over two nights, on November 15–16 and on December 3–4. These were even more encouraging, for the plates contained "a somewhat larger number" of spectral lines than had been recorded by the few other astronomers who had observed spirals spectrographically, notably Sir William Huggins in England, Max Wolf and Julius Scheiner in Germany, and Fath in the United States. "Of course the spectrum is very faint," Slipher conceded to Lowell, "and getting the velocity from the spectrograms would doubtless impress these observers as quite a hopeless undertaking, and maybe it is but I want to make the attempt."[89]

On December 28 Slipher advised Lowell that he planned to get "one good carefully made spectrogram" of the Andromeda nebula for velocity,[90] and the following night he began this spectrogram, exposing the plate over three nights and into the pre-dawn hours of January 1, 1913.[91] After a preliminary inspection of the plate, he reported, "I feel it safe to say here that the velocity bids fair to come out unusually high."[92]

Over the next two weeks, Slipher carefully measured all

four of his Andromeda plates, finding that the nebula was moving at a radial velocity some three times that of any other known object in the universe. The result seems to have caused him some concern, and even to have raised doubts in his mind that the Doppler shift was a valid indicator of radial velocity. To reinforce his conclusion, he sent a print of his Andromeda spectrum to Fath. "You will I think," he wrote, "be able to see the displacement of the nebular lines toward the violet with reference to such lines as 4325, 4308, and 4272 [Ångstroms] of the Fe [iron] and V [vanadium] comparison spectrum. Other plates show the same thing, which corresponds to a velocity of 275 km.... I cannot find any other explanation...."[93]

To further resolve his doubts, Slipher spent another two weeks painstakingly remeasuring his Andromeda plates and found the mean velocity to be slightly higher. On February 3, 1913 he wrote Lowell that the Great Nebula in Andromeda was approaching the earth at the then unheard-of speed of 300 km/sec, the value, incidentally, that is accepted today.[94] "It looks as if you had made a great discovery," Lowell replied. "Try some other spiral nebulae for confirmation."[95]

Slipher now turned his attention to a spindle-shaped, edge-on spiral in Virgo, designated NGC 4594, and by April his spectrograms showed that its spectral lines were shifted far toward the red, indicating that it was receding from the earth at about 1000 km/sec, an astounding velocity at that time.[96] "This nebula is leaving the solar system," he pointed out to Lowell, "hence it seems safe to conclude that motion in the line of sight is the real cause of these great displacements in their nebular spectra, for if there were some unknown agency akin to the pressure shifts but enormously magnified residing in the nebulae, we would not expect it to one time act one way, another time the opposite way."[97]

Slipher continued these observations through the next

year. In August 1914, at the American Astronomical Society's seventeenth meeting at Evanston, Illinois, he could announce radial velocities for fifteen spirals.[98] "In the great majority of cases," he reported, "the nebula is receding; the largest velocities are all positive.... The striking preponderance of the positive sign indicates a general fleeing from us or the Milky Way...."[99] Three years later, when Holland's Willem de Sitter first theorized that the universe might be expanding, Slipher's list contained twenty-five spiral nebulae and globular clusters, their velocities continuing to be "preponderantly positive."[100]

DISCOVERY OF NEBULAR ROTATION

Slipher's investigations of the spiral nebulae had one other important result. His 1913 spectrograms of the Virgo spiral had not only shown that its spectral lines were shifted toward the red, but that they were slightly inclined, indicating differential radial motion in the nebula itself, and thus rotation. With typical caution, Slipher waited a full year, until he could obtain a satisfactory confirmatory spectrogram, before telegraphing Lowell: "Spectrograms show Virgo nebula rotating."[101] Over the next few years he found that a number of other spirals, including Andromeda's, were rotating, and by late 1917 he concluded that they were all spinning in the same relative direction, "turning into the spiral arms like a winding spring."[102]

This discovery, however, conflicted with an earlier finding by Mount Wilson Observatory's Adriaan van Maanen, based on the comparative photography of nebulae, that the spirals' arms were, in effect, unwinding. Van Maanen's results were of great interest, because if angular motion within a nebula could be detected in photographs taken at relatively short intervals, then the nebula could be at no very great distance from the earth. Quite a few astronomers, then and in subsequent years, cited van Maanen's work to argue against the "island universe" theory and the proposition that spiral nebulae were distant galaxies of stars like the Milky Way itself.[103]

In the long debate over this issue, Slipher's work on nebular rotation was largely neglected in favor of van Maanen's. Slipher himself did nothing to bring it to the fore, preferring always to avoid controversy. This he managed to do even in his private correspondence, writing to an inquiring colleague, for example:

> It is unfortunately a fact that the results from the spectrographic observations of nebulae show the central parts of the spirals to be rotating in a direction opposite to that indicated by Van [sic] Maanen's observed motions of nebulae. No results have been got here since to modify the conclusions drawn from the earlier spectrographic rotations. . . . I have heard expressions of doubt as to whether Van Maanen's results might not be somehow in error. Then perhaps there are some astronomers who might think some other interpretations might be applied to the spectrographic observations. It is perhaps natural that I should not hear the spectrographic results questioned. . . .[104]

More than ten years would pass before astronomers in general would conclude that van Maanen's results were wrong, and van Maanen himself reject them.[105] The issue of nebular rotation, moreover, was complicated by the problem of which edge of the spiral was nearest the observer—Slipher opting for the edge showing dark, silhouetted lanes of absorbing material.[106] It was more than twenty years before this aspect of the controversy was settled—primarily by Hubble—and Slipher's reasoning shown to be sound.[107]

Slipher's work on nebulae was extremely difficult and laborious, and represented a major technical achievement for observational astronomy at the time. It required precise guidance of the 24-inch refractor for periods ranging from five to more than sixty hours, frequently extending over many nonconsecutive nights.[108] Slipher once remarked that he should have observed some of the bright planetary nebulae as "it would be a real recreation to be able to secure a satisfactory spectrogram of a nebula in one night's exposure." But to this he quickly added: "To do the best work one must limit himself to a few problems."[109] Some of his colleagues marvelled that he did not electrocute himself with the makeshift array of Leiden jars he used to create the spark for his comparison spectra. When Slipher described his equipment and techniques along with his results at the August 1914 AAS meeting at Evanston, he received an unprecedented standing ovation.[110]

Some of Slipher's early speculations on his nebular work were not as valid or as durable as the work itself. He did not at first think, for example, that the spirals were vast exterior galaxies, and his discovery of the reflection nature of the Pleiades nebula briefly reinforced this belief. "If this nebula shines by reflected light," he wondered, "why could not the nebula in Andromeda shine in the same way being lighted by a central sun obscurred [sic] by the fragmentary material around it?"[111] Again, he speculated briefly that the spirals might be "very advanced stars in old age undergoing a strange disintegration, brought about possibly by their swift flight through stellar space";[112] that novae, like the one that flared in Andromeda in 1885, might be explained by such a fast-moving nebula encountering a "dark sun."[113] He also suggested that the higher velocities he found for edge-on spirals might indicate that spirals in general moved "as a disk in a resisting medium."[114]

Slipher's own later work, as well as Lowell's quick grasp of the implication of high nebular velocities,[115] soon changed such ideas. By April 1917 Slipher declared that the "island universe" theory "gains favor in the present observations." He also noted that early in his nebular work he had discovered indications of group motion by both the spirals and clusters, and he now used his list of twenty-five velocities to compute the earth's motion relative to these objects. He reported that "our whole stellar system moves and carries us with it" at a velocity of about 700 km/sec in the direction of Capricorn. And he added: "It seems that if our solar system evolved from a nebula as we have long believed, that nebula was probably not one of the class of spirals here dealt with."[116]

By 1917 only four of Slipher's velocity measures had been confirmed,[117] but by the end of World War I, others began to take up the work and fully established the validity of his discoveries. Slipher, however, still dominated the field. In 1921—the year he was elected to the National Academy of Sciences—he found that the spiral NGC 584 in Cetus was receding at about 1800 km/sec, the fastest-moving object yet discovered, and added thirteen more objects to his list of velocities.[118] In 1922 he sent forty-one velocities to Eddington for use in a book on relativity. In requesting these, the English astrophysicist declared, "I do not trouble myself about measures which merely duplicate yours as I know the agreement is in general quite satisfactory."[119]

In 1929 Hubble derived his important velocity-distance relationship for nebulae using, as he later wrote Slipher, "your velocities and my distances."[120] Hubble acknowledged Slipher's seminal contribution to his own work by declaring that "the first steps in a new field are the most difficult and the most significant. Once the barrier is forced, further development is relatively simple."[121]

AURORAE AND NIGHT SKY LIGHT

After 1921 Slipher's work on nebulae dropped off sharply. He had by this time largely exhausted the brighter nebulae and clusters within reach of the 24-inch and his spectrograph. Also, after Lowell's death he necessarily devoted more time to the administrative affairs of the Lowell Observatory. After 1927 his supervision of the new search for Lowell's trans-Neptunian planet drew much of his attention. Finally, he was deep into another investigation, involving the aurorae and the light of the night sky, which had emerged serendipitously from his nebular studies.

On February 7, 1913, in reporting the Andromeda velocity to his friend, astronomer John C. Duncan, Slipher discussed the differences between the spectra of the Andromeda nebula and of globular clusters and added: "I want to get the spectrum of the integrated light of the night sky to see how well the composite features come out in it as a suggestion of what we might expect from a galaxy observed from a great distance."[122]

He did not get around to doing this until June 1915, and then he found that a bright, greenish-yellow line at about 5571 Å dominated his long-exposure plate. This line had been observed before as the most prominent line in the spectrum of an auroral display. Slipher made some more night sky plates, and in March 1916 Lowell announced his assistant's discovery of a "permanent aurora."[123] In November Slipher published the results of more than fifty such observations, reporting the "chief auroral line" in all of his plates, even though no auroral displays were evident during the exposures.[124]

The following year, using a three-prism spectrograph with the 24-inch refractor, he measured a series of night sky plates, one exposed 115 hours, and showed that this line was at 5578 Å, seven Ångstroms above the previously accepted value. From these observations he concluded that the line was not due to nitrogen, as others had hypothesized. In 1924 it was found to be the result of atomic oxygen.[125]

Through the 1920's Slipher continued his observations of the night sky and of the rare auroral displays visible at Flagstaff's latitude. He discovered many new features in their spectra that were soon shown to be due to nitrogen, sodium, and other components of the earth's upper atmosphere in various ionized states.[126] In the early 1930's he extended this work to the zodiacal light, finding faint auroral features in its spectrum and concluding that upper atmospheric radiations contributed to what was otherwise predominantly a reflection phenomenon.[127] In 1933 Slipher's night sky and auroral work was carried on from Antarctica, with one of his spectrographs, by Thomas C. Poulter, chief scientist of the Byrd Antarctic Expedition II. Slipher was one of ten members of the honorary scientific staff of the expedition.[128]

Marathon exposures—in one case 147 hours—were needed to record a readable spectrum of the night sky light.[129] Despite this, the work was far less time-consuming than his nebular work; there was no telescope to guide, and it was only necessary to point the spectrograph toward the desired region of the sky, and check it periodically.[130] Slipher continually sought better optics for his instruments in this work. In 1924 he was offered a $300 grant by the National Academy of Sciences' Henry Draper Committee for special lenses. He never used the money, however, explaining later that "it turned out that I was able personally to pay for the optical parts. . . . Thus, as it worked out, I felt I should leave the grant to cases that could not—or would not—go on without it."[131]

Slipher also found time to lead two Lowell Observatory eclipse expeditions—to Syracuse, Kansas in 1918, and Ensenada, Mexico in 1923[132]—and for spectrographic studies of "peculiar" objects. In 1913 and 1915 he observed the Crab Nebula (NGC 1952), later found to be the remnant of a brilliant supernova reported by Chinese astronomers in A.D. 1054, and found its spectrum "the most extraordinary one known."[133] Its spectral lines, he discovered, were split and displaced at equal distances on each side of their normal place, a phenomenon he erroneously attributed to the Stark effect involving radiation in a strong electric field.[134] In 1917 he found that Hubble's variable nebula (NGC 2261) and the variable nebula NGC 6729 both had nova-like spectra.[135]

Throughout his career, Slipher continued to carry out observations of the planets and to otherwise work on projects to which Lowell had given priority. These included such transient phenomena as comets and novae, and on one occasion a transit of Mercury. Of this latter event, he noted that while such transits were not particulary rare, "the individual's opportunity to observe one is rare enough that he should not let it go unimproved."[136]

INFLUENCE OF PERCIVAL LOWELL

Perhaps the most interesting aspect of Slipher's career was the extent to which his flamboyant employer, Percival Lowell, and Lowell's often sensational ideas influenced his work and thought. There can be no doubt that Slipher was a cautious but convinced Lowellian. Not even in private did he question Lowell's controversial theories of the habitability of Mars or of the probable existence of intelligent Martians. Rather, he considered them possibilities that had been neither proven nor disproven, and used them as working hypotheses around which he programmed much of the work of the Observatory. When this work and work elsewhere seemed to support Lowell's ideas, as it sometimes did in the 1920's, Slipher carefully pointed this out to correspondents. In 1926 for example, when a student asked him for a disclaimer of life on Mars to use in a class debate, Slipher replied: "Unfortunately for your side, recent investigations tend more and more to confirm Lowell's conclusions... by adding further evidence of atmosphere and water and temperature such as would sustain organic life. While the *canali* markings [the so-called "canals"] are best interpreted by assuming Mars possessed of intelligent beings, yet the great distance between us and Mars renders the telescope incapable of showing directly objective presence of living beings."[137]

Slipher did, in fact, believe that millions of other planets exist in the universe and that many of them could, and probably did, support some form of life. "A thousand million rose bushes and one rose!" he once exclaimed to a botanist who had inquired about extra-mundane life. "It is neither according to religious or scientific teaching, but reminds us of the time when the earth was regarded as the center of the universe."[138]

Slipher's discovery of the extraordinary velocities of spiral nebulae, however, remains the most important of his many contributions to knowledge, as President F. J. M. Stratton of the Royal Astronomical Society pointed out in presenting him with the Society's Gold Medal in 1933:

> In a series of studies of the radial velocities of these island galaxies he laid the foundations of the great structure of the expanding universe.... If cosmogonists today have to deal with a universe that is expanding in fact as well as in fancy, at a rate which offers them special difficulties, a great part of the blame must be borne by our medalist.[139]

Slipher's own assessment of his work was more modest. This same year, in accepting the Henry Draper Medal from the National Academy of Sciences, he acknowledged a debt to Lowell, to "my good teacher Doctor John A. Miller," and to "scientific friends," and added:

> Other helpful factors for me have been good instrumental equipment and favorable skies for observation.... Added to these was that of a rather free hand to choose my own program, which fit happily a spirit of exploration. Under such conditions, some one else might have accomplished much more, but surely no one could find more pleasure in doing it than I.[140]

THE PRIMARY reference materials used for this memoir are contained in the Lowell Observatory Archives and consist of letters, texts, and other documents relating to Slipher's tenure at the Observatory, 1901–1954. Letters dated prior to 1917 can also be found in W. G. Hoyt and A. Babbitt, eds., *The Early Correspondence of the Lowell Observatory 1894–1916* (microfilm ed.; Flagstaff: Lowell Observatory, 1973). I have also used Slipher's will, his Indiana University transcript, and several biographical notes in the Archives prepared at the time of his death by colleagues and members of his family.

Printed materials used were preeminently Slipher's own publications (listed in the Bibliography), as well as publications by others in the astronomical literature relating to his work. A number of general works on astronomy have also been used to provide background and set Slipher's work in the context of that of his contemporaries. These include, notably, A. M. Clerke, *A Popular History of Astronomy During the Nineteenth Century* (4th ed.; London: Adam and Charles Black, 1902); O. Struve and V. Zebergs, *Astronomy of the Twentieth Century* (New York: Macmillan, 1962); E. P. Hubble, *The Realm of the Nebulae* (New Haven: Yale University Press, 1936); and R. Berendzen, R. Hart, and D. Seeley, *Man Discovers the Galaxies* (New York: Science History Publications, 1976).

In addition I have also drawn on two of my own works which are the only fully documented volumes extant relating to Percival Lowell, his observatory, and his early assistants. These are: *Lowell and Mars* (Tucson: University of Arizona Press, 1976); and *Planets 'X' and Pluto* (Tucson: University of Arizona Press, 1980).

FOOTNOTES

[1] J. S. Hall, "V.M. Slipher's Trail-blazing Career," *Sky and Telescope*, 39(1970):84; "Vesto Melvin Slipher (1875–1916)," *American Philosophical Society Yearbook*, 1970, pp. 161–66.

[2] V. M. Slipher, "The Radial Velocity of the Andromeda Nebula," *Lowell Observatory Bulletin*, no. 58, 2(1913):56; "Spectrographic Observations of Nebulae," *Publications of the American Astronomical Society*, 3(1913):18(A); *Popular Astronomy*, 22 (1914):146.

[3] W. Bonner, *The Mystery of the Expanding Universe* (New York: Macmillan, 1964), p. 1; R. Berendzen, R. Hart, and D. Seeley, *Man Discovers the Galaxies* (New York: Science History Publications, 1976), pp. 104–7.

[4] E. P. Hubble, *The Realm of the Nebulae* (New Haven: Yale University Press, 1936),

pp. 102–5. See also E. P. Hubble to V. M. Slipher, April 11, 1930, and March 6, 1953, Lowell Observatory Archives, (LOA).

[5] V. M. Slipher, "The Detection of Nebular Rotation," *Lowell Observatory Bulletin,* no. 62, 2(1914):65.

[6] V. M. Slipher, "Spectrographic Observations of Nebulae," *Publications of the American Astronomical Society,* 3(1914):98(A); *Popular Astronomy,* 23(1915):21–24; "Nebulae," *Proceedings of the American Philosophical Society,* 56(1917):403–10; and "Spectrographic Observations of Star Clusters," *Publications of the American Astronomical Society,* 3(1918):331(A); *Popular Astronomy,* 26(1918):8.

[7] V. M. Slipher, "Peculiar Star Spectra Suggestive of Selective Absorption of Light in Space," *Lowell Observatory Bulletin,* no. 51, 2(1909):1; and "On the Spectrum of the Nebula in the Pleiades," *ibid.,* no. 55, 2(1913):26–27.

[8] V. M. Slipher, "A Spectrographic Investigation of the Rotation Velocity of Venus," *ibid.,* no. 3, 1(1903):9; and "Detection of the Rotation of Uranus," *ibid.,* no. 53, 2(1912):17–20.

[9] V. M. Slipher, "The Spectrum of the Major Planets," *ibid.,* no. 42, 1(1908):231; "The Spectrum of Mars," *Astrophysical Journal,* 28(1908):397; "Spectrographic Studies of the Planets," (George Darwin Lecture), *Monthly Notices of the Royal Astronomical Society,* 93(1933):657–68. See also Bibliography for papers with A. Adel, 1934–1936.

[10] V. M. Slipher and C. O. Lampland, "Preliminary Notes on Photographic and Spectrographic Observations of Halley's Comet," *Lowell Observatory Bulletin,* no. 47, 1(1910):252–54; Slipher, "The Spectrum of Halley's Comet as Observed at the Lowell Observatory," *ibid.,* no. 52, 2(1911):3–16. See also Bibliography for publications on comets in 1914, 1916, 1919, 1927, and 1938.

[11] V. M. Slipher, "Some Spectrographic Results of the Lowell Observatory Eclipse Expedition," *Publications of the American Astronomical Society,* 4(1918):49–50(A); *Popular Astronomy,* 27(1918):148; "The Spectrum of the Corona as Observed by the Expedition from Lowell Observatory of the Total Eclipse of June 8, 1918," *Astrophysical Journal,* 55(1922):73–84.

[12] V. M. Slipher, "A New Type of Nebular Spectrum. I. The Spectrum of Hubble's Variable Nebula NGC 2261. II. The Variable Nebula NGC 6729," *Lowell Observatory Bulletin,* no. 81, 3(1918):63.

[13] V. M. Slipher, "The Spectrum of Lightning," *ibid.,* no. 79, 3(1917):55.

[14] V. M. Slipher, "On the Spectrum of the Eclipsed Moon," *Astronomische Nachrichten,* 199(1914):103.

[15] V. M. Slipher, "Spectral Evidence of a Persistent Aurora," *Lowell Observatory Bulletin,* no. 76, 3(1916):1; "On the General Illumination of the Night Sky and the Wave-length of the Chief Auroral Line," *Astrophysical Journal,* 49(1919):266–75; "Emissions of the Spectrum of the Night Sky," *Publications of the American Astronomical Society,* 6(1931):241–42(A); "Preliminary Note on the Spectrum of the Zodiacal Light," *Lowell Observatory Circular,* Feb. 20, 1931. See also Bibliography for publications on night sky spectra in 1918, 1929, 1930, 1933, 1934, and 1938.

[16] W. G. Hoyt, *Planets 'X' and Pluto* (Tucson: University of Arizona Press, 1980), chaps. 7–12. See also C. W. Tombaugh, "The Discovery of Pluto," *Astronomical Society of the Pacific Leaflet,* no. 209, 1946; and "The Trans-Neptunian Planet Search," in *The Solar System: Planets and Satellites,* ed. G. P. Kuiper and B. Middlehurst (Chicago: University of Chicago Press, 1961), pp. 12–30.

[17] H. Shapley and H. D. Curtis, "The Scale of the Universe," *Bulletin of the National*

Research Council, 2(1921):217. See also O. Struve and V. Zebergs, *Astronomy of the Twentieth Century* (New York: Macmillan, 1962), pp. 416ff. and 441ff., and Berendzen, Hart, and Seeley, *Man Discovers the Galaxies*, pp. 35–47.

[18] Berendzen, Hart, and Seeley, *Man Discovers the Galaxies*, pp. 146–51.

[19] W. G. Hoyt, *Lowell and Mars* (Tucson: University of Arizona Press, 1976), *passim*. For a specific instance, see V. M. Slipher to P. Lowell, May 7, 1913, LOA.

[20] For example, Slipher's announcement of his initial nebular velocities was read to the Atlanta meeting of the American Astronomical Society in 1913 by Philip Fox of Dearborn Observatory in Illinois and "was greeted with some expression of incredulity, especially on the part of Professor [Henry Norris] Russell...." See P. Fox to V. M. Slipher, April 10, 1920, LOA.

[21] See correspondence between V. M. Slipher and H. Shapley, Oct. 31 and Nov. 13, 1917; between Slipher and A. S. Eddington, Nov. 11, 1921, Feb. 5, and March 8, 1922; Slipher to K. Lundmark, March 11, 1924; between Slipher and G. Strömberg, Sept. 30, Oct. 7 and 11, Nov. 29, and Dec. 8, 1924; between Slipher and L. Silberstein, Sept. 8 and 18, 1924; between Slipher and W. S. Adams, May 29 and 31, 1930; and between Slipher and E. P. Hubble, April 11, 1930, and July 22 and Aug. 4, 1932, LOA.

[22] See Slipher, Bibliography, *supra*.

[23] Slipher was not, however, a particularly prolific correspondent. Lick Observatory's Robert G. Aitken once complained: "I have as you know a very high regard for you as a man and as an astronomer, but you have one little failing that makes me want to curse you loud and deep; *you do not answer letters!*" See R. G. Aitken to V. M. Slipher, Sept. 16, 1931, LOA.

[24] J. S. Hall, "Slipher's Trail-blazing Career," "Vesto Slipher"; *Arizona Daily Sun* (Flagstaff), Nov. 9, 1969, p. 1; *ibid.*, Aug. 8, 1964, p. 1; and V. M. Slipher to F. R. Elliott, May 29, 1930, LOA.

[25] W. G. Hoyt, "Historical Note: Astronomy on the San Francisco Peaks," *Plateau*, 47(1975):116.

[26] A. Adel Feb. 1, 1978: personal communication.

[27] See, for example, V. M. Slipher to H. E. Knight, May 9, 1924, LOA; and C. W. Tombaugh, "Reminiscences of the Discovery of Pluto," *Sky and Telescope*, 19(1960):264–70.

[28] P. Lowell to V. M. Slipher, June 4, 1904, LOA: "I trust you have seen to the cow's calving regularly since I went away?" Lowell writes here. "If not, see to her at once please."

[29] Transcript of course work of V. M. Slipher, issued by the Alumni Office, Indiana University, Nov. 18, 1969. See also J. S. Hall, "Slipher's Trail-blazing Career," "Vesto Slipher."

[30] V. M. Slipher to F. R. Elliott, May 29, 1930, LOA.

[31] Miller and Cogshall, along with John C. Duncan of Wellesley College, who was on the Lowell staff in 1905–1906, were the only persons outside the Observatory circle to whom Slipher gave advance notice of Pluto's discovery. See Slipher to J. A. Miller and to W. A. Cogshall, March 8, 1930, and to J. C. Duncan, March 9, 1930, LOA.

[32] W. A. Cogshall to P. Lowell, June 24, 1901, LOA.

[33] P. Lowell to W. A. Cogshall, July 7, 1901, LOA.

[34] J. S. Hall, "Slipher's Trail-blazing Career," "Vesto Slipher"; *Arizona Daily Sun*, Nov. 9, 1969, p. 1.

[35] V. M. Slipher, last will and testament, dated Dec. 17, 1967, and filed for probate Nov. 12, 1969 in Coconino County (Arizona) Superior Court.

[36] Biographical note on V. M. Slipher, prepared Nov. 12, 1966, by K. J. Nicholson (Slipher's son-in-law), LOA.

[37] *Ibid.*

[38] *Ibid.*

[39] P. Lowell to H. S. Pritchett, Sept. 30, 1902, LOA.

[40] P. Lowell to V. M. Slipher, Sept. 17, 1901, LOA.

[41] P. Lowell to V. M. Slipher, Oct. 21 and 28, Nov. 14, and Dec. 18, 1901; and Jan. 4, March 10 and 26, 1902, LOA.

[42] P. Lowell, "Spectrographic Proof of the Rotations of Jupiter, Saturn and Mars," text (dated Dec., 1902) of paper for Washington, D.C. Meeting of the American Association for the Advancement of Science, LOA.

[43] See Bibliography for years 1902–1907.

[44] P. Lowell to V. M. Slipher, Oct. 4, 1902, LOA.

[45] V. M. Slipher, "An Attempt to Apply Velocity-Shift to Detecting Atmospheric Lines in the Spectrum of Mars," *Lowell Observatory Bulletin*, no. 17, 1(1905):118.

[46] H. Spinrad, G. Münch, and L. Kaplan, "Spectrographic Determination of Water Vapor on Mars," *Astrophysics Journal*, 137(1963):1319.

[47] V. M. Slipher, "The Spectrum of Mars," *Astrophysics Journal*, 28(1908):397. See also V. M. Slipher to P. Lowell, Feb. 4 and 20, 1908, and P. Lowell to V. M. Slipher, Feb. 26, 1908, LOA; and F. W. Very, "Measurements of the Intensification of Aqueous Bands in the Spectrum of Mars," *Lowell Observatory Bulletin*, no. 36, 1(1909):207–12.

[48] W. W. Campbell, "Note on the Spectrum of Mars," *The Observatory*, 51(1928): 322; V. M. Slipher, "On the Spectral Proof of Water and Oxygen on Mars," *ibid.*, 53(1930):79–81; and W. W. Campbell to V. M. Slipher, Oct. 5, 1932, LOA.

[49] W. S. Adams and C. St. John, "An Attempt to Detect Water Vapor and Oxygen Lines in the Spectrum of Mars with the Registering Microphotometer," *Publications of the Astronomical Society of the Pacific*, 37(1925):158–59.

[50] A. M. Clarke, *A Popular History of Astronomy During the Nineteenth Century*, 4th ed. (London: Adam and Charles Black, 1902), pp. 250–51.

[51] P. Lowell, "Detection of Venus' Rotation Period and of the Fundamental Physical Features of the Planet," *Popular Astronomy*, 4(1896):281; and "Determination of the Rotation and Surface Character of the Planet Venus," *Monthly Notices of the Royal Astronomical Society*, 57(1897):148.

[52] A. A. Belopolsky, "Ein versuch die Rotationgeschwindigkeit des Venusequators auf spectrographischen Wege zu bestimmen," *Astronomische Nachrichten*, 152(1900): 263–75.

[53] P. Lowell to V. M. Slipher, Nov. 5, 1902, LOA.

[54] P. Lowell to H. S. Pritchett, March 23, 1903, LOA.

[55] V. M. Slipher, "Spectrographic Investigation of the Rotation Velocity of Venus," *Lowell Observatory Bulletin*, no. 3, 1(1903):9; and *Astronomische Nachrichten*, 163(1903):35.

[56] V. M. Slipher, "The Spectrum of Venus," *Lowell Observatory Bulletin*, no. 84,

3(1922):85–89. See also V. M. Slipher to S. B. Nicholson, July 15 and Aug. 10, 1922, LOA.

[57] R. M. Goldstein, "Radar Observations of Venus," *Astrophysical Journal*, 69(1964):12; R. B. Dyce, G. H. Pettingill, and I. I. Shapiro, "Radar Determination of the Rotations of Venus and Mercury," *ibid.*, 72(1967):351; and R. L. Carpenter, "A Radar Determination of the Rotation of Venus," *ibid.*, 75(1970):61.

[58] V. M. Slipher, "The Spectra of the Major Planets," *Lowell Observatory Bulletin*, no. 42, 1(1908):231.

[59] R. Wildt, "Methan in den Atmosphäre der grossen Planeten," *Die Naturwissenschaften*, 20(1932):851; and "Ammoniakgas in der Atmosphäre des Planeten Jupiter," *Forschungen und Fortschritte*, 8(1932):223.

[60] See Bibliography for years 1934–1935 for papers with A. Adel.

[61] V. M. Slipher to W. A. Cogshall, Feb. 25, 1908, and to Guy Lowell, Oct. 4, 1924, LOA. See also G. P. Kuiper, "Planetary Atmospheres and Their Origin," in *The Atmospheres of the Earth and the Planets*, ed. G. Kuiper (Chicago: University of Chicago Press, 1952), p. 399.

[62] V. M. Slipher, "Detection of the Rotation of Uranus," *Lowell Observatory Bulletin*, no. 53, 2(1912):19. See also P. Lowell "Spectroscopic Discovery of the Rotation Period of Uranus," *ibid.*, 2(1912):17–18.

[63] S. H. Hayes and M. J. S. Belton, "The Rotational Period of Uranus and Neptune," paper (no. 133-5) read to the Eighth Meeting of the Division for Planetary Sciences of the American Astronomical Society, Honolulu, Hawaii, Jan. 22, 1977. Hayes' and Belton's result, however, has not yet been confirmed.

[64] V. M. Slipher to P. Lowell, Jan. 3, Feb. 3 and 5, 1913, LOA.

[65] V. M. Slipher to G. Lowell, March 22, and May 5, 1921; and G. Lowell to V. M. Slipher, April 4, 1921, LOA.

[66] P. Lowell to V. M. Slipher, May 23, 1904, LOA.

[67] J. F. Hartmann, "Investigations on the Spectrum and Orbit of δ [delta] Orionis," *Astrophysical Journal*, 19(1904):268–86.

[68] J. C. Kapteyn, "On the Absorption of Light in Space," *Astrophysical Journal*, 29(1909):46–54.

[69] V. M. Slipher, "Peculiar Star Spectra Suggestive of Selective Absorption of Light in Space." See also P. Lowell to J. C. Kapteyn, Oct. 1, 1909, LOA.

[70] J. Hartmann to V. M. Slipher, March 6, 1910; J. C. Kapteyn to V. M. Slipher, Oct. 20, 1909; E. Hertzsprung to V. M. Slipher, April 16, 1911; and correspondence between E. B. Frost and V. M. Slipher between Oct. 18, 1908 and Jan. 25, 1910, LOA.

[71] H. Shapley, *The View From a Distant Star* (New York: Basic Books, 1963), pp. 5–6, 21. See also Berendzen, Hart, and Seeley, *Man Discovers the Galaxies*, p. 76.

[72] J. S. Plaskett and J. A. Pearce, "The Problems of Diffuse Matter in the Galaxy," *Publications of the Dominion Astrophysical Observatory*, 5(1933):169; and A. S. Eddington, "Diffuse Matter in Interstellar Space," *Proceedings of the Royal Society of London*, Series A, 3(1926):424.

[73] Quoted in F. J. M. Stratton, "President's Speech on Presenting Gold Medal," *Monthly Notices of the Royal Astronomical Society*, 93(1933):476–77.

[74] V. M. Slipher, "On the Spectrum of the Nebula in the Pleiades."

[75] V. M. Slipher, "On the Spectrum of the Nebula About Rho Ophiuchi," *Lowell Observatory Bulletin*, no 75, 2(1916):155–56.

[76] V. M. Slipher, "Spectra of the Pleiades, Scorpio and Cygnus Nebulosities," *Publications of the American Astronomical Society*, 9(1938):168-69.

[77] V. M. Slipher to P. Lowell, Dec. 16 and 17, 1912; and to J. C. Duncan, Dec. 29, 1912, LOA.

[78] P. Lowell to V. M. Slipher, Jan. 29, and Feb. 8, 1909, LOA.

[79] V. M. Slipher to P. Lowell, Feb. 26, 1909, LOA.

[80] Hoyt, *Planets 'X' and Pluto*, chap. 5.

[81] See, for examples, V. M. Slipher correspondence with E. A. Fath between Nov. 11, 1910 and Jan. 18, 1913; with E. B. Frost between Aug. 12, 1909 and Oct. 23, 1913; and with J. M. Schaeberle, Aug. 3 and 23, 1911, LOA.

[82] V. M. Slipher to E. A. Fath, Dec. 5, 1910, LOA.

[83] V. M. Slipher to P. Lowell, Nov. 9, 1910, LOA.

[84] V. M. Slipher to P. Lowell, Dec. 3, 1910, LOA.

[85] V. M. Slipher to W. W. Campbell, undated, LOA.

[86] V. M. Slipher, "The Radial Velocity of the Andromeda Nebula." See also V. M. Slipher to F. W. Very, Sept. 20, 1912, LOA.

[87] W. W. Campbell to V. M. Slipher, June 6, 1911, LOA.

[88] V. M. Slipher to P. Lowell, Oct. 2, 1912, LOA.

[89] V. M. Slipher to P. Lowell, Dec. 19, 1912, LOA.

[90] V. M. Slipher to P. Lowell, Dec. 28, 1912, LOA.

[91] V. M. Slipher, "The Radial Velocity of the Andromeda Nebula."

[92] V. M. Slipher to P. Lowell, Jan. 2, 1913, LOA.

[93] V. M. Slipher to E. A. Fath, Jan. 18, 1913, LOA.

[94] V. M. Slipher to P. Lowell, Feb. 3, 1913, LOA.

[95] P. Lowell to V. M. Slipher, Feb. 8, 1913, LOA.

[96] V. M. Slipher, "Spectrographic Observations of Nebulae."

[97] V. M. Slipher to P. Lowell, April 12, 1913; and to J. A. Miller, May 16, 1913, LOA.

[98] V. M. Slipher, "Spectrographic Observations of Nebulae." See also text of paper read at the Seventeenth (Evanston) Meeting, American Astronomical Society, Aug. 14, 1914, LOA. It is interesting to note that Edwin P. Hubble, then a young astronomer at Yerkes Observatory, attended this meeting, was elected to membership, and heard Slipher deliver the paper.

[99] *Ibid.*

[100] V. M. Slipher, "Nebulae."

[101] V. M. Slipher to P. Lowell, cablegram, May 25, 1914, LOA. See also, V. M. Slipher, "The Detection of Nebular Rotation."

[102] V. M. Slipher, "The Spectrum and Velocity of the Nebula NGC 1068," *Lowell Observatory Bulletin*, no. 80, 3(1917):59.

[103] Shapley and Curtis, "The Scale of the Universe." See also Hubble, *The Realm of the Nebulae*, p. 85; Struve and Zebergs, *Astronomy of the Twentieth Century*, p. 439; and Berendzen, Hart, and Seeley, *Man Discovers the Galaxies*, pp. 108–131.

[104] V. M. Slipher to A. C. Gifford, Oct. 10, 1924, LOA. Slipher learned of van Maanen's conflicting result even before it was published; see J. C. Duncan to V. M. Slipher, July 14, 1916, LOA.

[105] E. P. Hubble, "Angular Rotations of Spiral Nebulae," *Astrophysical Journal*, 81(1935):334–35; and A. van Maanen, "Internal Motions in Spiral Nebulae," *ibid.*, 81(1935):336–37.

[106] V. M. Slipher, "Nebulae."
[107] E. P. Hubble, "The Direction of Rotation in Spiral Nebulae," *Astrophysical Journal*, 97(1943):112–18; V. M. Slipher, "The Direction of Rotation in Spiral Nebulae," *Science*, 99(1944):144–45. See also Berendzen, Hart, and Seeley, *Man Discovers the Galaxies*, pp. 151–52.
[108] V. M. Slipher, "Spectrographic Observations of Nebulae."
[109] V. M. Slipher to F. W. Very, Jan. 12, 1917, LOA.
[110] J. S. Hall, *op. cit.*
[111] V. M. Slipher to J. C. Duncan, Dec. 29, 1912, LOA.
[112] V. M. Slipher to E. Hertzsprung, May 8, 1914, LOA.
[113] V. M. Slipher to J. C. Duncan, Feb. 7, 1913; and J. C. Duncan to V. M. Slipher, Feb. 11 and 17, 1913, LOA.
[114] V. M. Slipher, "Spectrographic Observations of Nebulae"; and "Nebulae." See also V. M. Slipher to P. Lowell, May 16, 1913; and to E. B. Frost, Nov. 4, 1913, LOA.
[115] P. Lowell, "Nebular Motion," text (dated Nov. 23, 1915) of lecture for Melrose Club, Boston, LOA. See also E. Hertzsprung to V. M. Slipher, March 14, 1914, LOA.
[116] V. M. Slipher, "Nebulae."
[117] *Ibid.* See also W. W. Campbell to V. M. Slipher, March 30, 1914; M. Wolf to V. M. Slipher, June 13, 1914; and F. G. Pease to V. M. Slipher, July 13, 1916, LOA.
[118] V. M. Slipher, "Two Nebulae with Unparalleled Velocities," *Lowell Observatory Circular*, Jan. 17, 1921; *Astronomische Nachrichten*, 213(1921):391–93. Re election to National Academy, see W. S. Adams to V. M. Slipher, June 14, 1921, LOA.
[119] See correspondence between V. M. Slipher and A. S. Eddington, Nov. 5, 1921, Feb. 2, and March 8, 1922, LOA.
[120] E. P. Hubble to V. M. Slipher, March 6, 1953, LOA.
[121] Hubble, *The Realm of the Nebulae*, pp. 102–5, 113–15.
[122] V. M. Slipher to J. C. Duncan, Feb. 7, 1913, LOA.
[123] "Aurora," *Lowell Observatory Circular*, March 15, 1916.
[124] V. M. Slipher, "Spectral Evidence of a Persistent Aurora," *Lowell Observatory Bulletin*, no. 76, 3(1916):1.
[125] V. M. Slipher, "On the General Illumination of the Night Sky and the Wavelength of the Chief Auroral Line." See also correspondence between V. M. Slipher and W. W. Campbell, Aug. 17, 20, 27, 31, and Sept. 21, 1917, LOA.
[126] V. M. Slipher, "Emissions of the Spectrum of the Night Sky." See also V. M. Slipher to W. W. Campbell, Jan. 28, 1929, LOA.
[127] V. M. Slipher, "Preliminary Note on the Spectrum of the Zodiacal Light." See also V. M. Slipher to F. R. Moulton, Feb. 9, and 16, 1931; and E. A. Fath to V. M. Slipher, April 24, 1931, LOA.
[128] See correspondence between V. M. Slipher and T. C. Poulter from June 6, 1932 to Sept. 28, 1933, LOA.
[129] V. M. Slipher to D. Menzel, May 6, 1940, LOA.
[130] V. M. Slipher to J. W. Miles, May 18, 1922, LOA.
[131] W. W. Campbell to V. M. Slipher, Jan. 9, 1929; and V.M. Slipher to W. W. Campbell, Jan. 29, 1929; LOA.
[132] V.M. Slipher, "The Lowell Observatory Eclipse Expedition," *Popular Astronomy*, 30(1918):346–47; and V. M. Slipher to J. A. Miller and C. Lowell, Feb. 14, 1923; D. Roberts to V. M. Slipher, July 17, 1923; V. M. Slipher to D. Roberts, July 25, 1923;

and W. W. Campbell to V. M. Slipher, July 16, 1923, LOA.

[133] V. M. Slipher to C. Lowell, Jan. 18, 1919; and to E. A. Fath, March 19, 1921, LOA. See also N. U. Mayall, "The Story of the Crab Nebula," *Science*, 137(1962):91–102.

[134] V. M. Slipher to P. Lowell, Jan. 23, 25, and 26, 1915; to J. A. Miller, Dec. 10, 1915, Jan. 9, Feb. 3 and 23, and March 2, 1916; to F. R. Moulton, Feb. 9, 1916; and J. H. Moore to V. M. Slipher, March 1, 1915, LOA. See also R. Sanford, "The Spectrum of the Crab Nebula," *Publications of the Astronomical Society of the Pacific*, 31(1919): 108–9.

[135] V. M. Slipher, "A New Type of Nebular Spectrum."

[136] V. M. Slipher to E. W. Scott, April 28, 1924, LOA.

[137] V. M. Slipher to H. Wetherald, March 9, 1926, LOA.

[138] V. M. Slipher to F. O. Grover, Jan. 23, 1923, LOA.

[139] F. J. M. Stratton, "President's Speech."

[140] V. M. Slipher, text, response to citation and award of Henry Draper Medal of National Academy of Sciences, April 25, 1933, LOA.

HONORS AND DISTINCTIONS

MEDALS AND AWARDS

Lalande Prize, Académie des Sciences de Paris, 1919
Henry Draper Medal, National Academy of Sciences, 1933
Gold Medal, Royal Astronomical Society, 1933
Bruce Medal, Astronomical Society of the Pacific, 1935

HONORARY DEGREES

The University of Arizona, 1923, Sc.D.
Indiana University, 1930, LL.D.
The University of Toronto, 1935, Sc.D.
Northern Arizona University, 1957, Sc.D.

AMERICAN MEMBERSHIPS

American Academy of Arts and Sciences (Fellow)
American Association for the Advancement of Science (Fellow)
American Astronomical Society
American Philosophical Society
Astronomical Society of the Pacific
National Academy of Sciences
Phi Beta Kappa
Sigma Xi

FOREIGN MEMBERSHIPS

International Astronomical Union
Royal Astronomical Society (Associate)
Société Astronomique de France

BIBLIOGRAPHY

1902

On the variable velocity of ζ [zeta] Herculis in the line of sight. Astron. J., 22:190.

Spectrograms of Jupiter. Pop. Astron., 11:1–4.

The spectroscopic binary β [beta] Scorpii. Lowell Observ. Bull., 1(1):4.

A spectrographic investigation of the rotation velocity of Venus. Lowell Observ. Bull., 1(3):9–18. Also in: Astron. Nachr., 163:35–51.

Of the efficiency of the spectrograph for investigating planetary rotations and on the accuracy of the inclination method of measurement. Tests on the rotation of the planet Mars. Lowell Observ. Bull., 1(4):19–23.

Variable velocity of λ [lambda] Scorpii in the line of sight. Lowell Observ. Bull., 1(4):23.

With C. O. Lampland. Notes on visual experiment. Lowell Observ. Bull., 1(10):53–55.

1904

The Lowell spectrograph. Astrophys. J., 20:1–20.

A list of five stars having variable radial velocities. Lowell Observ. Bull., 1(11):57–58. Also in: Astrophys. J., 20:146–48.

On the spectra of Neptune and Uranus. Lowell Observ. Bull., 1(13):87–90. Also in: Bull. Soc. Astron. Fr., 19(1905):284–88.

1905

A photographic study of the spectrum of Jupiter. Lowell Observ. Bull., 1(16):111–15.

An attempt to apply velocity-shift to detecting atmospheric lines in the spectrum of Mars. Lowell Observ. Bull., 1(17):113.

The variable velocity of γ [gamma] Geminorum. Astrophys. J., 22:84–86.

Observations of standard velocity stars with the Lowell spectrograph. Lowell Observ. Bull., 1(23):139–56. Also in: Astrophys. J., 22:318–40.

1906

A photographic study of the spectrum of Saturn. Lowell Observ. Bull., 1(27):173–75. Also in: Astrophys. J., 26:59–62.

Variable radial velocity of δ [delta] Capricorni. Astrophys. J., 24:361.

Preliminary note on the spectrum of o [omicron] Ceti (Mira). Astrophys. J., 25:66–67.

1907

Variable velocity of U Cephei. Astrophys. J., 25:284.

The spectrum of ε [epsilon] Capricorni. Astrophys. J., 25:285.

1908

The spectra of the major planets. Lowell Observ. Bull., 1(42):231–38.

The spectrum of Mars. Astrophys. J., 28:397–404.

1909

Peculiar star spectra suggestive of selective absorption of light in space. Lowell Observ. Bull., 2(51):1–2. Also in: Astron. Nachr., 189:6–7.

1910

With C. O. Lampland. Preliminary notes on photographic and spectrographic observations of Halley's Comet. Lowell Observ. Bull., 1(47):252–54.

1911

The spectrum of Halley's Comet as observed at Lowell Observatory. Lowell Observ. Bull., 2(52):3–16.

1912

Detection of the rotation of Uranus. Lowell Observ. Bull., 2(53):17–20.

1913

On the spectrum of the nebula in the Pleiades. Lowell Observ. Bull., 2(55):26–27.

The radial velocity of the Andromeda nebula. Lowell Observ. Bull., 2(58):56–57. Also in: Pop. Astron., 22:19–21.

Spectrographic observations of nebulae (abstract of paper read at the Sixteenth AAS [Atlanta] Meeting). Publ. Am. Astron. Soc., 3:18. Also in: Pop. Astron., 22:146.

1914

The detection of nebular rotation. Lowell Observ. Bull., 2(62):66.

On the spectrum of the eclipsed moon. Astron. Nachr., 199:103.

The spectrum of comet b 1914 (Zlatinsky). Lowell Observ. Bull., 2(63):67–68.

The discovery of nebular rotation. Sci. Am., 110:501.

Spectrographic observations of nebulae (abstract of paper read at the Seventeenth AAS [Evanston] Meeting). Publ. Am. Astron. Soc., 3:98–100. Also in: Pop. Astron., 23(1915):21–24.

1916

The spectrum of comet a 1915 (Mellish). Lowell Observ. Bull., 2(74):151–53.

Aurora. Lowell Observ. Circ., March 15.

On the spectrum of the nebula about Rho Ophiuchi. Lowell Observ. Bull., 2(75):155–56. Also in: Pop. Astron., 24:542–53.

Spectrographic observations of Barnard's high proper motion star. Lowell Observ. Bull., 2(75):157.

Spectrographic observations of nebulae and star clusters. Publ. Astron. Soc. Pac., 28:191–92(A).

Spectrographic observations of nebulae and star clusters (abstract of paper read at the Nineteenth AAS [Swarthmore] Meeting). Publ. Am. Astron. Soc., 3:223. Also in: Pop. Astron., 25(1917):36–37.

Spectral evidence of a persistent aurora. Lowell Observ. Bull., 3(76):1. Also in: Publ. Am. Astron. Soc., 3:224; Pop. Astron., 25(1917):37.

1917

Nebulae. Proc. Am. Philos. Soc., 56:403–10.

The spectrum of lightning. Lowell Observ. Bull., 3(79):55–58.

With C. O. Lampland. The nebula NGC 2261. Lowell Observ. Circ., January 29. Also in: Pop. Astron., 25:213–14.

The spectrum of Wolf's Comet. Publ. Astron. Soc. Pac., 29:208.
Radial velocity observations of spiral nebulae. Observatory, 40:304–6.
The spectrum and velocity of the nebula NGC 1068. Lowell Observ. Bull., 3(80):59–62.

1918

Spectrographic observations of star clusters (abstract of paper read at the Twenty-first AAS [Albany] Meeting). Publ. Am. Astron. Soc., 3:331–32. Also in: Pop. Astron., 26:8.
Observations of the aurora spectrum (abstract of paper read at the Twenty-first AAS [Albany] Meeting). Publ. Am. Astron. Soc., 3:331. Also in: Pop. Astron., 26:8.
A new type of nebular spectrum. I. The spectrum of Hubble's variable nebula NGC 2261. II. The variable nebula NGC 6729. Lowell Observ. Bull., 3(81):63–67.
The spectrum of NGC 7023. Publ. Astron. Soc. Pac., 30:63–64.
The Lowell Observatory eclipse expedition. Pop. Astron., 26:462–66.
Unusual nebular spectra. Publ. Astron. Soc. Pac., 30:346–47.

1919

Some spectrographic results of the Lowell Observatory eclipse expedition (abstract of paper read at the Twenty-second AAS [Boston] Meeting). Publ. Am. Astron. Soc., 4:49–50. Also in: Pop. Astron., 27:148–49.
On the spectra of two variable nebulae: A new type of nebular spectrum (abstract of paper read at the Twenty-second AAS [Boston] Meeting). Publ. Am. Astron. Soc., 4:50–51. Also in: Pop. Astron., 27:149–50.
On the spectrum of the Orion nebulosities. Publ. Astron. Soc. Pac., 31:212–15.
The spectrum of comet b 1919 (Brorsen-Metcalf). Publ. Astron. Soc. Pac., 31:3–304.
The spectrum of the Milky Way (abstract of paper read at the Twenty-third AAS [Ann Arbor] Meeting). Publ. Am. Astron. Soc., 4:114–15. Also in: Pop. Astron., 27:676.
On the general illumination of the night sky and the wave-length of the chief auroral line. Astrophys. J., 49:266–75.

1920

On spectrographic methods for measuring diurnal rotation of planets. Observatory, 43:391–93.

1921

Two nebulae with unparalleled velocities. Lowell Observ. Circ., Jan. 17. Also in: Astron. Nachr., 213:47.
Dreyer nebula no. 584 inconceivably distant. The New York Times, Jan. 19.
Spectrographic observations of the rotation of spiral nebulae (abstract of paper read at the Twenty-fifth AAS [Chicago] Meeting). Publ. Am. Astron. Soc., 4:232–33. Also in: Pop. Astron., 29:272–73.

1922

The spectrum of the corona as observed by the expedition from the Lowell Observatory of the total eclipse of June 8, 1918. Astrophys. J., 55:73–84.
The spectrum of Venus. Lowell Observ. Bull., 3(84):85–89.
Further notes on spectrographic observations of nebulae and clusters (abstract of paper read at the Twenty-sixth AAS [Middletown] Meeting). Publ. Am. Astron. Soc., 4:284–85. Also in: Pop. Astron., 30:9–11.

1924

Spectrum observations of Mars. Publ. Astron. Soc. Pac., 36:261–62.
The radial velocity of additional globular star clusters (abstract of paper read at the Thirty-second AAS [Dartmouth] Meeting). Publ. Am. Astron. Soc., 5:192–93. Also in: Pop. Astron., 32:622–23.

1927

The Lowell Observatory. Publ. Astron. Soc. Pac., 39:143–54.
The spectrum of the Pons-Winneke Comet and the size of the cometary nucleus. Lowell Observ. Bull., 3(86):135–37.
With E. C. Slipher. Daylight observations of Skjellerup's Comet at the Lowell Observatory (abstract of paper read at the Thirty-ninth AAS [New Haven] Meeting). Publ. Am. Astron. Soc., 6:122–23.

1929

With L. A. Sommer. Zur Deutung des Nordlichtspektrums. Naturwissenschaften, 17:801–2.

1930

With L. A. Sommer. On the interpretation of the aurora spectrum (abstract of paper read at the Forty-second AAS [Ottawa] Meeting). Publ. Am. Astron. Soc., 6:280–81. Also in: Pop. Astron., 38:94.

The discovery of a solar system body apparently trans-Neptunian. Lowell Observ. Circ., March 13.

Untitled (reporting a preliminary orbit and proposing the name Pluto for the trans-Neptunian object). Lowell Observ. Circ., May 1.

On the spectral proof of water and oxygen on Mars. Observatory, 53:79–81.

1931

Preliminary note on the spectrum of the zodiacal light. Lowell Observ. Circ., February 20.

Emission of the spectrum of the night sky (abstract of paper read at the Forty-first AAS [New York City] Meeting). Publ. Am. Astron. Soc., 6:241–42.

Simple direct means of getting rapidly rough color indices of stars (abstract of paper read at the Forty-fifth AAS [New Haven] Meeting). Publ. Am. Astron. Soc., 7:15.

1932

With R. L. Putnam. Searching out Pluto—Lowell's trans-Neptunian planet X. Sci. Mon., 34:5–21.

1933

Spectrographic studies of the planets (George Darwin Lecture). Mon. Not. R. Astron. Soc., 93:657–68.

Spectra of the night sky, the zodiacal light, the aurora, and the cosmic radiations of the sky. J. R. Astron. Soc. Can., 27:365–69.

Planet studies at the Lowell Observatory. Nature, 133:10–13.

1934

With A. Adel. The atmospheres of the giant planets. Nature, 134:148–49.

With A. Adel. Concerning the carbon dioxide content of the atmosphere of the planet Venus. Phys. Rev., 46:240.

With A. Adel. On the identification of the methane bands in the solar spectra and of the major planets. Phys. Rev., 46:240–41.

Additional observations of the spectrum of the night sky (abstract of paper read at the Fifty-first AAS [Cambridge] Meeting). Publ. Am. Astron. Soc., 8:23–24.

1935

With A. Adel and E. Barker. The absorption of sunlight by the earth's atmosphere in the remote infrared region of the spectrum. Phys. Rev., 47:580–84.

With A. Adel. Difference bands in the spectrum of the major planets. Phys. Rev., 47:651–53.

With A. Adel. The methane content of the giant planet atmospheres. Phys. Rev., 47:787–88.

1936

Nova Herculis (abstract of paper read at the Fifty-third AAS [Philadelphia] Meeting). Publ. Am. Astron. Soc., 8:123.

With A. Adel. Fraunhofer's spectrum in the interval from 7700 and 11000 Å. Astrophys. J., 84:354–58.

With A. M. Rogers. The detection of stars of high color index with the Lawrence Lowell telescope (abstract of paper read at the Fifty-sixth AAS [Cambridge] Meeting). Publ. Am. Astron. Soc., 8:255.

1937

With A. Adel and R. Ladenburg. The sodium content of the head of the great daylight comet Skjellerup 1927k. Astrophys. J., 86:345–62.

1938

With A. Adel and R. Ladenburg. Remarks on the paper "The sodium content of the head of the great daylight comet Skjellerup 1927k." Astrophys. J., 88:207–8.

The trans-Neptunian planet search. Proc. Am. Philos. Soc., 79:435–40.

Spectra of the Pleiades, Scorpio and Cygnus nebulosities (abstract of paper read at the Sixtieth AAS [Ann Arbor] Meeting). Publ. Am. Astron. Soc., 9:168–69.

The night sky and twilight auroral radiation (abstract of paper read at the Sixtieth AAS [Ann Arbor] Meeting). Publ. Am. Astron. Soc., 9:169–70.

Dark bands in comet spectra (abstract of paper read at the Sixtieth AAS [Ann Arbor] Meeting). Publ. Am. Astron. Soc., 9:176.

The spectra of faint extended nebulae from Cepheus to Orion (abstract of paper read at the Sixty-first AAS [New York City] Meeting). Publ. Am. Astron. Soc., 9:229.

1939

The spectra of faint extended nebulae (abstract of paper read at the Sixty-second AAS [Berkeley] Meeting). Publ. Am. Astron. Soc., 9:251–52.

The spectrum of the variable nebula NGC 2261. Publ. Astron. Soc. Pac., 51:115–16.

1942

The surfaces of the major planets. Pop. Astron., 50:142–43.

1944

The direction of rotation in spiral nebulae. Science, 99:144–45.

Wilson S. Stone

WILSON STUART STONE
October 6, 1907–February 28, 1968

BY JAMES F. CROW

WILSON STUART STONE was born October 6, 1907 in Junction, Texas, and died February 28, 1968 in Austin. He was elected to the National Academy of Sciences in 1960.

Except for the years from 1942 to 1945, when he served in the U.S. Army Air Force, he spent his entire life in Texas. His academic career was at the University of Texas. His death, unexpected and coming after a very short illness, occurred as he was in the midst of one of the most active phases of his academic and research career.

EDUCATION AND MENTORS

Wilson Stone attended Brackenridge High School in San Antonio from 1921 to 1924. His family wanted him to be a preacher, and in this tradition he attended Baylor University, an institution with Baptist ties. After one year, however, he transferred to the University of Texas, receiving his B.A. in 1931. He received the master's degree in 1932 and the Ph.D. in 1935, both from the University of Texas. Immediately after graduation he joined the faculty, becoming an associate professor in 1936 and a professor in 1945.

His undergraduate career was initially undistinguished, and he had a mediocre academic record. This changed abruptly under the influence of H. J. Muller. In genetics,

Stone discovered a consuming interest; Muller discovered in Stone a keen, analytical mind. It is greatly to Muller's credit that he looked through Stone's weak background and poor academic record to recognize his intellectual power and creativity.

Prior to this time, J. T. Patterson, who was to be Stone's major professor, had spent summers at Woods Hole, Massachusetts, where he became acquainted with T. H. Morgan and his students. Although Patterson was working in embryology at the time, he acquired an increasing interest in genetics and brought some of Morgan's *Drosophila* cultures to the University of Texas. Soon after, he also brought H. J. Muller and arranged for him to have an X-ray machine. This led to the discovery of radiation-induced mutation in 1926, for which Muller received the Nobel Prize twenty years later.

Stone became Muller's assistant and helped with the *Drosophila* stocks. While still an undergraduate, he coauthored with Muller a paper on X-chromosome translocations. This shows how soon Stone became a productive researcher after entering genetics; it also shows Muller's high esteem for him.

Muller left Texas in the summer of 1932, the year Stone received his master's degree. Stone's Ph.D. thesis, begun under Muller's tutelage, was continued with Patterson. It was the beginning of an unusually rich collaboration that continued throughout the remainder of Patterson's active career.

It was while Stone was a graduate student that T. S. Painter discovered the giant salivary gland chromosomes in *Drosophila melanogaster*. The combination of producing chromosome rearrangements by radiation and analyzing these by salivary gland cytology became a powerful, and now standard, research technique. Stone played a crucial role at the very beginning by suggesting to Painter that one way of being sure that these giant objects in the salivary glands were indeed chromosomes was to show that cells from strains known by genetic analysis to have X-ray induced chromosome abnormalities also have visible structural changes. Stone had joined Muller, Patterson, and Painter in the great Texas school of *Drosophila* cytogenetics.

SCIENTIFIC WORK

Stone's thesis, as mentioned before, was based on a problem originally instigated by Muller, but carried on with Patterson. In this paper, he showed that when the X-chromosome is broken and the originally distal part is brought closer to the centromere, the amount of crossing-over is greatly reduced. On the other hand, the remainder of the X, which has had its tip removed but is unchanged as regards the centromere, has crossing-over that is nearly normal. He also demonstrated that flies survive despite a large degree of chromosomal unbalance for the X-chromosome. He did this by combining normal and rearranged chromosomes in such a way that identifiable chromosome regions were present too few or too many times.

Patterson and Stone, along with several of their students, then undertook a systematic study of translocations. The object was to understand the effects of aneuploidy on viability and fertility, to learn the effects of rearrangement on crossing-over and disjunction, and to search for a possible female sex-determining gene on the X-chromosome. The original paper in this series, written by Patterson, Stone, Bedichek, and Suche in 1934, is a classic; it is still studied and quoted.

At this time Patterson was especially interested in following an earlier idea of Muller's that one could use judicious combinations of broken X-chromosomes to locate the element that makes the X-chromosome the female determiner. Stone joined him in this effort and they devised a procedure for combining two different translocations between the X and the tiny fourth chromosome, broken at different places on the X, in such a way that the fly had the equivalent of one complete X-chromosome plus a fragment. If a major sex-determining gene was in the fragment, the fly should be female, otherwise it would be male. After a series of frustrating attempts (one duplicated region persistently killed the fly too early to determine its sex), the question was finally answered by others: no single region is responsible, so sex-determination must be polygenic.

During this period Stone also studied the variegated patterns that accompany rearrangements involving heterochromatin, the production of gynandromorphs by irradiating the parents, the effect of chiasma formation in reducing non-disjunction in rearranged chromosomes, and the viability and fertility reduction caused by aneuploidy.

In 1938 Patterson's interest, guided by Stone's repeated suggestions, turned to the study of *Drosophila* evolution. Together they began a systematic study of wild *Drosophila* species. One of the early studies, which has become a model, was the combination of data on geographical distribution with genetic and cytological analysis to work out the phylogeny and speciation mechanisms of the *virilis* group of *Drosophila*. A series of papers by Patterson and Stone, characteristically done in cooperation with a succession of graduate students, reported experiments on speciation, isolating mechanisms, and phylogeny for one *Drosophila* group after another. The culmination of this was Stone's only book, *Evolution in the Genus Drosophila,* coauthored with Patterson. However, he and Patterson edited a series of collected research papers published by the University of Texas.

Upon his return from military service in World War II, Stone devoted part of his time to collaborative experiments in bacterial mutagenesis. Along with Felix Haas and Orville

Wyss, he made the startling discovery that mutations could be induced by irradiating the culture medium *before* the bacteria were grown in it. This finding came almost immediately after the first realization that chemicals could be mutagenic. Subsequent analysis showed the effect to be most likely accounted for by peroxides and other chemicals induced by the radiation, which were acting as chemical mutagens. This work was followed by a series of studies with oxidants, antioxidants, sulfhydryl groups, and cyanide on mutation and repair mechanisms.

This never was a main issue with Stone, however, and he soon returned to evolutionary problems in various *Drosophila* species. In addition to writing the book with Patterson and continuing the pattern of genetic and cytological analysis of related Texas species, by then so well established, he branched out in three new directions.

One of these was a study of *Drosophila* from the Pacific Islands that had been the site of bomb testing. Cooperating as usual with colleagues and students, he was able to find the expected genetic variability induced by the radiation. Most of this was in the form of hidden recessive lethal mutations whose presence was revealed by inbreeding.

The second line of work grew out of his realization that the Hawaiian Islands had a particularly rich and diversified population of *Drosophila* species, many of them indigenous. The island structure offered an especially good chance to study species in the making. Stone was a leader, not only in the actual research, but in arranging for the organization, logistics, and funding of the cooperative program between Texas and Hawaii. His last paper, published posthumously, is a review of this work.

The third area of inquiry issued from his early realization that isozyme differences detected by gel electrophoresis provided a particularly sensitive indicator of variability in natural populations. Largely through Stone's initiative, the University of Texas acquired a number of people who were ready to exploit this field. Texas became a leader in experimental population genetics, thanks to his guidance.

It was while he was most active in these last two areas that his death occurred. It is indicative of his deep involvement that several papers on Hawaiian Drosophilidae and on isozyme variants have been published since his death—papers that had been in various stages of completion and were finished by his co-workers.

In the period before World War II, Stone was known outside the Texas laboratory mainly as a member of the great research group that included Muller, Painter, and Patterson. After Muller's departure for Russia in 1932, Stone became increasingly the intellectual leader of the group. As a graduate student there from 1937 to 1941, I quickly learned that the person with the deepest insights and most imaginative suggestions was Stone. After his return from military duties, he became recognized throughout the world of genetics as the force behind the Texas program. Over a period of years, he grew in influence from first being Muller's assistant; then the collaborator with Muller, Painter, and Patterson; then the man behind the scenes who was providing most of the ideas; and eventually the recognized leader.

Stone was an author of about sixty major articles and some twenty abstracts of papers presented at meetings, usually of the Genetics Society of America.

In summary, his work is not distinguished by one or two major discoveries, but rather by consistent production of high-quality work. Most of all it shows the evidence of his enormously fruitful collaboration with Patterson. It also demonstrates, time after time, his close working relationship with students.

SERVICE TO THE UNIVERSITY OF TEXAS AND TO THE NATION

Before he left for military service, Stone took little interest in administrative questions. He was mainly the idea man for the Patterson-Stone program, content to remain behind the scene while Patterson handled all the administrative details.

This changed abruptly on his return. Although he had little liking for administrative problems, it soon became apparent to him and to his colleagues that continued excellence of the Texas genetics program depended on his leadership. In 1952, largely through his own efforts and with the active cooperation of C. P. Oliver, then chairman of the Zoology Department, the Genetics Foundation was formed. Stone was its director from 1952 until his death. The Foundation provided the necessary organization for a coherent program of research and graduate teaching and a mechanism for soliciting and channeling funds. He was chairman of the Zoology Department from 1959 to 1963. In 1964 he became advisor to the Chancellor for Graduate and Research Programs. The next year he was Vice-Chancellor for Graduate Affairs, and a year later he became Vice-Chancellor of the University of Texas. He was largely responsible for obtaining the funds for a biology research building, named after J. T. Patterson and dedicated in 1969. In 1966 he relinquished his administrative duties and returned to his first love, research. He had planned to teach an undergraduate course, but death intervened.

Nationally, he served in many ways. He spent three years as first lieutenant and captain in the Army Air Force during World War II. He was active in the Genetics Society and the Society of Naturalists, and was secretary of the latter from

1947 to 1949. He served as a member of the first Genetics Study Section (1958–1962), Cell Biology Fellowship Section (1963–1964), and National Advisory Research Resources Council (1964–1968)—all for the National Institutes of Health. He was a consultant on genetics for the Atomic Energy Commission from 1955 to 1957. He was coeditor, with C. P. Oliver, of *Genetics* from 1956 to 1962. He also served on many state and local committees.

While doing all this administrative and committee work, he continued his research and teaching. Twenty-four students received the Ph.D. with Stone as their major professor. To this number should be added four who were working toward the doctorate under his direction at the time of his death and several others (including myself) who were officially students of Patterson, but who were influenced at least as much by Stone, and were the beneficiaries of their complementary abilities and friendly cooperation.

I don't think Stone liked administrative work. He found it hard. But he did it conscientiously and very successfully, and he did it because he thought that it needed to be done. Texas science, and genetics in particular, flourished during the time of his leadership.

WILSON STONE, THE MAN

The aspect of Stone's personality that first impressed me as a graduate student was his sharp intellect. I recall vividly his way of thinking through complex *Drosophila* breeding experiments without the pencil and paper on which others are so dependent. He simply sat back in his chair and thought it out, seemingly without effort.

He was absolutely honest and completely unaffected. He had no guile, nor pretense. He had almost no interest in small talk, although he loved to converse about politics, music, or any of his many other interests—including, of course, evolution and genetics. He enjoyed concocting evolutionary-selectionist explanations for any biological fact that came up in conversation, and for the quirks of human behavior. He never thought any of these worth publishing, although others would have.

As a classroom teacher, he did everything wrong by the ordinary standards. He spoke in a barely audible monotone; he paced back and forth in front of the class with an ameboid flowing motion; he looked out the window; he filled the blackboard with endless rows of numbers; and he didn't introduce the subject, nor summarize it. But it was somehow thrilling! For me, it was my first contact with a really first-class analytical mind. The class was pure intellectual excitement; it didn't require any trappings.

Another trait was his unselfishness and lack of desire for personal aggrandizement. He was intensely loyal to his colleagues and to his institution. He managed somehow to take his work seriously without taking himself seriously. He worked best as part of a team, at first with Patterson, later with others. But in every case, he furnished ideas.

Stone's quiet, almost shy manner kept him from making quick, superficial friendships. Yet, he took a genuine personal interest in his students. He had a deep love of music and those who shared his pleasure in listening to records were taken regularly to his home for an evening of his favorites. In the late 1930's these included Rimsky-Korsakov, Prokofieff, Shostakovich, Debussy, and Dohnanyi.

Wilson Stone was married to the former Jean Lampman, who also had been an assistant to H. J. Muller. She had an unusually quick, sharp, retentive, and inquisitive mind. She also had a strong, often consuming interest in political and social problems, which she shared with her husband and which she still retains. There were three children: Charles Stuart, Laurie Jean, and Michael. The great tragedy of

Stone's life was the death of his younger son, Michael, as a young boy in a vacation accident. The father and son were very close, and Michael's death had a deep effect on his father, one that was noticeable to close friends for several years.

In 1971 the University of Texas began an award, the Wilson S. Stone Memorial Award, for the outstanding achievement in the biomedical sciences accomplished by a student in the United States. Since that time it has been given annually as a memorial to Stone's great contributions to the University and to the nation.

BIBLIOGRAPHY

1930

With H. J. Muller. Analysis of several induced gene rearrangements involving the X-chromosome of *Drosophila*. Anat. Rec., 47:393–94 (A).

1931

With C. A. Offermann and H. J. Muller. Causes of interregional differences in crossover frequency, studied in individuals homozygous for gene rearrangements. Anat. Rec., 51 (Suppl.):109 (A).

1934

With J. T. Patterson, Sarah Bedichek, and Meta Suche. The production of translocations in *Drosophila*. Am. Nat., 68: 359–69.

Linkage between the X and IV chromosomes in *Drosophila melanogaster*. Genetica, 16:506–19.

1935

With Theophilus S. Painter. Chromosome fusion and speciation in *Drosophila*. Genetics, 20:327–41.

With J. T. Patterson and Sarah Bedichek. Further studies on X-chromosome balance. Am. Nat., 70:59–60 (A).

With J. T. Patterson. Some observations on the structure of the scute-8 chromosome of *Drosophila melanogaster*. Genetics, 20:172–78.

With J. T. Patterson and Sarah Bedichek. The genetics of X-hyperploid females. Genetics, 20:259–79.

With Isabel Thomas. Crossover and disjunctional properties of X-chromosome inversions in *Drosophila melanogaster*. Genetica, 17:170–84.

1937

With J. T. Patterson and Sarah Bedichek. Further studies on X-chromosome balance in *Drosophila*. Genetics, 22: 407–26.

1938

With A. B. Griffen. Gene position and mottling. Genetics, 23:149 (A).
With J. T. Patterson and Meta Suche. Aneuploidy of the second and third chromosomes of *Drosophila melanogaster*. Genetics, 23:162–63 (A).
With J. T. Patterson. Gynandromorphs in *Drosophila melanogaster*. Univ. Tex. Publ., 3825:1–67.
The Y-chromosome and pigment formation in *Drosophila melanogaster*. Genetics, 23:173 (A).
With A. B. Griffen. "Free" centromeres in *Drosophila melanogaster*. Genetics, 23:173 (A).

1939

With A. B. Griffen. The demonstration of a new chromosome arm in *Drosophila melanogaster*. Genetics, 24:73 (A).
With A. B. Griffen. Reverse mutation and the position effect. Genetics, 24:73 (A).
With J. T. Patterson and A. B. Griffen. Crosses between members of the *Drosophila virilis* group. Proc. Int. Congr. Genet., 7th, 1939:233 (A).
With A. B. Griffen. Studies in chromosome conversion. Genetics, 24:87–88 (A).

1940

With J. T. Patterson and A. B. Griffen. The *virilis* complex in *Drosophila*. Genetics, 25:131 (A).
With J. T. Patterson and Meta Suche Brown. Experimentally produced aneuploidy involving the autosomes of *Drosophila melanogaster*. Univ. Tex. Publ., 4032:167–89.
With A. B. Griffen. The w^{m5} and its derivatives. Univ. Tex. Publ., 4032:190–200.
With A. B. Griffen. The second arm of chromosome 4 in *Drosophila melanogaster*. Univ. Tex. Publ., 4032:201–7.
With A. B. Griffen. Changing the structure of the genome in *Drosophila melanogaster*. Univ. Tex. Publ., 4032:208–17.
With J. T. Patterson and A. B. Griffen. Evolution of the *virilis* group in *Drosophila*. Univ. Tex. Publ., 4032:218–50.

1941

With J. T. Patterson and A. B. Griffen. Studies in *Drosophila* speciation: IV. Extension of the *D. virilis* complex. Genetics, 26:164 (A).

Studies in *Drosophila* speciation. V. Mutations in wild strains of *Drosophila virilis*. Genetics, 26:171 (A).

1942

The Ix^B factor and sex determination. Univ. Tex. Publ., 4228: 146–52.

With J. T. Patterson and A. B. Griffen. Genetic and cytological analysis of the *virilis* species group. Univ. Tex. Publ., 4228: 162–200.

Heterosis in *Drosophila hydei*. Univ. Tex. Publ., 4228:16–22.

With A. B. Griffen and J. T. Patterson. *Drosophila montana*, a new species of the *virilis* group. Genetics, 27:172 (A).

1947

With J. T. Patterson and Linda Wharton McDonald. Sexual isolation between members of the *virilis* group of species. Univ. Tex. Publ., 4720:7–31.

With J. T. Patterson. The species relationships in the *virilis* group. Univ. Tex. Publ., 4720:157–160.

Gene replacement in the *virilis* group. Univ. Tex. Publ., 4720: 161–66.

With Orville Wyss and Felix Haas. The production of mutation in *Staphylococcus aureus* by irradiation of the substrate. Proc. Natl. Acad. Sci. USA, 33:59–66.

With Orville Wyss. Induced mutations in bacteria. J. Bacteriol., 54:4 (A).

With Orville Wyss and J. Bennett Clark. The production of mutations in *Staphylococcus aureus* by chemical treatment of the substrate. J. Bacteriol., 54:767–72.

1948

With Felix Haas, J. Bennett Clark, and Orville Wyss. The role of mutation and of selection in the frequency of mutants among microorganisms grown on irradiated substrate. Proc. Natl. Acad. Sci. USA, 34:142–49.

With Orville Wyss, J. Bennett Clark, and Felix Haas. The role of peroxide in the biological effects of irradiated broth. J. Bacteriol., 56:51–57.

With Felix Haas and Orville Wyss. The effect of irradiation on recombination in *Escherichia coli*. Proc. Natl. Acad. Sci. USA, 34:229–32.

1949

With J. Bennett Clark, Orville Wyss, and Felix Haas. Gasometric determination of hydrogen peroxide. Proc. Soc. Exp. Biol. Med., 72:32–33.

The survival of chromosomal variation in evolution. Univ. Tex. Publ., 4920:18–21.

1950

With J. Bennett Clark, Felix Haas, and Orville Wyss. The stimulation of gene recombination in *Escherichia coli*. J. Bacteriol., 59:375–79.

With R. P. Wagner, C. H. Haddox, and R. Fuerst. The effect of irradiated medium, cyanide and hydrogen peroxide on the mutation rate in Neurospora. Genetics, 35:137–38 (A).

With R. P. Wagner, C. H. Haddox, and R. Fuerst. The effect of irradiated medium, cyanide and hydrogen peroxide on the mutation rate in Neurospora. Genetics, 35:237–48.

With J. Bennett Clark and Orville Wyss. Induction of mutation in *Micrococcus pyogenes* by chemical inactivation of sulphhydryl groups. Nature (London), 166:340.

With Felix Haas, J. Bennett Clark, and Orville Wyss. Mutations and mutagenic agents in bacteria. Am. Nat., 84:261–74.

With Orville Wyss, Felix Haas, and J. Bennett Clark. Some effects of ultraviolet irradiation on microorganisms. J. Cellular Comp. Physiol., 35(Suppl. 1):133–40.

1952

With Mary L. Alexander and R. B. Lea. Interspecific gene variability in the *virilis* species group. Univ. Tex. Publ., 5204:106–13.

With Felix L. Haas, Frances E. Clayton, and Edna Dudgeon. Frequency of chromosomal rearrangements as related to rate of irradiation, temperature and gases. Genetics, 37:589–90 (A).

With J. T. Patterson. *Evolution in the Genus Drosophila.* N. Y.: Macmillan. 610 pp.

With C. L. Ward. Studies in the *repleta* group: the *melanopalpa* subgroup. Univ. Tex. Publ., 5204:137–57.

With T. L. Thompson, N. Durham, and O. Wyss. Low oxidation rate of ribose in streptomycin resistant *E. coli.* Microb. Genet. Bull., 6:22.

1953

With Heinz Berger, F. L. Haas, and O. Wyss. The effect of sodium azide on radiation damage and photoreactivation. J. Bacteriol., 65:538–43.

With Felix L. Haas, O. Wyss, and H. Berger. Induction of mutations to antibiotic resistance in bacteria. J. Bacteriol., 65:354.

1954

With Felix L. Haas, Edna Dudgeon, and Frances E. Clayton. Measurement and control of some direct and indirect effects of X-radiation. Genetics, 39:453–71.

With Mary L. Alexander and Frances E. Clayton. The induction of translocations by X-radiations at different stages of germ cell development in *Drosophila virilis.* Genetics, 39:956 (A).

With Mary L. Alexander and Frances E. Clayton. Heterosis studies with species of *Drosophila* living in small populations. Univ. Tex. Publ., 5422:272–307.

With Mary L. Alexander, Frances E. Clayton, and Edna Dudgeon. The production of translocations in *Drosophila virilis* by fast neutrons from a nuclear detonation. Am. Nat., 88:287–93.

With Felix Haas, Mary L. Alexander, and Frances E. Clayton. Comments on the mechanism of action of radiations on living systems. Univ. Tex. Publ., 5422:244–71.

With J. T. Patterson. Fertilizations in multiple matings of the *virilis* group. Univ. Tex. Publ., 5422:38–45.

1955

With Mary L. Alexander. Radiation damage in the developing germ cells of *Drosophila virilis.* Proc. Natl. Acad. Sci. USA, 41:1046–57.

Genetic and chromosomal variability in *Drosophila.* Cold Spring Harbor Symp. Quant. Biol., 20:256–70.

1956

Indirect effects of radiation on genetic material. Brookhaven Symp. Biol., 8:171–90.

1957

With Marshall R. Wheeler, Warren P. Spencer, Florence D. Wilson, June T. Neuenschwander, Thomas G. Gregg, Robert L. Seecof, and Calvin L. Ward. Genetic studies of irradiated natural populations of *Drosophila*. Univ. Tex. Publ., 5721:260–316.

1958

With Florence D. Wilson. Genetics studies of irradiated natural populations of *Drosophila*. II. 1957 tests. Proc. Natl. Acad. Sci. USA, 44:565–75.

1959

With Florence D. Wilson. Genetics studies of irradiated natural populations of *Drosophila*. IV. 1958 tests. Univ. Tex. Publ., 5914:223–33.

With Tsueng-Hsing Chang and Florence D. Wilson. Genetic radiation damage reversal by nitrogen, methane and argon. Proc. Natl. Acad. Sci. USA, 45:1397–1404.

1960

With William C. Guest and Florence D. Wilson. The evolutionary implications of the cytological polymorphism and phylogeny of the *virilis* group of *Drosophila*. Proc. Natl. Acad. Sci. USA, 46:350–61.

1962

The dominance of natural selection and the reality of super-species (species group) in the evolution of *Drosophila*. Univ. Tex. Publ., 6205:507–37.

With M. R. Wheeler and F. D. Wilson. Genetic studies of irradiated natural populations of *Drosophila*. V. Summary and discussion of tests of populations collected in the Pacific Proving Ground from 1955 through 1959. Univ. Tex. Publ., 6205:1–54.

1963

With Florence D. Wilson and Virginia L. Gerstenberg. Genetic studies of natural populations of *Drosophila: Drosophila pseudoobscura*, a large dominant population. Genetics, 48:1089–1106.

1964

With Irene M. Cotton, Robert R. Rinehart, and Ruby Petrusek. Nitric oxide protection of bacteriophage against X-radiation damage. Radiat. Res., 21:481–91.

1966

With F. M. Johnson, Carmen G. Kanapi, R. H. Richardson, and M. R. Wheeler. An analysis of polymorphisms among isozyme loci in dark and light *Drosophila ananassae* strains from American and Western Samoa. Proc. Natl. Acad. Sci. USA, 56:119–25.

With F. M. Johnson, Carmen G. Kanapi, R. H. Richardson, and M. R. Wheeler. An operational classification of *Drosophila* esterases for species comparisons. Univ. Tex. Publ., 6615:517–32.

With Marshall R. Wheeler, Florence D. Wilson, Virginia L. Gerstenberg, and Hei Yang. Genetic studies of natural populations of *Drosophila*. II. Pacific island populations. Univ. Tex. Publ., 6615:1–36.

1968

With F. M. Johnson, K. Kojima, and M. R. Wheeler. Isozyme variation in island populations of *Drosophila*. I. An analysis of a species of the *nasuta* complex in Samoa and Fiji. Univ. Tex. Publ., 6618:157–70.

With Ken-ichi Kojima and F. M. Johnson. Enzyme polymorphisms in animal populations. Proc. Int. Congr. Genet., 12th, 1968: 153–54.

With Marshall R. Wheeler, F. M. Johnson, and Ken-ichi Kojima. Genetic variation in natural island populations of members of the *Drosophila nasuta* and *Drosophila ananassae* subgroups. Proc. Natl. Acad. Sci. USA, 59:102–9.

1969

With Ken-ichi Kojima and F. M. Johnson. Enzyme polymorphisms in animal populations. Jpn. J. Genet., 44:166–71.

1970

With Hampton L. Carson, D. Elmo Hardy, and Herman T. Spieth. The evolutionary biology of the Hawaiian Drosophilidae. In: *Essays in Evolution and Genetics in Honor of Theodosius Dobzhansky*, ed. M. K. Hecht and W. C. Steere, pp. 437–543. N. Y.: Appleton-Century-Crofts.

With E. S. Rockwood, C. G. Kanapi, and M. R. Wheeler. Allozyme changes during the evolution of Hawaiian *Drosophila*. Univ. Tex. Publ., 7103:193–212.

LORANDE LOSS WOODRUFF

July 14, 1879–June 23, 1947

BY G. EVELYN HUTCHINSON

LORANDE LOSS WOODRUFF was born on July 14, 1879 in New York City, the son of Charles Albert and Eloise Clara (née Loss) Woodruff. His father and grandfather were clothing merchants; they came of a family of English descent that had settled near Farmington, Connecticut in 1641.

Woodruff was educated in public schools in New York and then at the College of the City of New York and at Columbia. He earned his B.A. at the latter institution in 1901, his M.A. in 1902, and his Ph.D. in 1905. His graduate work was done under Gary N. Calkins, partly *in absentia* as he obtained an assistantship at Williams College in 1903 and served as an instructor at that institution from 1904 to 1907. His great capacity as a teacher was recognized at Williams and was clearly a factor in his gaining an appointment as an instructor in biology at Yale in 1907. Though the College of the City of New York tried to lure him away in 1922, he remained at Yale for the rest of his life, apart from some service as a consulting physiologist in the Chemical Warfare Service during World War I and a sabbatical year spent with the National Research Council in 1928–1929. He became Assistant Professor in 1909 and Professor in 1915. In 1922 he was appointed Professor of Protozoology and in 1944 Colgate Professor of that subject; Colgate Professorships are primarily given to senior members of the Yale Faculty who have shown outstanding ability as undergraduate teachers. He was designated a fellow of Branford College in Yale University in 1934. He was acting Chairman of the Department of Zoology in 1927–1928 when R. G. Harrison was on sabbatical leave and succeeded Harrison as Chairman and Director of the Osborn Zoological Laboratory in 1938. He continued in these positions till his death, though he was given a leave of absence during his last year, having suffered a complete breakdown after his wife's death in March 1946. He died on June 23, 1947. His marriage to Margaret Louise Mitchell, also of New York City, was a singularly happy one, and without his wife he appeared to his colleagues and friends to have lost all incentive for life. They had a son and a daughter.

Although he wrote a number of articles on the history of science and some on more general biological matters, Woodruff's original scientific investigations all concerned the ciliate Protozoa.

At the opening of the twentieth century when he began his work, it had been long recognized, and indeed was logically obvious, that the family lines of unicellular, or as some later would have it, acellular organisms, are potentially immortal, though of course in any line most descendants are destined to perish. The meaning of this immortality was, however, subject to debate. It was widely believed that the process of conjugation observed in a number of protistan groups had something to do with the capacity of cell lines to continue perpetuating themselves, though not all observations supported this belief.

In his earlier papers, from 1905 to 1914, at first working with a variety of ciliates but later concentrating on *Paramecium aurelia* and *P. caudatum,* Woodruff showed that the inevitable extinction of lines that did not conjugate could be prevented by appropriate conditions of culture and was in fact almost certainly due to unidentified nutrient deficiencies. However, even under the best possible culture conditions, an irregularly rhythmical variation in division rate persisted. In a classical experiment involving an enormous tenacity of purpose over a period of eight years, he showed that more than 5,000 generations could be reared by cell division without the intervention of conjugation. Later under somewhat less rigorous control the culture was maintained for over 24,000 generations. The oscillations in division rate, however, persisted. In 1914 Woodruff and Rhoda Erdmann found that these variations were correlated with a process of nuclear reorganization which they termed *endomixis,* and which they realized had earlier been observed in a fragmentary way by Hertwig. In spite of the name that they used for the process, which etymologically would seem to imply fusion of gametes in a strictly internal process, Woodruff and Erdmann believed that the macronuclear replacement resulting from this process involved no such fusion. Later work, particularly by Diller in Woodruff's laboratory, showed, however, that in this they were mistaken. They had missed one micronuclear division and subsequent fusion, so that the reconstituted macronucleus was, as after conjugation, the result of a process that can, in the widest sense, be regarded as sexual. Such a process is now generally called *autogamy.* The result of the process that Woodruff and Erdmann discovered inevitably leads not merely to the replacement of the macronucleus, now known to be polyploid to a very high degree, but also to a continual reduction of the heterozygosity of any nuclei in the cell line, as Sonneborn soon demonstrated genetically. In this the internal reorganization process is in direct contrast to conjugation, which normally will lead to outcrossing and an increase in heterozygosity. These fundamental studies, though Woodruff at the time could not be fully aware of their implications, obviously played a great role in increasing our understanding of the cell physiology of the ciliates. In addition, he was naturally much interested in cases in which the micronucleus appeared to be absent or where, even though it was present, no reorganization seemed to take place. He also published on the appearance of various ciliates in hay infusions allowed to mature in the laboratory, giving rise to a kind of ecological succession.

Woodruff wrote a dozen notes and papers on the history of biology, of which the most important was on Sir John Hill, the pre-Linnaean author of the name *Paramecium*. Woodruff had an admirable collection of the works of this versatile Figaroesque Englishman, pharmacist, physician, actor, dramatist, botanist, zoologist, editor, and man-about-town. This part of his extensive collection of historic scientific books was fortunately not dispersed at his death and is now in the George Peabody Department of the Enoch Pratt Free Library in Baltimore. Woodruff could have resembled none of his predecessors less than Hill. No one would have supposed that had Woodruff not been elected to the National Academy of Sciences, as he was in 1924, he would have retaliated with an entertaining if mildly erotic parody of the scientific activities of our august body. Nevertheless, in private Woodruff could enjoy Hill's *Lucina Sine Concubitu,* directed at the Royal Society of London, which would not increase the prestige and wealth of its author by electing him and so making it possible for F.R.S. to follow his name on the title pages of his writings, an embellishment greatly desired by Hill's publishers.

From 1909 onward, Woodruff gave a very successful graduate course on the history of biology, which often attracted students from outside his own department and was for many years the only instruction in the history of science given in Yale.

Though Woodruff's influence as a protozoologist was great and his contribution enduring, it is possible that his real significance was as a teacher. Beginning in the academic year 1909–1910 he had charge of the introductory biology course at Yale which he built up until about 500 students were enrolled in 1927. His textbook, *Foundations of Biology,* was very widely used throughout the 1920's and 1930's and is said in an examination at another New England college to have been attributed, when the author's name was asked, mainly to Woodruff, but by more than one student apiece to Aristotle, Theophrastus, Vesalius, Hales, Buffon, Lamarck, and Wordsworth. Actually since the author was a very literate man, all of these putative authors had had some share in making the book.

As an example of Woodruff the teacher in action, the following reminiscences of Professor Daniel Merriman are of interest.

One of the requirements for Woodruff's graduate course in Protozoology was to collect in the wild and identify 50 species. On culture, a collection from the outskirts of New Haven yielded me an hypotrichous ciliate that defied identification, and after examining innumerable specimens both living and stained Woodruff agreed that it was a new species. Then came the task of drawing it and writing it up for publication. This was my first real lesson in *looking.* In the best manner of Louis Agassiz, Woodruff rejected sketch after sketch until finally I produced one that met his standard with respect to the number and position of the cirri and cilia. The species was named *Urostyla polymicronucleata* and its description was published in the *Archiv für Protistenkunde* [88,3(1937):427–430].

I also had the good fortune to take Woodruff's course on the History of Biology. This resulted in my first paper in the field ["Peter Artedi—Systematist and Ichthyologist," *Copeia,* 1(1938):33–39] and, more importantly, led to a life-long interest in the history of science that has been reflected both in my teaching and in the publication of a number of contributions on oceanography in the 19th century. The background and methodology from Woodruff's course were invaluable. His teaching, perhaps combined with a certain parental influence, clearly provided the stimulus for a highly rewarding field of endeavor.

Though in his later years rather reserved in manner, he

was an essentially friendly man, capable of great kindness. A few letters preserved in the departmental files in the Yale Archives testify to the trouble that he would take in answering questions from amateurs and high school students puzzled about biological matters. Essentially conservative by disposition, he was ultimately always in favor of any change promoting higher standards, and is said for a time to have been a member of an informal group of Young Turks who met for lunch in the Graduates Club on New Haven Green and discussed what was wrong with Yale and what should be done about it.

Outside Yale, Woodruff had an enduring interest in the Marine Biological Laboratory (MBL) at Woods Hole. He was an instructor in the invertebrate course from 1905 to 1909 and then joined the staff of the embryology course in which he taught until 1914. Later he took over the course in protozoology for the season of 1927 in the absence of his old teacher and friend Dr. Calkins. He had been a member of the Corporation of the MBL since 1905, was elected to the Board of Trustees, and in 1930–1932 served on the Executive Committee. The Woodruffs had a summer cottage at Woods Hole, and their hospitality is remembered by many of those who survive from the generations that were students and young investigators forty or fifty years ago. He also occasionally visited the Mountain Lake Laboratory of the University of Virginia where he had several close friends, and he lectured on protozoology at four summer sessions there.

In retrospect, Woodruff's career seems unspectacular but extremely useful. A true servant of science and education, his contributions are built solidly into the fabric of our culture but can now be identified only by those with long memories or an exceptional interest in the past. Yet in the 1920's he was one of the American biologists best known in Europe. The ciliates at that time seemed more primitive than we now believe them to be, and the processes by which they maintain the integrity of what is essentially a complicated mass of somatic chromatin dividing in a way that is likely to be rather untidy, appears less fundamental than it did in 1914. There was at times almost a feeling that Maupas, having overemphasized the life-giving properties of sexuality, was being appropriately corrected in puritan New England. Nevertheless, the patient and skillful work that Woodruff did has made possible all the later research in his chosen area, and some of this later work has been very important indeed. He belongs to history, which is what he would have wanted.

BIBLIOGRAPHY

1905

An experimental study on the life-history of hypotrichous infusoria. J. Exp. Zool., 2:585–632.

1907

Variation during the life-cycle of infusoria in its bearings on the determination of species. Science, 25:734–35.

1908

Effects of alcohol on the division-rate of infusoria. Science, 27: 442–43.
Increased susceptibility of protozoa to poison due to treatment with alcohol. Proc. Soc. Exp. Biol. Med., 5:124.
The life cycle of *Paramecium*. Proc. Soc. Exp. Biol. Med., 5:82–83.
Effects of alcohol on the life cycle of infusoria. Biol. Bull., 15: 85–104.
The life cycle of *Paramecium* when subjected to a varied environment. Am. Nat., 42:520–26.
The American Society of Zoologists. Science, 27:441.

1909

Duration of the cycle of *Paramecium*. Science, 29:425.
Studies on the life cycle of *Paramecium*. Proc. Soc. Exp. Biol. Med., 6:117–18.
Further studies on the life cycle of *Paramecium*. Biol. Bull., 17: 287–308.
The American Society of Zoologists. Science, 29:424.
With H. H. Bunzel. The relative toxicity of various salts and acids toward *Paramecium*. Am. J. Physiol., 25:190–94.

1910

On the power of reproduction without conjugation in *Paramecium*. Proc. Soc. Exp. Biol. Med., 7:144.
With M. S. Fine. The biological cycle of the hay infusion. Science, 31:467–68.

1911

The effect of culture medium contaminated with the excretion products of *Paramaecium* on its rate of reproduction. Proc. Soc. Exp. Biol. Med., 8:100.
Paramaecium aurelia and *Paramaecium caudatum*. J. Morphol., 22: 223–37.
Two thousand generations of *Paramaecium*. Arch. Protistenkd., 21: 263–66.
The effect of excretion products of *Paramaecium* on its rate of reproduction. J. Exp. Zool., 10:557–81.
Evidence on the adaptation of paramaecia to different environments. Biol. Bull., 22:60–65.
With G. A. Baitsell. Beef extract as a "constant" culture medium for *Paramaecium aurelia*. Proc. Soc. Exp. Biol. Med., 8:121–22.
With G. A. Baitsell. The reproduction of *Paramaecium aurelia* in a "constant" culture medium of beef extract. J. Exp. Zool., 11: 135–42.
With G. A. Baitsell. Rhythms in the reproductive activity of infusoria. J. Exp. Zool., 11:339–59.
With G. A. Baitsell. The temperature coefficient of the rate of reproduction of *Paramaecium aurelia*. Am. J. Physiol., 29: 147–55.

1912

The sequence of the protozoan fauna in hay infusions. Proc. Soc. Exp. Biol. Med., 9:65–66.
A five-year pedigreed race of *Paramaecium* without conjugation. Proc. Soc. Exp. Med., 9:121–23.
Observations on the origin and sequence of the protozoan fauna of hay infusions. J. Exp. Zool., 12:205–64.
A summary of the results of certain physiological studies on a pedigreed race of *Paramaecium*. Biochem. Bull., 1:396–412.

1913

The Kernplasmarelation during the life of a pedigreed race of *Oxytricha fallax*. Proc. Soc. Exp. Biol. Med., 10:74.
Dreitausend und dreihundert Generationen von *Paramaecium* ohne Konjugation oder künstliche Reizung. Biol. Zentralbl., 33:34–36.

The production of specific excretion products by infusoria. Biochem. Bull., 2:465.

The effect of excretion products of infusoria on the same and on different species, with special reference to the protozoan sequence in infusions. J. Exp. Zool., 14:575–82.

Cell size, nuclear size and the nucleo-cytoplasmic relation during the life of a pedigreed race of *Oxytricha fallax.* J. Exp. Zool., 15:1–22.

With F. P. Underhill. Protozoan protoplasm as an indicator of pathological changes. I. In nephritis. J. Biol. Chem., 15: 385–400.

With F. P. Underhill. Protozoan protoplasm as an indicator of pathological changes. II. In carcinoma. J. Biol. Chem., 15:401–14.

1914

Further light on the conjugation of *Paramaecium.* Proc. Soc. Exp. Biol. Med., 11:64.

So-called conjugating and non-conjugating races of *Paramaecium.* J. Exp. Zool., 16:237–40.

With R. Erdmann. Complete periodic nuclear reorganization without cell fusion in a pedigreed race of *Paramaecium.* Proc. Soc. Exp. Biol. Med., 11:73–74.

With R. Erdmann. A normal periodic reorganization process without cell fusion in *Paramaecium.* J. Exp. Zool., 17:425–518.

With R. Erdmann. Vollständige periodische Eineuerung des Kernapparates ohne Zellverschmelzung bei reinlinigen Paramaeciun. Biol. Zentralbl., 34:484–96.

With F. P. Underhill. Protozoan protoplasm as an indicator of pathological changes. III. In fatigue. J. Biol. Chem., 17:9–12.

1915

The problem of rejuvenescence in protozoa. Biochem. Bull., 4:371–78.

1916

Endomixis in diverse races of *Paramaecium aurelia.* Proc. Soc. Exp. Biol. Med., 13:161–62.

With R. Erdmann. The periodic reorganization process in *Paramaecium caudatum.* J. Exp. Zool., 20:59–97.

1917

Rhythms and endomixis in various races of *Paramaecium aurelia.* Biol. Bull., 33:51–56.
The influence of general environmental conditions on the periodicity of endomixis in *Paramecium aurelia.* Biol. Bull., 33:437–62.
Erasmus Darwin and Benjamin Franklin. Science, 46:291–92.

1918

Baker on the microscope and the polype. Sci. Mon., 7:212–26.
The origin of life. In: R. S. Lull, *The Evolution of the Earth and Its Inhabitants,* pp. 82–108. New Haven: Yale Univ. Press.

1919

The hay infusion microcosm. Guide to Nature, 11:288–89.
Didinium nasutum. Guide to Nature, 11:304–5.

1919

Hooke's Micrographia. Am. Nat., 53:247–64.

1920

With H. Laurens and G. A. Baitsell, eds. *Laboratory Directions for General Biology.* 63 pp. New Haven, Conn.: Osborn Zoological Laboratory.

1921

Amicronucleate infusoria. Proc. Soc. Exp. Biol. Med., 18:28–29.
Paramecium calkinsi sp. n. Proc. Soc. Exp. Biol. Med., 18:137–38.
The present status of the long-continued pedigree culture of *Paramecium aurelia* at Yale University. Proc. Natl. Acad. Sci. USA, 7:41–44.
The structure, life history and intrageneric relationships of *Paramecium calkinsi* sp. nov. Biol. Bull., 41:171–80.
Micronucleate and amicronucleate races of infusoria. J. Exp. Zool., 34:329–37.
History of biology. Sci. Mon., 12:253–81.

With H. Spencer. The food reactions of the infusorian *Spathidium spathula*. Proc. Soc. Exp. Biol. Med., 18:183–84.
With H. Spencer. The early effects of conjugation on the division rate of *Spathidium spathula*. Proc. Soc. Exp. Biol. Med., 18:240–41.
With H. Spencer. The survival value of conjugation in the life history of *Spathidium spathula*. Proc. Soc. Exp. Biol. Med., 18:303–4.

1922

Foundations of Biology. N.Y.: Macmillan. 476 pp. (7 editions and 1936 Chinese translation by World Book Co.)
With H. Spencer. Studies on *Spathidium spathula*. I. The structure and behavior of *Spathidium*, with special reference to the capture and ingestion of prey. J. Exp. Zool., 35:189–205.
With H. Spencer. On the method of macronucleic disintegration during endomixis in *Paramecium aurelia*. Proc. Soc. Exp. Biol. Med., 19:290–91.
With H. Spencer. Racial variations in *Blepharisma undulans*. Proc. Soc. Exp. Biol. Med., 19:339–40.

1923

Biology. In: Ernest W. Brown et al., *The Development of the Sciences*, ed. L. L. Woodruff, 1st series, pp. 215–59. New Haven: Yale Univ. Press.
With H. Spencer. *Paramecium polycaryum*, nov. Proc. Soc. Exp. Biol. Med., 20:338–39.
With W. W. Swingle. The effect of thyroid products on *Paramecium*. Proc. Soc. Exp. Biol. Med., 20:386.

1924

The protozoa and the problem of adaptation. In: M. R. Thorpe, *Organic Adaptation to Environment*, pp. 45–66. New Haven: Yale Univ. Press.
Biology. In: H. G. Black, *Paths to Success*, pp. 162–81. N.Y.: D.C. Heath.
With E. L. Moore. On the longevity of *Spathidium spathula* without endomixis or conjugation. Proc. Natl. Acad. Sci. USA, 10:183–86.

With H. Spencer. Studies on *Spathidium spathula*. II. The significance of conjugation. J. Exp. Zool., 39:133–96.
With W. W. Swingle. The effects of thyroid and some other endocrine products on *Paramecium*. Am. J. Physiol., 69:21–34.

1925

The physiological significance of conjugation and endomixis in the infusoria. Am. Nat., 59:225–49.

1926

Eleven thousand generations of *Paramecium*. Q. Rev. Biol., 1:436–38.
The versatile Sir John Hill, M.D. Am. Nat., 60:417–42.

1927

Studies on the life history of *Blepharisma undulans*. Proc. Soc. Exp. Biol. Med., 24:769–70.

1928

Further studies on the life history of *Blepharisma undulans*. Proc. Soc. Exp. Biol. Med., 25:683–84.

1929

Thirteen thousand generations of *Paramecium*. Proc. Soc. Exp. Biol. Med., 26:707–8.
The origin of life. In: G. A. Baitsell, *The Evolution of Earth and Man*, pp. 83–109. New Haven: Yale Univ. Press.

1930

Chairman. [Report of the] Division of Biology and Agriculture [of the National Research Council]. Report of Natl. Acad. Sci. USA, 1928/1929, 89–92.
The National Academy of Sciences. Yale Sci. Mag., 4:19–20, 35.

1931

Micronuclear variation in *Paramecium bursaria*. Q. J. Microscop. Sci., 74:537–45.
Variations in the micronuclear apparatus of *Paramecium bursaria*. Proc. Soc. Exp. Biol. Med., 28:818.

1932

Paramecium aurelia in pedigree culture for twenty-five years. Trans. Am. Microscop. Soc., 51:196–98.
Animal Biology. N.Y.: Macmillan. 513 pp. (2d ed., 1938.)

1935

Physiological significance of conjugation in *Blepharisma undulans*. J. Exp. Zool., 70:287–300.
Biology. In: *Nelson's Loose-Leaf Encyclopedia*, pp. 92–96. N.Y.: T. Nelson and Sons.

1937

Louis Joblot and the protozoa. Sci. Mon., 44:41–47.

1938

Philosophers in little things. Univ. Okla. Bull., No. 739:21–33.

1939

Some pioneers in microscopy with special reference to protozoology. Trans. N.Y. Acad. Sci., 1:74–77.
Microscopy before the nineteenth century. Am. Nat., 73:485–516.
Edmund Beecher Wilson. Am. J. Sci., 237:371–72.

1940

With E. J. Boell. Mating and metabolism of *Paramecium calkinsi*. Science, 92:417.

1941

Population problems in protozoa . . . Introduction. Am. Nat., 75:401–5.
Biology. In: Oystein Ore et al., *The Development of the Sciences,* ed. L. L. Woodruff, 2d series, pp. 197–246. New Haven: Yale Univ. Press.
Endomixis. In: Calkins and Summers, *Protozoa in Biological Research,* pp. 646–65. N.Y.: Columbia Univ. Press.
With E. J. Boell. Respiratory metabolism of mating types in *Paramecium calkinsi*. J. Exp. Zool., 87:385–402.

1942

Robert William Hegner, 1880–1942. Sci. Mon., 55:182–84.

1943

The pedigreed culture of *Paramecium aurelia* at Yale University. Proc. Natl. Acad. Sci. USA, 29:135–36.
The advent of the microscope at Yale College. Am. Sci., 31:241–45.
Gary Nathan Calkins. Collecting Net, 18:5–6.

1944

The advent of the microscope at Yale College. Conn. State Med. J., 8:93–95.

1945

Alexander Petrunkevitch, colleague and friend. Trans. Conn. Acad. Arts Sci., 36:7–8.
The early history of the genus *Paramecium* with special reference to *Paramecium aurelia* and *Paramecium caudatum*. Trans. Conn. Acad. Arts Sci., 36:517–31.